PoetryFocus 2025

Leaving Certificate poems and notes for **English Higher Level**

Martin Kieran & Frances Rocks

Gill Education
Hume Avenue
Park West
Dublin 12
www.gilleducation.ie

Gill Education is an imprint of M.H. Gill & Co.

© Martin Kieran & Frances Rocks 2023

ISBN: 978-0-7171-95404

All rights reserved. No part of this publication may be copied, reproduced or transmitted in any form or by any means without written permission of the publishers or else under the terms of any licence permitting limited copying issued by the Irish Copyright Licensing Agency.

Design: Graham Thew
Print origination: Carole Lynch

At the time of going to press, all web addresses were active and contained information relevant to the topics in this book. Gill Education does not, however, accept responsibility for the content or views contained on these websites. Content, views and addresses may change beyond the publisher or author's control. Students should always be supervised when reviewing websites.

For permission to reproduce photographs, the authors and publisher gratefully acknowledge the following:

© Adobe Stock: 5, 17, 19, 250, 252, 253, 276, 280, 372, 375, 407, 408, 409; © Alamy: 29, 36, 40, 50, 56, 59, 60, 63, 67, 68, 71, 80, 83, 84, 94, 118, 121, 124, 126, 127, 129, 131, 138, 141, 148, 168, 171, 179, 183, 186, 196, 199, 200, 203, 210, 212, 213, 215, 218, 226, 229, 230, 233, 234, 235, 283, 284, 285, 300, 303, 306, 308, 311, 314, 315, 318, 328, 332, 334, 362, 401; © Bridgeman Images: 357; © Capital Pictures: 219; © Getty Images: 13, 15, 206, 244, 246, 248, 249, 254, 257, 258, 262, 294, 342, 377, 382; © iStock/Getty Premium: 8, 11, 21, 24, 26, 32, 52, 55, 64, 66, 74, 77, 107, 111, 150, 153, 154, 158, 160, 161, 165, 166, 172, 174, 175, 178, 222, 225, 263, 268, 270, 272, 275, 297, 298, 320, 323, 326, 345, 383, 384, 385, 389; © National Library of Ireland: 194; © The Permissions Company, on behalf of Graywolf Press: 367; © RTÉ Archives: 2; © Shutterstock: 101, 103, 112, 133, 136, 351, 355; © Wikimedia Commons: 395.

The authors and publisher have made every effort to trace all copyright holders. If, however, any have been inadvertently overlooked, we would be pleased to make the necessary arrangement at the first opportunity.

Contents

Introduction v

Eavan Boland
- 'The War Horse' 4
- 'Child of Our Time' (OL) 8
- 'The Famine Road' 12
- 'The Shadow Doll' 16
- 'White Hawthorn in the West of Ireland' 20
- 'Outside History' 24
- 'The Black Lace Fan My Mother Gave Me' 28
- 'This Moment' (OL) 32
- 'The Pomegranate' 35
- 'Love' (OL) 39
- Sample Questions and Essay Material 43
- Revision Overview 49

Emily Dickinson
- '"Hope" is the thing with feathers' 52
- 'There's a certain Slant of light' 56
- 'I felt a Funeral, in my Brain' (OL) 60
- 'A Bird came down the Walk' 64
- 'I heard a Fly buzz—when I died' (OL) 67
- 'The Soul has Bandaged moments' 70
- 'I could bring You Jewels—had I a mind to' 74
- 'A narrow Fellow in the Grass' 77
- 'I taste a liquor never brewed' 80
- 'After great pain, a formal feeling comes' 84
- Sample Questions and Essay Material 87
- Revision Overview 93

T.S. Eliot
- 'The Love Song of J. Alfred Prufrock' 96
- 'Preludes' (OL) 106
- 'Aunt Helen' (OL) 112
- from 'The Waste Land': 'II. A Game of Chess' 116
- 'Journey of the Magi' 123
- from 'Landscapes': 'III. Usk' 129
- from 'Landscapes': 'IV. Rannoch, by Glencoe' 133
- from 'Four Quartets': 'East Coker IV' 137
- Sample Questions and Essay Material 142
- Revision Overview 147

Gerard Manley Hopkins
- 'God's Grandeur' 150
- 'Spring' (OL) 154
- 'As Kingfishers Catch Fire, Dragonflies Draw Flame' 158
- 'The Windhover' 161
- 'Pied Beauty' 165
- 'Felix Randal' 168
- 'Inversnaid' (OL) 172
- 'I Wake and Feel the Fell of Dark, Not Day' 175
- 'No Worst, There is None' 179
- 'Thou Art Indeed Just, Lord, if I Contend' 183
- Sample Questions and Essay Material 187
- Revision Overview 193

Patrick Kavanagh
- 'Inniskeen Road: July Evening' 196
- 'Shancoduff' (OL) 200
- from 'The Great Hunger' 204
- 'Advent' 210
- 'A Christmas Childhood' (OL) 214
- 'Epic' 219
- 'Canal Bank Walk' 222
- 'Lines Written on a Seat on the Grand Canal, Dublin' 226
- 'The Hospital' 230
- 'On Raglan Road' 233
- Sample Questions and Essay Material 237
- Revision Overview 243

(OL) indicates poems that are also prescribed for the Ordinary Level course.

Derek Mahon

- 'Grandfather' (OL) — 246
- 'Day Trip to Donegal' — 250
- 'Ecclesiastes' — 254
- 'After the *Titanic*' (OL) — 258
- 'As It Should Be' — 263
- 'A Disused Shed in Co. Wexford' — 267
- 'Rathlin' — 272
- 'The Chinese Restaurant in Portrush' — 276
- 'Kinsale' — 280
- 'Antarctica' (OL) — 283
- Sample Questions and Essay Material — 287
- Revision Overview — 293

Sylvia Plath

- 'Black Rook in Rainy Weather' — 296
- 'The Times Are Tidy' — 300
- 'Morning Song' — 303
- 'Finisterre' — 307
- 'Mirror' — 311
- 'Pheasant' — 315
- 'Elm' — 319
- 'Poppies in July' (OL) — 323
- 'The Arrival of the Bee Box' — 327
- 'Child' (OL) — 332
- Sample Questions and Essay Material — 335
- Revision Overview — 341

Tracy K. Smith

- 'Joy' — 344
- 'Dominion over the Beasts of the Earth' — 349
- 'The Searchers' (OL) — 356
- 'Letter to a Photojournalist Going-In' — 361
- 'The Universe is a House Party' — 366
- 'The Museum of Obsolescence' — 371
- 'Don't You Wonder, Sometimes?' — 376
- 'It's Not' (OL) — 383
- 'The Universe as Primal Scream' — 387
- 'The Greatest Personal Privation' (OL) — 393
- 'I am 60 odd years of age' — 399
- 'Ghazal' — 406
- Sample Questions and Essay Material — 411
- Revision Overview — 417

The Unseen Poem

- 'Autumn' — 420
- 'Roller-Skaters' — 423
- 'At Cider Mill Farm' — 426
- 'Lipstick' — 429
- 'Stalled Train' — 432

Acknowledgements — 433

(OL) indicates poems that are also prescribed for the Ordinary Level course.

Introduction

Poetry Focus is a modern poetry textbook for Leaving Certificate Higher Level English. It includes all the prescribed poems for the 2025 exam as well as succinct commentaries on each one. Well-organised study notes allow students to develop their own individual responses and enhance their skills in critical literacy. **There is no single 'correct' approach to answering the poetry question.** Candidates are free to respond in any appropriate way that shows good knowledge of and engagement with the prescribed poems.

- **Concise poet biographies** provide context for the poems.
- **List of prescribed poems** gives a brief introduction to each poem.
- **Personal response** questions follow the text of each poem. These allow students to consider their first impressions before any in-depth study or analysis. These questions provide a good opportunity for written and/or oral exercises.
- **Critical literacy** highlights the main features of the poet's subject matter and style. These discussion notes will enhance the student's own critical appreciation through focused group work and/or written exercises. Analytical skills are developed in a coherent, practical way to give students confidence in articulating their own personal responses.
- **Analysis (writing about the poem) is provided using graded sample paragraphs** which aid students in fluently structuring and developing valid points, using fresh and varied expression. These model paragraphs also illustrate effective use of relevant quotations and reference.
- **Class/homework exercises** for each poem provide focused practice in writing personal responses to examination-style questions.
- **Points to consider** provide a memorable snapshot of the key aspects to remember about each poem.
- **Full sample Leaving Certificate essays** are accompanied by marking-scheme guidelines and examiner's comments. These show the student exactly what is required to achieve a successful top grade in the Leaving Cert. The examiner's comments illustrate the use of the PCLM marking scheme and are an invaluable aid for the ambitious student.
- **Sample essay plans** on each poet's work illustrate how to interpret a question and recognise the particular nuances of key words in examination questions. Student evaluation of these essay plans increases confidence in developing and organising clear responses to exam questions.
- **Sample Leaving Cert questions** on each poet are given at the end of their particular section.
- **Revision overviews** provide a concise and visual summary of each poet's work, through highlighting and interlinking relevant themes.
- **Unseen poetry** provides guidelines for this 20-mark section of the paper. Included are numerous sample questions and answers, which allow students to practise exam-style answers.

 The FREE eBook contains:

- **Investigate Further** sections, which contain **useful weblinks** should you want to learn more.
- **Pop-up key quotes** to encourage students to select their own individual combination of references from a poem and to write brief commentaries on specific quotations.
- Additional sample graded paragraphs called '**Developing your personal response**'.
- Audio of a selection of the poetry read by the poets, including audio of all Eavan Boland and Derek Mahon poetry.

Further material can also be found on GillExplore.ie:

- **A glossary of common literary terms** provides an easy reference when answering questions.
- **A critical analysis checklist** offers useful hints and tips on how to show genuine engagement with the poetry.

How is the Prescribed Poetry Question Marked?

The Prescribed Poetry Question is marked out of 50 marks by reference to the PCLM assessment criteria:

- Clarity of purpose (P): 30% of the total (15 marks)
- Coherence of delivery (C): 30% of the total (15 marks)
- Efficiency of language use (L): 30% of the total (15 marks)
- Accuracy of mechanics (M): 10% of the total (5 marks)

Each answer will be in the form of a response to a specific task requiring candidates to:

- Display a clear and purposeful engagement with the set task (P)
- Sustain the response in an appropriate manner over the entire answer (C)
- Manage and control language appropriate to the task (L)
- Display levels of accuracy in spelling and grammar appropriate to the required/chosen register (M)

General

'Students at Higher Level will be required to study a representative selection from the work of eight poets: a representative selection would seek to reflect the range of a poet's themes and interests and exhibit his/her characteristic style and viewpoint. Normally the study of at least six poems by each poet would be expected.' (DES English Syllabus, 6.3)

The marking scheme guidelines from the State Examinations Commission state that in the case of each poet, the candidates have **freedom of choice** in relation to the poems studied. In addition, there is **not a finite list of any 'poet's themes and interests'**.

Note that in responding to the question set on any given poet, the candidates must refer to the poem(s) they have studied but are not required to refer to **any specific poem(s), nor are they expected to discuss or refer to all the poems they have chosen to study**.

In each of the questions in **Prescribed Poetry**, the underlying nature of the task is the invitation to the candidates to **engage with the poems themselves**.

Exam Advice

- **You are not expected to write about any set number of poems** in the examination. You might decide to focus in detail on a small number of poems, or you could choose to write in a more general way on several poems.
- Most candidates write one or two well-developed **paragraphs** on each of the poems they have chosen for discussion. In other cases, a paragraph will focus on one specific aspect of the poet's work. When discussing recurring themes or features of style, appropriate cross-references to other poems may be useful.
- Reflect on central **themes** and viewpoints in the poems you discuss. Comment also on the use of language and the poet's distinctive **style**. Examine imagery, tone, structure, rhythm and rhyme. Be careful not to simply list aspects of style, such as alliteration or repetition. There's little point in mentioning that a poet uses sound effects or metaphors without discussing the effectiveness of such characteristics.
- Focus on **the task** you have been given in the poetry question. Identify the key terms in the wording of the question and think of similar words for these terms. This will help you develop a relevant and coherent personal response in keeping with the PCLM marking scheme criteria.
- Always root your answers in the text of the poems. Support the points you make with **relevant reference and quotation**. Make sure your own expression is fresh and lively. Avoid awkward expressions, such as 'It says in the poem that …'. Look for alternatives: 'There is a sense of …', 'The tone seems to suggest …', 'It's evident that …', etc.
- Neat, **legible handwriting** will help to make a positive impression on examiners. Corrections should be made by simply drawing a line through the mistake. Scored-out words distract attention from the content of your work.
- Keep the emphasis on why particular poets **appeal to you**. Consider the continuing relevance or significance of a poet's work. Perhaps you have shared some of the feelings or experiences expressed in the poems. Avoid starting answers with prepared biographical sketches. Brief reference to a poet's life is better used when discussing how the poems themselves were shaped by their experiences.
- Remember that the examination encourages **individual engagement** with the prescribed poems. Poetry can make us think and feel and imagine. It opens our minds to the wonderful possibilities of language and ideas. Your interaction with the poems is what matters most. **Commentary notes and critical interpretations are all there to be challenged.** Read the poems carefully and have confidence in expressing your own personal response.

Eavan Boland
1944–2020

'Poetry begins – as all art does – where certainties end.'

Eavan Boland was one of the most prominent voices in Irish poetry and was the author of many highly acclaimed poetry collections. Born in Dublin but raised in London, she had early experiences with anti-Irish racism that gave her a strong sense of heritage and a keen awareness of her identity. She later returned to attend school and university in Dublin, where she published a pamphlet of poetry after her graduation. Boland received her BA from Trinity College in 1966. She held numerous teaching positions and published poetry, books of criticism and articles. She married in 1969 and had two children. Her experiences as a wife and mother influenced her to recognise the beauty and significance of everyday living. Boland wrote plainly and eloquently about her experiences as a woman, mother and exile.

She taught at several colleges in America and was a professor of English at Stanford University, California. In addition to traditional Irish themes, Eavan Boland explored a wide range of subjects, including incisive commentaries on contemporary subjects and intensely personal poems about history, womanhood and relationships.

Investigate Further

To find out more about Eavan Boland, or to hear readings of her poems not available in your eBook, you could search some useful websites, such as YouTube, BBC Poetry, poetryfoundation.org and poetryarchive.org, or access additional material on this page of your eBook.

Prescribed Poems

EAVAN BOLAND

○ **1 'The War Horse'**
A runaway horse in a quiet suburban estate is the starting point for Boland's explorations of attitudes to warfare and violence throughout Irish history. **Page 4**

○ **2 'Child of Our Time' (OL)**
Written in response to a newspaper photograph of a child killed in the 1974 Dublin bombings, this poem tries to draw some kind of meaning from the tragedy. **Page 8**

○ **3 'The Famine Road'**
The poet dramatically recreates a tragic period in Irish history. Boland also links the Famine with another traumatic experience, the story of a woman diagnosed as infertile by her doctor. **Page 12**

○ **4 'The Shadow Doll'**
Boland considers the changing nature of marriage since Victorian times. The silence and submission of women are signified by the porcelain doll in its airless glass dome. **Page 16**

○ **5 'White Hawthorn in the West of Ireland'**
The poet's journey into the West brings her into contact with a wildly beautiful landscape where she can explore Irish superstitions and a strange, unspoken language. **Page 20**

○ **6 'Outside History'**
Another poem addressing the experience of the marginalised ('outsiders') and reflecting Boland's own humanity as a female Irish poet. **Page 24**

○ **7 'The Black Lace Fan My Mother Gave Me'**
This poem was inspired by the first gift given by the poet's father to her mother back in 1930s Paris. The souvenir is a symbol of young love and the mystery of changing relationships. **Page 28**

○ **8 'This Moment' (OL)**
In this short lyric, Boland unobtrusively captures the mystery and magic of the natural world and the beauty of loving relationships. **Page 32**

○ **9 'The Pomegranate'**
Another personal poem in which Boland uses mythical references to examine the complexity of feelings experienced in mother–daughter relationships. **Page 35**

○ **10 'Love' (OL)**
This reflective poem is addressed to the poet's husband, and considers the changing nature of romantic love. In developing her themes, Boland draws on Greek mythology. **Page 39**

(OL) indicates poems that are also prescribed for the Ordinary Level course.

1 🔊 The War Horse

This dry night, nothing unusual
About the clip, clop, casual

Iron of his shoes as he stamps death
Like a mint on the innocent coinage of earth.

I lift the window, watch the ambling feather   5
Of hock and fetlock, loosed from its daily tether

In the tinker camp on the Enniskerry Road,
Pass, his breath hissing, his snuffling head

Down. He is gone. No great harm is done.
Only a leaf of our laurel hedge is torn –   10

Of distant interest like a maimed limb,
Only a rose which now will never climb

The stone of our house, expendable, a mere
Line of defence against him, a volunteer

You might say, only a crocus its bulbous head   15
Blown from growth, one of the screamless dead.

But we, we are safe, our unformed fear
Of fierce commitment gone; why should we care

If a rose, a hedge, a crocus are uprooted
Like corpses, remote, crushed, mutilated?   20

He stumbles on like a rumour of war, huge,
Threatening; neighbours use the subterfuge

Of curtains; He stumbles down our short street
Thankfully passing us. I pause, wait,

Then to breathe relief lean on the sill   25
And for a second only my blood is still

With atavism. That rose he smashed frays
Ribboned across our hedge, recalling days

Of burned countryside, illicit braid:
A cause ruined before, a world betrayed.   30

👤 Personal Response

1. Describe the atmosphere in the first ten lines of the poem. Is it edgy or relaxed? Refer to the text in your response.
2. Choose one image from the poem that is particularly vivid and dramatic. Briefly explain your choice.
3. Write your own personal response to the poem, highlighting the impact it made on you.

👁 Critical Literacy

'The War Horse' was written in 1972 by Eavan Boland after she had moved to the suburbs at the foothills of the Dublin Mountains. It was an icy winter and the 'sounds of death from the televisions were heard almost nightly' as the news about the Northern Ireland Troubles was broadcast. In this poem, Boland questions ambivalent attitudes towards war.

This poem is based on a **real event**, **the appearance of a 'loosed' Traveller horse**, described in lines 1–9. Boland has said, 'It encompassed a real event. It entered a place in my heart and moved beyond it.' An aural description of the innocuous noise, 'nothing unusual', heralds the arrival of the animal. The horse, a menacing intruder that suggests the opposition between force and formality, wreaked havoc on the neat order of **suburban gardens**. The rigid control of the rhyming couplets mirrors the desire for order in the suburbs.

Onomatopoeia and the alliteration of the hard 'c' vividly echo the horse's walk, like something out of a young child's story: 'clip, clop, casual'. The second couplet counteracts this sense of ordinariness as it describes the damage the animal inflicts. The brutal verb 'stamps' jolts the reader as the garden, **'the innocent coinage of earth'**, is being destroyed. The simile of a mint, which puts an indelible mark on metal to make coins, is used to highlight the destruction. The **consequences of war** are also permanent – people are wounded or killed ('stamps death').

The **poet is an observer**: 'I lift the window, watch'. A detailed description of the horse's leg, 'ambling feather/Of hock and fetlock', conceals its capacity for

'his breath hissing, his snuffling head'

POETRY FOCUS

violence. There then follows an explanation of where the horse came from, the 'tinker camp on the Enniskerry Road'. The **random nature of violence** is aptly contained in the verbs 'ambling', 'loosed' and also in the long run-on line 'I lift ... Down.' The sounds the animal makes are vividly conveyed using onomatopoeia: 'hissing', 'snuffling'. The moment of danger passes: 'He is gone'. We can feel the palpable relief: 'No great harm is done'. Colloquial language reduces the event to a trivial disruption.

Lines 10–16 show that the poet has adopted a **sensible approach** as she surveys the **damage**, minimising it with an emphasis on the word 'only': 'Only a leaf ... is torn', 'Only a rose', 'only a crocus'. These are all 'expendable'; they can be done without. The language becomes more unsettling as violent descriptions are used to show the mangled blooms: 'like a maimed limb ... which now will never climb', 'Blown from growth'. All describe a world that will never be the same again, potential that will never be realised and life that is cut short. From Boland's perspective, 'the screamless dead' can no longer command attention.

And who cares anyway? It is of 'distant interest'. This apathetic view can be taken by people as they watch atrocities in other countries. The **language of war** is prominent: 'a mere/Line of defence', 'a volunteer', the head is 'Blown'. The poet's focus has now shifted away from the horse and is concentrated on conflict, its consequences and the vulnerability of victims.

In lines 17–21, Boland realises that 'we are safe'. War calls for commitment; people must choose to take sides, to fight. This is frightening: 'our unformed fear'. It is there but not expressed, nor given substance or form. Here in this domestic incident is war in miniature, the entry of an intruder who perpetrates damage. The poet asks why the community should care about something so insignificant as a damaged rose or a crushed crocus. She is challenging people who are blasé and examining their **insularity**: 'why should we care ... corpses, remote, crushed, mutilated?' Are there consequences if people do not care?

Boland criticises her own community in lines 22–30, with the neighbours described as hiding behind curtains ('subterfuge'). This 'I don't want to know' attitude reflects the **ambivalence** about the Northern Troubles in the Irish Republic during the 1970s. The tension, 'I pause, wait', is followed by release: 'breathe relief'. At the conclusion, there are two insightful views. One is the suburban woman's; the other is an Irish person's awareness of connecting with history. There is an ancestral memory, 'atavism', which associates the smashed rose with Ireland's history. The ribbon trails back to the violence of English colonialism. Boland and her neighbours chose not to confront the horse, just as generations of Irish people did not successfully confront the invaders. The intruder (the horse, the British) destroyed something beautiful and precious (the rose, Irish culture and freedom). The mood here is one of regret. Should both intruders have been challenged? How right is it to live so indifferently? The poem ends on a bleak note, a lament for **'a world betrayed'**.

EAVAN BOLAND

✒ Writing About the Poem

'We are collectively involved in violence which occurs in our land.' Discuss how 'The War Horse' reflects this statement. Illustrate your response with reference to the poem.

Sample Paragraph

Boland uses an ordinary incident, the arrival of a Traveller's horse into a suburban Dublin garden, to explore the ambivalent attitude to wars that seem distant. The colloquial phrase 'No great harm is done' and the neighbours who use 'the subterfuge/ Of curtains' both illustrate this insular approach. Everything is all right so long as 'we' are safe. The consequences of war are listed as Boland itemises them: 'maimed limb', 'expendable', 'screamless dead'. The vulnerability of the innocent victims is exposed. Can we afford to be so indifferent? The implicit statement is that we should care. We are left feeling that perhaps due to Irish people's indifference and through a lack of commitment, 'A cause' was lost. The poem ends with a lament, 'a world betrayed', with its long echoing vowel sound. I think Boland is upset at people's lack of commitment in a time of trouble.

> **EXAMINER'S COMMENT**
> This response succinctly addresses the task through a discussion on the theme and style of the poem. It ranges from the local incident to war's inevitable consequences and people's indifference. Close engagement with the text is evident in the discussion of colloquial language and sound effects. Good use is made of the rhetorical question, 'Can we afford to be so indifferent?' This well-controlled answer merits the top grade.

✏ Class/Homework Exercises

1. Is 'The War Horse' a private poem, or does it have a wider significance? Use reference to the text in your answer.
2. Eavan Boland creates an underlying sense of threat throughout 'The War Horse'. Discuss this view using close reference to the poem.

⊙ Points to Consider

- Themes include attitudes to conflict and violence throughout Irish history.
- Inclusive personal pronouns and rhetorical questions used to involve readers.
- Use of observational details, vibrant language, striking comparisons.
- Contrasting atmospheres and tones – reflective, accusatory.
- Memorable onomatopoeic effects – assonance, alliteration, internal rhyme.

2. Child of Our Time

(for Aengus)

Yesterday I knew no lullaby
But you have taught me overnight to order
This song, which takes from your final cry
Its tune, from your unreasoned end its reason,
Its rhythm from the discord of your murder   5
Its motive from the fact you cannot listen.

We who should have known how to instruct
With rhymes for your waking, rhythms for your sleep,
Names for the animals you took to bed,
Tales to distract, legends to protect,   10
Later an idiom for you to keep
And living, learn, must learn from you, dead,

To make our broken images rebuild
Themselves around your limbs, your broken
Image, find for your sake whose life our idle   15
Talk has cost, a new language. Child
Of our time, our times have robbed your cradle.
Sleep in a world your final sleep has woken.

discord: lack of harmony among people; harsh, confused sounds; conflict.

idiom: turn of phrase; words which when used together have a different meaning from when used singly.

'our times have robbed your cradle'

👤 Personal Response

1. Boland believes that the 'murder of the innocent' is one of the greatest obscenities. How is this explored in the poem? Refer to the text in response.
2. Where are the two feelings, tenderness and outrage, evident in the poem? Use reference to the text in your response.
3. What is Boland implying about 'our times'? Is she satisfied or dissatisfied with what is happening? Refer closely to the poem in your answer.

👁 Critical Literacy

'Child of Our Time' was written in 1974 at the height of the Troubles in Northern Ireland. It was prompted by a harrowing newspaper picture of a fireman tenderly carrying a dead child from the rubble of a bomb explosion in Dublin. The poem is dedicated to Aengus, the infant son of the poet's friend, who had suffered cot death. This lyric is a response to the sudden and unexpected deaths of all young children. It also challenges adults to change their ways.

The title of this poem places the little child in a wider context than that of family and town – he is a child of 'our time'. He is our responsibility; he belongs to us. A child should be a **symbol of innocence**, growth, love, potential and the future, but this has been savagely and tragically cut short by 'our time'. Boland did not have children when she wrote this poem ('Yesterday I knew no lullaby'), but in the first stanza she describes how she has been taught to sing a lullaby which is different: 'you have taught me overnight to order/This song'.

The child's violent and tragic death demands a response, so she will form and order and 'reason' a poem from the child's 'unreasoned end'. It is a song made of harsh sounds, 'discord'. The tone moves from tender compassion ('lullaby') to indignation ('the fact you cannot listen'). There is no escaping the finality of death, yet the poet is a balanced, reasonable person trying to make **order out of disorder** in a poem that uses simple language and is carefully arranged in three stanzas.

The poem is also charged with both **sadness and awareness**. The compassionate voice of the poet is heard in 'rhythms for your sleep,/Names for the animals you took to bed'. However, Boland is aware of the awfulness of the event: 'final cry', 'end', 'murder'. The language is formal, as befits such a solemn occasion: 'We who should have known', 'Child/Of our time'. This poem has several elements of an elegy (a poem for the dead): it laments, praises and consoles. The poem's many half-rhymes mimic this discordant time: 'idle'/'cradle', 'order'/'murder'.

The collective 'We' in the second stanza is used to show the true context of the child as a member of the human family. **It is 'We' who are responsible** for not making society safer so that childhood could consist of 'Tales to distract, legends to protect'. The repetitive sound of 'rhymes' and 'rhythms' imitates the rocking sound of a mother nursing her child. Boland's aim is clear: we must learn from our mistakes and reconstruct a better world out of 'our broken images'.

In the third stanza, the poet is insistent that **society takes on this responsibility**, that we 'find ... a new language'. We have to engage in dialogue, not 'idle/Talk', so that we can deliver a safer world for our children. Ironically, it is the little child, who 'our time' has 'robbed' from his cradle, who will form the scaffold around which we can build a new and better society: 'rebuild/Themselves around your limbs'. The final line of the poem is a **prayer and a hope**: 'Sleep in a world your final sleep has woken'. It is a wish that the little child be at rest now and that the world may be woken to its senses by his death.

Writing About the Poem

'Eavan Boland is a "sensitive poet" who is "rarely thrown off balance by anger".' Discuss this view of the poet in relation to the poem 'Child of Our Time'. Develop your answer with reference to the text.

Sample Paragraph

'Child of Our Time' is an example of Boland's control in response to what must be the most horrific event that people can witness: the brutal murder of an innocent child. The poem is carefully ordered into three stanzas that act as balanced paragraphs in an argument. The first stanza emphasises the meaningless atrocity of 'your unreasoned end'. The second places responsibility on the adult society that should have provided a safe environment for the young: 'We who should have known'. The third stanza urges adults to do something now, to 'find for your sake whose life our idle/Talk has cost, a new language'. Boland's language is controlled, appropriate for an elegy. The poet makes order out of disorder rather than letting her anger explode. The poem lacks sentimentality or even consolation.

EXAMINER'S COMMENT

Boland's careful management of ideas is explored in this answer to advance the view that she explores the tragic event in a controlled, sensitive way. Attention is paid to the form of the poem: 'The poem is carefully ordered into three stanzas that act as balanced paragraphs in an argument.' The insightful critical commentary shows good personal engagement. Clear expression and effective use of accurate quotation enhances this highly successful top-grade response.

✒ Class/Homework Exercises

1. There is a 'difficult sort of comfort' in literature. Discuss this statement in relation to 'Child of Our Time'. Develop the points you make with reference to the poem.
2. In 'Child of Our Time', Boland explores the universal experience of tragic violence. To what extent do you agree with this view? Develop the points you make with reference to both the themes and language use in the poem.

⊙ Points to Consider

- Addresses issues surrounding the tragic death of a child.
- Striking images of innocence, poignant mood, repetition.
- Universal significance of random violence and tragedy.
- Solemn, didactic tone emphasised by extended uninterrupted lines.
- Simple childlike language and gentle sound effects.

EAVAN BOLAND

3 🔊 The Famine Road

Title: during the Irish Famine of 1845–48, the British authorities organised various relief schemes. The hungry were given a small wage to buy food for participating in road building and other community projects. Many of the new roads were constructed in remote areas and served little purpose other than controlling the starving population.

'Idle as trout in light Colonel Jones,
these Irish, give them no coins at all; their bones
need toil, their characters no less.' Trevelyan's
seal blooded the deal table. The Relief
Committee deliberated: 'Might it be safe,   5
Colonel, to give them roads, roads to force
from nowhere, going nowhere of course?'

    'one out of every ten and then
    another third of those again
    women – in a case like yours.'   10

Sick, directionless they worked; fork, stick
were iron years away; after all could
they not blood their knuckles on rock, suck
April hailstones for water and for food?
Why for that, cunning as housewives, each eyed –   15
as if at a corner butcher – the other's buttock.

    'anything may have caused it, spores,
    a childhood accident; one sees
    day after day these mysteries.'

Dusk: they will work tomorrow without him.   20
They know it and walk clear; he has become
a typhoid pariah, his blood tainted, although
he shares it with some there. No more than snow
attends its own flakes where they settle
and melt, will they pray by his death rattle.   25

    'You never will, never you know
    but take it well woman, grow
    your garden, keep house, good-bye.'

'It has gone better than we expected, Lord
Trevelyan, sedition, idleness, cured   30
in one; from parish to parish, field to field,
the wretches work till they are quite worn,
then fester by their work; we march the corn
to the ships in peace; this Tuesday I saw bones
out of my carriage window, your servant Jones.'   35

    'Barren, never to know the load
    of his child in you, what is your body
    now if not a famine road?'

Colonel Jones: army officer and Chairman of the Board of Works.
Trevelyan: Charles Trevelyan, a senior civil servant in overall charge of famine relief.
Relief Committee: groups usually consisting of landlords, the clergy and influential people were set up to distribute food.
deliberated: considered, discussed.
spores: germs.
typhoid pariah: someone shunned because of this deadly blood disease.
death rattle: last sound of the dying.
sedition: subversion, treachery.
corn/to the ships: throughout the famine years, corn was exported from Ireland.

👤 Personal Response

1. Describe the tone of voice in the opening stanza, using close reference to the text.
2. The poet links the abuse of famine victims with the mistreatment of women in modern society. Is this convincing? Briefly explain your response.
3. In your view, how chillingly pessimistic are the last three lines of the poem? Give reasons for your answer.

👁 Critical Literacy

The poem raises interesting questions about marginalised people, a favourite theme in Boland's work. Here she makes a connection between a famine road in the 1840s and an infertile woman in modern times. Boland presents the poem as a series of dramatic moments featuring a variety of characters.

Stanza one begins with the voice of Colonel Jones, a British official, reading from a letter written by Lord Trevelyan, who had overall responsibility for famine relief. The boorish tone of the opening comments about 'these Irish' is explicitly offensive. Trevelyan's generalised insults reflect the **depth of prejudice and suspicion** felt towards an entire population, who are 'Idle as trout in light'. Such ruthless disregard is further underlined by the vivid image of the official blood-red seal. The proposed solutions – 'toil' or hard labour building roads 'going nowhere' – could hardly be more cynical and are all the more ironic coming from the 'Relief Committee'.

Stanza two (like stanzas four and six) is italicised and introduces another speaker, the authoritative voice of a consultant doctor. The unidentified voice quoting statistics to an unnamed woman is casually impersonal. The situation becomes clearer as the poem continues: the medical expert is discussing the woman's failure to have children. Boland portrays him as insensitive and patronising: 'anything may have caused it'. His tone becomes increasingly **unsympathetic as he dismisses her disappointment**: 'You never will, never you know'. He almost seems to take delight in repeating the word 'never'. The doctor's final comments are as severe as some of the remarks made by any of the British officials: 'take it well woman, grow/your garden, keep house'.

'the wretches work till they are quite worn'

POETRY FOCUS

In stanza three, the poet imagines the terrible experiences of the famine victims. The language used to describe their struggle is disturbing: 'Sick, directionless they worked'. Prominent **harsh-sounding consonants**, especially 'c' and 'k' in such phrases as 'blood their knuckles on rock', emphasise the suffering. The alarming suggestion of cannibalism ('each eyed –/as if at a corner butcher – the other's buttock') is a reminder of how people were driven beyond normal standards of civilised human behaviour.

Stanza five focuses on the prevalence of death throughout the long famine years. Attitudes harden as disease becomes widespread and commonplace. The poet's direct description, steady rhythm and resigned tone combine to reflect the awful reality of the times: 'they will work tomorrow without him'. Boland illustrates the **breakdown of communities** with the tragic example of one 'typhoid pariah' abandoned to die without anyone to 'pray by his death rattle'.

This great human catastrophe is made all the more pathetic in stanza seven, which begins with an excerpt from Colonel Jones's response to Trevelyan: 'It has gone better than we expected'. **The offhand tone is self-satisfied** as he reports that the road-building schemes have succeeded in their real purpose of controlling the peasant population ('the wretches'). The horrifyingly detached admission – without the slightest sense of irony – of allowing the starving to 'fester' while 'we march the corn/to the ships' is almost beyond comprehension. The colonel's matter-of-fact comment about seeing 'bones/out of my carriage window' is a final reminder of the colossal gulf between the powerful and the powerless.

In the final stanza, Boland's **own feelings of revulsion** bring her back to the present when she sums up the 'Barren' reality of the childless woman 'never to know the load/of his child'. The famine road is reintroduced as a common symbol for the shared tragedies of the victims of both mass starvation and infertility. The concluding rhetorical question leaves us to consider important issues of authority and the abuse of power, whatever the circumstances.

✒ Writing About the Poem

'Eavan Boland uses evocative symbols to address important issues.' Discuss this statement in relation to 'The Famine Road', developing your points with suitable quotation or reference.

Sample Paragraph

The deserted famine road in Boland's poem is a haunting symbol through which we can examine aspects of power. The poet blends two narratives, one of a country road in the 1840s and the other of a modern-day visit to a doctor, in a series of dramatic scenes. Lord Trevelyan and the doctor abuse their power. Trevelyan's offensive comments, 'these Irish', 'Idle as trout in light', set the tone. This ignorance is mirrored in the doctor's response to his infertile patient, 'You never will, never you know'. The superior, patronising attitude of those in charge is captured in snippets of direct speech, 'It has gone better than we expected', 'but take it well woman'. None of the famine victims' voices are heard and this omission emphasises their vulnerability. Instead, the 'wretches work till they are quite worn'. Nothing changes.

> **EXAMINER'S COMMENT**
> This top-grade response traces the two interconnected narratives, focusing on the dramatic significance of these events. The similar tones of those in charge are well explored: Trevelyan's 'offensive' remarks are mirrored in 'the doctor's response to his infertile patient'. An interesting point is made about the omission of the victims' voices. Expression is controlled and confident throughout.

EAVAN BOLAND

✒ Class/Homework Exercises

1. To what extent does 'The Famine Road' show Eavan Boland's sympathies for the outsiders and the marginalised in society? Refer to the poem in your answer.
2. Eavan Boland makes effective use of several dramatic techniques in 'The Famine Road'. Discuss this view, developing your points with close reference to the poem.

⊙ Points to Consider

- **Dramatic recreation of famine suffering and exploitation.**
- **Updated comparison with the experience of an infertile woman.**
- **Authentic language, descriptive details, stark imagery, symbols.**
- **Sound effects echo the harsh, cynical atmosphere.**

4 The Shadow Doll

They stitched blooms from ivory tulle
to hem the oyster gleam of the veil.
They made hoops for the crinoline.

Now, in summary and neatly sewn –
a porcelain bride in an airless glamour –   5
the shadow doll survives its occasion.

Under glass, under wraps, it stays
even now, after all, discreet about
visits, fevers, quickenings and lusts

and just how, when she looked at   10
the shell-tone spray of seed pearls,
the bisque features, she could see herself

inside it all, holding less than real
stephanotis, rose petals, never feeling
satin rise and fall with the vows   15

I kept repeating on the night before –
astray among the cards and wedding gifts –
the coffee pots and the clocks and

the battered tan case full of cotton
lace and tissue-paper, pressing down, then   20
pressing down again. And then, locks.

Title: in Victorian times a bride-to-be's dressmaker would send her a shadow doll. It consisted of a figurine under a dome of glass modelling the proposed wedding dress.

tulle: fine net fabric.
oyster: off-white colour.
crinoline: hooped petticoat.

discreet: careful to avoid embarrassment by keeping confidences secret; unobtrusive.
quickenings: sensations; a woman's awareness of the first movements of the child in the womb.

bisque: unglazed white porcelain.

stephanotis: scented white flowers used for displays at both weddings and funerals.

👤 Personal Response

1. What style of language is used to describe the doll? Do you consider it beautiful or stifling, or both? Illustrate your response with reference to the poem.
2. Choose two phrases from the poem that you found particularly interesting. Briefly explain the reasons for your choice.
3. Do you think marriage has changed for the modern bride in today's world? Refer to the last two stanzas in your answer.

👁 Critical Literacy

'The Shadow Doll' is taken from the 1990 collection of poems, *Outside History*. The shadow doll wore a model of the wedding dress for the bride-to-be. Boland uses the doll as a symbol to explore the submission and silence surrounding women and women's issues by placing the late 20th century and Victorian times side by side.

The **first two stanzas** describe the doll vividly, with her 'ivory tulle' and 'oyster gleam'. The 'porcelain doll' is a **beautiful, fragile object**, but the 'ivory' and 'oyster' colours are lifeless. Passivity and restriction are being shown in the phrase 'neatly sewn'. The pronoun 'it' is used – the woman is seen as an object, not a real flesh-and-blood human being. Her community is described in the preparations: 'They stitched', 'They made'. Are they colluding in the constraint? The phrase 'airless glamour' conveys an allure that has been deprived of life-giving oxygen. The occasion of the marriage is long gone, but the doll remains as a reminder, a shadow of what was.

The **language of containment** and imprisonment is continued in **stanza three**: 'Under glass, under wraps'. The doll is silent and 'discreet'; it knows but does not tell. The bride would have kept the doll throughout her life, so the doll would have been present at all major events such as marriage, childbirth, sickness and intimate moments, 'visits, fevers, quickenings and lusts'. These experiences are not explored in poetry, which is why women and their issues are 'outside history'. They are neither recorded nor commented on.

Stanza four sees the **pronoun change to 'she'** as the poet imagines the Victorian bride considering her own wedding: 'she could see herself/inside it all'. It is as if she becomes like the doll, assuming a mask of 'bisque features' and unable to feel real life: 'holding less than real/stephanotis', 'never feeling/satin rise and fall with the vows'. The only remnant of her life is the silent doll.

EAVAN BOLAND

'a porcelain bride'

Stanza five ends with the word 'vows', and this is the link into the next stanza, which is a view from the modern-day bride where the narrative voice becomes 'I'.

The poet is 'repeating' the same vows as the Victorian bride. Are these entrapping and imprisoning women? Like the Victorian bride, the modern bride is surrounded by things ('cards and wedding gifts'), yet she is 'astray' (stanza six), with the same **sense of disorientation** coming over her. Is she feeling this because she is losing her individual identity as she agrees to become part of a couple?

Stanza seven increases the **feelings of restriction** when the suitcase is described as 'battered', and there is the added emphatic repetition of 'pressing down'. Finally, the single monosyllable 'locks' clicks the poem to an end. The onomatopoeic sound echoes through the years as Boland voices the silence in the depressing ending. For some women, little has changed since Victorian times.

✒ Writing About the Poem

'Boland's poems often end on a bleak note.' Discuss how 'The Shadow Doll' reflects this statement. Illustrate your response with reference to the text.

Sample Paragraph

The onomatopoeia of the word 'locks' echoes with frightening intensity at the end of 'The Shadow Doll'. It suggests the clang of a prison door. This poem explores the meaning of marriage for women. It starts with the description of the Victorian doll with its wedding dress, which seems to become a stifling mask fitted on a living woman, 'airless glamour', 'Under glass', 'under wraps'. Marriage is shown as confining, 'discreet'. The repetition of 'pressing down' has an almost nightmarish sense of claustrophobia. I find it strange that there is no mention of the groom, or friends or families. Instead there is a growing sense of intimidation culminating in the echoing phrase 'And then, locks'. What or who is locked in? What or who is locked out?

EXAMINER'S COMMENT

This succinct response carefully considers the effect of the poem's ending and Boland's exploration of the theme of marriage as a repressive and restricting force in women's lives. The paragraph also touches on interesting questions about the narrow views expressed in the poem. A real sense of individual engagement is evident, particularly in the comment about the final two rhetorical questions. Top-grade standard.

✏ Class/Homework Exercises

1. 'In her poetry, Boland uses concrete images of objects, colours and textures to explore themes.' In your opinion, how valid is this statement? Use reference to 'The Shadow Doll' in your answer.
2. In 'The Shadow Doll', Boland succeeds in highlighting the experience of women in patriarchal societies. Discuss this view using close reference to the poem.

EAVAN BOLAND

⊙ Points to Consider

- Themes include the changing nature of marriage and the oppression of women.
- Effective concrete details, symbolism, confinement imagery, repetition.
- Dreamlike sense of disorientation.
- Varying tones – reflective, sympathetic, critical and hopeful.

5 White Hawthorn in the West of Ireland

Title: hawthorn is a flowering tree that blossoms in springtime. It is associated with fairy tales and superstitions in Irish folklore. People believed that it was unlucky to cut hawthorn or to keep it indoors.

I drove West
in the season between seasons.
I left behind suburban gardens.
Lawnmowers. Small talk.

Under low skies, past splashes of coltsfoot, 5
I assumed
the hard shyness of Atlantic light
and the superstitious aura of hawthorn.

All I wanted then was to fill my arms with
sharp flowers, 10
to seem, from a distance, to be part of
that ivory, downhill rush. But I knew,

I had always known
the custom was
not to touch hawthorn. 15
Not to bring it indoors for the sake of

the luck
such constraint would forfeit –
a child might die, perhaps, or an unexplained
fever speckle heifers. So I left it 20

stirring on those hills
with a fluency
only water has. And, like water, able
to re-define land. And free to seem to be –

for anglers, 25
and for travellers astray in
the unmarked lights of a May dusk –
the only language spoken in those parts.

the season: between spring and summer.

coltsfoot: wild plant with yellow flowers.
assumed: became part of.
Atlantic light: unsettled weather causes the light to vary.
superstitious aura: disquiet associated with hawthorn stories.

forfeit: lose, risk.

heifers: cows which have not yet had calves.

👤 Personal Response

1. Describe the poet's changing mood as she travels from her suburban home to the West. Refer to the text in your answer.
2. There are many beautiful images in the poem. Choose two that you find interesting and briefly explain their appeal.
3. What is the significance of the white hawthorn? What might it symbolise? Refer closely to the poem in your answer.

👁 Critical Literacy

In this poem, the folklore associated with hawthorn in rural Ireland is seen as symbolic of an ancient 'language' that has almost disappeared. Boland structures her themes around the image of a journey into the West. It seems as though she is hoping to return to her roots in the traditional landscape of the West of Ireland.

The poem opens on a conversational note. Boland's clear intention is to leave the city behind: 'I drove West/in the season between seasons'. Her tone is determined, dismissing the **artificial life of suburbia** ('Lawnmowers. Small talk.') in favour of the freedom awaiting her. Stanza one emphasises the poet's strong desire to get away from her cultivated suburban confines, which seem colourless and overly regulated. The broken rhythm of line 4 adds to the abrupt sense of rigidity.

EAVAN BOLAND

'the superstitious aura'

POETRY FOCUS

This orderly landscape is in stark contrast with the world of 'Atlantic light' Boland discovers on her journey. Stanzas two and three contain **striking images of energy and growth**. The 'splashes of coltsfoot' suggest a fresh enthusiasm for the wide open spaces as she becomes one with this changing environment. The prominent sibilant 's' underpins the rich stillness of the remote countryside.

She seems both fearful and fascinated by the hawthorn's 'superstitious aura'. The experience is similar to an artist becoming increasingly absorbed in the joy of painting. Run-on lines and the frequent use of the pronoun 'I' accentuate our appreciation of the **poet's own delight** in 'that ivory, downhill rush'.

Stanzas four and five focus on the mystery and superstition associated with hawthorn in Irish folk tradition. Boland's awareness of the **possible dangers** check her eagerness as she considers the stories that have been handed down: 'a child might die, perhaps'. The poet is momentarily caught between a desire to fill her arms with these wild flowers and her own disquieting belief in the superstitions. Eventually, she decides to follow her intuition and respect the customs of the West: 'So I left it'.

The personification ('stirring') of the hawthorn in stanza six reinforces Boland's regard for this unfamiliar landscape as a **living place**. The poet's imagination has also been stirred by her journey. In comparing the hawthorn to water, she suggests its elemental power. Both share a natural 'fluency' which can shape and 're-define land'.

The poet links the twin forces of superstition and landscape even more forcibly in stanza seven. They both defy time and transcend recorded history. The hawthorn trees give the poet a **glimpse of Ireland's ancient culture**. Although nature remains elusive, Boland believes that for outsiders like herself – visiting 'anglers' and tourists – it is 'the only language spoken in those parts'. Her final tone is one of resignation as she accepts that she can never fully understand Ireland's unique landscape or the past.

✒ Writing About the Poem

'Boland uses a variety of poetic techniques to create poems which allow readers to contemplate the beauty and mystery of nature.' Discuss this statement, with particular reference to 'White Hawthorn in the West of Ireland'.

Sample Paragraph

Boland creates vivid word pictures of two contrasting landscapes, the ordered urban and the wild rural. She decisively sets off on her journey, 'I left behind suburban gardens'. Suddenly the view opens out to the big western skyline, 'the hard shyness of Atlantic light'. The magic of the countryside is conveyed in the 'superstitious aura of hawthorn'. The lush assonance of this line's broad vowels contrasts abruptly with the sharp sounds of the town's descriptive details. But there is another aspect to nature foreshadowed in the adjective, 'sharp'. Cutting the hawthorn is considered bad luck in the countryside and Boland respects the local tradition, 'So I left it'. She, like the other tourists, can enjoy, but not fully understand the wild beauty of nature, 'the only language spoken in those parts'.

EAVAN BOLAND

> **EXAMINER'S COMMENT**
>
> *This answer focuses on how aspects of Boland's style contribute to communicating her message that nature may be appreciated but never entirely understood. A developed discussion encompasses the poet's use of varying tones and sound effects: 'The lush assonance of this line's broad vowels contrasts abruptly with the sharp sounds of the town's descriptive details.' Accurate quotation supports the discussion throughout. A confident top-grade standard.*

✒ Class/Homework Exercises

1. What do you think Eavan Boland has learned from her journey to the West of Ireland? Refer to the poem, 'White Hawthorn in the West of Ireland', in your answer.
2. Boland makes effective use of both visual and aural imagery to celebrate the Irish landscape in this poem. Discuss this statement, using close reference to the text.

◎ Points to Consider

- **Beauty of the native landscape and Irish traditions are central themes.**
- **Contrast between urban and rural landscapes.**
- **Reflective tone reveals the poet's personal feelings and attitudes.**
- **Vivid visual imagery, free rhythm, striking onomatopoeia and sibilant effects.**

6  Outside History

There are outsiders, always. These stars –
these iron inklings of an Irish January,
whose light happened

thousands of years before
our pain did: they are, they have always been   5
outside history.

They keep their distance. Under them remains
a place where you found
you were human, and

a landscape in which you know you are mortal.   10
And a time to choose between them.
I have chosen:

out of myth into history I move to be
part of that ordeal
whose darkness is   15

only now reaching me from those fields,
those rivers, those roads clotted as
firmaments with the dead.

How slowly they die
as we kneel beside them, whisper in their ear.   20
And we are too late. We are always too late.

inklings: slight idea or suspicion; clues.

history: record or account of past events and developments; the study of these.

mortal: destined to die.

myth: tale with supernatural characters; untrue idea or explanation; imaginary person; story with a germ of truth in it.
ordeal: painful experience.

clotted: clogged up.
firmaments: sky or heavens.

'These stars'

👤 Personal Response

1. How are the stars 'outsiders'? Do you think they are an effective symbol for those who are marginalised and regarded as being of no importance? Briefly explain your answer.
2. In your opinion, what does Boland mean by the final line of the poem?
3. Write a short personal response to 'Outside History', highlighting the impact the poem made on you.

👁 Critical Literacy

'Outside History' was written in 1990 as part of a collection of poems that were arranged to reflect the changing seasons. This poem is set in January. Boland believes that it is important to remember the experiences of those who have not been recorded in history. These are the outsiders, the lost, the voiceless, the silent, to whom she gives a hauntingly beautiful voice.

Lines 1–6. The poem opens with an **impersonal statement**: 'There are outsiders, always'. The poet is referring to those who have not been recorded in history. The stars are also outsiders, standing outside and above human history. At their great distance, they are shown as cold and remote ('iron', 'Irish January'). They have a permanence and longevity that are in contrast to human life: 'whose light happened/thousands of years before/our pain did'. The run-on line suggests the light that travels thousands of years to reach us. The phrase 'outside history' is placed on its own to emphasise how the stars do not belong to human history.

Lines 7–11. The poet stresses **the remoteness of the stars**: 'They keep their distance'. They don't want to be involved. Now she turns to 'you', a member of the human race, and places 'you' in context with the words 'place' and 'landscape'. This is where 'you found/you were human' and 'mortal'. Unlike the stars; 'you' are a suffering member of the human race who is subject to ageing and death. The line 'And a time to choose between them' could refer to choosing between the perspective of the stars, i.e. remaining at an uninvolved distance, or the perspective of a member of the human race, i.e. involved and anguished.

Lines 12–18. The phrase 'I have chosen' marks a **turning point** in the poem. Boland has made a deliberate decision, moving away from 'myth' and tradition. She felt that myth obscures history. She regarded figures like Caitlín Ní Houlihán and Dark Rosaleen, female symbols of Ireland, as passive, simplified and decorative emblems in male poems. For the poet, history is laced with myths, which, in her opinion, are as unreal, cold and distant as the stars are from reality. She regarded these mythic emblems as false and limiting, a corruption. Boland is trying to achieve a sense of belonging and wholeness by unwinding the myth and the stereotype. She wants reality rather than the glittering image of the stars: 'out of myth into history I move to be/part of that ordeal'.

Just as the stars' light travelled vast distances to reach us, so the darkness of unwritten history is travelling to reach her 'only now'. The run-on stanza again suggests great distances that had to be covered for the poet to connect with the past. There follows a description that recalls the **Irish famine**: 'those fields', 'those rivers', 'those roads' which were covered with 'the dead'. The paradoxical phrase 'clotted as/firmaments' uses the language of the stars to describe the numberless bodies strewn everywhere as a result of the famine. This condensed image evokes a poignant sense of the unmarked graves of countless victims, as numberless as the stars.

Lines 19–21. The concluding stanza changes to the collective 'we'. Is this referring to the Irish people accepting responsibility for **honouring the dead** and being part of history? The rite of contrition is being said: 'as we kneel beside them, whisper in their ear'. It was believed that the person's soul would go to rest in heaven as he or she had made their peace with God, but the repetition of the last line stresses that the words of comfort have come 'too late'. The people don't know they are being honoured by the poet. Nevertheless, the poem stands as a testament to them and their unrecorded history. Has Boland changed her attitude from the beginning of the poem: 'There are outsiders, always'? Has she brought them in from the cold sidelines, including them into history? Or has she (and we) left it too late?

Writing About the Poem

'Eavan Boland's poetry gives a haunting voice to the marginalised and dispossessed in society.' Discuss this statement, with particular reference to 'Outside History'.

Sample Paragraph

I found the symbol of the stars effective because they represented the cold distance the outsiders must feel 'they have always been/outside history'. The sympathetic tone and the alliterative phrase, 'iron inklings of an Irish January' capture the predicament facing marginalised people. The stars show no human empathy with the dispossessed, 'They keep their distance'. But Boland has 'chosen' to embrace her humane side. She gives them an unforgettable voice, recalling their tragic story, 'those roads clotted as/firmaments with the dead'. The poem ends with the sad realisation, 'And we are too late'. They won't know that they are being remembered. The dispossessed may not, but Boland has given them a voice.

EXAMINER'S COMMENT

As part of a full essay this perceptive reading of Boland's poem addresses the task directly in a series of accurately referenced arguments. Excellent use of quotation throughout supports the thoughtful discussion points. Expression is also clear and impressive, 'But Boland has "chosen" to embrace her humane side'. An informed exploration of the poet's language also ensures the top-grade standard.

EAVAN BOLAND

✒ Class/Homework Exercises

1. Does 'Outside History' make a compelling case on behalf of voiceless and marginalised people? Develop your answer with close reference to the text of the poem.
2. In your opinion, what does the dominant tone throughout the poem reveal about Eavan Boland as a person? Develop your answer with close reference to the text.

◉ Points to Consider

- **Key themes – exclusion of the marginalised.**
- **Boland's distrust of myth, history and stereotypes.**
- **Varying tones – reflective, regretful, didactic.**
- **Effective use of repetition, striking imagery.**

7 The Black Lace Fan My Mother Gave Me

It was the first gift he ever gave her,
buying it for five francs in the Galeries
in pre-war Paris. It was stifling.
A starless drought made the nights stormy.

They stayed in the city for the summer. 5
They met in cafés. She was always early.
He was late. That evening he was later.
They wrapped the fan. He looked at his watch.

She looked down the Boulevard des Capucines.
She ordered more coffee. She stood up. 10
The streets were emptying. The heat was killing.
She thought the distance smelled of rain and lightning.

These are wild roses, appliquéd on silk by hand,
darkly picked, stitched boldly, quickly.
The rest is tortoiseshell and has the reticent, 15
clear patience of its element. It is

a worn-out, underwater bullion and it keeps,
even now, an inference of its violation.
The lace is overcast as if the weather
it opened for and offset had entered it. 20

The past is an empty café terrace.
An airless dusk before thunder. A man running.
And no way now to know what happened then –
none at all – unless, of course, you improvise:

The blackbird on this first sultry morning, 25
in summer, finding buds, worms, fruit,
feels the heat. Suddenly she puts out her wing –
the whole, full, flirtatious span of it.

Galeries: Galeries Lafayette is a store in Paris.

appliquéd: embroidered.

tortoiseshell: clear decorative material.
reticent: reserved, restrained.

bullion: treasure.

improvise: make up, imagine.

flirtatious: enticing, playful.
span: extent, measure.

👤 Personal Response

1. The setting is important in this poem. Briefly explain what it contributes to the atmosphere, referring to the text in your answer.
2. Comment briefly on the effect of the short sentences and irregular rhythms in the first three stanzas.
3. Did you like this poem? Give reasons for your response, referring to the poem in your answer.

👁 Critical Literacy

Set in pre-war Paris in the 1930s, the incident that occurs is the giving of a gift, a black lace fan that the poet's father gave to her mother. A fan was usually seen as a sign of romantic love and desire. However, its significance here is never entirely explained to us. Maybe this is in recognition of our inability to fully understand other people's relationships or to recall the past and the effect it has on us. Boland's poem is one of those attempts.

Stanza one begins on a narrative note as the poet recreates a significant moment in her parents' lives back in the 1930s. **The fan was a special symbol of young love** and was important because it was 'the first gift' from her father to her mother. Other details of the precise cost and the 'stifling' weather add to the importance of the occasion. Although the Parisian

EAVAN BOLAND

'And no way now to know what happened then'

setting is romantic, the mood is tense. Their courtship is framed in a series of captured moments, as though Boland is flicking through an old photo album.

In stanzas two and three, short sentences and the growing unevenness of the rhythm add to this cinematic quality: 'They met in cafés. She was always early'. The hesitant relationship between the lovers is conveyed repeatedly through their nervous gestures: 'He looked at his watch', 'She stood up'. Boland builds up the tension through references to the heat wave: 'the distance smelled of rain and lightning'. The image might also suggest the **stormy nature of what lay ahead** for the couple.

Stanzas four and five focus on the elegant lace fan in **vivid detail**. The poet notes its decorative qualities, carefully embroidered with the most romantic 'wild roses' and fine 'tortoiseshell'. She seems fascinated by the painstaking craft ('stitched boldly') involved in creating this beautiful token of love. But the poet's appreciation of the fan becomes diminished with guilt. The tortoiseshell has suffered 'violation' at the expense of the gift. In Boland's mind, the delicate colours decorating the fan came from 'a worn-out, underwater bullion'. The tone is suddenly downbeat as the thought throws a shadow ('The lace is overcast') on her parents' relationship.

In stanza six, the poet imagines the romantic Parisian drama of the 'empty café terrace', but admits that she can never know what really happened that fateful evening in the 'airless dusk before thunder'. Instead, she must 'improvise' it. But at least the romantic moment is preserved in her imagination. Not for the first time, however, there is an underlying suggestion of the reality of relationships over time, and the balance of joy and disappointment that is likely. For Boland, the fan is only a small part of her parents' story. Perhaps she realises that **the past can never be completely understood**.

The striking image of a blackbird dominates the final stanza. The poet returns to the present as she observes the bird 'in summer, finding buds'. The movement of the blackbird's wing is an unexpected link with the black lace fan all those years ago. While the souvenir is old, its significance as a symbol of youthful romance can still be found elsewhere. For the first time, **Boland now seems to understand the beauty of her parents' love** for each other. The last lines are daring and appear to describe both the blackbird and her mother as a young girl holding her new gift: 'Suddenly she puts out her wing –/the whole, full, flirtatious span of it'. The energetic pace of the lines combine with the alliterative sounds and sibilant music to produce a lively sense of celebration at the end.

✒ Writing About the Poem

'Eavan Boland takes a balanced, unsentimental view of relationships.' To what extent is this true of 'The Black Lace Fan My Mother Gave Me'? Develop your answer with reference to the poem.

Sample Paragraph

This poem is not a typical love poem. The poet imagines the intense heat of Paris: 'It was stifling.' References to the weather hint at her parents' uncomfortable relationship: 'The heat was killing.' Boland might be referring indirectly to the future problems in the couple's marriage. Having said that, the gift of the fan is a symbol of the attraction the couple felt. It is a traditional image of true romance. Eavan shows the reality of the relationship by noting the unsentimental details: 'He was late', 'She stood up'. There was nervousness when they were first infatuated with each other, but their love was to change over time. This gives us a final impression that Boland is happy to imagine the love between her parents back in the 1930s. In a way, the poem is as much about the love Boland herself feels for her parents as about their love.

> **EXAMINER'S COMMENT**
> This paragraph focuses well on the way love is presented throughout the poem. Good use is made of suitable quotations and this high-grade response is well rounded off with an effective point about the poet's own enduring love for her parents.

✎ Class/Homework Exercises

1. Comment on Eavan Boland's use of symbolism in 'The Black Lace Fan My Mother Gave Me', referring to the text in your answer.
2. What does Boland's poem reveal about her parents' relationship? Develop the points you make with reference to both the subject matter and language use in the poem.

⊙ Points to Consider

- Themes include romantic love and changing family relationships.
- Striking language – central symbol of the fan, dramatic image of the blackbird.
- Evocative atmosphere of 1930s Paris.
- Vivid detail; varying tones – reflective, nostalgic, realistic.

8 🔊 This Moment

A neighbourhood.
At dusk.

Things are getting ready
to happen
out of sight.   5

Stars and moths.
And rinds slanting around fruit.   **rinds:** peels.

But not yet.

One tree is black.
One window is yellow as butter.   10

A woman leans down to catch a child
who has run into her arms
this moment.

Stars rise.
Moths flutter.   15
Apples sweeten in the dark.

'this moment'

👤 Personal Response

1. Choose either one visual or one aural image from the poem, and briefly comment on its effectiveness. Develop your answer by referring to the text.
2. Comment briefly on how Boland manages to create drama within the poem.
3. What do you think is the central theme in the poem? Refer to the text in your answer.

👁 Critical Literacy

In this short lyric poem, Eavan Boland captures the experience of a passing moment in time. It is clear that she is moved by the ordinariness of suburban life, where she glimpses the immeasurable beauty of nature and human nature. The occasion is another reminder of the mystery and wonder of all creation, as expressed by the American poet Walt Whitman, who wrote, 'I know of nothing else but miracles'.

The poem's **opening lines** introduce a suburban area in any part of the world. Boland pares the scene down to its essentials. All we learn is that it is dusk, a time of transition. The atmosphere is one of quiet intensity. Full stops break the rhythm and force us to evaluate what is happening. Although we are presented with an **anonymous setting**, it seems strangely familiar. The late evening – especially as darkness falls – can be a time for reflecting about the natural world.

The stillness and dramatic anticipation intensify further in **lines 3–8**. Something important is about to happen 'out of sight'. Boland then considers some of nature's wonders: 'Stars and moths'. In the twilight, everything seems mysterious, even 'rinds slanting around fruit'. The poet's eye for detail is like that of an artist. The rich, sensory image of the cut fruit is exact and tactile. She uses simple language precisely to create a **mood of natural calmness** that is delayed for a split second ('But not yet').

There is time for two more **vivid images** in **lines 9–10**. The startling colour contrast between the 'black' tree and the window that is 'yellow as butter' has a cinematic effect. The simile is homely, in keeping with the domestic setting. Repetition of 'One' focuses our attention as the build-up continues. Again, Boland presents the sequence of events in a series of brief glimpses. It is as if she is marking time, preparing us for the key moment of revelation.

This occurs in **lines 11–13**. The central image of the mother and child intuitively reaching out for each other is a powerful symbol of unconditional love. It is every bit as wonderful as any of life's greatest mysteries. The three lines become progressively condensed as the child reaches the mother. The syntax suggests their eagerness to show their love for each other. Boland's decision to generalise ('A woman' and 'a child') emphasises the **universal significance** of 'this moment'. The crucial importance of people's feelings transcends time and place.

EAVAN BOLAND

There is a slight tone of anti-climax about the last three lines. However, Boland rounds off her description of the moment by placing it within a wider context. The constant expression of family love is in harmony with everything else that is beautiful in nature. This feeling is suggested by the recurring sibilant 's' sounds and the carefully chosen verbs ('rise', 'flutter' and 'sweeten'), all of which celebrate the excitement and **joy of everyday human relationships**.

✒ Writing About the Poem

'Eavan Boland's poetry deals effectively with important contemporary issues.' Discuss this statement, with particular reference to her poem 'This Moment'.

Sample Paragraph

Boland places her poem in a contemporary setting, a Dublin suburb at dusk. The short lines, 'A neighbourhood./At dusk', set a modern tone for this anonymous, yet familiar scene which is played out worldwide. 'Things are getting ready/to happen/out of sight'. In this 'not yet' moment, the mysterious powers of nature are observed, 'rinds slanting around fruit'. Yet, I also feel there is a slight tinge of danger, reminding me of the serpent in the Garden of Eden waiting to pounce. Suddenly a child runs into a waiting mother's arms, 'A woman leans down to catch a child'. The general terms used emphasise the universal significance of this experience of a child returning to the security of a mother's arms. Boland's poem describes a common social issue – how in this uncertain modern world, every parent gives a sigh of relief when a child returns safely home.

> **EXAMINER'S COMMENT**
>
> *This competent response addresses both the theme and style of the poem. A developed discussion deals with Boland's use of free verse and economical language. An interesting personal reading of the poem is given in the line, 'I also feel there is a slight tinge of danger ...'. This well-written, successful answer engages closely with the text of the poem. Top-grade standard.*

✒ Class/Homework Exercises

1. Comment on the poet's tone in 'This Moment'. Refer to the text in your discussion.
2. A sense of intense mystery is often found in Boland's poetry. To what extent is this true of 'This Moment'? Develop your answer with reference to the poem.

⊙ Points to Consider

- **Themes include the mystery of nature and the beauty of loving relationships.**
- **Effective use of simple language and succinct dramatic style.**
- **Vivid, sensuous imagery; sibilant and assonant effects.**
- **Varying moods – subdued, reflective, celebratory.**

9 The Pomegranate

EAVAN BOLAND

The only legend I have ever loved is
the story of a daughter lost in hell.
And found and rescued there.
Love and blackmail are the gist of it.
Ceres and Persephone the names.   5
And the best thing about the legend is
I can enter it anywhere. And have.
As a child in exile in
a city of fogs and strange consonants,
I read it first and at first I was   10
an exiled child in the crackling dusk of
the underworld, the stars blighted. Later
I walked out in a summer twilight
searching for my daughter at bed-time.
When she came running I was ready   15
to make any bargain to keep her.
I carried her back past whitebeams
and wasps and honey-scented buddleias.
But I was Ceres then and I knew
winter was in store for every leaf   20
on every tree on that road.
Was inescapable for each one we passed.
And for me.
          It is winter
and the stars are hidden.   25
I climb the stairs and stand where I can see
my child asleep beside her teen magazines,
her can of Coke, her plate of uncut fruit.
The pomegranate! How did I forget it?
She could have come home and been safe   30
and ended the story and all
our heart-broken searching but she reached
out a hand and plucked a pomegranate.
She put out her hand and pulled down
the French sound for apple and   35
the noise of stone and the proof
that even in the place of death,
at the heart of legend, in the midst
of rocks full of unshed tears
ready to be diamonds by the time   40

Title: the pomegranate (from a French word meaning an apple with many seeds) is a pulpy oriental fruit.

Ceres and Persephone: mythological figures. Ceres was the goddess of earth and motherhood. Persephone was her beautiful daughter who was forced by Pluto to become his wife and was imprisoned in Hades, the underworld. Ceres was determined to find Persephone and threatened to prevent anything from growing on the earth until she was allowed to rescue her daughter. But because Persephone had eaten sacred pomegranate seeds in Hades, she was condemned forever to spend part of every year there.

city of fogs: London, where the poet once lived.

buddleias: ornamental bushes with small purple flowers.

the story was told, a child can be
hungry. I could warn her. There is still a chance.
The rain is cold. The road is flint-coloured.
The suburb has cars and cable television.
The veiled stars are above ground. 45
It is another world. But what else
can a mother give her daughter but such
beautiful rifts in time?
If I defer the grief I will diminish the gift.
The legend will be hers as well as mine. 50
She will enter it. As I have.
She will wake up. She will hold
the papery flushed skin in her hand.
And to her lips. I will say nothing.

rifts: gaps, cracks.
defer: delay.

👤 Personal Response

1. Boland conveys a sense of the city of London in this poem. How does she succeed in doing this? Refer to the text in your answer.
2. From your reading of this poem, what do you learn about the relationship between the poet and her daughter? Refer to the text in your response.
3. Comment on the poet's mood in the last five lines of the poem.

'my child asleep'

👁 Critical Literacy

In the poem, narrated as one unrhymed stanza, Boland explores the theme of parental loss by comparing her own experiences as a mother and daughter with the myth of Ceres and Persephone. Although it is a personal poem, it has a much wider relevance for families everywhere.

EAVAN BOLAND

Boland presents this exploration of the mother–child relationship as a dramatic narrative. In the **opening lines**, the poet tells us that she has always related to 'the story of a daughter lost in hell'. This goes back to her early experience as 'a child in exile' living in London. Her **sense of displacement** is evident in the detailed description of that 'city of fogs and strange consonants'. Like Persephone trapped in Hades, Boland yearned for home. But the myth has a broader relevance to the poet's life – she 'can enter it anywhere'. Years later, she recalls a time when, as a mother, she could also identify with Ceres, 'searching for my daughter'.

Lines 13–18 express the intensity of Boland's feelings for her child: she was quite prepared 'to make any bargain to keep her'. The **anxious tone** reflects the poet's awareness of the importance of appreciating the closeness between herself and her teenage daughter while time allows. She expresses her maternal feelings through rich natural images: 'I carried her back past whitebeams'. But she is also increasingly aware that both she and her daughter are getting older. This is particularly evident in **line 20**, as she anticipates an 'inescapable' change in their relationship: 'winter was in store for every leaf'.

Line 24 marks a defining moment ('It is winter') for them both. Observing her daughter asleep in her bedroom, Boland now sees herself as Ceres and the 'plate of uncut fruit' as the pomegranate. This marks the realisation that **her child has become an adult**. The poet imagines how different it might have been had Persephone not eaten the fruit – 'She could have come home' and ended all the 'heart-broken searching'. But Persephone deliberately made her choice, a decision that is emphasised by the repeated mention of her gesture ('she reached/out a hand', 'She put out her hand'). Significantly, Boland is sympathetic: 'a child can be/hungry'.

In **line 42**, the poet considers alerting her daughter ('I could warn her') about the dangers and disappointments that lie ahead. **Harsh imagery** suggests the difficulties of modern life: 'The rain is cold. The road is flint-coloured'. Boland wonders if 'beautiful rifts in time' are the most a mother can offer. Such delaying tactics may only postpone natural development into adulthood.

In the end, she decides to 'say nothing'. There is a clear sense of resignation in the **final lines**. The poet accepts the reality of change. Boland's daughter will experience the same stages of childhood and motherhood as the poet herself: 'The legend will be hers as well as mine'. This truth is underlined by the recurring use of 'She will', a recognition that her daughter's destiny is in her own hands. The **poem ends on a quietly reflective note** as Boland respectfully acknowledges the right of her daughter to mature naturally and make her own way in life.

Writing About the Poem

'Eavan Boland's use of mythical references vividly illuminates her own personal experiences.' Discuss this statement, with particular reference to Boland's poem 'The Pomegranate'.

Sample Paragraph

Eavan Boland has been very successful in blending her own life as a child and mother with Persephone and Ceres. The fact that she uses an ancient legend adds mystery to the theme of mother–daughter relationships. First, she compares herself to Persephone, when the poet was an exiled child in London. This links the grimy city life to the underworld of Hades. But Boland is more concerned with the present and her fears of losing her own daughter who is growing up fast. By describing her fears through the story of Ceres, she increases our understanding of how anxious she was feeling. Both parents were 'searching' desperately. Together, the legend and the true life story of the poet and her reluctance to come to terms with her daughter growing up really show how parents have to let go of their children and give them the freedom to make their own mistakes and learn for themselves.

> **EXAMINER'S COMMENT**
> *There are some very good discussion points here in this top-grade response to a challenging question. Although the answer shows personal engagement, it could be rooted a little more thoroughly in the text through the use of direct quotation. Expression is very well controlled.*

Class/Homework Exercises

1. What image of Eavan Boland herself emerges from 'The Pomegranate'? Refer to the text in your answer.
2. Boland manages to create a series of powerfully evocative moods throughout this poem. Discuss this statement, developing your answer with close reference to the text.

Points to Consider

- **Boland considers the complexity of mother–daughter relationships.**
- **Striking images – nature, family and the difficulties of modern life.**
- **Mythical references reflect a timeless, universal sense of loss.**
- **Tones vary – empathetic, anxious, resigned.**

10 Love

Dark falls on this mid-western town
where we once lived when myths collided.
Dusk has hidden the bridge in the river
which slides and deepens
to become the water
the hero crossed on his way to hell.

Not far from here is our old apartment.
We had a kitchen and an Amish table.
We had a view. And we discovered there
love had the feather and muscle of wings
and had come to live with us,
a brother of fire and air.

We had two infant children one of whom
was touched by death in this town
and spared: and when the hero
was hailed by his comrades in hell
their mouths opened and their voices failed and
there is no knowing what they would have asked
about a life they had shared and lost.

I am your wife.
It was years ago.
Our child was healed. We love each other still.
Across our day-to-day and ordinary distances
we speak plainly. We hear each other clearly.

And yet I want to return to you
on the bridge of the Iowa river as you were,
with snow on the shoulders of your coat
and a car passing with its headlights on:

I see you as a hero in a text –
the image blazing and the edges gilded –
and I long to cry out the epic question
my dear companion:

EAVAN BOLAND

mid-western town: in 1979, Boland lived in the United States and attended the prestigious Iowa Writers' Workshop.
myths: fictitious tales with supernatural characters and events.
hero: Aeneas was a hero in the Aeneid. He visited the underworld by crossing the River Styx, where he saw his dead companions, but they could not communicate with him.
Amish: strict American religious sect that makes functional, practical furniture without decoration.

epic: great, ambitious.

Will we ever live so intensely again?
Will love come to us again and be
so formidable at rest it offered us ascension 35
even to look at him?

But the words are shadows and you cannot hear me.
You walk away and I cannot follow.

formidable: very impressive.

'comrades in hell'

👤 Personal Response

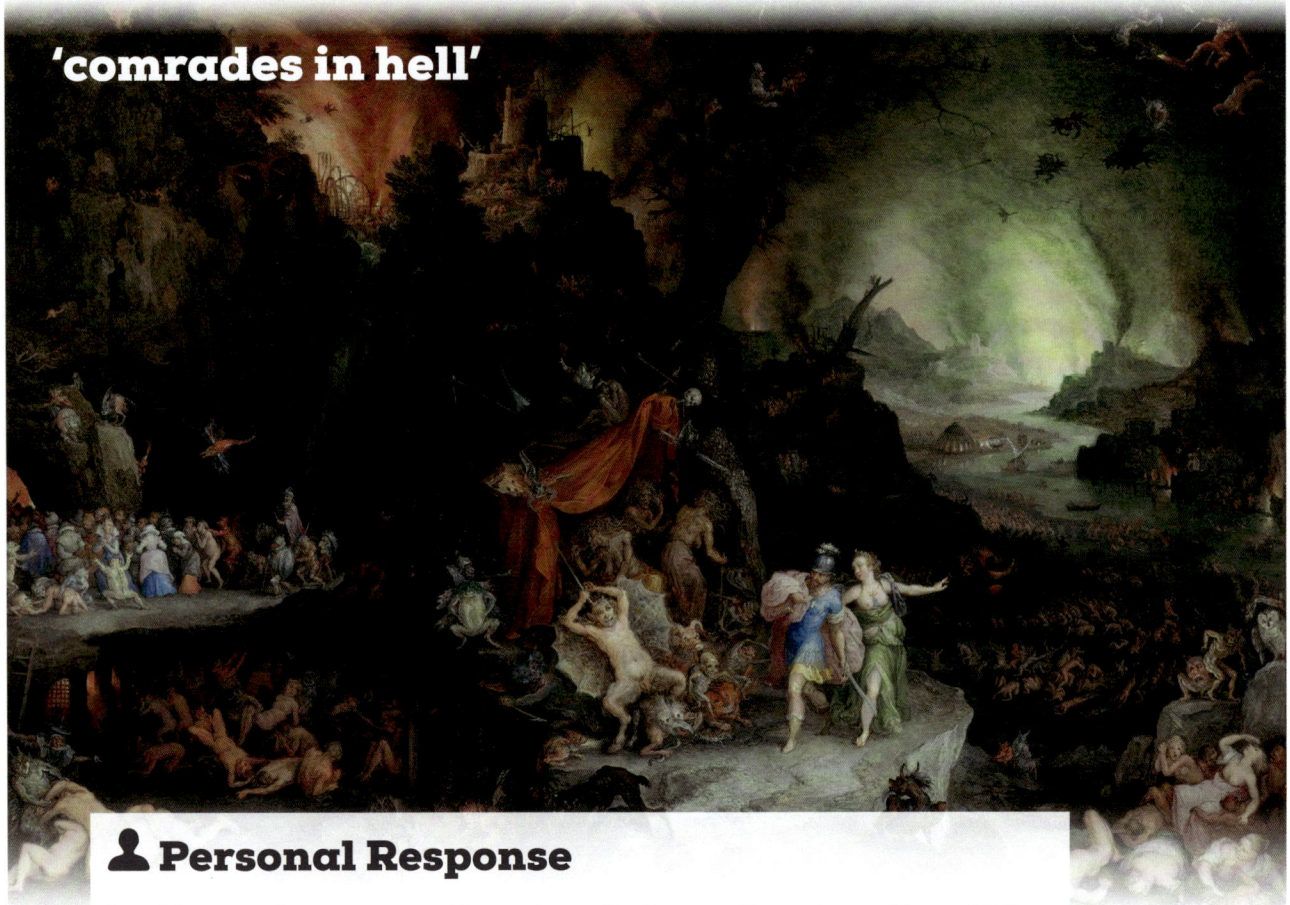

1. This poem is an open and honest meditation on the nature of love. Write your own personal response to it, referring to the text in your answer.
2. Choose one image from the poem that you think is particularly effective. Briefly explain your choice.
3. Explain the significance of the last section of the poem: 'But the words are shadows and you cannot hear me./You walk away and I cannot follow'. In your opinion, is this a positive or negative ending?

👁 Critical Literacy

'Love' is part of a sequence of poems called 'Legends' in which Boland explores parallels between myths and modern life. She records her personal experience of family life in Iowa at a time when her youngest daughter was seriously ill and came close to death. This is interwoven with the myth of Aeneas returning to the underworld. The narrative poem explores the nature of human relationships and how they change over time. It also shows the unchanging nature of human experience down through the ages.

Lines 1–6. The poem opens in darkness, **remembering the past**. Boland's personal experience was in 'this mid-western town' in Iowa, and she connects this with the myth of Aeneas visiting the underworld. Aeneas crosses the bridge on the River Styx to reach Hades, the land of the Shades ('the hero crossed on his way to hell'). Boland and her husband were also experiencing their own hell as they visited their very sick little girl in hospital.

Lines 7–12. These lines give us a **clear, detailed picture of their domestic life**: 'a kitchen', 'an Amish table', 'a view'. The poem is written in loose, non-rhyming stanzas, which suits reminiscences. The couple's internal emotional life is shown in the **striking metaphor** 'love had the feather and muscle of wings'. Love was beating, alive, vibrant. The word 'feather' suggests it could soar to great heights, while 'muscle' signifies that it was extraordinarily powerful. This natural, graceful love was palpable, substantial, elemental, 'a brother of fire and air'.

Lines 13–19. The **personal drama** of the sick daughter who 'was touched by death' is recalled. But Boland did not lose her child. The verb 'spared' links us with the myth again. Aeneas is in the underworld, but because his comrades are shadows, they cannot ask the questions they are longing to ask about the life they once shared. This mythical reference reflects the couple's inability to express their intense feelings at such a critical time. The moment of communication is lost: 'there is no knowing what they would have asked'.

Lines 20–36. The poet goes on to consider the **changing nature of love**. The 'we' becomes 'I' – 'I am your wife'. Do they, as husband and wife, communicate as deeply as they did before? Her tone is matter-of-fact, almost businesslike. She wants to recapture the intensity of their love and shared times, when she saw her husband as 'a hero in a text'. In her memory of him, he is outlined by the cars' lights as they pass on the bridge. Described as 'blazing' and 'gilded', he is contrasted with the darkness of the night, as Aeneas is contrasted with the darkness of the underworld. Boland longs to experience that special time, that transcendence, again.

The closing lines are dominated by rhetorical questions: 'Will we ever live so intensely again?' The inference is no. She can imagine asking these questions about the life they shared, but she cannot actually articulate them. This is **similar to Aeneas's dilemma** – his comrades wished to ask questions about the life they shared with him, but 'their voices failed'. Neither Boland nor the 'comrades' could express their feelings. The words of the questions remain unformed, unspoken, 'shadows'.

Lines 37–38. The poem ends with a two-line stanza in which the poet accepts that the **gap cannot be bridged**: 'You walk away and I cannot follow'. There is a real sense of loss and resignation in Boland's final tone.

✒ Writing About the Poem

Memory is one of the central themes in Boland's poem 'Love'. In your opinion, does the poet convey this theme effectively? Refer to the text in your answer.

Sample Paragraph

By blending myth and personal experience, Boland gives her poems a true sense of universality. But she also blends timelines, the past and the present tenses to give a quality of timelessness. In 'Love', the freshness of a strong memory is captured by her use of the present tense: 'Dark falls', 'here is our old apartment'. The recent past is shown in the past tense as she recalls: 'We had two infant children'. In the past they had a life together which was lived very intensely. Are they missing any of this now? The tense then changes to the present 'I am your wife'. The changing tenses add a compelling timeless quality to the experience of memory, as time shared is recalled. The poem ends with the realisation that time cannot be relived.

> **EXAMINER'S COMMENT**
>
> *An unusual approach is taken as the response focuses on the use of tenses as a stylistic feature to communicate theme: 'The changing tenses add a compelling timeless quality to the experience of memory'. There is evidence of close reading of the poem and effective use of quotation throughout this assured top-grade answer. Expression is varied and fluent.*

✒ Class/Homework Exercises

1. The poem 'Love' illustrates Boland's subtle skill in conveying significant universal truths through her exploration of personal relationships. Discuss this view, developing your points with close reference to the text.
2. 'When myths collided.' Do you consider Boland's use of myths in her work effective in exploring her themes? Discuss, referring closely to the poem 'Love'.

◎ Points to Consider

- **The changing nature of romantic love is a central theme.**
- **References to Greek mythology used to explore parallels with modern life.**
- **Use of detailed description, striking metaphors, rhetorical questions.**
- **Contrasting tones of relief, nostalgia, reflection and resignation.**

Sample Leaving Cert Questions on Boland's Poetry

1. 'Eavan Boland's poetic narratives often examine contemporary themes through effective comparisons from the shadowlands of myth and history.' Discuss this statement, developing your answer with reference to the poetry of Eavan Boland on your course.
2. 'Boland's intensely personal poems address issues that have a timeless quality and a universal significance.' To what extent do you agree or disagree with this statement? Develop your answer with reference to the poetry of Eavan Boland on your course.
3. From your study of the poetry of Eavan Boland on your course, select the poems that, in your opinion, best demonstrate her skilful use of language and imagery to explore aspects of identity and human rights. Justify your selection by demonstrating Boland's skilful use of language and imagery to explore aspects of identity and human rights in the poems you have chosen.

How do I organise my answer?

(Sample question 1)

'Eavan Boland's poetic narratives often examine contemporary themes through effective comparisons from the shadowlands of myth and history.' Discuss this statement, developing your answer with reference to the poetry of Eavan Boland on your course.

Sample Plan 1

Intro: (*Stance: agree with viewpoint in the question*) Boland explores modern and universal issues – e.g. changing nature of relationships and marginalised victims – through powerful references to history and myth.

Point 1: (*Myth – Ceres and Persephone*) 'The Pomegranate' acknowledges difficulty for parents to give children their freedom ('I will say nothing').

Point 2: (*History – Irish Famine*) 'The Famine Road' connects a modern-day infertile woman with an 1840s famine road to show the gap between power and powerlessness. Both are 'Barren', incapable of supporting life. Contrasting voices illustrate the cold sense of dismissal.

Understanding the Prescribed Poetry Question

Marks are awarded using the PCLM Marking Scheme: P = 15; C = 15; L = 15; M = 5 Total = 50

- **P** (Purpose = 15 marks) refers to the set question and is the launch pad for the answer. This involves engaging with all aspects of the question. Both theme and language must be addressed, although not necessarily equally.
- **C** (Coherence = 15 marks) refers to the organisation of the developed response and the use of accurate, relevant quotation. Paragraphing is essential.
- **L** (Language = 15 marks) refers to the student's skill in controlling language throughout the answer.
- **M** (Mechanics = 5 marks) refers to spelling and grammar.
- Although no specific number of poems is required, students usually discuss at least 3 or 4 in their written responses.
- Aim for at least 800 words, to be completed within 45–50 minutes.

NOTE

In keeping with the PCLM approach, the student has to take a stance by agreeing and/or disagreeing that Boland's poetic stories examine:

– **present-day issues** (love, war, death, oppression, marginalisation, transition, identity, tradition, victimisation, etc.)

... examined through:

– **comparisons from myth and history** (references to myth and the mysterious past, symbolism and powerful imagery, offering new perspectives on modern themes; enhancing tones, etc.)

Point 3: (*History – unrecorded Irish victims*) 'Outside History' honours the outsiders' place in history through vivid imagery ('roads clotted as/firmaments with the dead'). The excluded are finally included.

Point 4: (*Myth – Aeneas and the Underworld*) 'Love' examines difficulties of communication in a relationship through dramatic metaphors ('the words are shadows and you cannot hear me').

Conclusion: Effective references to myth/history explore specific personal moments that transcend the particular. Boland often highlights the universality of human experience.

Sample Paragraph: Point 1

In 'The Pomegranate', Boland explores the protectiveness of the modern mother towards her child. The vivid image of the 'plate of uncut fruit' reminds the poet of the pomegranate seeds that Persephone ate in Hades which caused her tragic separation from her mother. The timeless experience of the desperate mother 'searching for my daughter', eager to 'make any bargain to keep her' is vividly recalled. Boland too has to accept the loss of her daughter to adult maturity. In this intensely personal moment of transition and loss, vividly captured in the poet's subdued, reflective tone, Boland respectfully comes to terms with the reality that some things are beyond her control, 'I will say nothing'.

> **EXAMINER'S COMMENT**
>
> This well-written top-grade response succinctly addresses the question through focusing on the central myth used in the poem. Close engagement with the text is evident in the critical discussion which draws comparisons between the mythical references and Boland's own maternal feelings. Comments on tone and imagery respond to the 'poetic' element of the question.

NOTE

In keeping with the PCLM approach, the student has to take a stance by justifying his/her selection of Boland's poems which best demonstrate the poet's:

- **skilful use of language** (carefully crafted observational details, striking imagery and symbolism, memorable aural effects, engaging tones, etc.)

... to explore:

- **features of identity and basic human rights** (uniqueness of self, nationality, belonging, freedom, power, submission, violence, innocent suffering, victimisation, etc.)

(Sample question 3)

From your study of the poetry of Eavan Boland on your course, select the poems that, in your opinion, best demonstrate her skilful use of language and imagery to explore aspects of identity and human rights. Justify your selection by demonstrating Boland's skilful use of language and imagery to explore aspects of identity and human rights in the poems you have chosen.

Sample Plan 2

Intro: (*Stance: agree with viewpoint in the question*) Boland explores aspects of identity and human rights – importance of self, innocent victims of violence – through evocative language, symbolism, forceful verbs, poetic structure and varying tones.

Point 1: (*Identity – woman*) In 'The Shadow Doll' the dreamlike description of a Victorian doll models a bride's confined position in society ('airless glamour', 'under wraps'). Repetition ('pressing down') and strong verbs ('locks') emphasise suppression.

Point 2: (*Identity – woman*) 'The Black Lace Fan' is a symbol of freedom and romance ('flirtatious span') and is contrasted with the 'stifling' Parisian atmosphere. The couple's uncertain relationship is subtly explored.

Point 3: (*Human rights – innocent victim*) 'Child of Our Time' powerfully reflects on an innocent death during the Northern Ireland Troubles. Tone varies from compassion ('rhymes for your waking') to indignation ('you cannot listen'). A didactic voice ('must learn') completes a poem whose carefully ordered three-stanza structure mirrors Boland's attempt to put order on disorder.

Point 4: (*Human rights – innocent victim*) 'The War Horse' also examines the brutal consequences of war and aspects of national identity, using emphatic verbs, rhetorical questions and vivid imagery ('screamless dead').

Conclusion: Poet memorably explores the themes of woman's identity and the human rights of innocent victims. Through skilful use of language and imagery, Boland creates visionary moments to enrich the reader's experience.

Sample Paragraph: Point 4

'The War Horse' addresses the destruction of human rights through Boland's detailed observation of a 'loosed' horse wreaking havoc on suburban gardens. The consequences of the actions of a warlike intruder are conveyed through dramatic language. It 'smashed' a rose. Boland's reference ('illicit braid') to the Ribbonmen recalls the destruction caused by another earlier intruder, the British, who invaded Ireland. A chilling rhetorical question ('why should we care/If a rose, a hedge, a crocus are uprooted/Like corpses, remote, crushed, mutilated?') seeks to

EXAMINER'S COMMENT

Top-grade response showing close engagement with the poet's use of language in conveying powerfully held views on aspects of Irish history. Excellent expression ('detailed observation', 'implicate') and effective use of key quotes, well integrated into the commentary, add to the impressive quality of the answer. The paragraph is rounded off effectively with two thought-provoking questions.

implicate readers in these terrible events. The poet wishes us to consider why no-one challenged the intruder. Does indifference cause a 'world' to be 'betrayed'?

> **EXAM FOCUS**
> - As you may not be familiar with some of the poems referred to in the sample plans, substitute poems that you have studied closely.
> - Key points about a particular poem can be developed over more than one paragraph.
> - Paragraphs may also include cross-referencing and discussion of more than one poem.
> - Remember that there is no single 'correct' answer to poetry questions, so always be confident in expressing your own considered response.

INDICATIVE MATERIAL

Boland's fascinating world, influenced by both history and the present day:
- engaging exploration of Irish history, superstition, past and present relationships, power/powerlessness, enduring natural beauty, etc.

... is created through:
- a carefully controlled style
- striking use of places, people, precise tones/moods, sound effects, detailed imagery, structure, etc.

Leaving Cert Sample Essay

'Boland creates a fascinating world that is often influenced by both history and the present day, in a carefully controlled poetic style.' To what extent do you agree or disagree with this statement? Develop your answer with reference to the poetry of Eavan Boland on your course.

Sample Essay

1. I agree completely that Boland creates a very interesting poetic world through her precisely controlled language and imagery. But I do not fully agree that she is influenced by both the present day and history. In many poems, she identifies herself only with the marginalised and dispossessed, those written out of history. She gives a compelling voice to these unrecorded victims in poems like 'Outsiders' and 'The Famine Road'. Boland also creates moments of intense beauty in her celebration of family relationships, nature and tradition.

2. In 'This Moment', Boland writes about a moment when she records a common experience. It's a moment of love in an ordinary, suburban setting. She presents us with the love between a mother and young child. The poet uses a lot of onomatopoeia, including sibilant sounds, 'Star and moths and rinds'. This is an image of nature. She uses very simple language, 'One window is yellow as butter', and this paints a homely scene. The mood is harmonious, 'Stars rise. Moths flutter. Apples sweeten'. This is a very dramatic poem that is influenced by the modern world. We should appreciate the simple things in family life. The poem records a special time and offers a moment of relief and security in our tense modern world.

3. 'White Hawthorn in the West of Ireland' is a reflection on the differing relationships Boland has with the orderly suburban world and the wild, mystical country landscape. Her exact language describes the tidy, modern, urban environment, 'I left suburban gardens. Lawnmowers. Small talk'. In contrast, dynamic images of growth portray the abundant countryside. She glories in being 'part of that ivory downhill rush'. She intrigues readers with the unlucky 'sharp flowers' of the hawthorn. In Irish folklore, hawthorn was believed to bring misfortune to those who cut it or keep it indoors, 'for the sake of the luck such constraint would forfeit'. The run-on lines capture the wild countryside where the hawthorn stirs 'on those hills with a fluency only water has'. Boland describes a fascinating world shaped by the present day and Irish folklore.

4. In both 'Outside History' and 'The Famine Road', the poet focuses on those dispossessed not only in life but in history. It is with these marginalised victims that Boland empathises. Her critical eye forms vivid imagery and forces us to confront the reality of the victims' experience in the past ('roads clotted as firmaments with the dead'). She makes a deliberate conscious effort to shed light on the 'darkness' which destroys the memory of those who 'have always been outside history'. She wishes to move 'out of myth', away from the historical, passive myths of Caitlín Ní Houlihán and Dark Rosaleen. While Boland admits that those dead won't be aware that they are now honoured in her repetitive phrase, 'and we are too late. We are always too late', the poet has brought the victims in from 'outside history' – those in the present and the future.

5. Boland also focuses on the marginalised victims of the Irish Famine. In her dramatic recreation of this terrible time, we can only imagine the voices of these 'Sick, directionless' people. Harsh consonant 'c' and 'k' sounds compel her readers to experience the suffering of these unrecorded victims ('blood on their knuckles on rock, suck April hailstones for water and for food'). She quotes the recorded words in the letter of the British civil servant, Trevelyan, to Colonel Jones, 'Idle as trout in light Colonel Jones, these Irish'. The ironically named 'Relief Committee' decided to have the starving Irish build roads 'going nowhere of course'. Boland has deliberately excluded the voices of the 'wretches' in a chilling account of how the suffering of the Famine victims was omitted. Instead they will 'fester by their work' while the British remove food from the land, 'March the corn to the ships in peace'.

6. In this poem, Boland also records the experiences of a modern-day infertile woman who is powerless. She does not allow the woman's voice to be heard. Instead, the tone of the doctor dominates, 'take it well woman, grow your garden'. Similar tones are heard from both the British and the doctor. Boland's voice now interrupts the two narratives. She uses the adjective 'Barren' to link the two experiences.

7. Eavan Boland has constructed a fascinating world which is affected by modern times and the past. She has said, 'The rich and interesting part, for me, was the past, not history'. So she records the 'outsiders' from the past, those left out of history. Her critical eye produces carefully crafted poetry which resonates with readers long after the poems have been read.

(740 words)

> **EXAMINER'S COMMENT**
>
> Succinct personal response to the question, showing close engagement with Boland's poetry. Some aspects of the poet's style are explored throughout. There is good focused analysis in paragraphs 3–5 that addresses all elements of the question ('fascinating world', links to past and present, poet's 'controlled language'). Accurate quotes and references are used effectively to support points throughout, expression is notelike and repetitive at times.

GRADE: H1
P = 15/15
C = 14/15
L = 13/15
M = 5/5
Total = 47/50

👀 Revision Overview

'The War Horse'
Central themes of violence, warfare, death, suburban domestic incident and memory.

'Child of Our Time'
Elegy, response to theme of random tragedy unleashed by lack of communication.

'The Famine Road'
Two parallel narratives explore themes of oppression and victimisation, the Irish famine and the infertile woman.

'The Shadow Doll'
Theme of women's oppression, emotions and sexuality suppressed.

'White Hawthorn in the West of Ireland'
Journey into the West becomes reflection on contrast between orderly suburbia and wild, mystical beauty of Irish landscape.

'Outside History'
Compelling examination of theme of the marginalised.

'The Black Lace Fan My Mother Gave Me'
Challenging alternative account of the relationship between men and women.

'This Moment'
Reflection on theme of traditional role of women as mothers.

'The Pomegranate'
Insightful examination of themes of complex mother–daughter relationship and ageing process.

'Love'
Two narratives address theme of changes in relationships, personal story of young love and Aeneas's return to the underworld.

💬 Last Words

'Eavan Boland's work continues to deepen in both humanity and complexity.'
Fiona Sampson

'Memory, change, loss, the irrecoverable past – such are the shared conditions of humankind, with which she scrupulously engages.'
Anne Stevenson

'Poets are those who ransack their perishing mind and find pattern and form.'
Eavan Boland

EAVAN BOLAND

CONFLICT | DEATH | SUFFERING | HISTORY/MEMORY | RELATIONSHIPS | TRAVEL/JOURNEYS | NATURE | TIME | LOVE

POETRY FOCUS

Emily Dickinson

1830–1886

'Forever is composed of nows.'

Emily Dickinson was born on 10 December 1830 in Amherst, Massachusetts. Widely regarded as one of America's greatest poets, she is also known for her unusual life of self-imposed social seclusion. An enigmatic figure with a fondness for the macabre, she was a prolific letter-writer and private poet, though fewer than a dozen of her poems were published during her lifetime. It was only after her death in 1886 that her work was discovered. It is estimated that she wrote about 1,770 poems, many of which explored the nature of immortality and death, with an almost mantric quality at times. Ultimately, however, she is remembered for her distinctive style, which was unique for the era in which she wrote. Her poems contain short lines, typically lack titles and often ignore the rules of grammar, syntax and punctuation, yet she expressed far-reaching ideas in compact phrases. Amidst paradox and uncertainty, her poetry has an undeniable capacity to move and provoke.

Investigate Further

To find out more about Emily Dickinson, or to hear readings of her poems, you could do a search of some of the useful websites available such as YouTube, BBC Poetry, poetryfoundation.org and poetryarchive.org, or access additional material on this page of your eBook.

Prescribed Poems

○ 1 '"Hope" is the thing with feathers'
In this optimistic poem, Dickinson addresses the experience of hope and imagines it as having some of the characteristics of a small bird. **Page 52**

○ 2 'There's a certain Slant of light'
A particular beam of winter light puts the poet into a depressed mood in which she reflects on human mortality and our relationship with God. **Page 56**

○ 3 'I felt a Funeral, in my Brain' (OL)
Dickinson imagines the experience of death from the perspective of a person who is about to be buried. **Page 60**

○ 4 'A Bird came down the Walk'
The poet observes a bird and tries to establish contact with it, revealing both the beauty and danger of nature. **Page 64**

○ 5 'I heard a Fly buzz– when I died' (OL)
Another illustration of Dickinson's obsession with the transition of the soul from life into eternity. **Page 67**

○ 6 'The Soul has Bandaged moments'
This intricate poem explores the soul's changing moods, from terrified depression to delirious joy. **Page 70**

○ 7 'I could bring You Jewels– had I a mind to'
In this short love poem, Dickinson celebrates nature's simple delights and contrasts the beauty of an everyday flower with more exotic precious gifts. **Page 74**

○ 8 'A narrow Fellow in the Grass'
Using a male perspective, the poet details the fascination and terror experienced in confronting a snake. **Page 77**

○ 9 'I taste a liquor never brewed'
Dickinson uses an extended metaphor of intoxication in this exuberant celebration of nature in summertime. **Page 80**

○ 10 'After great pain, a formal feeling comes'
A disturbing examination of the after-effects of suffering and anguish on the individual. **Page 84**

(OL) indicates poems that are also prescribed for the Ordinary Level course.

EMILY DICKINSON

1 'Hope' is the thing with feathers

'Hope' is the thing with feathers—
That perches in the soul—
And sings the tune without the words—
And never stops—at all—

And sweetest—in the Gale—is heard— 5
And sore must be the storm—
That could abash the little Bird
That kept so many warm—

I've heard it in the chillest land—
And on the strangest Sea— 10
Yet, never, in Extremity,
It asked a crumb—of Me.

And sweetest—in the Gale—is heard: hope is most comforting in times of trouble.
abash: embarrass; defeat.

in Extremity: in terrible times.

'And sweetest—in the Gale—is heard—'

👤 Personal Response

1. What are the main characteristics of the bird admired by Dickinson?
2. Dickinson uses an extended metaphor to explore her theme of hope. Comment on the effectiveness of this technique in the poem.
3. In your view, what is the purpose of the poem – to instruct, to explain, to express a feeling? Support your response by reference to the text.

👁 Critical Literacy

Few of Emily Dickinson's poems were published during her lifetime and it was not until 1955, 69 years after her death, that an accurate edition of her poems was published, with the original punctuation and words. This instructive poem explores an abstraction: hope. It is one of her 'definition' poems, wherein she compares hope to a little bird, offering comfort to all.

In stanza one, Dickinson explores hope by using the **metaphor of a little bird** whose qualities are similar to those of hope: non-threatening, calm and powerful. Just like the bird, hope can rise above the earth with all its troubles and desperate times. Raised in the Puritan tradition, Dickinson, although rejecting formal religion, would have been aware of the religious symbolism of the dove and its connection with divine inspiration and the Holy Spirit or Holy Ghost, as well as the reference to doves in the story of Noah's Ark and the Flood. Hope appears against all odds and 'perches in the soul'. But this hope is not easily defined, so she refers to it as 'the thing', an inanimate object.

Hope's silent presence is able to **communicate** beyond reason and logic and far **beyond the limitations of language**: 'sings the tune without the words'. Hope's permanence is highlighted by the unusual use of dashes in the punctuation: 'never stops—at all', suggesting its continuity and endurance.

Stanza two focuses on the tangible qualities of hope (sweetness and warmth) and shows the spiritual, emotional and psychological **comfort found in hope**. The 'Gale' could refer to the inner state of confusion felt in the agony of despair. The little bird that comforts and shelters its young offers protection to 'so many'. The energy of the word 'abash' suggests the buffeting wind of the storm against which the little bird survives. The last two run-on lines convey the protective, welcoming circle of the 'little bird's wing'.

Stanza three refers to a personal experience of hope in times of anguish ('I've heard'). Extreme circumstances are cleverly expressed in the phrases 'chillest land' and 'strangest Sea'. This reclusive poet spent most of her life indoors in her father's house. She then explains that hope is not demanding in bad times; it is generous, giving rather than taking: 'Yet, never, in Extremity,/It asked a crumb—of Me.' The central paradox of hope is expressed in the metaphor of the bird, delicate and fragile, yet strong and unbeatable. The tiny bird is an effective image for the first stirring of hope in a time of despair. The solemn ending gives hope its deserved dignified celebration.

Dickinson was a unique and original talent. She used the regular rhythm of hymns. She also used their form of the four-line verse. Yet this is not conventional poetry, due to Dickinson's use of the dash to slow the line and make the reader pause and consider. Ordinary words like 'at all' and 'is heard' assume a tremendous importance and their position is to be considered and savoured. **Her unusual use of capital letters has the same effect, as it highlights the dangers ('Gale', 'Sea')**. The alliteration of 's' in 'strangest Sea' and the run-on line to suggest the circling comfort of the little bird all add to the curious music of Dickinson's poems. The uplifting, self-confident tone of the poem is in direct contrast to the strict Puritanical tradition of a severe, righteous God, with which she would have been familiar in her youth and which she rejected, preferring to keep her Sabbath 'staying at home'.

Writing About the Poem

'Emily Dickinson's poetry contains an intense awareness of the private, inner self.' Discuss this view with particular reference to '"Hope" is the thing with feathers'.

Sample Paragraph

Everyone has experienced moments when it seems that nothing is ever going to go right again. Dickinson, with her simple image of the bird singing, provides an optimistic response to this dark state of mind. She develops this metaphor, comforting us with the thought that the bird (symbolising hope) can communicate with us without the need for language, 'sings the tune without words'. Dickinson understands despair, 'in the Gale', 'the strangest Sea'. But the bird of hope provides comfort ('sweetest'). The poet uses enjambment effectively in the lines 'That could abash the little Bird/That kept so many warm'. The run-on rhythm suggests the protection of hope encircling us, just as the bird protects her young in the nest. The phrase 'perches in the soul' suggests to me that the poet regards hope as coming of its own choice.

EXAMINER'S COMMENT

This coherent and focused response shows a good understanding of the poem and a clear awareness of Dickinson's reflective tone. Effective use of accurate quotations. The commentary on enjambment and movement ('run-on rhythm suggests the protection of hope encircling us') is impressive. A solid top-grade answer.

Class/Homework Exercises

1. 'Dickinson is a wholly new and original poetic genius.' Do you agree or disagree with this statement? Develop your response with reference to '"Hope" is the thing with feathers'.
2. 'Emily Dickinson often uses concrete language to communicate abstract ideas in her unusual poems.' Discuss this view with reference to '"Hope" is the thing with feathers'.

Points to Consider

- The poem explores the concept of hope and its impact on human life.
- Effective use of the extended metaphor of 'the little Bird'.
- Symbols represent the challenges people face in life.
- Variety of tones: assured, personal, reflective, optimistic, etc.

2 There's a certain Slant of light

There's a certain Slant of light,
Winter Afternoons—
That oppresses, like the Heft
Of Cathedral Tunes—

Heavenly Hurt, it gives us—   5
We can find no scar,
But internal difference,
Where the Meanings, are—

None may teach it—Any—
'Tis the Seal Despair—   10
An imperial affliction
Sent us of the Air—

When it comes, the Landscape listens—
Shadows—hold their breath—
When it goes, 'tis like the Distance   15
On the look of Death—

Slant: incline; fall; interpretation.
oppresses: feels heavy; overwhelms.
Heft: strength; weight; influence.
Any: anything.
Seal Despair: sign or symbol of hopelessness.
imperial affliction: God's will for mortal human beings.

'Heavenly Hurt, it gives us—'

👤 Personal Response

1. Describe the mood and atmosphere created by the poet in the opening stanza.
2. Comment on Dickinson's use of personification in the poem.
3. Write your own personal response to the poem, developing your views with reference or quotation.

👁 Critical Literacy

Dickinson was a keen observer of her environment, often dramatising her observations in poems. In this case, a particular beam of winter light puts the poet into a mood of depression as the slanting sunlight communicates a sense of despair. The poem illustrates her creeping fascination with mortality. But although the poet's subject matter is intricate and disturbing, her own views are more difficult to determine. Ironically, this exploration of light and its effects seems to suggest a great deal about Dickinson's own dark consciousness.

From the outset, Dickinson creates an uneasy atmosphere. The setting ('Winter Afternoons') is dreary and aimless. Throughout stanza one, there is an underlying sense of time weighing heavily, especially when the light is compared to solemn cathedral music ('Cathedral Tunes'). We usually expect church music to be inspirational, but in this case, its 'Heft' simply 'oppresses' and adds to the **downcast mood**.

In stanza two, the poet considers the significance of the sunlight. For her, its effects are negative, causing pain to the world: 'Heavenly Hurt, it gives us.' The paradoxical language appears to reflect Dickinson's ironic attitude that **human beings live in great fear of God's power**. Is there a sense that deep down in their souls ('Where the Meanings, are'), people struggle under the weight of God's will, fearing death and judgement?

This feeling of humanity's helplessness is highlighted in stanza three: 'None may teach it' sums up the predicament of our limitations. Life and death can never be fully understood. Perhaps this is our tragic fate – our 'Seal Despair'. Dickinson presents **God as an all-powerful royal figure** associated with suffering and punishment ('An imperial affliction'). Is the poet's tone critical and accusatory? Or is she simply expressing the reality of human experience?

Stanza four is highly dramatic. **Dickinson personifies a terrified world** where 'the Landscape listens'. The earlier sombre light is now replaced by 'Shadows' that 'hold their breath' in the silence. The poet imagines the shocking moment of death and the mystery of time ('the Distance'). While the poem's ending is open to speculation, it seems clear that Dickinson is exploring the transition from life into eternity, a subject that is central to her writing. The only certain conclusion is an obvious one – that death is an inescapable reality beyond human understanding, as mysterious as it is natural. The poet's final tone is resigned, almost relieved. The 'Slant of light' offers no definitive answers to life's questions and the human condition is as inexplicable as death itself.

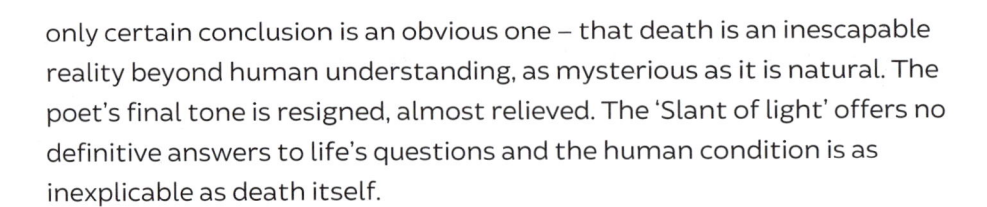

Throughout the poem, Dickinson's fragmented style is characterised by her **erratic punctuation and repeated use of capital letters**. She uses the dash to create suspense and drama. For the poet, the winter light is seen as an important sign from God, disturbing the inner 'Landscape' of her soul. In the end, the light (a likely metaphor for truth) causes Dickinson to experience an inner sadness and a deep sense of spiritual longing.

Writing About the Poem

In your view, what is the central theme in 'There's a certain Slant of light'? Support the points you make with suitable reference to the text.

Sample Paragraph

I think death is the main theme in Dickinson's poems. The poem is atmospheric, but the light coming through the window can be interpreted as a symbol of hope. However, Dickinson's language is quite negative and it could be argued that our lives are under pressure and that fear of eternal damnation is also part of life. 'Heavenly Hurt' and 'imperial affliction' suggest that we are trying to avoid sin in order to find salvation after death. I believe the central message is that death comes to us all and we must accept it. The mood is oppressive, like the sunlight coming in through the church window and the depressing 'Cathedral Tunes'. Dickinson's theme is distressing and images such as 'Seal Despair' and 'Shadows' add to the uneasiness of the reality that death is unavoidable.

EXAMINER'S COMMENT

A well-written, top-grade response that shows good engagement with both the poem and the question. References and succinct quotations used effectively to illustrate the poet's startling consideration of death. Confident and varied discussion of the poet's style throughout.

✒ Class/Homework Exercises

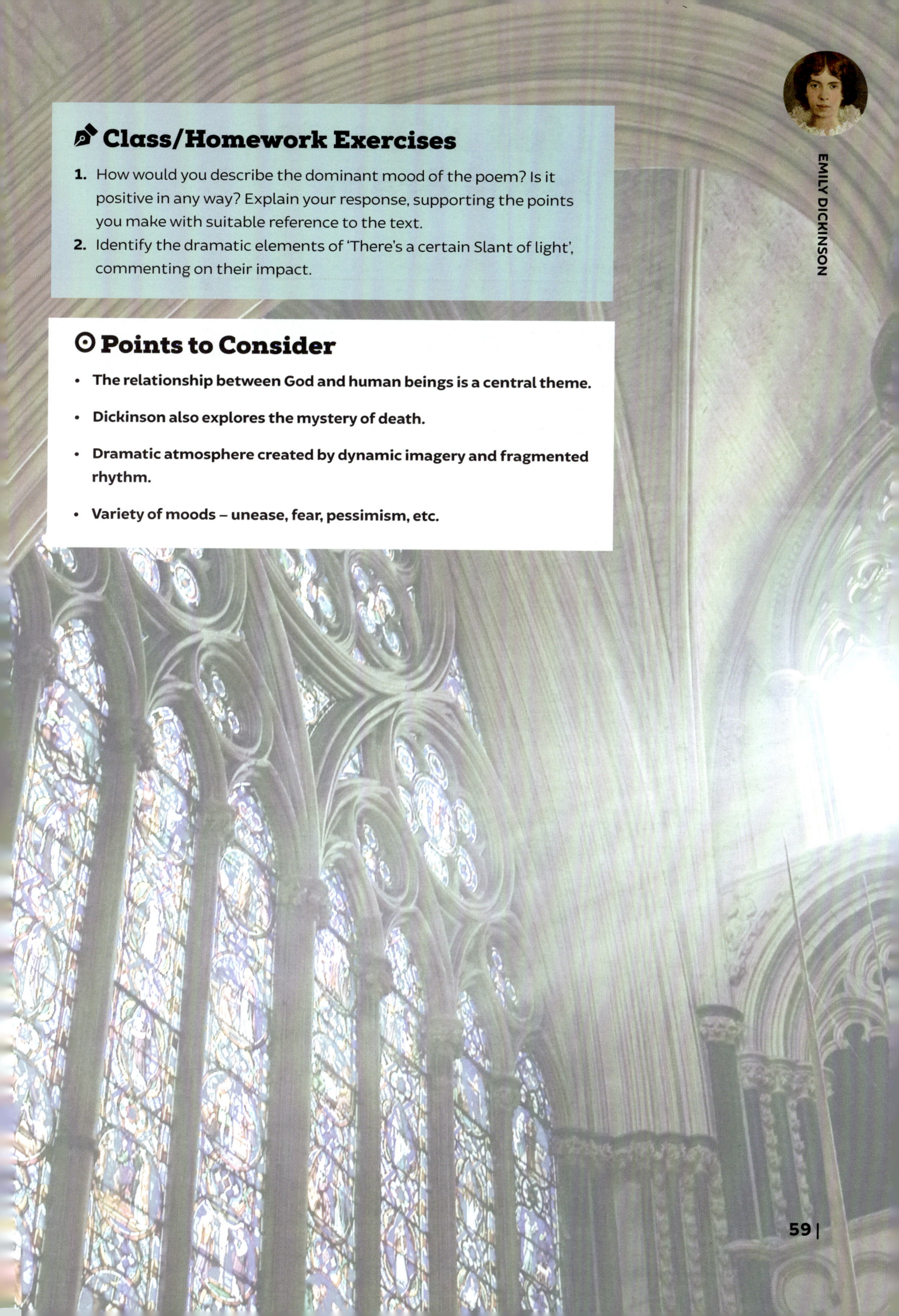

1. How would you describe the dominant mood of the poem? Is it positive in any way? Explain your response, supporting the points you make with suitable reference to the text.
2. Identify the dramatic elements of 'There's a certain Slant of light', commenting on their impact.

☉ Points to Consider

- The relationship between God and human beings is a central theme.
- Dickinson also explores the mystery of death.
- Dramatic atmosphere created by dynamic imagery and fragmented rhythm.
- Variety of moods – unease, fear, pessimism, etc.

3 I felt a Funeral, in my Brain

I felt a Funeral, in my Brain,
And Mourners to and fro
Kept treading—treading—till it seemed
That Sense was breaking through—

And when they all were seated,   5
A Service, like a Drum—
Kept beating—beating—till I thought
My Mind was going numb—

And then I heard them lift a Box
And creak across my Soul   10
With those same Boots of Lead, again,
Then Space—began to toll,

As all the Heavens were a Bell,
And Being, but an Ear,
And I, and Silence, some strange Race   15
Wrecked, solitary, here—

And then a Plank in Reason, broke,
And I dropped down, and down—
And hit a World, at every plunge,
And Finished knowing—then—   20

treading: crush by walking on.
Sense: faculty of perception; the senses (seeing, hearing, touching, tasting, smelling); sound, practical judgement.

toll: ring slowly and steadily, especially to announce a death.
As all: as if all.
And Being, but an Ear: all senses, except hearing, are now useless.

'And then a Plank in Reason, broke'

👤 Personal Response

1. Do you find the images in this poem frightening, gruesome or coldly realistic? Give reasons for your answer, supported by textual reference.
2. Where is the climax of the poem, in your opinion? Refer to the text in your answer.
3. Write a short personal response to the poem, highlighting the impact it made on you.

👁 Critical Literacy

This poem is thought to have been written in 1861, at a time of turbulence in Dickinson's life. She was having religious and artistic doubts and had experienced an unhappy time in a personal relationship. This interior landscape paints a dark picture of something falling apart. It is for the reader to decide whether it is a fainting spell, a mental breakdown or a funeral. That is the mystery of Dickinson.

The startling perspective of this poem in stanza one can be seen as the view experienced by a person in a coffin, if the poem is read as an **account of the poet imagining her death**. Alternatively, it could refer to the suffocating feeling of the breakdown of consciousness, either through fainting or a mental breakdown. Perhaps it is the death of artistic activity. Whichever reading is chosen, and maybe all co-exist, the **interior landscape of awareness is being explored**. The use of the personal pronoun 'I' shows that this is a unique experience, although it has relevance for all. The relentless pounding of the mourners walking is reminiscent of a blinding migraine headache. The repetition of the hard-sounding 't' in the verb 'treading—treading' evocatively describes this terrible experience. The 'I' is undergoing an intense trauma beyond understanding: 'Sense was breaking through.' This repetition and disorientation are closely associated with psychological breakdown.

Stanza two gives a **first person account of a funeral**. The mourners are seated and the service has begun. Hearing ('an Ear') is the only sense that is functioning. All the verbs refer to sound: 'tread', 'beat', 'heard', 'creak', 'toll'. The passive 'I' receives the experience, hearing, not actively listening. The experience is so overwhelming that 'I' thought the 'Mind was going numb', unable to endure any more. The use of the past tense reminds the reader that the experience is over, so is the first-person narrative told from beyond the grave? Is this the voice of someone who has died? Or is it the voice of someone in the throes of a desperate personal experience? The reader must decide.

The reference to 'Soul' in stanza three suggests a **spiritual dimension** to the experience. The 'I' has started to become disoriented as the line dividing an external experience and an internal one is breaking. The mourners 'creak across my Soul'. The oppressive, almost suffocating experience is captured in the onomatopoeic phrase 'Boots of Lead' and space becomes filled with the tolling bell. Existence in stanza four is reduced totally to hearing. The fearful transitory experience of crossing from awareness to unconsciousness, from life to death, is being imagined. The 'I' in stanza four is now stranded, 'Wrecked', cut off from life. The person is in a comatose state, unable to communicate: 'solitary, here'. The word 'here' makes the reader feel present at this awful drama.

Finally, in stanza five, a new sensation takes over, **the sense of falling uncontrollably**. The 'I' has finished knowing and is now no longer aware of their surroundings. Is this the descent into the hell of the angels in 'Paradise Lost'? Is it the descent of the coffin into the grave? Or is it the descent into madness or oblivion? The 'I' has learned something, but it is not revealed. The repetition of 'And' advances the movement of the poem in an almost uncontrollable way, mimicking the final descent. The 'I' is powerless under the repetitive verbs and the incessant rhythm punctuated by the ever-present dash. This poem is extraordinary, because before the study of psychology had defined it, it is a step-by-step description of mental collapse. Here is 'the drama of process'.

Writing About the Poem

'"I felt a Funeral, in my Brain" is a detailed and intense exploration of the experience of death.' Discuss this statement, using references from the text to support your views.

Sample Paragraph

Dickinson's imagined funeral suggests the losing of the grip on life by the individual 'I'. The noise ('treading', 'beating') induces an almost trance-like state as the brain becomes numb. The poet suggests that awareness is reduced to a single sense – hearing – 'an Ear'. I also find the poetic voice chilling. But the most compelling line in the poem is 'And then a Plank in Reason, broke'. This conveys the end of reason as the 'I' loses consciousness, hurtling away into another dimension. Even the punctuation, with the use of commas, conveys this reality. But the most unnerving word is yet to come – 'then'. What exactly does the poet know? Dickinson leaves us with unanswered questions.

EXAMINER'S COMMENT

A sustained personal response which attempts to stay focused throughout. The intensity within the poem is conveyed through a variety of expressions ('compelling', 'unnerving') and there is some worthwhile discussion on how features of the poet's style advance the theme of death. A solid high-grade answer.

✒ Class/Homework Exercises

1. 'She seems as close to touching bottom here as she ever got.' Discuss this view of Emily Dickinson with reference to the poem 'I felt a Funeral, in my Brain'.
2. Comment on the conclusion of the poem. Did you think it is satisfactory? Or does it leave unanswered questions?

⊙ Points to Consider

- **Themes include the imagined experience of loss of control and death.**
- **Vivid imagery depicts funeral scene.**
- **Introspective tones of uncertainty, shock and terror.**
- **Insistent rhythms, anguished tone, abrupt syntax all create dramatic impact.**
- **Striking use of onomatopoeia, assonance, repetition, etc.**

4 A Bird came down the Walk

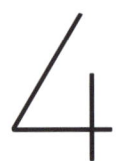

A Bird came down the Walk—
He did not know I saw—
He bit an Angleworm in halves
And ate the fellow, raw,

And then he drank a Dew   5
From a convenient Grass—
And then hopped sidewise to the Wall
To let a Beetle pass—

He glanced with rapid eyes
That hurried all around—   10
They looked like frightened Beads, I thought—
He stirred his Velvet Head

Like one in danger, Cautious,
I offered him a Crumb
And he unrolled his feathers   15
And rowed him softer home—

Than Oars divide the Ocean,
Too silver for a seam—
Or Butterflies, off Banks of Noon
Leap, plashless as they swim.   20

Angleworm: small worm used as fish bait by anglers.

the Ocean: Dickinson compares the blue sky to the sea.
silver: the sea's surface looks like solid silver.
a seam: opening; division.
plashless: splashless; undisturbed.

'He glanced with rapid eyes'

👤 Personal Response

1. In your view, what does the poem suggest about the relationship between human beings and nature?
2. What is the effect of Dickinson's use of humour in the poem? Does it let you see nature in a different way? Support the points you make with reference to the text.
3. 'Emily Dickinson expresses her admiration for nature through evocative sound effects.' To what extent do you agree with this statement? Develop your answer with reference to the poem.

👁 Critical Literacy

In this short descriptive poem, Dickinson celebrates the beauty and wonder of animals. While the bird is seen as a wild creature at times, other details present its behaviour and appearance in human terms. The poem also illustrates Dickinson's quirky sense of humour as well as offering interesting insights into nature and the exclusion of human beings from that world.

The poem opens with an everyday scene. Because the bird is unaware of the poet's presence, it behaves naturally. Stanza one demonstrates the **competition and danger of nature**: 'He bit an Angleworm in halves.' Although Dickinson imagines the bird within a human context, casually coming 'down the Walk' and suddenly eating 'the fellow, raw', she is amused by the uncivilised reality of the animal kingdom. The word 'raw' echoes her self-critical sense of shock. Despite its initial elegance, the predatory bird could hardly have been expected to cook the worm.

The poet's comic portrayal continues in stanza two. She gives the bird certain social qualities, drinking from a 'Grass' and politely allowing a hurrying beetle to pass. The tone is relaxed and playful. The slender vowel sounds ('convenient') and soft sibilance ('sidewise', 'pass') add to the seemingly refined atmosphere. However, the mood changes in stanza three, reflecting the bird's cautious fear. Dickinson observes the rapid eye movement, 'like frightened Beads'. Such **precise detail increases the drama of the moment**. The details of the bird's prim movement and beautiful texture are wonderfully accurate: 'He stirred his Velvet Head.' The simile is highly effective, suggesting the creature's natural grace.

The danger becomes more explicit in stanza four. Both the spectator and the observed bird are 'Cautious'. The crumb offered to the bird by the poet is rejected, highlighting the **gulf between their two separate worlds**. The description of the bird taking flight evokes the delicacy and fluidity of its movement: 'And he unrolled his feathers/And rowed him softer home.' The confident rhythm and emphatic alliteration enrich our understanding of the harmony between the creature and its natural environment. The sensual imagery captures the magnificence of the bird, compared to a rower moving with ease across placid water.

Stanza five develops the metaphorical description further, conveying the bird's poise and mystery: 'Too silver for a seam.' Not only was its flying seamless, it was smoother than that of butterflies leaping 'off Banks of Noon' and splashlessly swimming through the sky. The **breathtaking image and onomatopoeic language** remind us of Dickinson's admiration for nature in all its impressive beauty and is one of the most memorable descriptions in Dickinson's writing.

✒ Writing About the Poem

In your view, does Dickinson have a sense of empathy with the bird? Support your response with reference to the poem.

Sample Paragraph

Dickinson is both fascinated and amused by the small bird in her garden. She seems honoured that out of nowhere 'A Bird came down the Walk'. When it swallows a worm 'raw', she becomes even more interested. The fact that she admits 'He did not know I saw' tells me that she really has empathy for the bird. Her tone suggests she feels privileged to watch and she certainly doesn't want to disturb it in its own world. The poet also finds the bird's antics funny. Although it devours the worm, it behaves very mannerly towards the beetle. Dickinson shows her feelings for the bird when it becomes frightened and she notices it is 'in danger'. At the very end, she expresses her admiration for the beauty of the bird as it flies off to freedom – to its 'softer home'. The descriptions of it like a rower or a butterfly suggest that she admires its grace.

> **EXAMINER'S COMMENT**
>
> *Apt references and short quotations are effectively used to illustrate the poet's regard for the bird. The answer ranges well over much of the poem and considers various tones (including fascination, amusement, reverence, concern and admiration). A confident top-grade response.*

🔎 Class/Homework Exercises

1. Comment on Dickinson's use of imagery in 'A Bird came down the Walk'. Develop the points you make with the aid of suitable reference.
2. In your opinion, what does the poem suggest about the differences (or similarities) between animals and humans? Develop your response with reference to the text.

◎ Points to Consider

- **Exploration of the wonder of nature.**
- **Interesting use of personification gives the bird social graces.**
- **Impact of sensuous imagery, metaphorical language, sibilant effects.**
- **Contrasting tones – bemused, concerned, surprised, upbeat, etc.**

5. I heard a Fly buzz—when I died

EMILY DICKINSON

I heard a Fly buzz—when I died—
The Stillness in the Room
Was like the Stillness in the Air—
Between the Heaves of Storm—

The Eyes around—had wrung them dry— 5
And Breaths were gathering firm
For that last Onset—when the King
Be witnessed—in the Room—

I willed my Keepsakes—Signed away
What portion of me be 10
Assignable—and then it was
There interposed a Fly—

With Blue—uncertain stumbling Buzz—
Between the light—and me—
And then the Windows failed—and then 15
I could not see to see—

Heaves: lift with effort.

Onset: beginning.
the King: God.

Keepsakes: gifts treasured for the sake of the giver.

interposed: inserted between or among things.

'And then the Windows failed—'

👤 Personal Response

1. How would you describe the atmosphere in the poem? Pick out two phrases which, in your opinion, are especially descriptive and explain why you chose them.
2. Do you think Dickinson uses contrast effectively in this poem? Discuss one contrast you found particularly striking.
3. Write a brief personal response to the poem, highlighting its impact on you.

⊙ Critical Literacy

Dickinson was fascinated by death. This poem examines the moment between life and death. At that time, it was common for family and friends to be present at deathbed vigils. It was thought that the way a person behaved or looked at the moment of death gave an indication of the soul's fate.

The last moment of a person's life is a solemn and often sad occasion. The perspective of the poem is that of the person dying and this significant moment is dominated by the buzzing of a fly in the room in the first stanza. This is **absurdly comic and distorts** this moment into something strange. Surely the person dying should be concerned with more important matters than an insignificant fly: 'I heard a Fly buzz—when I died.' The room is still and expectant as last breaths are drawn. The word 'Heaves' suggests the force of the storm that is about to break.

In the second stanza, the mourners no longer cry but hold their breath, steadfast ('firm') in their religious belief as they await the entrance of God ('King'). 'Be witnessed' refers to both the mourners and the dying person, conjuring up the deep solemnity of a court. The word 'firm' also suggests these people's steadfast religious beliefs. The third stanza is concerned with putting matters right. The dying person has made a will – 'What portion of me be/Assignable' – and what is not assignable belongs to God. The person is awaiting the coming of his/her Maker, 'and then it was/There interposed a Fly' – the symbol of decay and corruption appeared. Human affairs cannot be managed; real life intervenes. The **fly comes between ('interposed') the dying person and the moment of death, which trivialises** the event.

The fractured syntax of the last stanza shows the **breakdown of the senses** at the moment of death: 'Between the light—and me.' Sight and sound are blurring. The presence of the fly is completely inappropriate, like a drunken person at a solemn ceremony, disturbing and embarrassing and interrupting proceedings. The fly is now between the dying person and the source of light. Does this suggest that the person has lost concentration on higher things, distracted by the buzzing fly? The sense of sight then fails: 'And then the Windows failed.' The moment of death has come and gone, dominated by the noisy fly. Has the fly prevented the person from reaching another dimension? Is death emptiness, just human decay, as signified by the presence of the fly, or is there something more? Do we need comic relief at overwhelming occasions? Is the poet signalling her own lack of belief in an afterlife with God? Dickinson, as usual, intrigues, **leaving the reader with more questions than answers**, so that the reader, like the dying person, is struggling to 'see to see'.

Writing About the Poem

'Dickinson's poems on mortality often lead to uncertainty or despair.' Discuss this statement with particular reference to 'I heard a Fly buzz—when I died'.

Sample Paragraph

The view of this deathbed scene is from the dying person's perspective. Dickinson seems to be saying that life and death are random – and this goes against the human desire for order, 'Signed away/What portion of me be/Assignable'. I feel the poet may be suggesting that the dying person, distracted by the fly is, therefore, cheated. The occasion has passed, dominated by a buzzing fly. Dickinson's voice is far from reassuring. Instead, she draws a deathbed scene and lets us 'see to see'. The divided voice, that of the person dying and that of the person after death leaves us with a question – is death just the final stage in the meaningless cycle of life? In the end, this poem leaves me with uncertainties about the human condition and our ability to exercise control.

> **EXAMINER'S COMMENT**
> This solid, high-grade response includes interesting and thought-provoking ideas on a challenging question. Comments show some good personal engagement with the poem and the issues raised by Dickinson. Expression is impressive and apt quotations are used effectively throughout the answer. References to the dramatic style and tone would have improved the standard.

Class/Homework Exercises

1. Comment on how Dickinson's style contributes to the theme or message in this poem. Refer closely to the text in your response.
2. Is there any suggestion that the speaker in this poem believes in a spiritual afterlife? Give a reason for your response, supporting your views with reference to the text.

Points to Consider

- Dickinson raises questions about death and the possibility of an afterlife.
- Surreal sense of the absurd throughout.
- Dramatic elements – the deathbed scene, still atmosphere, observers, noises, etc.
- Contrasting tones include disbelief, confusion, resignation and helplessness.
- Effective use of contrast and symbols (light, the fly) and repetition.

6 The Soul has Bandaged moments

The Soul has Bandaged moments—
When too appalled to stir—
She feels some ghastly Fright come up
And stop to look at her—

Salute her—with long fingers— 5
Caress her freezing hair—
Sip, Goblin, from the very lips
The Lover—hovered—o'er—
Unworthy, that a thought so mean
Accost a Theme—so—fair— 10

The soul has moments of Escape—
When bursting all the doors—
She dances like a Bomb, abroad,
And swings upon the Hours,

As do the Bee—delirious borne— 15
Long Dungeoned from his Rose—
Touch Liberty—then know no more,
But Noon, and Paradise—

The Soul's retaken moments—
When, Felon led along, 20
With shackles on the plumed feet,
And staples, in the Song,

The Horror welcomes her, again,
These, are not brayed of Tongue—

Bandaged moments: painful experiences.
appalled: shocked, horrified.
stir: act; retaliate.

Accost: address.

Escape: freedom.

like a Bomb: dramatically.
abroad: in unusual directions.

Dungeoned: imprisoned in the hive.

Felon: criminal.
shackles: chains, ropes.
plumed: decorated.
staples: fastenings.

brayed of Tongue: spoken of.

👤 Personal Response

1. What details in the poem evoke the feelings of 'ghastly Fright' experienced by the soul? Support your answer with quotation or reference.
2. Choose one comparison from the poem that you find particularly effective. Explain your choice.
3. Comment on Dickinson's use of dashes in this poem, briefly explaining their effectiveness.

👁 Critical Literacy

In much of her poetry, Dickinson focuses on the nature of consciousness and the experience of being alive. She was constantly searching for meaning, particularly of transient moments or changing moods. This search is central to 'The Soul has Bandaged moments', where the poet takes us through a series of dramatic images contrasting the extremes of the spirit and the conscious self.

Stanza one introduces the soul as being fearful and vulnerable, personified as a terrified female who 'feels some ghastly Fright', with the poem's stark

'As do the Bee—delirious borne—'

EMILY DICKINSON

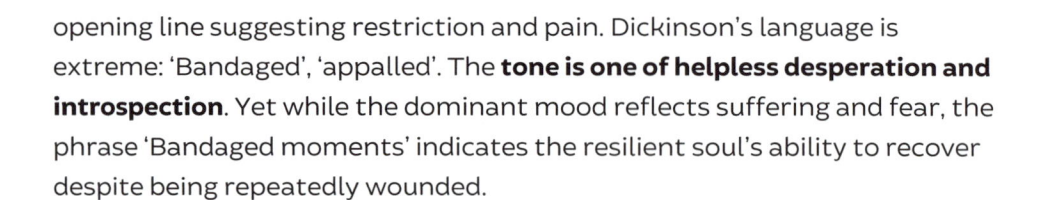

opening line suggesting restriction and pain. Dickinson's language is extreme: 'Bandaged', 'appalled'. The **tone is one of helpless desperation and introspection**. Yet while the dominant mood reflects suffering and fear, the phrase 'Bandaged moments' indicates the resilient soul's ability to recover despite being repeatedly wounded.

Stanza two is unnervingly dramatic. The poet creates a mock-romantic scene between the victimised soul and the 'ghastly Fright' figure, now portrayed as a hideous goblin and her would-be lover, their encounter depicted in terms of gothic horror. The soul experiences terrifying fantasies as the **surreal sequence becomes increasingly menacing** and the goblin's long fingers 'Caress her freezing hair'. The appearance of an unidentified shadowy 'Lover' is unexpected. There is a sense of the indecisive soul being caught between two states, represented by the malevolent goblin and the deserving lover. It is unclear whether Dickinson is writing about the choices involved in romantic love or the relationship between herself and God.

The stanza ends inconclusively, juxtaposing two opposites: the 'Unworthy' or undeserving 'thought' and the 'fair' (worthy) 'Theme'. The latter might well refer to the ideal of romantic love. If so, it is confronted by erotic desire (the 'thought'). Dickinson's disjointed style, especially her frequent use of dashes within stanzas, isolates key words and intensifies the overwhelmingly **nightmarish atmosphere**.

The feeling of confused terror is replaced with ecstatic 'moments of Escape' in stanzas three and four. The soul recovers in triumph, 'bursting all the doors'. This **explosion of energy** ('She dances like a Bomb') evokes a rising mood of riotous freedom. Explosive verbs ('bursting', 'dances', 'swings') and robust rhythms add to the sense of uncontrollable excitement. Dickinson compares the soul to a 'Bee—delirious borne'. After being 'Long Dungeoned' in its hive, this bee can now enjoy the sensuous delights of 'his Rose'.

The mood is short-lived, however, and in stanzas five and six, 'The Horror' returns. The soul becomes depressed again, feeling bound and shackled, like a 'Felon led along'. **Dickinson develops this criminal metaphor** – 'With shackles on the plumed feet' – leaving us with an ultimate sense of loss as 'The Horror welcomes her, again'. Is this the soul's inevitable fate? The final line is unsettling. Whatever horrible experiences confront the soul, they are simply unspeakable: 'not brayed of Tongue.'

As always, Dickinson's poem is open to many interpretations. Critics have suggested that the poet is dramatising the turmoil of dealing with the loss of creativity. Some view the poem's central conflict as the tension between romantic love and sexual desire. Others believe that the poet was exploring the theme of depression and mental instability. In the end, readers must find their own meaning and decide for themselves.

✒ Writing About the Poem

Comment on the dramatic elements that are present in the poem, developing the points you make with reference to the text.

Sample Paragraph

'The Soul has Bandaged moments' is built around a conflict between the 'Soul', or spirit, and its great enemy, 'Fright'. Dickinson sets the dramatic scene with the Soul still recovering – presumably from the last battle. It is 'Bandaged' after the fight with its arch enemy. The descriptions of the soul's opponent are startling. Fright is 'ghastly', a 'Horror' who is trying to seduce the innocent soul. Dickinson's images add to the tension. In the seduction scene, the goblin is described as having 'long fingers'. The goblin uses its bony claws to 'Caress her freezing hair'. The drama continues right to the end. The soul is compared to a 'Felon' being led away in 'shackles'. Finally, Dickinson's stop-and-start style is unsettling. Broken rhythms and condensed language increase the edgy atmosphere throughout this highly dramatic poem.

> **EXAMINER'S COMMENT**
>
> An assured and focused top-grade response, showing a clear understanding of the poem's dramatic features. The answer addressed both subject matter and style, using back-up illustration and integrated quotes successfully. Expression throughout was also excellent.

✐ Class/Homework Exercises

1. In your opinion, what is the dominant tone of 'The Soul has Bandaged moments'? Use reference to the text to show how the tone is effectively conveyed.
2. Identify the poem's surreal aspects and comment on their impact.

⊙ Points to Consider

- **An intense exploration of the nature of spiritual awareness.**
- **Dickinson focuses on a series of traumatic experiences.**
- **Effective use of dramatic verbs and vivid imagery.**
- **The soul is personified to convey various states – fear, joy, terror, etc.**

7 I could bring You Jewels—had I a mind to

I could bring You Jewels—had I a mind to—
But You have enough—of those—
I could bring You Odors from St. Domingo—
Colors—from Vera Cruz—

Berries of the Bahamas—have I— 5
But this little Blaze
Flickering to itself—in the Meadow—
Suits Me—more than those—

Never a Fellow matched this Topaz—
And his Emerald Swing— 10
Dower itself—for Bobadilo—
Better—Could I bring?

Odors: fragrances, perfumes.
St. Domingo: Santo Domingo (now the Dominican Republic) in the Caribbean.
Vera Cruz: city on the east coast of Mexico.
Bahamas: group of islands south-east of Florida.
Blaze: strong fire or flame; very bright light.
Dower: part of her husband's estate allotted to a widow by law.
Bobadilo: braggart; someone who speaks arrogantly or boastfully.

'Never a Fellow matched this Topaz—'

👤 Personal Response

1. Does the poet value exotic or homely gifts? Briefly explain your answer.
2. How effective, in your opinion, is Dickinson's use of visual imagery in her celebration of nature? Support your views with reference to the poem.
3. What is the tone in this poem: arrogant, humble, gentle, strident, confident? Briefly develop your answer with reference to the text.

👁 Critical Literacy

Although described as a recluse, Dickinson had a wide circle of friends. She wrote letter-poems to them, often representing them as flowers, 'things of nature which had come with no practice at all'. This poem is one without shadows, celebratory and happy, focusing out rather than in as she concentrates on a relationship.

In the first stanza, the poem opens with the speaker **considering the gift she will give** her beloved, 'You'. The 'You' is very much admired, and is wealthy ('You have enough'), so the gift of jewels is dismissed. The phrase 'had I a mind to' playfully suggests that maybe the 'I' doesn't necessarily wish to present anything. There is a certain flirtatious air evident here. A world of privilege and plenty is shown as, one after another, expensively exotic gifts are considered and dismissed. These include perfumes and vibrant colours from faraway locations, conjuring up images of romance and adventure: 'Odors from St. Domingo.'

The second stanza continues the list, with 'Berries of the Bahamas' being considered as an option for this special gift, but they are not quite right either. The tense changes to 'have I' and the laconic listing and dismissing stops. A small wildflower 'in the Meadow', 'this little Blaze', is chosen instead. This 'Suits Me'. Notice that it is not that this suits the other person. **This gift is a reflection of her own unshowy personality**. The long lines of considering exotic gifts have now given way to shorter, more decisive lines.

In the third stanza, the speaker's strength of feeling is evident, as she confidently states that 'Never a Fellow matched' this shining gift of hers. No alluring, foreign gemstone, be it a brilliant topaz or emerald, shines as this 'little Blaze' in the meadow. The gift glows with colour; it is natural, inexpensive and accessible. The reference to a dower might suggest a gift given by a woman to a prospective husband. This **gift is suitable** for a Spanish adventurer, a 'Bobadilo'. The assured tone is clear in the word 'Never' and the jaunty rhyme 'Swing' and 'bring'. The final rhetorical question suggests that this is the best gift she could give. The poem shows that **the true value of a present cannot be measured in a material way**.

EMILY DICKINSON

✍ Writing About the Poem

'Dickinson is fascinated by moments of change.' Discuss this statement with reference to 'I could bring You Jewels—had I a mind to'.

Sample Paragraph

In this lively poem, the speaker considers what present would be most suitable to give to her arrogant lover. The first change occurs when this confident woman dismisses expensive, exotic gifts, 'But You have enough' and chooses something which is natural – and, more importantly – which is to her liking: 'Suits Me –' The simple flower she offers is unexpectedly beautiful – this 'little Blaze' suggests the hidden passion of the woman herself. The changing breathless tone reflects the love she feels. The flower is brighter than any precious stone of 'Topaz' or 'Emerald'. Short lines express the self-belief of a woman who knows best. Even the rhyme changes from where she is considering her options ('those'/'Cruz') in the first stanza, to the more definite jaunty rhyme of 'Swing' and 'bring' in the final stanza. Dickinson is fascinated by the spontaneity of life.

> **EXAMINER'S COMMENT**
>
> *A confident top-grade response to the question, backed up with a convincing use of quotation. Good discussion about changes in thought and tone. The point about the change in line length was particularly interesting. Assured, varied vocabulary is controlled throughout and the paragraph is rounded off impressively.*

✒ Class/Homework Exercises

1. 'Dickinson disrupts and transforms our accepted view of things.' What is your opinion of this statement? Refer to 'I could bring You Jewels—had I a mind to' in support of your response.
2. Comment on the impact of Dickinson's use of sound effects in the poem.

⊙ Points to Consider

- **Central themes include the wonder and beauty of nature.**
- **Celebratory mood conveyed by powerful visual imagery and lively rhythm.**
- **Simplicity of the wildflower contrasted with extravagant glamour.**
- **Confident, optimistic tone contrasts with the poet's downbeat poems.**

8 A narrow Fellow in the Grass

EMILY DICKINSON

A narrow Fellow in the Grass
Occasionally rides—
You may have met Him—did you not
His notice sudden is—

The Grass divides as with a Comb— 5
A spotted shaft is seen—
And then it closes at your feet
And opens further on—

He likes a Boggy Acre
A Floor too cool for Corn— 10
Yet when a Boy, and Barefoot—
I more than once at Noon
Have passed, I thought, a Whip lash
Unbraiding in the Sun
When stooping to secure it 15
It wrinkled, and was gone—

Several of Nature's People
I know, and they know me—
I feel for them a transport
Of cordiality— 20

But never met this Fellow
Attended, or alone
Without a tighter breathing
And Zero at the Bone—

a spotted shaft: patterned skin of the darting snake.
Whip lash: sudden, violent movement.
Unbraiding: straightening out, uncoiling.
transport: heightened emotion.
cordiality: civility, welcome.
Zero at the Bone: cold terror.

'His notice sudden is—'

👤 Personal Response

1. Select two images from the poem that suggest evil or menace. Comment briefly on the effectiveness of each.
2. How successful is the poet in conveying the snake's erratic movement? Refer to the text in your answer.
3. Outline your own feelings in response to the poem.

◉ Critical Literacy

In this poem, one of the few published during her lifetime, Dickinson adopts a male persona remembering an incident from his boyhood. Snakes have traditionally been seen as symbols of evil. We still use the expression 'snake in the grass' to describe someone who cannot be trusted. Central to this poem is Dickinson's own portrayal of nature – beautiful, brutal and lyrical. She seems fascinated by the endless mystery, danger and unpredictability of the natural world.

The opening lines of stanza one casually introduce a 'Fellow in the Grass'. (Dickinson never refers explicitly to the snake.) The **conversational tone immediately involves readers** who may already 'have met Him'. However, there is more than a hint of warning in the postscript: 'His notice sudden is.' The menacing adjective 'narrow', and the disjointed rhythm foreshadow an underlying sense of caution.

Dickinson focuses on the volatile snake's dramatic movements in stanza two. The verbs 'divide', 'closes' and 'opens' emphasise its dynamic energy. The snake suddenly emerges like a 'spotted shaft'. The poet's **comparisons are particularly effective**, suggesting a lightning bolt or a camouflaged weapon. Run-on lines, a forceful rhythm and the repetition of 'And' contribute to the vivid image of the snake as a powerful presence to be treated with caution.

Stanza three reveals even more about the snake's natural habitat: 'He likes a Boggy Acre.' It also divulges the speaker's identity – an adult male remembering his failed boyhood efforts to capture snakes. The memory conveys something of the intensity of childhood experiences, especially of dangerous encounters with nature. The boy's innocence and vulnerability ('Barefoot') contrasts with the 'Whip lash' violence of the wild snake. **Dickinson's attitude to nature is open to interpretation**. Does the threat come from the animal or the boy? Did the adult speaker regard the snake differently when he was young? The poet herself clearly appreciates the complexities found within the natural world and her precisely observed descriptions ('Unbraiding', 'It wrinkled') provide ample evidence of her interest.

From the speaker's viewpoint in stanza four, nature is generally friendly. This positive image is conveyed by the affectionate tribute to 'Nature's People'. The familiar personification and personal tone underline the mutual 'cordiality' that exists between nature and human nature. Despite this, **divisions between the two worlds cannot be ignored**. Indeed, the focus in stanza five is on the sheer horror people experience when confronted by 'this Fellow'. The poet's sparse and chilling descriptions – 'tighter breathing', 'Zero at the Bone' – are startling expressions of stunned terror.

As in other poems, Dickinson attributes human characteristics to nature – the snake 'Occasionally rides', 'The Grass divides' and the bogland has a 'Floor'. One effect of this is to highlight the **variety and mystery of the natural environment**, which can only ever be glimpsed within limited human terms. The snake remains unknowable to the end, dependent on a chance encounter, a fleeting glance or a trick of light.

✒ Writing About the Poem

Comment on the effectiveness of Dickinson's use of the male persona voice in 'A narrow Fellow in the Grass'. Develop the points you make with reference to the poem.

Sample Paragraph

In some poems, Dickinson chose to substitute her own voice with a fictional narrator. This is the case in 'A narrow Fellow in the Grass', where she uses a country boy to tell the story of his experiences trying to catch snakes. It is obvious that he has a great love for nature, but neither is he blind to the fear he felt when he came face to face with the 'spotted shaft'. Dickinson's language emphasises terror. The images are disturbing: 'a tighter breathing.' The boy remembers shuddering with fright, 'Zero at the Bone'. The poem is all the more effective for being centred around one terrified character, the young boy. I can visualise the child in his bare feet trying to catch a frightened snake in the grass. By using another persona, Dickinson explores the excitement and danger of nature in a wider way.

> **EXAMINER'S COMMENT**
>
> *A sustained response that includes some good personal engagement and a great deal of insightful discussion – particularly regarding the conflict between the boy and the snake. References and quotations are well used throughout the answer to provide a very interesting high-grade standard.*

✎ Class/Homework Exercises

1. In your opinion, how does Dickinson portray nature in 'A narrow Fellow in the Grass'? Develop your points with reference to the poem.
2. Identify the dramatic moments in this poem and comment on their impact.

◉ Points to Consider

- Dickinson explores contrasting aspects of the natural world.
- Effective use of everyday conversational language.
- The poet adopts the persona of a young boy who encounters a snake.
- Dramatic atmosphere concludes on a note of terror.

9 I taste a liquor never brewed

I taste a liquor never brewed—
From Tankards scooped in Pearl—
Not all the Vats upon the Rhine
Yield such an Alcohol!

Inebriate of Air—am I— 5
And Debauchee of Dew—
Reeling—thro endless summer days—
From inns of Molten Blue—

When 'Landlords' turn the drunken Bee
Out of the Foxglove's door— 10
When Butterflies—renounce their 'drams'—
I shall but drink the more!

Till Seraphs swing their snowy Hats—
And Saints—to windows run—
To see the little Tippler 15
Leaning against the—Sun—

Tankards: one-handled mugs, usually made of pewter, used for drinking beer.
Vats: large vessels used for making alcohol.

Debauchee: someone who has overindulged and neglected their duty.

Seraphs: angels who are of the highest spiritual level.
Tippler: a person who drinks often, but does not get drunk.

'Not all the Vats upon the Rhine/
Yield such an Alcohol!'

👤 Personal Response

1. What is the mood in this poem? Does it intensify or change? Refer to the text in your response.
2. Which stanza appeals to you most? Discuss both the poet's style and the poem's content in your answer.
3. Dickinson creates a slapstick cartoon-like scene in this poem. Why, in your opinion, does the poet use this technique to convey the exuberance of summer?

👁 Critical Literacy

This 'rapturous poem about summer' uses the metaphor of intoxication to capture the essence of this wonderful season. Dickinson's family were strict Calvinists, a religion that emphasised damnation as the consequence of sin. Her father supported the Temperance League, an organisation that warned against the dangers of drink.

This poem is written as a **joyful appreciation of this wonderful life**. The tone is playful and exaggerated from the beginning, as the poet declares this drink was never 'brewed'. The reference to 'scooped in Pearl' could refer to the great, white frothing heads of beer in the 'Tankards'. The poet certainly conveys the merriment of intoxication, as the poem reels along its happy way. The explanation for all this drunkenness is that the poet is drunk on life ('Inebriate', 'Debauchee'). The pubs are the inns of 'Molten Blue', i.e. the sky (stanza two). It is like a cartoon, with little drunken bees being shown the door by the pub owners as they lurch about in delirious ecstasy. The drinkers of the natural world are the bees and butterflies, but she can drink more than these: 'I shall but drink the more!' This roots the poem in reality, as drunken people always feel they can manage more.

But this has caused uproar in the heavens, as the angels and saints run to look out at this little drunk, 'the little Tippler'. She stands drunkenly leaning against the 'Sun', a celestial lamppost. The final dash suggests the crooked stance of the little drunken one. **There is no heavy moral at the end of this poem. In fact, there seems to be a slight note of envy for the freedom and happiness being experienced by the intoxicated poet**. Are the angels swinging their hats to cheer her on in her drunken rebellion? Is this poem celebrating the reckless indulgence of excess? Or is the final metaphor of the sun referring to Christ or to the poet's own arrival in heaven after she self-indulgently enjoys the beauty of the natural world?

Nature is seen as the spur for high jinks and good humour. The riddle of the first line starts it off: how was the alcohol 'never brewed'? The exaggerated imagery, such as the metaphor of the flower as a pub and the bee as the drunk, all add to the fantasy-land atmosphere. The words 'Inebriate',

EMILY DICKINSON

'Debauchee' and 'renounce' are reminiscent of the language that those who disapprove of the consumption of alcohol might use for those who do indulge. Is the poet having a sly laugh at the serious Temperance League to which her father belonged? The ridiculous costumes, 'snowy Hats', and the uproar in heaven ('swing' and 'run') all add to the impression of this land of merriment. The juxtaposition of the sacred ('Seraphs') and the irreverent ('Tippler') in stanza four also adds to the comic effect. However, it is the verbs that carry the sense of mad fun most effectively: 'scooped', 'Reeling', 'drink', 'swing', 'run' and 'Leaning'. The poem lurches and flows in an almost uncontrollable way as the ecstasy of overindulging in the delirious pleasure of nature is vividly conveyed.

There are two different types of humour present in this irrepressible poem – the broad humour of farce and the more **subversive humour of irony**. Dickinson seems to be standing at a distance, smiling wryly, as she gently makes fun of people who take life too seriously.

Writing About the Poem

'Dickinson was always careful to avoid expressing excessive emotion, even of joy.' Discuss this statement with reference to 'I taste a liquor never brewed'.

Sample Paragraph

This is a funny poem and the poet is enjoying herself. She is drunk on nature and it is humourous when the angels are waving their caps, egging her on. I think this is really a happy poem, unlike Dickenson's disturbing poems we studied about funerals and souls. It goes to show she also writes happier poetry when she wants. Dickenson hardly ever uses normal punctuation. Her poems are hard as they don't have normal sentences but use capital letters. There is a comparison for drinking all through to describe being drunk on nature. The poem is definately full of joy, eg the story about the bee. The lines describing the tippler are joyful. I think everyone should be able to enjoy Emily's brilliant poem as it has happy images.

EXAMINER'S COMMENT

This note-like answer shows limited engagement with the poem. While there is a recognition of the poem's joyful tone and some supportive reference, the lack of substantial analysis is noticeable. Language use is repetitive, expression is flawed and there are several mechanical mistakes. The over-enthusiastic ending is not convincing. Closer study of the poem and greater care in writing the response would raise the standard from a basic grade.

✒ Class/Homework Exercises

1. 'Hypersensitivity to natural beauty produced Dickinson's poetry.' Do you agree or disagree with this statement? Refer to the poem 'I taste a liquor never brewed' in your response.
2. Identify the childlike elements of the poem and comment on their impact.

⊙ Points to Consider

- The poem highlights Dickinson's close relationship with nature.
- Exuberant mood conveyed by sibilant sounds, vivid images, lively rhythm, etc.
- Extended metaphor of intoxication used effectively throughout.
- Dominant sense of delight, celebration and good humour.

EMILY DICKINSON

10 After great pain, a formal feeling comes

After great pain, a formal feeling comes—
The Nerves sit ceremonious, like Tombs—
The stiff Heart questions was it He, that bore,
And Yesterday, or Centuries before?

The Feet, mechanical, go round— 5
Of Ground, or Air, or Ought—
A Wooden way
Regardless grown,
A Quartz contentment, like a stone—

This is the Hour of Lead— 10
Remembered, if outlived,
As Freezing persons, recollect the Snow—
First—Chill—then Stupor—then the letting go—

formal: serious; exact.
ceremonious: on show.
He: the stiff Heart, or possibly Christ.
bore: endured; intruded.

Ought: anything.

Quartz: basic rock mineral.

Hour of Lead: traumatic experience.

Stupor: numbness; disorientation.

Personal Response

1. Comment on the poet's use of personification in the opening stanza. Does it add drama?
2. How does the language used in the second stanza convey the condition of the victim in pain?
3. How, in your opinion, does Dickinson's use of punctuation in the last line of the poem heighten the sense of descending into nothingness?

'First—Chill—then Stupor'

👁 Critical Literacy

Dickinson wrote 'After great pain, a formal feeling comes' in 1862, at a time when she was thought to have been experiencing severe psychological difficulties. The poet addresses the effects of isolation and anguish on the individual. Ironically, the absence of the personal pronoun 'I' gives the poem a universal significance. The 'great pain' itself is never fully explained and the final lines are ambiguous. Like so much of Dickinson's work, this dramatic poem raises many questions for consideration.

From the outset, Dickinson is concerned with the emotional numbness ('a formal feeling') that follows the experience of 'great pain'. The poet's authoritative tone in stanza one reflects a first-hand knowledge of trauma, with the adjective 'formal' suggesting self-conscious recovery from some earlier distress. Dickinson personifies the physical response as order returns to body and mind: 'The Nerves sit ceremonious, like Tombs'. The severe pain has also shocked the 'stiff Heart', which has become confused by the experience. Is the poet also drawing a parallel with the life and death of Jesus Christ (the Sacred Heart), crucified 'Centuries before'? The images certainly suggest timeless suffering and endurance. This **sombre sense of loss** is further enhanced by the broad vowel assonance of the opening lines.

The feeling of being in a dazed standstill continues into stanza two. In reacting to intense pain, 'The Feet, mechanical, go round'. It is as if the response is unfocused and indifferent, lacking any real purpose. Dickinson uses two **analogies to emphasise the sense of pointless alienation**. The reference to the 'Wooden way' might be interpreted as a fragile bridge between reason and insanity, or this metaphor could be associated with Christ's suffering as he carried his cross to Calvary. The level of consciousness at such times is described as 'Regardless grown', or beyond caring. Dickinson's second comparison is equally innovative: 'A Quartz contentment' underpins the feeling of complete apathy that makes the victims of pain behave 'like a stone'. Is she being ironic by suggesting that the post-traumatic state is an escape, a 'contentment' of sorts?

There is a disturbing sense of resignation at the start of stanza three: 'This is the Hour of Lead'. The dull weight of depression is reinforced by the insistent monosyllables and solemn rhythm, but the devastating experience is not 'outlived' by everyone. Dickinson defines the aftermath of suffering by using one final comparison: 'As Freezing persons.' This shocking simile evokes the unimaginable hopelessness of the victim stranded in a vast wasteland of snow. The poem's last line traces the tragic stages leading to oblivion: 'First—Chill—then Stupor—then the letting go—.' The inclusion of the dash at the end might indicate a possibility of relief, though whether it is through rescue or death is not revealed. In either case, **readers are left with an acute awareness of an extremely distraught voice**.

EMILY DICKINSON

✒ Writing About the Poem

One of Dickinson's great achievements is her ability to explore the experience of deep depression. To what extent is this true of her poem 'After great pain, a formal feeling comes'? Refer closely to the text in your answer.

Sample Paragraph

'After great pain, a formal feeling comes' is a good example of Dickinson's skill in addressing distressing subjects. Although she never explains the 'pain' in the first line, she deals with the after-effects of suffering. What Dickinson does well is to explain how depression can lead to people becoming numb, beyond all emotion. I believe this is what she means by 'a formal feeling'. She uses an interesting image of a sufferer's nerves sitting quietly at a funeral service. This same idea is used to describe the mourners – 'Feet mechanical'. I get the impression that grief can destroy people's confidence. Dickinson's images suggest the coldness experienced by patients who have depression. The best description is when she compares sufferers to being lost in the snow. They will slowly fade into a 'stupor' or death wish. Dickinson is very good at using images and moods to explore depression.

EXAMINER'S COMMENT

Although the expression is slightly awkward in places, there are a number of interesting points in the response – particularly the discussion of 'a formal feeling' and the exploration of key images in the poem. Apt quotations and supportive references are used effectively. A solid high-grade standard.

✒ Class/Homework Exercises

1. In your opinion, what is the dominant mood in 'After great pain, a formal feeling comes'? Is it one of depression, sadness or acceptance? Refer closely to the text in your answer.
2. In your view, which metaphor in the poem best conveys a sense of deep depression? Briefly explain your choice.

⊙ Points to Consider

- **Intense exploration of depression and psychological suffering.**
- **Effective use of vivid imagery, personification and serious tone.**
- **Disturbing mood throughout is solemn and sombre.**
- **Ambiguous, open-ended conclusion.**

Sample Leaving Cert Questions on Dickinson's Poetry

1. 'Emily Dickinson's unique poetic style is perfectly suited to the extraordinary themes which she explores in her poems.' Do you agree with this assessment of Dickinson's poetry? Develop your answer with suitable reference to the poems by Dickinson on your course.
2. 'Dickinson's exploration of profound life experiences is effectively conveyed through her innovative style.' Discuss this statement, developing your answer with reference to the poetry of Emily Dickinson on your course.
3. 'A dark, eccentric vision is at the heart of Emily Dickinson's most dramatic poems.' Discuss this view, developing the points you make with reference to the poems by Dickinson on your course.

How do I organise my answer?

(Sample question 1)

'Emily Dickinson's unique poetic style is perfectly suited to the extraordinary themes which she explores in her poems.' Do you agree with this assessment of Dickinson's poetry? Develop your answer with suitable reference to the poems by Dickinson on your course.

Sample Plan 1

Intro: *(Stance: agree with viewpoint in the question)* Dickinson is an original voice who addresses abstract subject matter, such as states of consciousness, hope, death and the relationship between nature and human nature. Her energetic style is in keeping with the intense approach to her extraordinary themes.

Point 1: *(Positive approach in keeping with spontaneous enthusiastic tone)* '"Hope" is the thing with feathers' – metaphorical language reflects the small bird's presence to illustrate and highlight various aspects of hope and human resilience.

Point 2: *(Evocative language matches startling sense of self-awareness)* Dramatic atmospheres in 'I felt a Funeral, in my Brain' and 'I Heard a Fly buzz—when I died'. Surreal imagery, haunting aural effects and fragmented rhythms effectively convey disorientation and powerlessness.

Understanding the Prescribed Poetry Question

Marks are awarded using the PCLM Marking Scheme:
P = 15; C = 15; L = 15; M = 5
Total = 50

- **P** (Purpose = 15 marks) refers to the set question and is the launch pad for the answer. This involves engaging with all aspects of the question. Both theme and language must be addressed, although not necessarily equally.
- **C** (Coherence = 15 marks) refers to the organisation of the developed response and the use of accurate, relevant quotation. Paragraphing is essential.
- **L** (Language = 15 marks) refers to the student's skill in controlling language throughout the answer.
- **M** (Mechanics = 5 marks) refers to spelling and grammar.
- Although no specific number of poems is required, students usually discuss at least 3 or 4 in their written responses.
- Aim for at least 800 words, to be completed within 45–50 minutes.

NOTE

In keeping with the PCLM approach, the student has to take a stance by agreeing, disagreeing or partially agreeing with the statement that:

- **Dickinson's unique poetic style** (condensed poetic forms, compressed language, unconventional punctuation, broken rhythms, haunting aural effects, unsettling humour, intriguing perspectives, insightful reflection, vivid dramatisation, surreal imagery, quirky precise details, etc.)

... is perfectly suited to the exploration of:

- **her extraordinary themes** (hope/despair, loss, death/afterlife, consciousness/disorientation, the natural world, etc.)

Point 3: *(Unusual view of the natural world in line with off-beat dramatisation)* The poet's strangely realistic view of nature evident in 'A Bird came down the Walk'. Use of odd, precise details, onomatopoeic language and comic moments enhance the reader's understanding of Dickinson's attitude.

Point 4: *(Playful poetic voice enhances the ecstatic portrayal of nature)* Extended metaphor of drunkenness to reflect the poet's celebration of nature in 'I taste a liquor never brewed' reveals an idiosyncratic sense of humour. Strikingly imaginative images, forceful rhythms and enthusiastic tones all echo the poet's response to natural beauty.

Conclusion: Condensed poetic forms, compressed syntax and daring language use is entirely appropriate to Dickinson's insightful reflections and themes. Readers can engage more immediately with the intensity of the poet's heightened experiences.

Sample Paragraph: Point 2

In both 'I felt a Funeral, in my Brain' and 'I heard a Fly buzz—when I died', Dickinson creates a disturbing account of the sensation of dying. The two poems are dramatic, with terrifying images. I thought the poet's style is in keeping with this alarming subject in 'I felt a Funeral', especially her presentation of the 'Mourners' who keep 'treading' as the coffin is lowered – ' I dropped down, and down'. Repetition – the drum 'beating—beating' – and broken phrasing emphasised the feeling of helplessness. Dickinson's vivid imagery and sounds add to the feeling of being overpowered. There is a more absurd atmosphere in 'I heard a Fly buzz'. The exaggerated scene seems distorted, particularly when the insect became the centre of attention, an 'uncertain stumbling Buzz'. The ending stops abruptly, 'I could not see to see', a line suggesting the dreadful frustration and struggle for clarity.

EXAMINER'S COMMENT

As part of a full examination essay, this is a clear personal response that addresses the question directly. The sustained focus on Dickinson's language use is aptly supported with effective use of quotation. Both poems were treated succinctly and included some thoughtful discussion. Well-controlled expression added to the quality of the response. Top-grade answer.

(Sample question 2)

'Dickinson's exploration of profound life experiences is effectively conveyed through her innovative style.' Discuss this statement, developing your answer with reference to the poetry of Emily Dickinson on your course.

Sample Plan 2

Intro: *(Stance: agree with viewpoint in the question)* Dickinson looks to understand death, mental anguish and intensely vivid moments of joy. Through her inventive approach to language, she invites readers to join her as she tells 'the truth, but tells it slant'.

Point 1: *(The shock of intense self-consciousness – powerful language use)* 'After great pain, a formal feeling comes' – surreal sequence, alliteration, unusual syntax and monosyllabic words create a vivid exploration of disorientation.

Point 2: *(Original, vibrant poetic voice – deep appreciation of nature)* 'I could bring You Jewels—had I a mind to' – unusual appreciation of nature's simple joys. Chooses a simple, modest meadow flower ('But this little Blaze/Flickering to itself'). Alliteration, onomatopoeia, a run-on line and the monosyllabic broad vowel sound describe the strong impact of the flower. The dynamic verb 'Flickering' suggests its lively movement.

Point 3: *(Intensity of emotion – fresh comparative effects)* 'I taste a liquor never brewed' – another poem delighting in the natural world's everyday delights. Startling extended metaphor of stages of intoxication irrepressibly conveys the delirious pleasures of nature ('When landlords turn the drunken Bee/out of the Foxglove's door'). Unconventional use of capital letters evokes a fantastical landscape.

Point 4: *(Unique poetic style – confronting fear and intrigue)* 'A narrow Fellow in the Grass' – contrasting description of the brutal, unpredictable aspects of nature. Personification increases the surreal unnerving quality, 'the Grass divides', the bogland has a 'Floor'. The discomfiting experience and extreme fright conveyed in the cryptic phrase 'Zero at the Bone' alarms readers.

Conclusion: Dickinson's disconcerting use of humour, unconventional punctuation, dramatic use of personification coupled with unusual imagery disrupt the reader's conventional awareness of life experiences.

NOTE

In keeping with the PCLM approach, the student has to take a stance by agreeing, disagreeing or partially agreeing with the statement that:

- **Dickinson's exploration of profound life experiences** (loneliness/depression, death, mental anguish, joy, appreciation of life/relationships, deep response to the world of nature, etc.)

… is conveyed through:

- **her innovative style** (disruptive perspectives, innovative syntax, surreal sequences, dynamic verbs, colloquial language, memorable sound effects, unusual imagery, extended metaphor, dramatic personification, subversive humour.)

Sample Paragraph: Point 1

Dickinson's poem, 'After great pain, a formal feeling comes', uses surreal images to examine how emotional numbness, 'a formal feeling', often follows 'great pain'. Emphatic alliteration ('formal feeling') underlines the constrictive paralysis of emotion into which a person sinks after trauma. There is a sense of losing control as the 'Feet, mechanical, go round'. The line suggests a lack of purpose in the body's movements. The bridge between sanity and insanity, 'A Wooden way', is breaking, leaving the individual incapable of rational thought – 'regardless grown'. Monosyllables describe this nightmarish experience of sinking into inertia, 'First—Chill'. The final dash marks the disorientating awareness of the swirling 'Snow'. By this stage, all sense of direction has been lost. Dickinson is exploring the numbing effects of tragedy.

EXAMINER'S COMMENT

As part of a full essay answer to question 2, this is an impressive top-grade standard that shows close engagement with Dickinson's poetry. Incisive discussion of the poet's curious style (sound effects, syntax, punctuation, etc.) is also commendable. Excellent use of quotations and the expression is exceptionally good throughout (e.g. 'the constrictive paralysis of emotion', 'disorientating awareness').

EXAM FOCUS

- As you may not be familiar with some of the poems referred to in the sample plans, substitute poems that you have studied closely.
- Key points about a particular poem can be developed over more than one paragraph.
- Paragraphs may also include cross-referencing and discussion of more than one poem.
- Remember that there is no single 'correct' answer to poetry questions, so always be confident in expressing your own considered response.

Leaving Cert Sample Essay

'Emily Dickinson's distinctly eccentric poems explore intense emotions that range from stark desolation to giddy delight.' Discuss this view, developing your answer with reference to the poetry of Dickinson on your course.

Sample Essay

1. Emily Dickinson writes poems about emotions that everyone has. These can go from stark desolation to giddy delight. She always uses language in a strange way, especially using capital letters, personification and a weird order of words. Her poems can be very eccentric and depressing, but she also writes with a giddy sense of humour. I will examine four poems, 'There's a certain Slant of light', 'I felt a Funeral, in my Brain', '"Hope" is the thing with feathers' and 'A narrow Fellow in the Grass'.

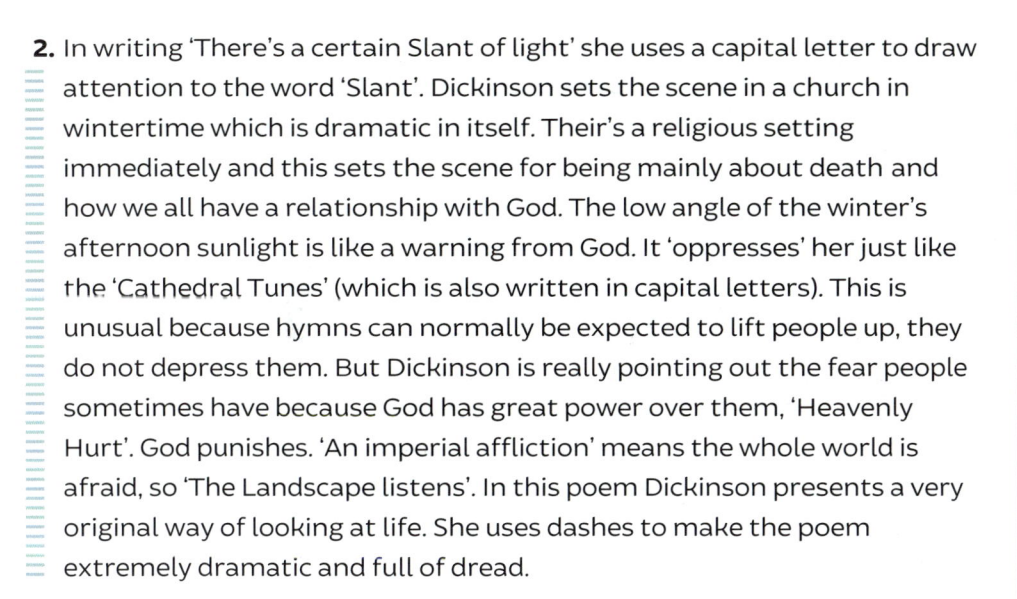

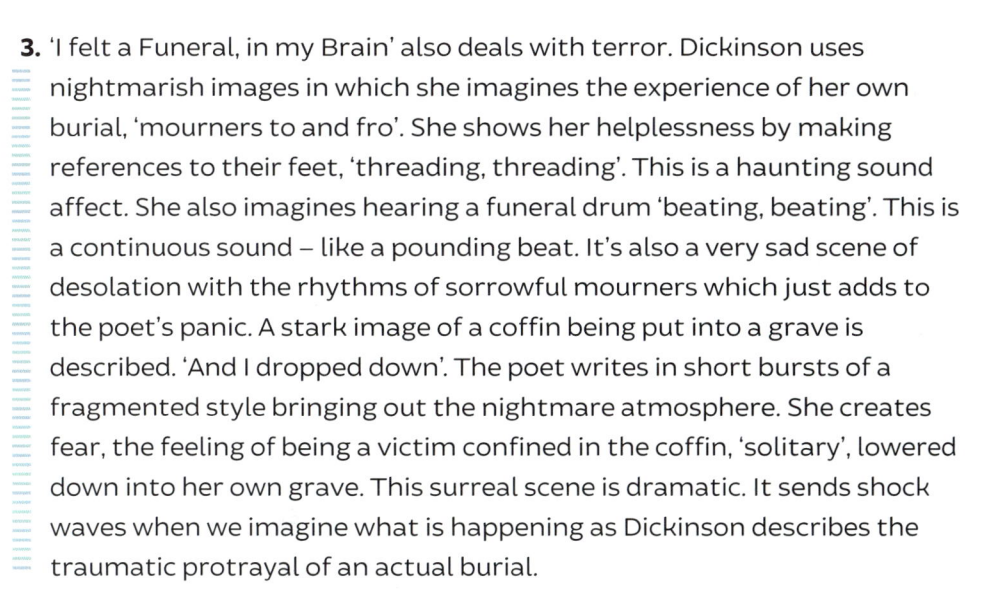

2. In writing 'There's a certain Slant of light' she uses a capital letter to draw attention to the word 'Slant'. Dickinson sets the scene in a church in wintertime which is dramatic in itself. Their's a religious setting immediately and this sets the scene for being mainly about death and how we all have a relationship with God. The low angle of the winter's afternoon sunlight is like a warning from God. It 'oppresses' her just like the 'Cathedral Tunes' (which is also written in capital letters). This is unusual because hymns can normally be expected to lift people up, they do not depress them. But Dickinson is really pointing out the fear people sometimes have because God has great power over them, 'Heavenly Hurt'. God punishes. 'An imperial affliction' means the whole world is afraid, so 'The Landscape listens'. In this poem Dickinson presents a very original way of looking at life. She uses dashes to make the poem extremely dramatic and full of dread.

3. 'I felt a Funeral, in my Brain' also deals with terror. Dickinson uses nightmarish images in which she imagines the experience of her own burial, 'mourners to and fro'. She shows her helplessness by making references to their feet, 'threading, threading'. This is a haunting sound affect. She also imagines hearing a funeral drum 'beating, beating'. This is a continuous sound – like a pounding beat. It's also a very sad scene of desolation with the rhythms of sorrowful mourners which just adds to the poet's panic. A stark image of a coffin being put into a grave is described. 'And I dropped down'. The poet writes in short bursts of a fragmented style bringing out the nightmare atmosphere. She creates fear, the feeling of being a victim confined in the coffin, 'solitary', lowered down into her own grave. This surreal scene is dramatic. It sends shock waves when we imagine what is happening as Dickinson describes the traumatic protrayal of an actual burial.

4. '"Hope" is the thing with feathers' is a poem full of giddy delight. The bird suggests hope, as a positive symbol high above the world's stark desolation. This is another of Dickinson's eccentric poems. It is like the dove in the Bible story of Noah's Ark and the Flood. In this Bible story, a dove let Noah know that the waters were going down and people would be able to survive. Therefore, the bird is 'sweetest' because it would of always brought good news.

5. In 'A Narrow Fellow in the Grass', Dickinson uses the voice of a young boy to tell a story of surprise and fear. She mixes up the order of words in a very eccentric way, 'His sudden notice is'. This shows the effect the unexpected snake had on the boy. This event is dramaticed. The setting is the strange field, the event is the meeting of the snake and the 'Barefoot' boy, the action is the snake 'Unbraiding in the sun'. The boy is 'stooping to secure it'. I thought the image of the snake as 'A spotted shaft' was

---

INDICATIVE MATERIAL

- **Dickinson's distinctly eccentric poems** (inventive style, vivid/surreal imagery, dramatic personification, fragmented syntax, unconventional punctuation, unusual settings, unnerving sense of humour, etc.)

... explore:

- **intense emotions from stark desolation to giddy delight** (mental anguish, death, loneliness and depression, moments of surprise and joy, love and loss, profound reactions to the natural world, etc.)

EMILY DICKINSON

unusual. It suggested lightning or a hidden weapon, both conveying danger. Nature is filled with mystery. I also thought the personification in the line 'The Grass divides as with a Comb' was very unusual. I could imagine the snake slithering along, the only movement is the grass parting as if someone was combing their hair. I thought this was surreal but Dickinson is also celebrating nature.

6. Dickinson's poems vary from terror of dying to intense feelings about the natural world. She looks at everything 'Slant', whether it is winter sunshine, hymns, a little bird or a snake. She made me think twice about nature and death. She also writes about the beauty and mystery of nature. Dickinson's language is eccentric. She is by far the most unusual of the poets we have studied.

(750 words)

EXAMINER'S COMMENT

A solid mid-grade standard, with reasonably focused engagement and analysis – particularly in paragraphs 2, 3 and 5. More emphasis on the element of 'giddy delight' would be expected. Expression varies greatly from fluent to awkward and the essay included several mechanical errors ('Their's', 'affect', 'protrayal', 'would of', 'dramaticed'). Some personal engagement evident at times and the essay was rounded off well in the concluding paragraph.

GRADE: H3
P = 12/15
C = 12/15
L = 10/15
M = 4/5
Total = 38/50

👀 Revision Overview

'"Hope" is the thing with feathers'
Theme of hope, extended metaphor, unusual punctuation, reflective, optimistic tones.

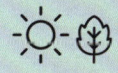

'There's a certain Slant of light'
Reflection on human mortality and our relationship with God, personification, fragmented rhythm and style add to unease and pessimism.

'I felt a Funeral, in my Brain' (OL)
Shocking introspection on loss and death, first-person perspective, onomatopoeia and repetition.

'A Bird came down the Walk'
Bemused observation of nature, personification, rich imagery and sound effects.

'I heard a Fly buzz—when I died' (OL)
Dramatic exploration of death and the afterlife, surreal, use of contrast and symbols add to feeling of helplessness.

'The Soul has Bandaged moments'
Unsettling examination of nature of consciousness, central conflict, changing moods.

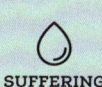

'I could bring You Jewels—had I a mind to'
Treatment of relationship, celebration of nature, vivid imagery, optimistic tone.

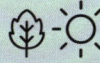

'A narrow Fellow in the Grass'
Danger and beauty in nature, use of persona, colloquial language, concluding tone of terror.

'I taste a liquor never brewed'
Joyful celebration of nature, extended metaphor, subversive humour.

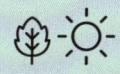

'After great pain, a formal feeling comes'
Disquieting exploration of depression, rich imagery, sombre tone, ambiguous ending.

💬 Last Words

'The Dickinson dashes are an integral part of her method and style ... and cannot be translated ... without deadening the wonderful naked voltage of the poems.'
Ted Hughes

(On her determination to hide secrets)
'The price she paid was that of appearing to posterity as perpetually unfinished and wilfully eccentric.'
Philip Larkin

'The Brain—is wider than the Sky—
The Brain is deeper than the sea—'
Emily Dickinson

EMILY DICKINSON

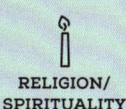

JOY/HOPE · NATURE · RELIGION/SPIRITUALITY · SUFFERING · DEATH · MEANING OF LIFE

POETRY FOCUS

T. S. Eliot
1888–1965

'Humankind cannot stand very much reality'

Thomas Stearns Eliot, the American–British poet, playwright and literary critic, was born in St Louis, Missouri in 1888. He was educated at Harvard before settling in England, where he worked as a teacher and publisher. In 1927, Eliot took British citizenship at about the same time he became an Anglican.

T. S. Eliot is one of the most daring innovators of modern literature. Indeed, his experiments in diction, style and versification revitalised English poetry. His collections, from *Prufrock* (1917) to the *Four Quartets* (1943), largely reflect the development of a Christian poet and dramatist.

Eliot's early writing depicts a bleak and barren soullessness, often in spare yet finely crafted modern verse. Much of his work deals with unsettling themes of individual consciousness and spiritual desolation against the decline of civilisation. His poems, which often lack any obvious narrative structure, include numerous cultural allusions.

Although some critics found his poetry esoteric and disconnected, he has been increasingly praised for his originality and is now widely recognised as one of the most significant poetic voices of the 20th century. An intensely private man, Eliot separated from his first wife in 1933 following an unhappy marriage. He remarried in 1956. T. S. Eliot received the Nobel Prize for Literature in 1948 and died in London in 1965.

Investigate Further

To find out more about T. S. Eliot, or to hear readings of his poems not already available in your eBook, you could search some useful websites, such as YouTube, BBC Poetry, poetryfoundation.org and poetryarchive.org, or access additional material on this page of your eBook.

Prescribed Poems

○ **1 'The Love Song of J. Alfred Prufrock'**
Eliot's most famous poem touches on fascinating aspects of human experience. For many people in the 1920s, Prufrock seemed to summarise the uncertainty of the modern individual. He is a man who feels isolated and incapable of decisive action. His poignant monologue is filled with irony since this is not a conventional love song. Prufrock would like to speak about love with a woman, but he does not dare. Hopelessly insecure about rejection and fearful of old age, Prufrock is never able to assert himself by asking the mysterious 'overwhelming question'. **Page 96**

○ **2 'Preludes'(OL)**
Throughout the four sections of this atmospheric poem, Eliot presents a dark vision of the failure of modern secular society, exploring human despair and feelings of failure. Using a stream of consciousness style, the poet reveals a variety of solitary lives that are played out against the backdrop of a dispiriting urban setting. **Page 106**

○ **3 'Aunt Helen'(OL)**
Eliot's unusually accessible poem portrays a prim 'maiden aunt'. Even after her death, there was 'silence in heaven'. The poet's gentle ridicule is directed at the cultural lifelessness and self-satisfaction of Miss Helen Slingsby's sterile lifestyle.
Page 112

○ **4 from 'The Waste Land': II. 'A Game of Chess'**
Using numerous literary allusions, Eliot focuses on the failure of relationships. In this chilling vision, human interaction is reduced to a set of movements on a chessboard. Characteristically, the poet depicts a false and meaningless world, in keeping with his disillusioned view of modern life. **Page 116**

○ **5 'Journey of the Magi'**
Eliot's version of the three kings who visited the newborn Messiah in Bethlehem is narrated by one of the elderly magi (wise kings). Christ's birth marked the end of their old pagan religion. The painful transition mirrors the poet's own doubts about his spiritual conversion to Christianity. Throughout the poem, Eliot interweaves the real and symbolic journeys of life and death. **Page 123**

○ **6 from 'Landscapes': III. 'Usk'**
This evocative landscape sketch records Eliot's response to the Welsh landscape after a short holiday there. The countryside is associated with the legend of King Arthur. However, the most likely reading of this 11-line poem sees it as a search for religious faith. **Page 129**

○ **7 from 'Landscapes': IV. 'Rannoch, by Glencoe'**
Written after a visit to the Scottish Highlands, Eliot's poem evokes the atmosphere of the remote moor, which provides a compelling backdrop to the poet's message that old conflicts become entrenched in the places where they once occurred. **Page 133**

○ **8 from 'Four Quartets': 'East Coker IV'**
This didactic poem is another illustration of Eliot's critical view of Christianity. He uses the field hospital as a compelling metaphor for the world's suffering patients who are in the hands of Jesus, the 'wounded surgeon'. Striking imagery and thought-provoking paradoxes emphasise the poet's severe view of the Christian experience. **Page 137**

(OL) indicates poems that are also prescribed for the Ordinary Level course.

1 The Love Song of J. Alfred Prufrock

*S'io credesse che mia risposta fosse
a persona che mai tornasse al mondo,
questa fiamma staria sanza più scosse;
ma però che già mai di questo fondo
non tornò vivo alcun, s'i'odo il vero,
sanza tema d'infamia ti rispondo.*

Let us go then, you and I,
When the evening is spread out against the sky
Like a patient etherised upon a table;
Let us go, through certain half-deserted streets,
The muttering retreats   5
Of restless nights in one-night cheap hotels
And sawdust restaurants with oyster-shells:
Streets that follow like a tedious argument
Of insidious intent
To lead you to an overwhelming question …   10
Oh, do not ask, 'What is it?'
Let us go and make our visit.

In the room the women come and go
Talking of Michelangelo.

The yellow fog that rubs its back upon the window-panes,   15
The yellow smoke that rubs its muzzle on the window-panes,
Licked its tongue into the corners of the evening,
Lingered upon the pools that stand in drains,
Let fall upon its back the soot that falls from chimneys,
Slipped by the terrace, made a sudden leap,   20
And seeing that it was a soft October night,
Curled once about the house, and fell asleep.

And indeed there will be time
For the yellow smoke that slides along the street
Rubbing its back upon the window-panes;   25
There will be time, there will be time
To prepare a face to meet the faces that you meet;
There will be time to murder and create,
And time for all the works and days of hands
That lift and drop a question on your plate;   30

Epigraph: 'If I thought that my response would be to someone who would ever return to earth, this flame would remain without further movement; but as no one has ever returned alive from this depth, if what I hear is true, I can answer you with no fear of disgrace.' This Italian epigraph is taken from Dante's 'Inferno'. The speaker was imprisoned in hell and is filled with hopelessness.

you and I: the public self and the inner man represent Prufrock's divided personality.

etherised upon a table: anaesthetised and unconscious on an operating table.

retreats: places of security.

sawdust restaurants with oyster-shells: cheap hotels with sawdust on the floor and oyster shells as ashtrays.

insidious intent: deceptive purpose.

Michelangelo: famous Italian Renaissance artist who portrayed heroic figures.

yellow: cowardly; London was also known for its dense fogs.

muzzle: animal's nose and mouth.

And indeed there will be time: biblical reference to each event having a correct time; 'A time to be born, and a time to die' (Book of Ecclesiastes).

Time for you and time for me,
And time yet for a hundred indecisions,
And for a hundred visions and revisions,
Before the taking of a toast and tea.

   In the room the women come and go
Talking of Michelangelo.

   And indeed there will be time
To wonder, 'Do I dare?' and, 'Do I dare?'
Time to turn back and descend the stair,
With a bald spot in the middle of my hair –
(They will say: 'How his hair is growing thin!')
My morning coat, my collar mounting firmly to the chin.
My necktie rich and modest, but asserted by a simple pin –
(They will say: 'But how his arms and legs are thin!')
Do I dare
Disturb the universe?
In a minute there is time
For decisions and revisions which a minute will reverse.

   For I have known them all already, known them all –
Have known the evenings, mornings, afternoons,
I have measured out my life with coffee spoons;
I know the voices dying with a dying fall
Beneath the music from a farther room.
   So how should I presume?

   And I have known the eyes already, known them all –
The eyes that fix you in a formulated phrase,
And when I am formulated, sprawling on a pin,
When I am pinned and wriggling on the wall,
Then how should I begin
To spit out all the butt-ends of my days and ways?
   And how should I presume?

   And I have known the arms already, known them all –
Arms that are braceleted and white and bare
(But in the lamplight, downed with light brown hair!)
Is it perfume from a dress
That makes me so digress?
Arms that lie along a table, or wrap about a shawl.
   And should I then presume?
   And how should I begin?

morning coat: a formal tailed coat.

dying fall: Shakespearean reference to fading music; 'That strain again, it had a dying fall' (*Twelfth Night*).

formulated phrase: prepared, dismissive expression.

butt-ends: discarded cigarette remains.

digress: stray from the point.

   Shall I say, I have gone at dusk through narrow streets   70
And watched the smoke that rises from the pipes
Of lonely men in shirt-sleeves, leaning out of windows? …

   I should have been a pair of ragged claws
Scuttling across the floors of silent seas.

    .   .   .   .   .

   And the afternoon, the evening, sleeps so peacefully!   75
Smoothed by long fingers,
Asleep … tired … or it malingers,
Stretched on the floor, here beside you and me.
Should I, after tea and cakes and ices,
Have the strength to force the moment to its crisis?   80
But though I have wept and fasted, wept and prayed,
Though I have seen my head (grown slightly bald) brought
   in upon a platter,
I am no prophet – and here's no great matter;
I have seen the moment of my greatness flicker,
And I have seen the eternal Footman hold my coat, and snicker,   85
And in short, I was afraid.

   And would it have been worth it, after all,
After the cups, the marmalade, the tea,
Among the porcelain, among some talk of you and me,
Would it have been worth while,   90
To have bitten off the matter with a smile,
To have squeezed the universe into a ball
To roll it towards some overwhelming question,
To say: 'I am Lazarus, come from the dead,
Come back to tell you all, I shall tell you all' –   95
If one, settling a pillow by her head,
   Should say: 'That is not what I meant at all.
   That is not it, at all.'

   And would it have been worth it, after all,
Would it have been worth while,   100
After the sunsets and the dooryards and the sprinkled streets,
After the novels, after the teacups, after the skirts that trail along
   the floor –
And this, and so much more? –
It is impossible to say just what I mean!
But as if a magic lantern threw the nerves in patterns
   on a screen: 105
Would it have been worth while

---

a pair of ragged claws: image of a dismembered crab.

malingers: pretends to be ill.

my head … upon a platter: biblical reference to John the Baptist, whose head was the price Salome demanded for performing her dance (Matthew).

the eternal Footman: Death.

porcelain: fine chinaware.

squeezed the universe into a ball: literary reference; 'Let us roll all our strength … into one ball' ('To His Coy Mistress' by Andrew Marvell).
Lazarus: biblical reference to a man Jesus brought back to life.

dooryards: American gardens.

magic lantern: instrument used to project enlarged moving images.

If one, settling a pillow or throwing off a shawl,
And turning toward the window, should say:
    'That is not it at all,
     That is not what I meant, at all.'   110

   .   .   .   .   .

  No! I am not Prince Hamlet, nor was meant to be;
Am an attendant lord, one that will do
To swell a progress, start a scene or two,
Advise the prince; no doubt, an easy tool,
Deferential, glad to be of use,   115
Politic, cautious, and meticulous;
Full of high sentence, but a bit obtuse;
At times, indeed, almost ridiculous –
Almost, at times, the Fool.

  I grow old ... I grow old ...   120
I shall wear the bottoms of my trousers rolled.

  Shall I part my hair behind? Do I dare to eat a peach?
I shall wear white flannel trousers, and walk upon the beach.
I have heard the mermaids singing, each to each.

I do not think that they will sing to me.   125

I have seen them riding seaward on the waves
Combing the white hair of the waves blown back
When the wind blows the water white and black.

We have lingered in the chambers of the sea
By sea-girls wreathed with seaweed red and brown   130
Till human voices wake us, and we drown.

Prince Hamlet: the indecisive hero of Shakespeare's tragic play.

swell a progress: make up part of the crowd.

Deferential: courteous, submissive.
Politic: diplomatic, expedient.
meticulous: scrupulously careful, fussy.
Full of high sentence: speaking in a pompous way (a literary reference to a character in Chaucer's *Canterbury Tales*).
obtuse: dull, insensitive.
Fool: in Shakespearean drama, the court jester or clown often spoke wisely.

I have heard the mermaids singing: literary reference to a poem by John Donne where the mermaids symbolise romance and danger.

👤 Personal Response

1. Eliot once considered 'Prufrock among the Women' as the title for this poem. Would you prefer that title or the present one, 'The Love Song of J. Alfred Prufrock'? Give reasons for your choice.
2. Choose a short section of the poem that you consider particularly rich in sensuous lyrical language. Briefly explain why you found it appealing.
3. Comment briefly on one of the three settings used in this poem: the seedy cityscape, the elegant drawing room and the romantic seashore.

👁 Critical Literacy

'The Love Song of J. Alfred Prufrock' (commonly known as 'Prufrock') was first published in 1915. This period saw Europe lose an entire generation of young men during World War I. The British Empire was breaking up and the certainty of Victorian ideals was still being shaken by the evolutionary theories of Darwin. Society seemed to be in crisis, with signs that cultural and spiritual values were crumbling in the new urban age. Eliot's dramatic monologue traces Prufrock's uneasy stream of consciousness. Through a series of compulsive cadences, the poem explores the tortured soul of modern man: educated, eloquent, alienated and emotionally paralysed by indecisiveness.

The title immediately raises the question about who is being addressed: possibly the unnamed woman in the poem, or Prufrock himself, or even the reader. What is not in doubt is that the name 'J. Alfred Prufrock' suggests a conceited, pretentious character, one who wishes to be seen as more important than he actually is. The epigraph (from Dante's 'Inferno') makes us think that the love song is not being sung in the real world at all, but in an interior 'Hell' of Prufrock's own making. From the outset, there are signs that the protagonist's torment comes from the division of his own self into a timid public person and a passionate private individual.

This is certainly suggested in the opening section (lines 1–12), where Prufrock proposes setting out on a journey: 'Let us go then, you and I'. The two pronouns might well refer to his divided personality: the reserved, careful outer man and the colourful, emotional inner soul. The initial mood is lethargic. Eliot uses a startling simile to describe the evening sky ('Like a patient etherised upon a table'), emphasising its distant, lifeless quality. Prufrock's own emotional state informs what he sees. There is **an uncomfortable sense of restlessness and dissatisfaction about Prufrock's life**, as though he is struggling with dark secrets. The impersonal streetscape suggests meaningless encounters 'in one-night cheap hotels'. Sea imagery ('oyster-shells') also seems slightly distasteful within the context of the furtive setting. Eliot's unsettling image of the 'half-deserted streets' compared to 'a tedious argument/Of insidious intent' conveys the agitation of modern living. Run-on lines lead Prufrock to momentarily think about an undisclosed 'overwhelming question' that is just too unbearable to consider at length.

Lines 13–14 stand alone. The **location has changed to a more sophisticated world** – probably a fashionable social event – where the smart conversation centres on an important sculptor of heroic figures: 'In the room the women come and go/Talking of Michelangelo'. The almost childlike jingling rhythm and rhyme raise the possibility that these cultured socialites are affected and frivolous. But why should Prufrock be intimidated by a group of sophisticated women discussing Renaissance art? Perhaps he fears that if these people are interested in the celebrated artist Michelangelo, they could never relate to somebody as undistinguished as himself. This disquieting feeling of exclusion becomes an increasingly defining characteristic of Prufrock.

In lines 15–22, the scene changes again, moving away from the trivial conversation of the social gathering. Using **a developed metaphor**, Eliot describes the foggy urban district through which Prufrock walks in terms of the sinuous movement of a cat, using sensuous verbs: 'rubs', 'Licked', 'Lingered', 'Slipped', 'Curled' and 'fell asleep'. Images suggesting the sleek movements of the cat combine with soft 'l' and 's' sounds to create a soporific mood. Does the 'yellow fog' convey the blurred vision of humanity in the 20th century?

Prufrock hypnotically repeats the phrase 'there will be time' to adopt a public mask that he can use to 'meet the faces that you meet'. Lines 23–34 convey a feeling of irritation with his surroundings and the people he encounters in public. He seems unnerved by the 'smoke that slides along the street' and his thoughts turn to the stark choices that any individual might face in extreme circumstances, 'to murder and create'. **The pressing rhythm marks Prufrock's growing nervousness** as he looks forward to but also fears meeting with the woman, when he will 'lift and drop a question on your plate'. Anxiously, he delays, hesitating and considering a 'hundred visions and revisions' before concluding with the mock-heroic action of 'the taking of a toast and tea'.

Lines 35–36 repeat the rhymed couplet, 'In the room the women come and go', further emphasising **the tedium of the women's conversation** as they endlessly discuss the same topic. The refrain might also indicate Prufrock's own inability to join in the social discourse of the elegant drawing room.

'after tea and cakes and ices'

He becomes increasingly more self-conscious in lines 37–48, mainly about his own insecurity ('Do I dare?'). Seemingly obsessed by his ageing appearance, Prufrock speculates about the way other people view him. He particularly **fears hearing the truth**, even about the most trivial matters: 'How his hair is growing thin!' For a moment, he tries to bolster his confidence by relating how carefully he pays attention to the details of his dress: 'My necktie rich and modest, but asserted by a simple pin'. However, the women's gaze seems relentless to Prufrock, who cannot stop imagining their derogatory comments: 'how his arms and legs are thin'. He exaggerates dramatically in the broken line, 'Do I dare/Disturb the universe?' Characteristically, the irony of his pretentious question reflects his self-deprecating humour. But as always, he is tormented by an uncontrollable inadequacy and paralysed by over-thinking. Despite all his self-delusion about future plans, Prufrock does nothing at all but sit and watch as time goes by.

Lines 49–54 present the first of three arguments against asking the 'overwhelming question'. Prufrock is only too aware that his complete lack of confidence stems from the **meaningless life** he leads. Its pointless routine is demonstrated by the repetition of the listless, broad-vowelled phrasing, 'For I have known them all already, known them all'. His earlier apprehension has gradually been replaced by the disillusionment of his wasted years: 'I have measured out my life with coffee spoons'. There is something acutely dismal about the admission of an entirely ineffective existence. Prufrock's social phobias now prevent any type of spontaneity. Feeling so distanced from human contact, he has reached the stage where he is no longer sure about anything, even the right to ask: 'So how should I presume?'

This **sensation of personal failure** increases in lines 55–61. Prufrock is constantly afraid of appearing foolish, which in itself always makes him feel that way. He is terrified of the contemptuous eyes of the women around him, who 'fix you in a formulated phrase'. He feels reduced to an insignificant insect pinned and coldly dissected as if in a laboratory experiment. His pointless lifestyle is further diminished, comparable to an ashtray filled with discarded cigarettes: 'the butt-ends of my days and ways'. Even the forlorn repetition of the question 'And how should I presume?' peters out. For Prufrock, the second argument against addressing the significant question is that he cannot face any further ridicule. It is typical of Eliot's portrayal that while we have sympathy for this pathetic man, we are also irritated by him.

Lines 62–69 reveal the third reason why Prufrock avoids life's most serious questions: he is both **attracted and repulsed** by the physical reality of the women around him. While he admires the perfect ideal of 'Arms that are braceleted and white and bare', he is also put off by the fact that they are 'in the lamplight, downed with light brown hair'. The poet's description of the apparently disembodied woman is impersonal. The sensuous movement of their arms 'that lie along a table, or wrap about a shawl' recalls the feline grace of the yellow fog. Caught between such thoughts of romance and revulsion, Prufrock's dilemma is unresolved. Yet again, he finds himself unable to do anything: 'And how should I begin?'

This intense sense of helplessness persists throughout lines 70–74. Prufrock rehearses what he might say if forced to make conversation. He wonders whether he might describe the 'narrow streets' he has just passed through and the 'lonely men in shirt-sleeves, leaning out of windows'. But his line of thought diminishes into silence, concluding with an ellipsis. It is as though **he is crushed by all the isolation he sees around him** – a feeling that accurately mirrors his own alienation. As always, in moments of desperate self-loathing, he reverts to using sea imagery: 'I should have been a pair of ragged claws'. Comparing himself to a crab scavenging on the floor of the ocean reduces him even further to an inanimate object, the very opposite of his present excruciating position. The renewed onomatopoeic effect of 'Scuttling' and the hauntingly alliterative 'silent seas' clearly depict this fantastical image of self-disgust.

Prufrock's random reflections continue in lines 75–86, which introduce a soft, trance-like, reflective atmosphere. The afternoon 'sleeps', 'malingers', is 'Stretched on the floor' like the earlier cat-like fog. Not for the first time, he debates whether he can ever have sufficient courage to display his true feelings and desires. For an instant, Prufrock imagines himself as a biblical figure, but soon dismisses this idea, accepting that his personal humiliation is simply ridiculous, especially when compared to such a celebrated martyr as John the Baptist. Arguably, this is the turning point of the poem, marking **the protagonist's stark realisation that his life is essentially insignificant**. His brief 'flicker' of youth and hope has gone. Death is all that lies ahead, personified as a sneering 'eternal Footman' who mocks Prufrock's unproductive past and his fear of the unknown.

Lines 87–98, however, mark yet another of the protagonist's attempts to excuse his failure to take control of his life. Prufrock tries to convince himself that the stylish setting – 'Among the porcelain', a delicate and easily damaged china – inhibits him. In such refined surroundings, an immense effort would be required to express his secret desires openly and squeeze 'the universe into a ball', a self-mocking reference to a poem by Andrew Marvell, who believed in seizing the moment and enjoying life's pleasures. But the **fear of rejection keeps restraining Prufrock**. He has become so self-deluded that he exaggerates his predicament, comparing his task of tackling his questions about the meaning of life to Lazarus coming back from the dead. Tortured by incessant thoughts of failure, he imagines an embarrassing misunderstanding between himself and an unnamed woman who tells him, 'That is not what I meant at all'. Once again, the pained awkwardness of the invented scene stops Prufrock in his tracks.

An edgy mood of growing frustration dominates lines 99–119. The sensuous language and fragmented style become even more evident as Prufrock cries out in exasperation at his inability to communicate: 'It is impossible to say just what I mean!' Almost completely demoralised, he creates an image of his true personality projected onto a screen by a 'magic lantern' for the derision of the woman he wishes to impress. He also admits that **he is no hero** like Prince Hamlet, even though they both share the characteristic of indecisiveness. If anything, Prufrock feels that he is more like the 'attendant lord' Polonius, a relatively minor character who is 'almost ridiculous'. In the end, he accepts that he is much more like 'the Fool' (or court jester), another dramatic stereotype whose quick wit often contained serious criticisms of life's absurdity.

The poem's closing lines (lines 120–131) **show a man anxiously trying to come to terms with ageing and death**: 'I grow old … I grow old'. Having completely failed to confront the 'overwhelming question', the only decision Prufrock will make is about his appearance: 'I shall wear the bottoms of my trousers rolled'. Nonetheless, in this agonising postscript, he indulges in one last flight of fancy set on an idyllic beach.

To the end, however, Eliot seems intent on trivialising the anxieties of a man who knows he is facing death but still cannot 'dare to eat a peach'. Yet, whatever time he has left may not be taken up entirely with mundane considerations. Prufrock can also dream of hearing the seductive 'mermaids singing'. Eliot's mysterious image – possibly symbolising both desire and danger – signals that Prufrock has come close to experiencing something wonderful, yet ultimately unattainable. A single line (the only isolated one in the entire poem) highlights the sad truth for this unfortunate individual: 'I do not think that they will sing to me'.

It could be argued that having the courage to dream is Prufrock's only triumph. Dramatic run-on lines depict a picture of the elusive mermaids through haunting sound effects: 'riding seaward on the waves/Combing the white hair of the waves blown back'. Their ability to enjoy the moment in harmony with their environment is the very antithesis of the neurotic Prufrock. Like so much of this mesmerising poem, **the conclusion is open to various interpretations**. It seems that Prufrock's divided self becomes united in the plural personal pronoun 'We'. He is suddenly awakened from his vision of 'sea-girls'. The heart-rending final line ends Prufrock's tragic fantasy and he is brought back to reality by 'human voices'. With his last words, 'we drown', he invites us into his own private hell. Is Eliot suggesting that all of us are lost in daydreams and desires that we can never realise?

Most critics agree that 'The Love Song of J. Alfred Prufrock' offers **a pessimistic vision of the modern spiritual condition**. The anti-hero of Eliot's ironic love song glimpses redemptive beauty, but settles for a life of indecision and triviality rather than boldly searching for personal fulfilment. This is likely to reflect the poet's own disenchanted outlook on modern secular civilisation, lacking any religious faith or meaningful love, and paralysed by anxiety. Yet nothing is resolved in this poem. Perhaps it is easier not to ask the 'overwhelming question' about life's meaning after all – particularly if there is no satisfactory answer.

✒ Writing About the Poem

'The sense of isolation and detachment in personal relationships is often evoked in the poetry of T. S. Eliot.' Do you agree with this view? Give reasons for your response, referring to Eliot's poem 'The Love Song of J. Alfred Prufrock'.

Sample Paragraph

'The Love Song of J. Alfred Prufrock' depicts the character of modern man weakened by over-analysis into a state of inaction: 'Do I dare/Disturb the universe?'. Prufrock is an insecure loner constantly searching for answers. His scattered thoughts wander from the important philosophical questions about life's meaning to the trivial reality of his mundane existence: 'Is it perfume from a dress/That makes me so digress?' The desperate tone of his random question reveals an inner trauma. The tone of self-disgust is conveyed in excruciating detail: 'When I am pinned and wriggling on the wall'. Fear of rejection keeps isolating Prufrock, 'That is not what I meant at all', and prevents him from even making the attempt to communicate.

EXAMINER'S COMMENT

A well-supported top-grade response that addresses the question directly. Revealing quotes illustrate Prufrock's distressing loneliness effectively and the comments on tone show a good understanding of the poem. Expression is impressive, varied and well controlled throughout.

✒ Class/Homework Exercises

1. 'T. S. Eliot's distinctive poetic voice presents troubled characters in an unsettled world.' Discuss this statement with reference to both the subject matter and style of 'The Love Song of J. Alfred Prufrock'.
2. 'T. S. Eliot explores the disturbing realities of modern life through inventive imagery.' Do you agree with this assessment of his poetry? Write a response, developing your points with suitable reference to the poem 'The Love Song of J. Alfred Prufrock'.

⊙ Points to Consider

- Character of Prufrock – ageing romantic, indecisive, divided self, unheroic.
- Inability to articulate shown in digressions, hesitations, mock-heroic tone.
- Key themes include human alienation, emotional and spiritual emptiness.
- Fragments of sections convey stream of consciousness in this dramatic monologue.
- Images of seedy city life, fog/cat, sea; literary, artistic and genteel imagery.

2 Preludes

Prelude: an introductory event that precedes something longer and more important; a short introductory piece of music.

I

The winter evening settles down
With smell of steaks in passageways.
Six o'clock.
The burnt-out ends of smoky days.
And now a gusty shower wraps   5
The grimy scraps
Of withered leaves about your feet
And newspapers from vacant lots;
The showers beat
On broken blinds and chimney-pots,   10
And at the corner of the street
A lonely cab-horse steams and stamps.

And then the lighting of the lamps.

II

The morning comes to consciousness
Of faint stale smells of beer   15
From the sawdust-trampled street
With all its muddy feet that press
To early coffee-stands.

With the other masquerades
That time resumes,   20
One thinks of all the hands
That are raising dingy shades
In a thousand furnished rooms.

III

You tossed a blanket from the bed,
You lay upon your back, and waited;   25
You dozed, and watched the night revealing
The thousand sordid images
Of which your soul was constituted;
They flickered against the ceiling.
And when all the world came back   30
And the light crept up between the shutters

gusty shower: strong windy rush of rain.

vacant lots: empty or abandoned building sites.

consciousness: awareness.

masquerades: pretences.

dingy shades: soiled window blinds.
furnished rooms: small apartments, often rented for a short time.

sordid: filthy, sleazy.
constituted: brought together, composed.

And you heard the sparrows in the gutters,
You had such a vision of the street
As the street hardly understands;
Sitting along the bed's edge, where   35
You curled the papers from your hair,
Or clasped the yellow soles of feet
In the palms of both soiled hands.

papers: small papers used as hair curlers.

IV

His soul stretched tight across the skies
That fade behind a city block,   40
Or trampled by insistent feet
At four and five and six o'clock;
And short square fingers stuffing pipes,
And evening newspapers, and eyes
Assured of certain certainties,   45
The conscience of a blackened street
Impatient to assume the world.

Assured: secure, confident.

assume: take responsibility; pretend.

I am moved by fancies that are curled
Around these images, and cling:
The notion of some infinitely gentle   50
Infinitely suffering thing.

fancies: dreams, fantasies, illusions.

Wipe your hand across your mouth, and laugh;
The worlds revolve like ancient women
Gathering fuel in vacant lots.

'The conscience of a blackened street'

👤 Personal Response

1. Based on your reading of Part I of 'Preludes', describe the atmosphere and mood Eliot creates in this opening section. Refer closely to the text in your answer.
2. Choose one interesting image from the poem that you found particularly effective. Briefly explain your choice.
3. Write your own personal response to this poem, referring closely to the text in support of the points you make.

👁 Critical Literacy

'Preludes' was composed between 1910 and 1911 and published in *Prufrock and Other Observations* (1917). Eliot considered these early poems 'the most satisfactory to myself'. Four sections of uneven, irregular verse provide a stream of consciousness, a literal and impressionistic view of various solitary lives as they play out against the backdrop of a seedy urban setting. There is an underlying awareness of the failure of modern secular civilisation throughout the sequence. Each prelude refers to the city as it moves from dusk to morning to night and back to dusk again.

The first prelude begins with vivid personification, 'The winter evening settles down', reminiscent of 'The Love Song of J. Alfred Prufrock'. Eliot blends various sensuous images, imagining the customary end of another unremarkable day. The 'smell of steaks in passageways' exemplifies the monotonous nature of city life and establishes the **dejected tone** for the rest of the poem. Repeated sibilant 's' sounds conjure up the habitual evening rituals of countless urban inhabitants. This is a place of conformity, where both the people and the day itself are exhausted, aptly evoked through the cigarette metaphor: 'burnt-out ends of smoky days'. An unrelenting sense of wasteful neglect and futile living is found everywhere within the dismal urban landscape, with its 'withered leaves' and 'vacant lots'.

Run-on lines mimic the relentless wintry weather while the abrupt rhyming of 'wraps' and 'scraps' suggests the recurring hardships of modern living. The explosive alliteration in lines 9–10, 'showers beat/On broken blinds', forcefully captures the insistent downpour of rain. Eliot presents readers with a range of symbols of alienation and helpless frustration, introducing the 'lonely cab-horse' waiting impatiently at a deserted street corner. Into this **uncomfortable scene of ugly sterility**, a flicker of hope appears in the stand-alone line, 'And then the lighting of the lamps'. Is something about to happen? Will something change? Or is the night closing in?

Eliot opens the second prelude by personifying a new day: 'The morning comes to consciousness'. Ironically, instead of a fresh start, **images of decay**

and desolation amplify the weariness of modern city living. Precisely descriptive language denotes emptiness, depression and quiet despair, a recurring theme throughout much of Eliot's poetry. This is skilfully evoked through the detail of 'faint stale smells of beer' left over from the previous night's drinking. Under pressure to conform to society's expectations, the anonymous occupants of the 'thousand furnished rooms' continue their daily routines, perhaps to mask their own unhappiness. The headlong rush of everyday life is suggested by the forward movement of run-through lines and the crushing verbs 'trampled' and 'press'.

Within all this urban chaos, individuality is submerged. People slavishly perform the same action at the same time: 'all the hands … raising dingy shades'. The poet clearly regards their routine lifestyles as 'masquerades', a daily pretence. It is as if they are raising a theatrical curtain on their artificial, unreal lives in this **soulless setting**. The rhyme of 'masquerades' and 'shades' reinforces this theme of pretence. By describing the people as mere body parts – 'feet', 'hands' – the individuals are depersonalised.

The third prelude addresses an unnamed woman who is plainly ill at ease: 'You tossed a blanket from the bed'. Eliot's description of her robotic movements develops the growing mood of despair. Indolent verbs describe a restless night: 'lay', 'waited' and 'dozed'. There is a disturbing sense of the woman's personal degeneration, disclosed by flickering patterns – 'The thousand sordid images' of which her soul is composed. Repetition of the conjunction 'And' in lines 30–32 emphasises the monotony of an unfulfilled existence. The morning's intrusion into this bedroom is unwelcome: 'the light crept up between the shutters'. Not unexpectedly, the early morning birdsong ('sparrows in the gutters') only adds to the atmosphere of gloom in this disreputable place. Meanwhile, a somewhat vulnerable and pathetic figure, the woman sits 'along the bed's edge' with her artificially curled hair, 'yellow soles' and 'soiled hands'. Once again, Eliot focuses on the **absence of personal identity**, reducing her to a mere collection of body parts. As morally degraded as her drab environment, she is only capable of a 'vision of the street/As the street hardly understands'.

The poet introduces a surreal image of spiritual torture in the fourth prelude: 'His soul stretched tight across the skies'. The monosyllabic 'tight' is precisely placed in the centre of line 39, suggesting that the tension is so great that it might snap at any moment. It is dusk and the unrelenting march of time is highlighted – 'At four and five and six o'clock' – when people return home from work. The ritual of pipe-filling is conveyed by the close-up image of 'short square fingers stuffing pipes' as the city's male inhabitants seek to relax after a day's toil and begin to read their newspapers. Eliot points out **the irony of their monotonous lives, where they are fed 'certain certainties'**. Does this suggest that these people always accept what they are told? Are they so powerless that they never question anything? Is their environment so 'blackened' that they 'assume the world' and accept it without any real understanding?

Lines 48–51 mark another change of mood to a **dreamlike atmosphere**. For the first time in the poem, a more personal voice emerges: 'I am moved by fancies'. Is this Eliot himself wondering if human life might have some worthwhile significance after all? Does he feel sympathy for all those people who have lost touch with their spiritual selves? Some critics have linked the 'infinitely gentle' reference to the presence of a Christ-like saviour destined to redeem a sinful world. But whatever it is that causes the poet to be 'moved' is wounded: 'Infinitely suffering thing'.

The momentary sense of hopefulness is quickly dismissed in the last three lines. Eliot reverts to cynicism, heralded by the derisive gesture 'Wipe your hand across your mouth', as if a gross appetite has just been satisfied. The vacant lot from the opening section is here again, and now old women are rummaging through the litter of urban desolation. We are left with **a bleak vision of an indifferent universe**.

Writing About the Poem

'T. S. Eliot presents an insightful and downbeat portrayal of the human condition.'
Discuss this statement in relation to the poem 'Preludes', developing your views with suitable reference and quotation.

Sample Paragraph

'Preludes' offers a pessimistic view about the lack of individuality, and the impossibility for spiritual growth in modern society. The poem's mood is depressing, set in the sleaze of a godless urban environment, which reminded me of Prufrock's dismal surroundings. With vivid imagery, Eliot painted a disturbing picture of city life. Nauseating odours ('smell of steaks in passageways'), dirty rooms ('dingy shades') and repugnant characters convey this unglamorous lifestyle. The human condition is described as one of conformity, where everyone is expected to put on an act all the time, whether they are rushing with 'muddy feet that press/To early coffee-stands' or 'raising dingy shades/In a thousand furnished rooms'. No one seems capable of looking upwards to something better. The image of old women hunting for fuel to keep them warm is truly startling.

EXAMINER'S COMMENT

A very well-focused personal response that tackles this question confidently. The range of accurate quotations are used effectively to support discussion points. Cross-references to other settings in Eliot's work broaden the scope of the answer. The writing is clear, fluent and assured throughout. Top-grade standard.

✒ Class/Homework Exercises

1. 'T. S. Eliot believed that human love offered rescue from a lifetime of misery and isolation.' Discuss this view with reference to 'Preludes'.
2. 'Eliot depicts broken individuals and spiritual emptiness through vivid images and arresting sound effects.' To what extent do you agree or disagree with this view of his poetry? Develop your points with reference to the poem 'Preludes'.

T. S. ELIOT

◉ Points to Consider

- Moral decay and isolation of 20th-century life.
- Paralysis of woman and city expressed in use of precise verbs.
- Dramatic journey through the minds and senses, stream of conciousness.
- Olfactory and tactile imagery – the lonely woman, debris of street.
- Use of rhyme to satirise theme of pretence; enjambment conveys movement of people and pressure of time.

3 Aunt Helen

Aunt Helen: a wealthy, unmarried lady who lived in a stylish Boston neighbourhood.

Miss Helen Slingsby was my maiden aunt,
And lived in a small house near a fashionable square
Cared for by servants to the number of four.
Now when she died there was silence in heaven
And silence at her end of the street.   5
The shutters were drawn and the undertaker wiped his feet –
He was aware that this sort of thing had occurred before.
The dogs were handsomely provided for,
But shortly afterwards the parrot died too.
The Dresden clock continued ticking on the mantelpiece,   10
And the footman sat upon the dining-table
Holding the second housemaid on his knees –
Who had always been so careful while her mistress lived.

handsomely provided for: supplying sufficient money to ensure a comfortable life.

Dresden clock: superior china clock from the German town of Dresden.

second housemaid: servant whose duties included cleaning and polishing.

'my maiden aunt'

👤 Personal Response

1. In your opinion, what is the speaker's attitude to Miss Helen Slingsby? Refer to the text in support of your views.
2. Consider the image of the footman and housemaid. How does it contrast with the life Aunt Helen lived? Develop your response with reference to the poem.
3. Based on your reading of the poem, do you think that T. S. Eliot is mocking respectable middle-class society? Briefly explain your response.

👁 Critical Literacy

'Aunt Helen' is included in T. S. Eliot's poetry collection *Prufrock and Other Observations*, published in 1917. The poet paints a satirical portrait of the rigid, conventional society of upper-class Boston in this short piece. What's left unsaid is almost as important as what is said. Boston offended Eliot's sensibilities. He regarded this world as 'quite uncivilised, but refined beyond the point of civilisation'. His critical view of polite society is from an insider's perspective and highlights its tragicomic outcome.

The poem's title, 'Aunt Helen', suggests a close family relationship between the poet and this lady, yet this is immediately dispelled by the formal address in the opening line, 'Miss Helen Slingsby'. Her unmarried status is carefully noted: 'maiden aunt'. This woman lived her life alone without close intimate relationships. Was she too proud to marry? Was she not asked? Her life is described in a three-line sentence that details where she lived. Aunt Helen did not reside in a large house, as Boston society would deem this vulgar and ostentatious. Her home was not on the 'fashionable square', but 'near' it. Such discretion was called for. **She carefully observed all the nuances of the secret codes of her social class.** However, there is no mention of friends. Nobody looks after Helen Slingsby except those she paid: 'servants to the number of four'. Eliot's quaint expression mirrors the old-world aunt and her affected language. Rolling 'r' and 'o' sounds allow the reader to hear the genteel tones of this superior person.

A series of short sentences deal with **the impact of the old lady's death**. The momentous adverb 'Now' in line 4 announces her passing. The poet adopts the persona of a detached observer rather than a regretful nephew, dryly observing that his aunt's death caused 'silence in heaven'. Is the silence indifference on the part of heaven to the death of this self-absorbed lady? Or does the silence suggest hushed awe at the passing of an important individual? We are left to wonder about who, apart from herself, might have regarded Miss Slingsby as a person of note. Eliot humorously concludes that there was 'silence at her end of the street'. Was her death really of sufficient importance to bring the whole street to stillness?

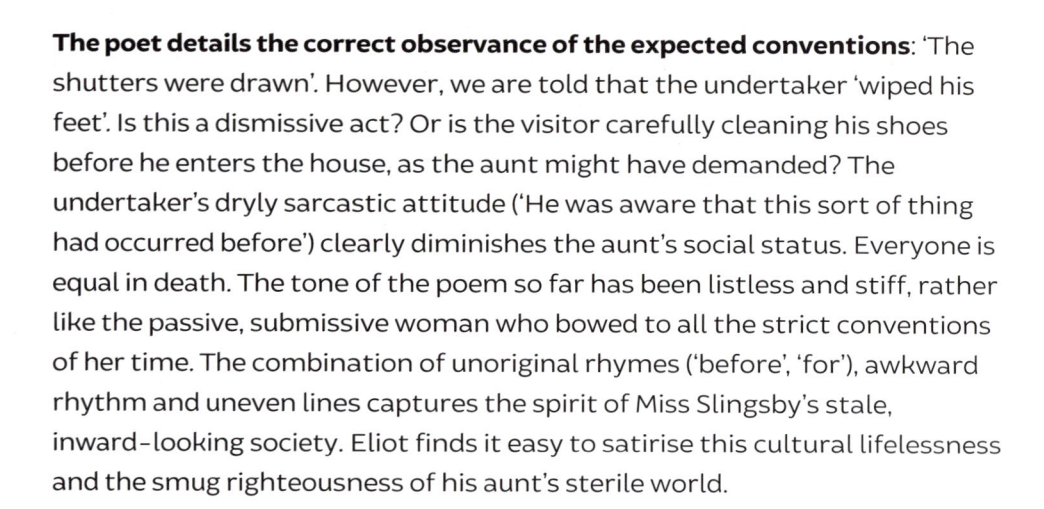

The poet details the correct observance of the expected conventions: 'The shutters were drawn'. However, we are told that the undertaker 'wiped his feet'. Is this a dismissive act? Or is the visitor carefully cleaning his shoes before he enters the house, as the aunt might have demanded? The undertaker's dryly sarcastic attitude ('He was aware that this sort of thing had occurred before') clearly diminishes the aunt's social status. Everyone is equal in death. The tone of the poem so far has been listless and stiff, rather like the passive, submissive woman who bowed to all the strict conventions of her time. The combination of unoriginal rhymes ('before', 'for'), awkward rhythm and uneven lines captures the spirit of Miss Slingsby's stale, inward-looking society. Eliot finds it easy to satirise this cultural lifelessness and the smug righteousness of his aunt's sterile world.

Line 8 **cleverly suggests where the nephew's real interest lay**: 'The dogs were handsomely provided for'. What was left to him is omitted. Is it likely that he was excluded from her will? We also learn that his aunt's parrot died. A pet parrot spends its life imitating its owner. Was this action in sympathy with the elderly lady's passing? Or does it suggest that the aunt's and the parrot's deaths were equally insignificant? Again, the emphasis is on a woman's empty, barren life, which was spent concerned with protocol and etiquette rather than with people.

Eliot reminds us that **everyday life goes on** in the extended line 10: 'The Dresden clock continued ticking on the mantelpiece'. Aunt Helen's fine possessions survived her passing implacably. The poem's somewhat humorous and risqué ending conveys a picture of sound, movement and life ('And the footman sat upon the dining-table/Holding the second housemaid on his knees'), clearly showing that the aunt's distorted sense of values does not survive. The servants ('Who had always been so careful') are finally free of the confines of the aunt's lifeless, artificial world. A new order has been established in the remnants of this proper world. The repeated sibilant 's' mirrors the hushing secrecy upheld while the aunt lived.

In this unusual poem, **Eliot, the dramatist, creates a caricature caught up in her own world from a few detailed images**. He even captures the pompous tones of the aunt in phrases such as 'fashionable square' and 'this sort of thing'. Through the use of a distorted sonnet structure, one line short of the conventional 14-line form, Eliot reflects the failed notions of Aunt Helen's sense of her own importance and grandeur. The random, prosaic rhymes ('four', 'before', 'for') accentuate the dreary tone, leaving readers with an uneasy sense of the old lady's futile existence. Nevertheless, there is an underlying mischief and optimism in the poem's final lines. Now that Miss Slingsby has gone, at least the servants can begin to enjoy life.

✒ Writing About the Poem

'Eliot's poetry unveils a sharply observant picture of ordinary people.'
Discuss this statement with reference to 'Aunt Helen'.

Sample Paragraph

Eliot paints a revealing caricature of a lady who is trapped inside a rigid, conservative society. The poet launches a quietly blistering attack on the joyless life of the self-absorbed Miss Slingsby, who required 'servants to the number of four' to look after her in her 'small house near a fashionable square'. Using just a few details, Eliot captures her upper-class voice in the repeated 'r' and 'o' sounds. She is not described, but her possessions are – her 'Dresden clock', her parrot and her dogs. Her real lack of importance is evident in the fact that there was silence in heaven at her passing and the undertaker 'was aware that this sort of thing had occurred before'.

> **EXAMINER'S COMMENT**
>
> *This well-focused high-grade short paragraph shows a very close reading of the poem. Suitable quotations are effectively used to highlight the poet's portrayal of the central character's lonely life. The fluent, controlled expression is sustained throughout.*

✒ Class/Homework Exercises

1. 'Eliot's poetry is filled with quiet despair.' Discuss this statement in relation to 'Aunt Helen'.
2. 'Eliot explores human activity as habitual and futile through carefully chosen details and an innovative use of form.' Discuss this view of the poetry of T. S. Eliot with reference to the poem 'Aunt Helen'.

⊙ Points to Consider

- Self-righteous, emotional and spiritual void.
- Mockery of distorted values of Aunt Helen and servants, appearance is paramount.
- Detached, banal tone, innovative sound effects.
- Imagery of silence, animals, time and servants.
- Unusual structure, effective use of caricature, dead-pan humour.

4 from The Waste Land: II. A Game of Chess

A Game of Chess: Eliot's poem is based on two plays by the Jacobean playwright Thomas Middleton: *A Game of Chess* and *Women Beware Women*. In the second play, a young woman is seduced while her mother-in law unknowingly plays a game of chess with another woman who has facilitated the seduction. Every move in the game of chess represents a stage in the seduction. The audience sees both scenes at once as the action takes place in a gallery above the chess game.

    The Chair she sat in, like a burnished throne,
Glowed on the marble, where the glass
Held up by standards wrought with fruited vines
From which a golden Cupidon peeped out
(Another hid his eyes behind his wing)   5
Doubled the flames of sevenbranched candelabra
Reflecting light upon the table as
The glitter of her jewels rose to meet it,
From satin cases poured in rich profusion.
In vials of ivory and coloured glass   10
Unstoppered, lurked her strange synthetic perfumes,
Unguent, powdered, or liquid – troubled, confused
And drowned the sense in odours; stirred by the air
That freshened from the window, these ascended
In fattening the prolonged candle-flames,   15
Flung their smoke into the laquearia,
Stirring the pattern on the coffered ceiling.
Huge sea-wood fed with copper
Burned green and orange, framed by the coloured stone,
In which sad light a carvèd dolphin swam.   20
Above the antique mantel was displayed
As though a window gave upon the sylvan scene
The change of Philomel, by the barbarous king
So rudely forced; yet there the nightingale
Filled all the desert with inviolable voice   25
And still she cried, and still the world pursues,
'Jug Jug' to dirty ears.
And other withered stumps of time
Were told upon the walls; staring forms
Leaned out, leaning, hushing the room enclosed.   30
Footsteps shuffled on the stair.
Under the firelight, under the brush, her hair
Spread out in fiery points
Glowed into words, then would be savagely still.

The Chair she sat in: a paraphrase of the description of Cleopatra's barge from Shakespeare's play of love and betrayal, *Antony and Cleopatra*: 'The barge she sat in, like a burnished throne/Burned on the water'. Antony decides to marry another woman for political reasons and Cleopatra dies by suicide.
standards: banners, upright supports.
wrought: twisted, formed.
Cupidon: Cupid, the young god of love in classical mythology.
candelabra: large branched candlestick.
vials: small containers.
Unstoppered: opened.
synthetic: artificial, fake.
Unguent: balm, ointment.
laquearia: panelled ceiling, referencing the story of the Queen of Carthage, Dido, and her betrayal by Aeneas in Virgil's famous Latin poem, 'The Aeneid'. The ceiling of the hall in which Dido gave a banquet for Aeneas is described: 'flaming torches hang from the gold-panelled ceiling, and the night is pierced by the flaming lights'.
coffered: decorated with sunken panels.
sylvan scene: a wooded area. In John Milton's great poem 'Paradise Lost', Satan sees a similar scene upon entering the Garden of Eden. Corruption and treachery ensue.
Philomel: an allusion to Ovid's epic poem 'Metamorphoses', which tells the tragic story of Philomel's rape and mutilation by her brother-in-law, Tereus, the King of Thrace. He cut off her tongue to prevent her telling, but she communicated the horrific event to his wife, her sister Procne, by weaving a tapestry. She killed their son and fed him to Tereus in a terrible act of revenge. The gods then turned Philomel into a nightingale and she fills the desert with her song.
inviolable: secure, beyond corruption.
Jug Jug: way of representing birdsong in Elizabethan poetry; also a crude expression for lovemaking.
Glowed into words: reference to Dante's 'Inferno', where the damned souls can only speak through the tip of the flame that engulfs them.

'My nerves are bad tonight. Yes, bad. Stay with me.   35
Speak to me. Why do you never speak? Speak.
   What are you thinking of? What thinking? What?
I never know what you are thinking. Think.'

   I think we are in rats' alley
Where the dead men lost their bones.   40

'What is that noise?'
           The wind under the door.
'What is that noise now? What is the wind doing?'
           Nothing again nothing.

                    'Do   45
You know nothing? Do you see nothing? Do you remember
Nothing?'

   I remember
Those are pearls that were his eyes.
'Are you alive, or not? Is there nothing in your head?'   50
           But
O O O O that Shakespeherian Rag –
It's so elegant
So intelligent
'What shall I do now? What shall I do?   55
I shall rush out as I am, and walk the street
With my hair down, so. What shall we do tomorrow?
What shall we ever do?'
           The hot water at ten.
And if it rains, a closed car at four.   60
And we shall play a game of chess,
Pressing lidless eyes and waiting for a knock upon the door.

   When Lil's husband got demobbed, I said –
I didn't mince my words, I said to her myself,
HURRY UP PLEASE ITS TIME   65
Now Albert's coming back, make yourself a bit smart.
He'll want to know what you done with that money he gave you
To get yourself some teeth. He did, I was there.
You have them all out, Lil, and get a nice set,
He said, I swear, I can't bear to look at you.   70
And no more can't I, I said, and think of poor Albert,
He's been in the army four years, he wants a good time,
And if you don't give it him, there's others will, I said.
Oh is there, she said. Something o' that, I said.
Then I'll know who to thank, she said, and give me a
 straight look.   75

rats' alley: slang term for World War I trenches.
the dead men lost their bones: soldiers felt great anguish when their fallen comrades were left unburied.
What is that noise?: from the revenge tragedy *The Duchess of Malfi*; the duchess's brother sends madmen to torment her.

Those are pearls that were his eyes: reference to Shakespeare's *The Tempest*, referring to the transformation of the dead into something beautiful and magical.
that Shakespeherian Rag: a popular American tune from *Ziegfeld Follies* (1912).

demobbed: demobilised, retired from the army.

HURRY UP PLEASE ITS TIME: the call of bartenders at closing time in British pubs.

HURRY UP PLEASE ITS TIME
If you don't like it you can get on with it, I said.
Others can pick and choose if you can't.
But if Albert makes off, it won't be for lack of telling.
You ought to be ashamed, I said, to look so antique.   80
(And her only thirty-one.)
I can't help it, she said, pulling a long face,
It's them pills I took, to bring it off, she said.
(She's had five already, and nearly died of young George.)
The chemist said it would be all right, but I've never been
   the same.   85
You *are* a proper fool, I said.
Well, if Albert won't leave you alone, there it is, I said,
What you get married for if you don't want children?
HURRY UP PLEASE ITS TIME
Well, that Sunday Albert was home, they had a hot gammon,   90
And they asked me in to dinner, to get the beauty of it hot –
HURRY UP PLEASE ITS TIME
HURRY UP PLEASE ITS TIME
Goonight Bill. Goonight Lou. Goonight May. Goonight.
Ta ta. Goonight. Goonight.   95
Good night, ladies, good night, sweet ladies, good night,
   good night.

gammon: cured ham.

Good night, ladies: Ophelia's poignant farewell before she dies by suicide in Shakespeare's *Hamlet*. She has been driven mad by the deception and corruption of people around her.

'The Chair she sat in'

👤 Personal Response

1. Choose one image from the poem that you found particularly interesting. Briefly explain your choice.
2. The poet introduces us to various characters whose voices we hear. In your opinion, are they happy or unhappy? Explain your response with reference to the poem.
3. Write your own personal response to the poem, highlighting its impact on you.

👁 Critical Literacy

'A Game of Chess' is the second section in T. S. Eliot's masterpiece, 'The Waste Land'. It was written in 1921, when the poet was recovering from a nervous breakdown in Lausanne, Switzerland. Section II, 'A Game of Chess', explores themes of misdirected love and its destructive consequences. It also examines the insistent march of time and how the past haunts the present. The poem's fragmentary form, irregular punctuation and content respond to the mayhem and devastation caused by World War I. Eliot's many cultural and literary references universalise his themes. This modernist approach in literature also occurred in art with Pablo Picasso and in music with Arnold Schönberg. Such artists struggled to find a voice for this frenetic world of the post-war period. As Eliot's friend, the American poet Ezra Pound, commented, they were attempting to 'make it new'.

The poem presents us with two main scenes, both of which are concerned with deception and betrayal. On an initial reading, there appear to be striking differences between the characters of the first and the second drama in terms of social class, wealth and education. On closer examination, however, interesting similarities emerge. The first half of the poem shows an unnamed, sophisticated woman surrounded by beautiful furnishings – resembling props in a stage play. Eliot's opening line rephrases the account of Cleopatra's arrival on her magnificent barge in Shakespeare's play *Antony and Cleopatra*. The **elaborate language** ('burnished', 'marble', 'wrought') suggests the lavish opulence of the setting. In line 4, the poet describes the mirror decorated with a 'golden Cupidon', like Cleopatra's 'smiling Cupids'. The atmosphere is formal and oppressive. But why is one of the Cupid figurines depicted as hiding 'his eyes behind his wing'? Is there a suggestion of something inappropriate or illicit?

The reference to the 'sevenbranched candelabra' shows Eliot mixing images of the sacred with the profane. God had ordered the Temple of Jerusalem to be furnished with a golden chair and seven ornate candles. The elegant diction is filled with such a 'rich profusion' of lush images that the reader is almost disoriented. However, an **unsettling note** is struck when the woman's 'synthetic perfumes' are described as 'Unstoppered' on her dressing table.

T.S. ELIOT

Something seems wrong and out of control in this apparently luxurious setting. It is likely that the reader becomes 'troubled, confused'. Eliot depicts a stale, stifling atmosphere through the stressed extended sentences of the first nine lines and the evocative assonance of 'Unguent, powdered, or liquid'.

The sumptuously decorated ceiling (the 'laquearia') alludes to the tragic story of the mythical Queen of Carthage. Dido gave a splendid banquet for her lover, Aeneas, who subsequently deserted her. She then threw herself onto a funeral pyre as his ship sailed out of the harbour. Eliot is illustrating how **tragedy and destruction follow misplaced love**. This is an unavoidable reality for the stylish modern woman who is central to the poem's opening section. At every stage, she is viewed in terms of threat and betrayal. With the reference to Philomel (line 23), readers are introduced to another legendary scene of corruption as the seduced heroine, whose tongue was cut off, is eventually changed into a nightingale, allowing her to sing 'with inviolable voice'. Is Eliot himself like the songbird revealing the truth about deception and how it inevitably destroys relationships?

The emphasis on the present tense in line 26 ('still the world pursues') suggests that nothing changes. Beauty and love will always be tainted. The bird's pure song is caught in the Elizabethan 'Jug Jug', yet to 'dirty ears', it has a vulgar sexual meaning.

The disappointments of real life are emphasised. Suddenly, the gaudy decorations are dismissed for what they really are – 'withered stumps of time'. **This is the infertility of the wasteland.** Is Eliot also expressing his cynicism towards those people who possess wonderful works of art but who don't really appreciate them? Is he hinting that the modern world is unaware of its rich cultural inheritance? There is no denying the poet's sharper tone as the earlier longer lines of lavish description now give way to the curt expressions in lines 27–30.

Line 32 focuses on the modern woman, showing her under severe emotional strain while she sits alone. A surreal image, 'her hair/Spread out in fiery points', seems to speak: 'Glowed into words'. This frightening Medusa-like figure appears to be trapped in her own personal hell as she retreats into neurotic silence: 'savagely still'. Anonymous and faceless, she seems to lose control over the safe space of her beautiful dressing room when she hears 'Footsteps shuffled on the stair' – her husband, presumably. She begins to voice her paranoid concerns: 'My nerves are bad tonight'. Her nervous tension is played out in a **staccato rhythm** with the jumpy, erratic repetition of 'Speak', 'What' and 'Think'. Aimless questions and panicky commands show the lack of purpose in her speech. Is Eliot suggesting that she is just like Cleopatra and Dido, an emotional wreck who is depending on the attentions of a man? The man's response is indirect and dismissive, indicating that he thinks but does not voice a reply to the petulant woman.

Caught in his own desperate psychological state, **he is haunted by images of death**: 'I think we are in rats' alley', a reference to World War I trenches. The woman's whining voice intrudes as she wonders, 'What is that noise?' He thinks 'Nothing again nothing' and retreats from the tense questions, blotting out her voice with snippets of Shakespeare and an American hit tune. The syncopated rhythm of ragtime is indicated by the repetition of 'O O O O' and the extra syllable 'he' in 'Shakespeherian' (line 52). Such erratic movement and trite rhyme ('elegant'/'intelligent') reflect the couple's obvious inability to interconnect.

The woman becomes even more hysterical and threatens to 'rush out' and 'walk the street/With my hair down'. Her anxious questioning, 'What shall we ever do?', is characteristic of Eliot's recurring commentary on **the loss of religion and spirituality in modern life**. The sense of meaninglessness is emphasised when the man contemplates the banality of his daily routine. He will rise late, as if to shorten the day, 'hot water at ten' (line 59) before going for a pointless car ride in the rain and playing another dull game of chess. Is he simply waiting, with 'lidless' eyes, for something to happen? Who will make the 'knock upon the door'? Death, perhaps? The boredom and lack of communication of this living hell are enacted by the frightened, loveless woman and the self-centred, nihilistic man.

The second scene opens in a typical working-class British pub (line 63): 'When Lil's husband got demobbed'. A prayer-like mantra of 'I said' breaks up the bar room monologue in which the speaker recalls an earlier dialogue between herself and her friend Lil. The snapshot of post-war British society places ordinary individuals in difficult situations, just like pieces in a game of chess. Marriage between Lil and her husband Albert is reduced to a sexual level. She is advised to 'make yourself a bit smart', otherwise she risks losing her man, who is returning from the war. Albert had given her money to buy false teeth, but she had used it for an abortion: 'She's had five already, and nearly died of young George'. Her relationship is as unsatisfactory as those mentioned in the first section of the poem. **Loneliness and human misery are shared by all social classes.** It is clear from the gossip that the speaker is sympathising with 'poor Albert'. Is this another case of 'Women Beware Women'? Is the speaker taking a perverse delight in Lil's predicament, almost blaming her in advance for what might happen: 'You *are* a proper fool' (line 86)?

The barman's insistent call, 'HURRY UP PLEASE ITS TIME', stresses the sinister absence of hope. Ironically, this urgency is not picked up by any of the other pub characters as they bid each other 'Goonight' (line 95). The bleak ending echoes one of Shakespeare's most unfortunate victims, the naive Ophelia, who dies by suicide, surrounded by heartless manipulation and betrayal. Like so much in the poem, these final lines depict a false and meaningless world, in keeping with Eliot's dark vision of modern life as a wasteland devoid of lasting love or moral values.

✒ Writing About the Poem

'T. S. Eliot's challenging poetic voice makes him inaccessible to the modern reader.' Discuss this view with reference to 'A Game of Chess'.

Sample Paragraph

From my study of 'A Game of Chess', I can understand the criticism of Eliot as a difficult poet. However, I enjoyed his references to Cleopatra, 'The Chair she sat in, like a burnished throne', and to the unfortunate Dido and Philomel. By referring to these mythical women and then comparing them to Lil, the unhappy modern wife, I think Eliot succeeded in exploring sexuality very effectively. All of these women try to defy this cruel world with a determined search for communication: 'Speak to me'. But Tereus cut off Philomel's tongue to prevent her speaking. The self-absorbed modern man also blots out the woman's attempts to connect by responding to her questions with unspoken thoughts: 'we shall play a game of chess'. In my opinion, Eliot is playing a game of chess with his reader as he moves his women, the pawns in this game of love or sex, through their stories.

> **EXAMINER'S COMMENT**
>
> *This is a good top-grade personal response that takes a clear thematic view in support of Eliot's use of cultural and literary allusions. The focus is sustained throughout and aided effectively with accurate quotations. Expression is also varied, fluent and well controlled.*

✎ Class/Homework Exercises

1. 'Eliot's poem "A Game of Chess" moves characters like chess pieces towards destinations they cannot see as they perform in a drama they do not control or understand.' Discuss this statement with reference to the text.
2. 'Eliot often showed people's sense of defeat through the effective use of powerful imagery.' Discuss this view with reference to his poem 'A Game of Chess'.

◎ Points to Consider

- Splendour of the past contrasts sharply with the squalid nature of the present.
- Inhibiting effect of improperly directed love/lust.
- Failure of modern man to get to grips with cultural heritage.
- Past haunts the present, purposelessness in modern life.
- Juxtaposition of cultural imagery and dingy bar culture.
- Effective use of rich allusions.
- Snatches of contrasting dialogue.

5 Journey of the Magi

T.S. ELIOT

'A cold coming we had of it,
Just the worst time of the year
For a journey, and such a long journey:
The ways deep and the weather sharp,
The very dead of winter.'   5
And the camels galled, sore-footed, refractory,
Lying down in the melting snow.
There were times we regretted
The summer palaces on slopes, the terraces,
And the silken girls bringing sherbet.   10
Then the camel men cursing and grumbling
And running away, and wanting their liquor and women,
And the night-fires going out, and the lack of shelters,
And the cities hostile and the towns unfriendly
And the villages dirty and charging high prices: 15
A hard time we had of it.
At the end we preferred to travel all night,
Sleeping in snatches,
With the voices singing in our ears, saying
That this was all folly.   20

   Then at dawn we came down to a temperate valley,
Wet, below the snow line, smelling of vegetation,
With a running stream and a water-mill beating the darkness,
And three trees on the low sky.
And an old white horse galloped away in the meadow.   25
Then we came to a tavern with vine-leaves over the lintel,
Six hands at an open door dicing for pieces of silver,
And feet kicking the empty wine-skins.
But there was no information, so we continued
And arrived at evening, not a moment too soon   30
Finding the place; it was (you may say) satisfactory.

   All this was a long time ago, I remember,
And I would do it again, but set down
This set down
This: were we led all that way for   35
Birth or Death? There was a Birth, certainly,

We had evidence and no doubt. I had seen birth and death,
But had thought they were different; this Birth was
Hard and bitter agony for us, like Death, our death.
We returned to our places, these Kingdoms,   40
But no longer at ease here, in the old dispensation,
With an alien people clutching their gods.
I should be glad of another death.

dispensation: prevailing religion.
clutching: retaining, clinging to.

'and such a long journey'

👤 Personal Response

1. In your opinion, what is the mood of the magi as revealed in lines 19–20?
2. The poem is filled with striking imagery. Choose the image that most appeals to you and briefly explain why you found it interesting.
3. Based on your reading of the poem, what does the speaker mean when he declares: 'I should be glad of another death'? In your response, consider whether he is referring to physical or spiritual death – or both.

👁 Critical Literacy

'Journey of the Magi' was published in 1927 as part of a selection of poems that were to be included later in a series of Christmas cards. T. S. Eliot had converted to Anglicanism in August of that year and had been baptised into his new faith. The poem reflects Eliot's state of mind in transition between his old and new faiths. It fuses past and present as one of the magi, now an old man, recalls his experience of the journey undertaken to witness the birth of Jesus. This dramatic monologue is riddled with ambiguity. Throughout the narrative, Eliot interweaves the real and symbolic journeys of life and death.

The poem recreates the story of the three magi who travelled to Bethlehem from the East to honour the infant Jesus. Eliot's version is based on the gospel of St Matthew and takes the form of a dramatic monologue describing **a painful and life-changing experience**. The opening section (lines 1–20) recounts the arduous journey through the persona of one of the unnamed kings. He is caught between the past and present, no longer at ease in his old world, yet unsure about his new Christian life choice. The narrative tone is tired and unenthusiastic, as though the ageing magus has already told the tale too many times.

Eliot's first five lines are based on a celebrated sermon given by an English clergyman, the Bishop of Winchester, on Christmas Day 1622: 'A cold coming we had of it,/Just the worst time of the year/For a journey'. Such strong **colloquial phrases ground the account of this extraordinary journey in reality**, although the gruelling trek itself was undertaken to find a mystery that was impenetrable to human wisdom. The details of the suffering camels, 'galled, sore-footed, refractory', add to the authenticity of the story.

Lines 11–16 contrast the **world of ease and luxury** that the magi had left behind with the challenging expedition and uncertainty ahead. They had rejected all their earlier comfort and sensuous pleasure: 'The summer palaces on slopes, the terraces,/And the silken girls bringing sherbet'. Frequent pauses in these lines convey the unhurried pace of their former lives. The recurring soft letter 's' floats as effortlessly as the youthful girls, enabling the language to glide by – a stark contrast to the hazardous mountain journey. This harsh trek is vividly captured by the strikingly familiar imagery and run-on lines mimicking the fleeing camel men. Their coarse speech is graphically caught by the emphatic hard 'c' sound and broad assonance in the phrase 'cursing and grumbling'.

Memories tumble from the elderly magus, who reminisces about the various hardships endured: 'And the cities hostile and the towns unfriendly/And the villages dirty and charging high prices'. The impetus of the narrative is driven forward by an insistent rhythm emphasised by the evident repetition of 'And'. A short monosyllabic line curtly sums up his frustration: 'A hard time we had of it'. For the magi, however, there were more serious concerns than the physical discomforts. Along the way, all three kings faced agonising moments of self-doubt: 'voices singing in our ears, saying/That this was all folly'. In many ways, **their difficult experience symbolises every individual's search for spiritual meaning**, particularly Eliot's own painful journey into the Anglican faith.

The poem's second stanza (lines 21–31) describes the arrival of the three wise men. Eliot's version of events is unusual for all the well-known details it omits. There is no talk of a stable or any mention of gold, frankincense and myrrh. Instead, **present and future time blends** as Christ's adult life is predicted. The early morning descent into the 'temperate valley' evokes three significant Christian events: the Nativity, Easter and the Second Coming of Christ. A bewildering range of images follows. Some are positive, such as the 'running stream', 'meadow' and 'vine-leaves', all of which suggest hope, freedom and fruitfulness. However, these are juxtaposed with negative imagery: the winter's 'low sky', the horse 'galloped away', 'feet kicking'.

Ambiguity fills this vivid dream-like state. **Eliot liked to use symbolism to represent philosophical ideas** through simple images. His description of 'three trees on the low sky', for example, implies the spiritual truth of the future (the skies lowered and heaven opened). The trees, of course, are likely representations of the three crosses on Calvary, where Jesus was to be crucified alongside two common criminals. Does the 'old white horse' signify Christ the conqueror? And if so, why is it galloping away? Might the poet be suggesting that true faith is always elusive? Are the 'Six hands … dicing for pieces of silver' foreshadowing the betrayal of Christ by Judas?

The magi eventually found 'the place' where the new Messiah was born. There is a clear impression of anticlimax: 'it was (you may say) satisfactory'. All of the prophecies had been fulfilled, but there is an edge, an uncertain reticence in tone. The event was no more than adequate or acceptable. The material discomfort of the poem's opening section is replaced by **a growing awareness of a more mysterious discomfort**. Why is the magus so unsure about the importance of what he has witnessed? Undoubtedly, something crucial has happened, but there is a lingering sense of loss. The reader is also left wondering. Why was there no sense of the joyous excitement that is recounted in the Bible at the birth of the infant Jesus?

The final section, lines 32–43, of this typically multi-layered poem conveys the enduring effect that the journey had on the three magi. Emphatic repetition is used to stress that Christ's Nativity must be recorded carefully: 'but set down/This set down/This'. The unusual line placing echoes the breakdown of the old order resulting from this recent momentous event. Eliot highlights **the poem's central paradox**: 'were we led all that way for/Birth or Death?' For the poet, the two experiences are inseparable. The birth of Christ marked the death of all previous religious beliefs. Through the experience of the three kings, Eliot also reveals the trauma of his personal spiritual journey. To an extent, this reflective monologue is that of any individual who has made his choice and achieved belief in the Incarnation, but who is nonetheless linked to the life that Christianity has come to replace.

The poem's conclusion is one of acceptance of a destiny that is the only possible answer, but still seems unbearably painful. The elderly magus admits that he 'should be glad of another death'. After they returned home, the three kings felt 'no longer at ease'. The new order that they witnessed makes them regard 'our places' as full of 'alien people clutching their gods'. The ageing narrator grows to understand that the birth of the Christ child changed everything. He has reached the end of his old pagan life, but despite his acknowledgment of the epiphany, he is still faced with the overwhelming mystery of his new Christian faith. The poem ends on a note of **mystified resignation**, serving as a metaphor for Eliot's own search to find meaning in the modern world.

✒ Writing About the Poem

'Eliot's fondness for using references can make his poetry seem difficult and dense.' Discuss this statement in relation to 'Journey of the Magi'.

Sample Paragraph

I would agree that 'Journey of the Magi' can be demanding, but I did not find it baffling. Eliot explores two journeys simultaneously, that undertaken by the magi to witness the birth of Jesus who was to bring in a new 'dispensation', a new religion. The second journey is Eliot's own spiritual conversion to Anglicanism. He was realising, just as the magi had, that when moving from one faith to another, there is regret for the old familiar ways – 'no longer at ease here'. Both Eliot and the magi found 'an alien people clutching their gods'. I found the poem's content complex, but understandable. Similarly, its many images are by no means

> **EXAMINER'S COMMENT**
>
> This succinct top-grade paragraph addresses a challenging question effectively. There is a good sense of confident engagement with the poem's central theme. Impressive use is made of relevant quotations and the expression is well controlled throughout.

obscure. The 'three trees on the low sky' represent the lush vegetation of the 'temperate valley', the promise of heaven. But they also contain a foreshadowing of the crucifixion on Calvary. For me, Eliot's poetry is understandable in its treatment of difficult themes and ingenious in his use of imagery.

✒ Class/Homework Exercises

1. 'Eliot's poetry is modern in outlook yet old in allusions.' Do you agree or disagree with this assessment of his poetry? Develop your response with close reference to the poem.
2. 'Symbolism and dialogue play a large part in Eliot's examination of alienation in his poetry.' Discuss this view with reference to the poem 'Journey of the Magi'.

◎ Points to Consider

- Journey symbolising spiritual search.
- Alienation, life on the periphery.
- Suffering required to enable new birth.
- Journey, birth, death and biblical imagery.
- Dramatic monologue, natural speech, voice of magus.
- Changing tones – critical, regretful, nostalgic, incantatory, anxious, self-pitying.

6 from Landscapes: III. Usk

T.S. ELIOT

Do not suddenly break the branch, or
Hope to find
The white hart behind the white well.
Glance aside, not for lance, do not spell
Old enchantments. Let them sleep. 5
'Gently dip, but not too deep',
Lift your eyes
Where the roads dip and where the roads rise
Seek only there
Where the grey light meets the green air 10
The hermit's chapel, the pilgrim's prayer.

Usk: small town in South Wales located on the river Usk, an ancient crossing point. Caerleon-Upon-Usk is reputed to be the site of the legendary court of King Arthur.
hart: male adult deer, associated with Arthurian legends.
white well: St Cybi's Well was a place of pilgrimage, where the water was reputed to cure various ailments.
Glance aside: have a quick look secretly.
lance: a long spear used by horsemen when jousting in medieval tournaments.
Old enchantments: legends and superstitions.
'Gently dip, but not too deep': do not pry. The quotation comes from an Elizabethan play, *The Old Wives' Tale*, about old superstitions.
Lift your eyes: 'I will lift up mine eyes unto the hills, from whence cometh my help.' (Psalm 21, Old Testament)
hermit's chapel: prayer-room of someone who lives alone for religious reasons.
pilgrim: traveller who goes on a spiritual journey to a holy place.

'The white hart behind the white well'

👤 Personal Response

1. In the poem 'Usk', Eliot uses some effective images to create the atmosphere of the Welsh countryside. Choose one image that you particularly liked and explain its impact.
2. Sound effects, such as alliteration, assonance and rhyme, are used in this brief lyric. In your opinion, what contribution do they make?
3. Did you find the conclusion of the poem satisfactory or not? Give reasons for your view, supporting it with reference to the poem.

👁 Critical Literacy

'Usk' is the third of five short lyrics by Eliot entitled 'Landscapes', published in 1935. Each poem describes a specific place steeped in history. This evocative landscape sketch records Eliot's response to the Welsh landscape after a 10-day holiday spent there. It is the climax of the sequence, representing summer to autumn, symbolising the speaker's search for true tranquillity and spiritual happiness through prayer. The theme of spiritual fulfilment occupies much of Eliot's later poetry.

This is one of Eliot's least well known and most puzzling poems. Typically, it can be seen as a conversation, both with the reader and the poet himself. To an extent, it is simply a very short landscape or pastoral description of the Welsh countryside around Usk. There was also a pub here called The White Hart Inn and behind it a once-whitewashed well that was so shallow that water was procured by dipping a container in it. However, **Eliot's poem is primarily spiritually instructive**. The first line opens with an abrupt command, 'Do not', rather in the manner of an instruction given to a wayward child. Readers are warned not to seek romantic fantasy in such a landscape. The harsh alliteration ('break the branch') introduces the poet's attitude to 'Old enchantments'. We are strongly advised not to pursue the traditions and superstitions of the past: 'white hart', 'white well', 'lance'. All these symbols figure prominently in the Arthurian legend of the Quest for the Holy Grail. Eliot clearly mocks the medievalism of some of his contemporaries with a self-assured tone suggesting that his advice comes from one who is confident about his own religious faith.

Line 4 issues another ringing instruction, 'Glance aside', its internal rhyme echoing the medieval word 'lance' and emphasising that the old superstitious beliefs must be avoided: 'Let them sleep'. But line 6 introduces a second thought with the quotation, 'Gently dip, but not too deep'. This forms the pivotal point of the poem. The quotation comes from an old Elizabethan play that satirised popular romantic dramas of the time. In the play a mysterious head appears from a well warning not to intrude too closely. As far as the poet is concerned, **legend and tradition are appealing, but should be treated with caution**. In a recording of the poem, Eliot spoke this line in a sing-song voice reminiscent of a remembered childhood song. The jaunty rhythm forces readers forward. Is the poet suggesting that our relationship with the landscape should not be escapist or full of romantic fantasy, but should lead us towards the spiritual?

Unlike the restless opening, with its recurring musical effects, the second half of the poem begins with a prayer-like exhortation from the Old Testament: 'Lift your eyes'. The reader is being invited to go on a pilgrimage, a spiritual journey, 'Where the roads dip and where the roads rise', a reference to the smooth rolling countryside of Brecon. The repetition of 'Where' emphasises the need to seek 'The hermit's chapel, the pilgrim's prayer'. But these will only be found 'Where the grey light meets the green air'. This evocative phrase conjures up the misty countryside and green forest, an insubstantial place of light and space. The assertive triple rhyme ('there', 'air', 'prayer') reinforces the sense that the destination is within sight. Is this the symbolical meeting of the two traditions, Arthurian legend and Christianity? While the early section of the poem included repeated punctuation breaks, giving it a disruptive force, the second part flows much more smoothly through several run-on lines. **The poem concludes with a note of hope, firmly rooted in Christian imagery.** Characteristically, Eliot demonstrates his skill at evoking the reverential atmosphere of the 'hermit's chapel'.

The poem's principal tone is one of incantation – 'Hope to find', 'Lift your eyes', 'Seek only there' – which is emphasised by musical sounds and insistent rhyme. Eliot makes good use of both end-rhyme (such as 'well' and 'spell') and internal rhyme ('find', 'behind'). The colours used suggest peace and rejuvenation. White is usually associated with brightness and purity. The 'grey light' hints at the misty past, while 'green' is a natural, soothing shade. **Eliot creates a mysterious, mystical atmosphere** by blending simple images with sibilant sounds.

Some critics have argued that 'Usk' reflects the poet's continuing search for an answer to the 'overwhelming question' first asked in 'The Love Song of J. Alfred Prufrock'. If we accept that **the search for spiritual meaning is central to the poem**, then the chapel of the hermit would seem to represent the pilgrim's destination and the poet's confidence in the 'spell' of Christian faith.

Writing About the Poem

'T. S. Eliot's interest in religion and the spiritual journey people make are important elements in his poetry.' Discuss this statement in relation to his poem 'Usk'.

Sample Paragraph

In 'Usk', readers are instructed to 'Glance aside' and not to become involved with the escapist fantasy of the Arthurian legend of 'white hart' and 'lance'. This is not where to look for spiritual fulfilment. The central quotation from an old play, 'Gently dip, but not too deep', pushes the reader away from the mythological past and instead points the way forward with the following Old Testament command: 'Lift your eyes'. The last four lines of the poem advise that we should look for fulfilment of our spiritual journey by turning to the mysteries of the Christian faith. The poem concludes with two simple symbols of Christianity, the 'hermit's chapel' and the 'pilgrim's prayer'. 'Usk' clearly demonstrates the significance for Eliot of the spiritual journey.

EXAMINER'S COMMENT

A focused and succinct top-grade paragraph showing close engagement with the text. Suitable quotes are used very effectively to trace the progress of thought through the poem. There are impressive references to key lines which emphasise Eliot's Christian viewpoint.

Class/Homework Exercises

1. 'T. S. Eliot's presentation of Christianity can be surprisingly positive at times'. To what extent is this the case in the poem 'Usk'?
2. 'Eliot investigates how the present contains the past in fragmented memories, effective imagery and striking sound effects.' Discuss this statement with reference to the poem 'Usk'.

Points to Consider

- **Pastoral poem, descriptive and spiritually instructive.**
- **'Old enchantments' of Arthurian legend contrasted with spiritual quest.**
- **Old Testament tone of exhortation, use of imperatives.**
- **Insistent energy, hopeful note. Evocative sound effects.**
- **Use of colour suggests peace and energy.**

7. from Landscapes: IV. Rannoch, by Glencoe

T.S. ELIOT

Here the crow starves, here the patient stag
Breeds for the rifle. Between the soft moor
And the soft sky, scarcely room
To leap or soar. Substance crumbles, in the thin air
Moon cold or moon hot. The road winds in   5
Listlessness of ancient war,
Langour of broken steel,
Clamour of confused wrong, apt
In silence. Memory is strong
Beyond the bone. Pride snapped,   10
Shadow of pride is long, in the long pass
No concurrence of bone.

Rannoch: a moor in the Scottish Highlands, near the valley of Glencoe. It was the location of a terrible battle in 1692 when the Campbell clan massacred the MacDonalds.

Substance: material, solidity.

Listlessness: without energy or enthusiasm.
Langour: tiredness; pain.

Clamour: loud noise, outcry.
apt: appropriate, suitable.

pass: gap, route over mountains.
concurrence: agreement, co-operation.

'Substance crumbles, in the thin air'

👤 Personal Response

1. In your opinion, what do the animal images of the first two lines contribute to the impression of Rannoch being presented by Eliot?
2. Trace how the poet develops his theme that the present is weighed down by the past. Support your answer with suitable quotation from the text.
3. How effective are the poem's sound effects in conveying the atmosphere of Glencoe? Illustrate your response using reference to the text.

👁 Critical Literacy

'Rannoch, by Glencoe' is the fourth poem in T. S. Eliot's five-part series 'Landscapes' (1935). After visiting the Scottish Highlands, he composed this poem evoking the essence of the remote moor in condensed images, and its geography provides a compelling backdrop to the poet's message. Eliot was struck by Rannoch's pervading atmosphere, which he felt was a consequence of a 17th-century battle between two Scottish clans, the Campbells and the MacDonalds. Set during the winter season, this marvellously compressed poem captures the eerie sense of dislocation that is often found on old battlefields.

The opening lines convey an uninviting image of death. Rannoch's barren terrain presents nature at its worst: even 'the crow starves'. The long-suffering deer is fodder for the hunter's 'rifle'. This is a place of brooding menace and extreme harshness, both from nature and from man, captured in the startling death-in-life imagery. Eliot's dismal tone is in keeping with the slow-moving pace. Yet the insistent 's' alliteration hints at the rugged beauty of the bleak surroundings: 'Between the soft moor/And the soft sky'. But **it is a claustrophobic and oppressive place**. The cloudy sky hangs so low above the landscape that there is no room for the stag to leap or the crow to fly. Strangely, the references to softness appear negative, almost tyrannical. Nothing can be relied on in this place – the moon is changeable ('cold' or 'hot') and the rock is being eroded ('Substance crumbles, in the thin air').

Even the lazy description of the winding road in lines 5–6 is misleading. Unlike the routeways symbolising salvation in Eliot's poem 'Usk', there is only 'Listlessness' and 'Languor' here. The countryside is weighed down and **haunted by disturbing memories of the past**, the notorious massacre of 1692. The 'broken steel' of an 'ancient war' still remains in the landscape. This locality is devoid of hope, rooted in the endless cycles of past violence. For Eliot, the silence of the place resonates with memories of the 'Clamour' of warfare, which occurred due to transgressions on both sides ('confused wrong'). The alliterative sharp 'c' effect emphasises the uproar of battle. In the poem's closing lines, Eliot captures the closeness of the past. There is no underlying peace in this land. Instead, disharmony remains between the bones of the dead enemies. The Scottish hills are darkened by the 'Shadow of pride'. This clearly suggests that the descendants of both clans have never become truly reconciled. The repetition of 'long' (line 11) stresses the brutal consequence of such a terrible event that took place over three centuries ago. In contrast to the hard mountain rock, which can be broken down over time, pride and self-worth do not crumble. Like a shadow blighting the landscape, **memory discourages healing**. This is the stark truth about human pride that Eliot uncovers in the rugged terrain of Rannoch. There is no sign of hope and certainly no religious perspective here.

The poem ends on a discordant note that bristles with tension and the lines run on to finish abruptly: 'Memory is strong/Beyond the bone'. The insistent force of Eliot's monosyllables, 'Pride', 'pass' and 'bone', create a stumbling rhythm. Assonant sounds – particularly the long mournful 'o' within line 12 ('in the long pass/No concurrence of bone') – highlight **the sadness that suffuses the beautiful landscape** damaged for all time by the cruelty of nature and man. Readers are left in no doubt about the poem's central theme – historical events and old conflicts become entrenched in the places where they once occurred.

✒ Writing About the Poem

'Landscape or setting is an important symbol that T. S. Eliot uses to great effect in his poetry.' Discuss this statement in relation to Eliot's poem 'Rannoch, by Glencoe'.

Sample Paragraph

Eliot uses landscape to represent much more than local scenery in 'Rannoch, by Glencoe'. He captures the spirit of Glencoe in dark, vivid imagery associated with death and the winter season: 'the crow starves' and the 'patient stag' destined 'for the rifle'. This cruel place offers no opportunity to escape. Eliot references the battle of 1692, the Massacre of Glencoe, which took place between two rival Scottish clans. I found Eliot's description of the unchanged, winding road revealing, suggesting that there is no hope. Eliot uses landscape to show the outer world's bleak beauty, with its crumbling stone and haunting moonlight. But he also captures the dark workings of the human heart, which won't let go of the past.

EXAMINER'S COMMENT

A very assured top-grade response to the question, tracing the progress of thought in the poem. The connections between past and present are explored effectively, using suitable references and accurate quotations. Expression is clear and coherent throughout.

✒ Class/Homework Exercises

1. 'The poetry of T. S. Eliot is depressing and anguished.' Discuss this statement in relation to 'Rannoch, by Glencoe'. Refer to both the poet's subject matter and style in your response, using suitable quotation from the poem to develop your views.
2. 'In Eliot's poetry, the harshness and beauty of nature is evoked through startling imagery.'
   Discuss this view with reference to the poem 'Rannoch, by Glencoe'.

⊙ Points to Consider

- **Relation between human beings and nature; old unresolved rivalries.**
- **Impact of human beings on the natural world – war, erosion, destruction.**
- **Dysfunctional landscape, discordant poetic structure.**
- **Closed system of strong memories of confused wrongs.**
- **Vivid imagery, off-rhyme.**

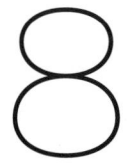

from Four Quartets: East Coker IV

T.S. ELIOT

East Coker: a village in Somerset, near Yeovil. It is Eliot's ancestral home. Family and family history feature in the poem. He had found information on his family from 'Sketch of the Eliot Family', which described how his family had lived in East Coker for 200 years. Andrew Eliot left in 1669, disrupting the family history. Eliot also broke away from his family in America. In the poem, he stresses the need for a journey and the need for inward change.

The wounded surgeon plies the steel
That questions the distempered part;
Beneath the bleeding hands we feel
The sharp compassion of the healer's art
Resolving the enigma of the fever chart.   5

Our only health is the disease
If we obey the dying nurse
Whose constant care is not to please
But to remind of our, and Adam's curse,
And that, to be restored, our sickness must grow worse.   10

The whole earth is our hospital
Endowed by the ruined millionaire,
Wherein, if we do well, we shall
Die of the absolute paternal care
That will not leave us, but prevents us everywhere.   15

The chill ascends from feet to knees,
The fever sings in mental wires.
If to be warmed, then I must freeze
And quake in frigid purgatorial fires
Of which the flame is roses, and the smoke is briars.   20

The dripping blood our only drink,
The bloody flesh our only food:
In spite of which we like to think
That we are sound, substantial flesh and blood –
Again, in spite of that, we call this Friday good.   25

wounded surgeon: Jesus Christ, the Son of God, who suffered for our sins, yet healed humanity.
plies: works steadily using a tool.
steel: scalpel, a knife with a small, sharp blade used by a surgeon.
questions: probes, cross-examines.
distempered: diseased.
bleeding hands: the hands of Jesus were nailed to the Cross.
Resolving: sorting out what man could only 'chart' and observe.
enigma: puzzle, mystery, problem.
dying nurse: the Church.
Adam's curse: original sin. Adam disobeyed the commandment of God and was banished from the Garden of Eden and he and all his descendants were now prone to disease and death.
Endowed: provided, donated.
ruined millionaire: Adam.
paternal care: God's care.
prevents: leads on, stops.

mental wires: mind's torment.

quake: tremble, cower.
frigid: cold, icy.
purgatorial fires: the soul burns in purgatory to be cleansed from sin before ascending to heaven.

substantial: of considerable importance, strongly built.

'the flame is roses'

👤 Personal Response

1. Select one image from the poem that you find particularly unsettling and briefly describe its impact on you.
2. What, in your opinion, is the tone of the poem: devotional, assured, searching, frightened, etc.? Support your views with reference to the poem.
3. Do you consider the final stanza a satisfactory conclusion to the poem? Explain the reasons for your opinion, using reference to the text.

👁 Critical Literacy

'East Coker' forms part of the cycle of four poems titled *Four Quartets*, widely regarded as Eliot's masterpiece. The poems were first published individually with place names as titles: 'Burnt Norton' (1936), 'East Coker' (1940), 'The Dry Salvages' (1941) and 'Little Gidding' (1942). This sequence is loosely based on the four seasons and the four elements. The title, 'Four Quartets', suggests a musical quartet, where themes and images are repeated as the meanings accumulate through the different instrumentation used. Time, experience, purgation, prayer and unity are the themes that are common to each poem.

There is a historical dimension to 'East Coker', as Eliot's ancestor Sir Thomas Elyot was baptised in St Michael's Church in East Coker in 1627. Another ancestor, Andrew Eliot, left East Coker for America in 1669. Eliot visited this village in the 1930s and his ashes are buried in the same church with the inscription, 'In my beginning is my end. Of your kindness, pray for the soul of Thomas Stearns Eliot, poet. In my end is my beginning.' Critics have described 'East Coker' as a poem of late summer, earth and faith. It is also seen by some as signifying hope that English communities would survive World War II. The village is an idyll of England at the start of the war. In Eliot's view, the end of all exploring is 'to arrive where we started/And know the place for the first time' ('Little Gidding').

The poem 'East Coker' is divided into five sections. 'East Coker IV' is a formal, elegant section that uses **elaborate paradoxes**. It is full of personal and collective despair paired with the gloom of Good Friday. This religious meditation focuses on the central Christian doctrines of original sin (humanity's state after the fall of Adam), redemption (salvation through the sacrifice of Jesus on the Cross) and atonement (penance undertaken to purge sin). The poem is focused on the magnitude of Christ's death on the Cross as a way of securing salvation for mankind.

Eliot enjoyed the Metaphysical poets, such as Donne, who used intricate comparisons in their work. In this poem, in stanza one, Eliot uses the hospital as a metaphor for the world. The suffering patients are mankind. The 'wounded surgeon' is Jesus Christ, who operates to save sinful/diseased man. Stern love is shown by the surgeon as he skilfully 'plies the steel' to cure the 'distempered part'. He is 'wounded' like Jesus on the Cross. The surgeon's 'bleeding hands' recall how Christ's hands were nailed to the Cross. Through his suffering the puzzle, 'enigma', of sin, denoted by the 'fever chart', is being sorted out, 'Resolving'. This 'sharp compassion' is needed to solve the mystery of our ailing, sinful existence. Metaphysical poetry had a real sense of **argument** running through it, as here: we need to reject the demands of the body and achieve salvation through curing the body's ills. Suffering leads to grace. Eliot saw a close similarity between the poetry of the 17th century and that of the 20th century – both saw the disintegration of old traditions and the arrival of new learning.

In stanza two **the comparison is extended**: 'Our only health is the disease'. This refers to a poem by Andrew Marvell where the soul speaks of being 'Constrained not only to endure/Diseases, but, what's worse, the cure'. According to the poet, we have to do what the 'dying nurse', the Church, says. Its role is 'not to please', but to remind us of our morality. This is a direct consequence of 'our, and Adam's curse'. We have to recognise that **we are sinful and that we need to be redeemed** and then we can be spiritually healthy. This is inspired by 'Dark Night of the Soul' by Saint John of the Cross, which told of the journey of the soul from its bodily home to its union with God. Purification is needed for spiritual growth.

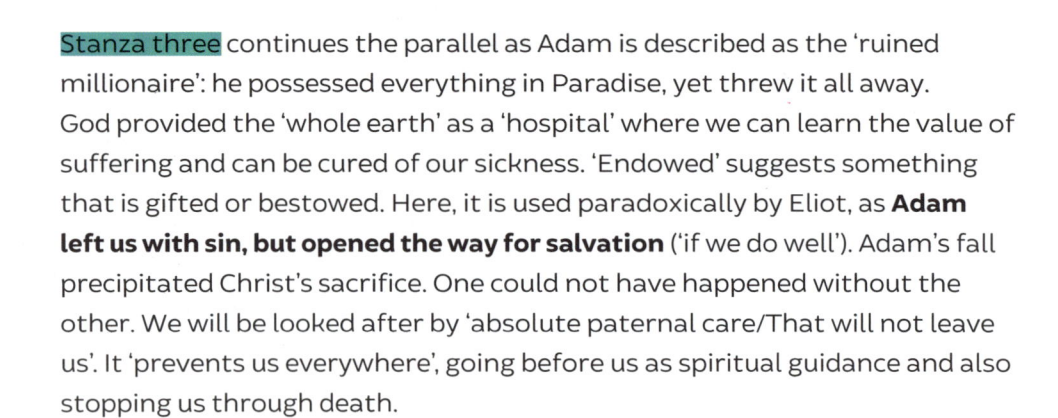

Stanza three continues the parallel as Adam is described as the 'ruined millionaire': he possessed everything in Paradise, yet threw it all away. God provided the 'whole earth' as a 'hospital' where we can learn the value of suffering and can be cured of our sickness. 'Endowed' suggests something that is gifted or bestowed. Here, it is used paradoxically by Eliot, as **Adam left us with sin, but opened the way for salvation** ('if we do well'). Adam's fall precipitated Christ's sacrifice. One could not have happened without the other. We will be looked after by 'absolute paternal care/That will not leave us'. It 'prevents us everywhere', going before us as spiritual guidance and also stopping us through death.

Rich, sensuous images in stanza four describe the fever of sickness: 'The chill ascends from feet to knees'. We feel the icy coldness of death. We experience the shrill sound of mental anguish in the assonance of 'The fever sings in mental wires'. In order to triumph, 'If to be warmed', the individual must suffer, 'freeze/And quake', as the disease of sin is purified through suffering. This results in the experience of **divine love**, 'Of which the flame is roses'. This was the sacrifice of Jesus on the Cross. The 'briars' suggest the crown of thorns placed on Christ's head as he was crucified. The emblems of martyrdom are 'roses' and 'briars'.

The fifth stanza concludes with sensational, vivid images of the **Eucharist**. 'The dripping blood' (the wine) and 'The bloody flesh' (the host) form the only sustenance we need for eternal life. Eliot criticises our blindness, 'In spite of which we like to think' that we are whole and complete without this 'sound, substantial flesh and blood'. Nevertheless, he acknowledges that we do realise the value of Jesus' suffering because 'we call this Friday good'.

The **tone** of this poem is one of calm, detached humility. Its **devotional, assured voice** is contained in five stanzas of five lines. Each stanza concludes with a full stop, a complete syntactical unit on its own. The rhyme scheme is regular, *ababb*, *cdcdd*, etc. This polished, formal yet private voice expresses the concerns of an entire generation in the midst of war and doubt.

Writing About the Poem

'T. S. Eliot's poem "East Coker IV" is a bitter poem concluding in resignation.' Discuss this statement, referring to both the content and style of the poem. Develop your response with suitable reference to the text.

Sample Paragraph

I do not agree that this is a bitter poem. Instead Eliot sets out in a dazzling display of elaborate comparisons the reality of this violent, sinful world which needs healing by the 'wounded surgeon', Jesus Christ. Eliot believed in the Christian doctrine of penance and salvation. In my opinion, that is why he speaks of purging sin and sickness 'in frigid purgatorial fires'. I do not consider that the poem ends in resignation, as there is hope because of Jesus Christ's sacrifice on the Cross which won us our salvation. This is captured in the quite shocking images of the Eucharist's wine and host, 'The dripping blood' and 'The bloody flesh'. Eliot concludes his poem by acknowledging that man does appreciate the sacrifice as 'we call this Friday good', a very positive end note!

EXAMINER'S COMMENT

This is a robust high-grade personal response to the question and presents a number of arguments that show close engagement with the poem. Accurate quotations and contextual references are used effectively throughout.

Class/Homework Exercises

1. '"East Coker IV" is a poem whose lines fail to come to life.' To what extent do you agree or disagree with this view? Develop your response with reference to the poem.
2. 'Eliot surveys the dominant emotion of despair through paradoxical comparisons in his poems.' Discuss this view with reference to 'East Coker IV'.

Points to Consider

- **Necessary evil, suffering is redemptive.**
- **God's caring love.**
- **Imagery taken from medical world, martyrdom, cross and Eucharist.**
- **Precise use of language, play of opposites, didactic tone.**
- **Metaphysical elements – developed argument, paradoxes, conceits and wit.**

Understanding the Prescribed Poetry Question

Marks are awarded using the PCLM Marking Scheme:
P = 15; C = 15; L = 15; M = 5
Total = 50

- **P** (Purpose = 15 marks) refers to the set question and is the launch pad for the answer. This involves engaging with all aspects of the question. Both theme and language must be addressed, although not necessarily equally.
- **C** (Coherence = 15 marks) refers to the organisation of the developed response and the use of accurate, relevant quotation. Paragraphing is essential.
- **L** (Language = 15 marks) refers to the student's skill in controlling language throughout the answer.
- **M** (Mechanics = 5 marks) refers to spelling and grammar.
- Although no specific number of poems is required, students usually discuss at least 3 or 4 in their written responses.
- Aim for at least 800 words, to be completed within 45–50 minutes.

> **NOTE**
>
> In keeping with the PCLM approach, the student has to explore poems of Eliot's on the course that include:
> - **serious issues of universal significance** (the search for spiritual fulfilment, transience, personal experience, purification, 20th-century moral decline, estrangement, etc.)
>
> ... explored through:
> - **a fresh and innovative style** (dramatic monologue, stream of consciousness, fragmentary dialogue, vivid and disturbing imagery, engaging satire, startling contrasts, rich cultural and religious allusions, intense atmospheres, etc.)

Sample Leaving Cert Questions on Eliot's Poetry

1. 'The poetry of T. S. Eliot explores serious issues of universal significance in a fresh and innovative style.' Discuss this statement, developing your answer with suitable reference to the poems by Eliot on your course.
2. 'T. S. Eliot can be a challenging poet to understand, both in terms of language use and central themes.' To what extent do you agree with this statement? Develop your answer with suitable reference to the poems by Eliot that you have studied.
3. 'Eliot's pessimistic vision of life is conveyed in poems that are both interesting and atmospheric.' Discuss this view, developing your answer with suitable reference to the poems by Eliot on your course.

How do I organise my answer?

(Sample question 1)

'The poetry of T. S. Eliot explores serious issues of universal significance in a fresh and innovative style.' Discuss this statement, developing your answer with suitable reference to the poems by Eliot on your course.

Sample Plan 1

Intro: (*Stance: agree with viewpoint in the question*) Eliot's poetry examines serious questions which are important to everyone through an innovative use of descriptive details, discordant poetic structure, cultural and religious allusions and digressions.

Point 1: (*Lack of spirituality – descriptive details*) 'Preludes' provides disturbing examples of a spiritual emptiness in modern society, conveyed by detailed description.

Point 2: (*Destructive experience – dysfunctional landscape, harsh poetic structure*) 'Rannoch, by Glencoe' shows the damaging effect of man on the landscape. Disturbing memories have created a bleak landscape. Abrupt ending and insistent monosyllables emphasise the damage.

Point 3: (*Failure of modern man – rich fragmentary allusions*) 'A Game of Chess' shows man's problems in dealing with his cultural heritage. Fragmentary cultural allusions to Shakespeare and Greek legends show how man struggles to find a voice in today's society.

Point 4: (*Emotional emptiness – digressions, mock-heroic tone*) 'The Love Song of J. Alfred Prufrock' traces Prufrock's paralysing indecision through random asides about his appearance and a mock-heroic tone as he attempts to come to a decision, 'Shall I part my hair behind?'

Conclusion: Unsettling issues which are both profound and universal are intelligently examined through Eliot's original and challenging poetic style.

Sample Paragraph: Point 1

Lack of a meaningful personal life is a universal theme addressed in 'Preludes'. A woman is described in a series of unattractive body parts, 'yellow soles of feet', 'soiled hands'. This reduction of a human being suggests a spiritual yearning. Her spirit is defeated by constantly moving patterns of 'The thousand sordid images'. The use of the definite article, 'The', suggests that this woman has experienced these shames. Her lack of a name further reduces her to an insignificant status. The verbs 'lay' and 'dozed' create a mood of quiet despair. The woman lacks spiritual vision, even the birds do not fly in the sky but are confined by the 'gutters'. These sleazy descriptions of the woman and her environment convey Eliot's bleak vision of spiritual and moral emptiness.

EXAMINER'S COMMENT

As part of a full essay, this top-grade response shows close engagement with the question and Eliot's poetry. Focused analysis of the poet's fresh writing style in depicting a character who is seeking spiritual fulfilment. Varied, controlled expression and apt quotations add to the quality of the response.

(Sample question 2)

"T. S. Eliot can be a challenging poet to understand, both in terms of language use and central themes." To what extent do you agree with this statement? Develop your answer with suitable reference to the poems by Eliot that you have studied.

Sample Plan 2

Intro: (*Stance – partially agree with viewpoint in question*) Eliot's irregular writing style is interesting – always inviting the reader to explore the possibilities of language. The wide-ranging subject matter can be difficult at times, but it reflects the multi-layered experience in the modern age.

Point 1: (*Meaning of life in secular world – personification, images of decay*) 'Preludes' addresses complex spiritual and philosophical questions, confronting the modern secular world through vivid personification and sordid images of spiritual desolation.

Point 2: (*Lack of personal fulfilment – dramatic vignettes*) Readers are engaged by the dramatic scenes and intriguing atmospheres in 'Prufrock'. In his alienation and insecurity, the unhappy central character raises disturbing questions about contemporary urban society.

NOTE

In keeping with the PCLM approach, the student has to take a stance by agreeing, disagreeing or partially agreeing that Eliot can be a challenging poet:

- **in terms of language** (innovative poetic style, complex religious references, multi-layered narratives, demanding cultural and literary allusions, shifting moods and atmospheres, etc.)

... and

- **in terms of central themes** (fruitless search for personal and spiritual meaning in life, alienation, insecurity, paralysis, etc.)

Point 3: (*Less challenging content – satire*) Some of the shorter poems, 'Aunt Helen' for example, are more easily understood. This gentle satire is critical of aspects of polite society.

Point 4: (*Religious experience – demanding references*) Cultural allusions and literary references can be difficult, but they enrich our understanding of important themes, such as the Christian experience in 'Journey of the Magi' and 'East Coker IV'.

Conclusion: Eliot's original poetic voice challenges and his thought-provoking poems have much to interest the modern reader in a rapidly changing world.

Sample Paragraph: Point 3

Not all of Eliot's poems are difficult to understand. In 'Aunt Helen', he paints a satirical pen portrait of his 'maiden aunt', a 'fashionable' lady whose fussy ways are seen as quite absurd. The 'silence in heaven' summed her up well. Eliot is daring in ways – especially as he doesn't take death too seriously: 'the undertaker wiped his feet' when he visited, as if Helen would expect good manners even after she had died. This dry ironic humour is also evident where all the aunt's puritanical rules no longer have any effect on the servants who enjoy their new freedom: 'the footman sat upon the dining-table holding the second housemaid on his knees'. The poet's writing is suggestive but down-to-earth and clear. The two servants are lower class, but they are certainly enjoying life – unlike the lonely spinster.

> **EXAMINER'S COMMENT**
>
> *Short and succinct top-grade response to the question. Some good personal engagement with the poem and perceptive discussion of Eliot's satirical approach and use of subtle irony. Points are well supported by apt quotation and the expression is clear throughout.*

EXAM FOCUS

- As you may not be familiar with some of the poems referred to in the sample plans, substitute poems that you have studied closely.
- Key points about a particular poem can be developed over more than one paragraph.
- Paragraphs may also include cross-referencing and discussion of more than one poem.
- Remember that there is no single 'correct' answer to poetry questions, so always be confident in expressing your own considered response.

Leaving Cert Sample Essay

'T. S. Eliot's distinctive poetry is concerned with the search for meaning in an uncertain world.' Develop your response with reference to the poems of Eliot on your course.

Sample Essay

1. Eliot addresses the exploration for life's meaning in several poems I studied, 'Journey of the Magi', 'The Love Song of J. Alfred Prufrock' and 'Preludes'. Eliot's writing style is very distinctive. He uses modern-day language and his poems are often broken into fragments. Revealing contrasts, dramatic imagery and stream of consciousness style are all used in an original way to convey the poet's observations on modern society's faults and failings.

2. A lot of Eliot's poems are concerned with religion and reflect his own spiritual search. 'Journey of the Magi' is a dramatic account of the three kings who visited the infant Jesus in Bethlehem. They seem to symbolise every person who is seeking spiritual or religious meaning in life. But Eliot's approach contrasts to the traditional Bible story. He focuses a lot on the physical hardships the magi faced in 'the very dead of winter'. The elderly king who narrates the story admits 'there were times we regretted' the journey.

3. Powerful sibilant images convey the pleasures and sensual life they had left behind, 'Summer places on the slope', 'silken girls carrying sherbet'. Eliot shows us that Christianity is not an easy religion to follow. The magi describe their destination in Bethlehem – 'Finding the place, it was you may say satisfactory'. The understatement shows the troubled minds of the magi in this clash between their old lives as wealthy pagan kings and a strange new religion.

4. The final lines describe the changing mindset of the magi who are not at all sure about this new Christianity: 'This birth was hard and bitter agony for us just like death'. The journey marked the end of their old easy-going pagan religion. Yet it did not give them a lot of contentment or deep faith in God. The poem has three different storylines – the actual journey of the magi, Eliot's personal journey from doubts about God's existance to Anglican faith and, finally, the journey of any individual in search of religious belief. 'Journey of the Magi' examines the idea that faith can never be free of serious doubt, 'this was all folly'.

5. Eliot's often addresses alienation and powerlessness in a world that is constantly in transition. The absence of any widespread sense of religion in secular 20th-century society is the background to his great poem, 'The Love Song of J. Alfred Prufrock'. The poem's insecure central figure is unable to take control of his life. His need for fulfilment and his anxiety toward watching his time fade away make him a tragic character. Prufrock's fear of rejection stops him from obtaining a lover or any future hopes of happiness. In this dramatic monologue, Prufrock brings us on a journey to meet an unnamed woman. He hopes to ask her 'an overwhelming question'. Possibly to propose marriage.

INDICATIVE MATERIAL

- **Eliot's distinctive poetry:** (original poetic style, powerful imagery, revealing literary allusions, complex cultural references, dramatic use of multiple narrative voices/personae, varied moods – ironic, poignant, weary, satirical, etc.)

... is concerned with:

- **the search for meaning in an uncertain world** (disillusioned vision of urban life in the 20th century, unsettling themes of alienation, failure, spiritual yearning, longing for satisfying personal relationships, etc.)

T.S. ELIOT

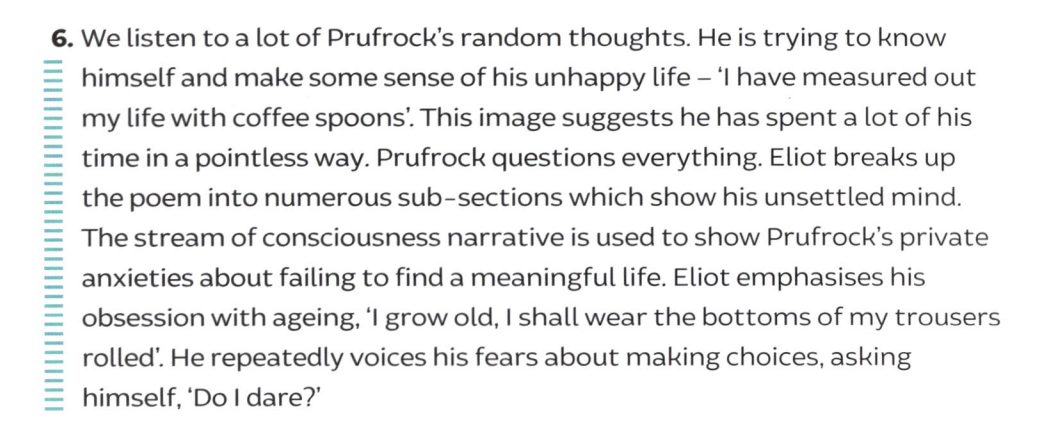

6. We listen to a lot of Prufrock's random thoughts. He is trying to know himself and make some sense of his unhappy life – 'I have measured out my life with coffee spoons'. This image suggests he has spent a lot of his time in a pointless way. Prufrock questions everything. Eliot breaks up the poem into numerous sub-sections which show his unsettled mind. The stream of consciousness narrative is used to show Prufrock's private anxieties about failing to find a meaningful life. Eliot emphasises his obsession with ageing, 'I grow old, I shall wear the bottoms of my trousers rolled'. He repeatedly voices his fears about making choices, asking himself, 'Do I dare?'

7. Prufrock cannot fully express what he really wants to say, 'It is impossible to say just what I mean!' I found the poem's ending bitter and sad. A haunting image of Prufrock abandoning his secret dreams of finding a girlfriend or wife is described. He imagines being near the ocean and hearing mermaids singing. Unfortunatly he realises, 'I do not think they will sing to me'.

8. 'Preludes' explores the solitary, ordinary lives of unhappy people against the backdrop of a drab run-down modern city. The poet is very effective at creating unsettling moods. Dramatic images of 'grimy scraps of whithered leaves', 'newspapers in vacant lots' and 'broken blinds and chimney-pots' capture the anonymous lives of dingy back-streets. The nameless characters go through daily routines in their own seperate and silent desperation – 'With the other masquerades that time resumes'. The poem's outlook was pessimistic and summed up Eliot's view that a lot of urban life these days can be dreary and dissappointing.

9. Overall, I liked Eliot's distinctive poetry. Individuals seeking meaningful relationships, either human or spiritual, in contrast to the pressures of their day-to-day lives is the main theme of these poems. The dark view of modern life in these poems expresses the unhappiness of people through vivid scenes and memorable characters.

(790 words)

> **EXAMINER'S COMMENT**
> Sustained response showing clear engagement with Eliot's poetry. The poems chosen for discussion allowed for well-supported analysis of the question's three elements (distinctive poetry, search for meaning, uncertain world). There are some slight misquotations, some spelling errors ('existance', 'Unfortunatly', 'whithered', 'seperate', 'dissappointing') and overuse of the phrase, 'a lot'. However, expression is generally controlled throughout.
>
> **GRADE: H1**
> P = 15/15
> C = 14/15
> L = 13/15
> M = 4/5
> Total = 46/50

👀 Revision Overview

'The Love Song of J. Alfred Prufrock'
Dramatic inner monologue of an indecisive man tormented by feelings of isolation and inadequacy. Central themes include the impact of modern city life on lonely individuals, alienation and fear of death.

'Preludes' (OL)
Complex narrative about the dark and depressing nature of today's urban lifestyle and the uncertain state of the human soul.

'Aunt Helen' (OL)
In this satirical portrayal of a recently deceased woman who appears to have been unloved, Eliot addresses themes of life, death, relationships and solitude.

from 'The Waste Land': II. 'A Game of Chess'
Critical view of today's unfulfilling, shallow world where people are often unable to connect meaningfully with others.

'Journey of the Magi'
Symbolic poem about the pain of spiritual rebirth. Alienation from a meaningless past is another central theme.

from 'Landscapes': III. 'Usk'
Eliot's instructive poem urges people to live a simple life and to continue seeking spiritual fulfilment through prayer.

from 'Landscapes': IV. 'Rannoch, by Glencoe'
Dramatic evocation of Scotland and its tragic history are merged in a haunting landscape.

from 'Four Quartets': 'East Coker IV'
Eliot focuses on man's place in the universe and emphasises the prospect of renewal and spiritual salvation through Christianity.

💬 Last Words

'Although the idea of a life not fully lived is central to his poetry, T. S. Eliot was not the dry old stick of his self-caricature.'
Craig Raine

'As a schoolboy in a Catholic boarding school in Derry, I was daunted by T. S. Eliot and all that he stood for.'
Seamus Heaney

'Genuine poetry can communicate before it is understood.'
T. S. Eliot

RELIGION/SPIRITUALITY | MEANING OF LIFE | MODERN WORLD | ISOLATION | RELATIONSHIPS | HISTORY/MEMORY

T. S. ELIOT

Gerard Manley Hopkins 1844–1889

'Every poet must be original.'

Gerard Manley Hopkins, a priest and poet, was born in Stratford, outside London, in 1844. In 1863 he began studying classics at Balliol College, Oxford, where he wrote a great deal of poetry. Hopkins converted to Catholicism and was later ordained a Jesuit priest in 1877. It was while studying for the priesthood that he wrote some of his best-known religious and nature poems, including 'The Windhover' and 'Pied Beauty'. His compressed style of writing, especially his experimental use of language, sound effects and inventive rhythms, combined to produce distinctive and startling poetry. In 1884 Hopkins was appointed Professor of Greek at University College, Dublin. He disliked living in Ireland, where he experienced failing health and severe depression. In 1885 he wrote a number of the so-called 'terrible sonnets', including 'No Worst, There is None', which have desolation at their core. Hopkins died of typhoid fever in June 1889 without ever publishing any of his major poems. He is buried in Glasnevin Cemetery.

Investigate Further

To find out more about Gerard Manley Hopkins, or to hear readings of his poems, you could search some useful websites, such as YouTube, BBC Poetry, poetryfoundation.org and poetryarchive.org, or access additional material on this page of your eBook.

Prescribed Poems

☐ **1 'God's Grandeur'**
Hopkins's sonnet welcomes the power of the Holy Ghost to rescue people from sin and hopelessness.
Page 150

☐ **2 'Spring' (OL)**
This poem celebrates the natural beauty of springtime. However, Hopkins also regrets humanity's loss of innocence because of sin.
Page 154

☐ **3 'As Kingfishers Catch Fire, Dragonflies Draw Flame'**
In recognising the uniqueness of everything that exists in the world, Hopkins praises God as the unchanging source of all creation.
Page 158

☐ **4 'The Windhover'**
This was one of Hopkins's favourite poems and describes a bird in flight. Its powerful Christian theme focuses on the relationship between God and mankind.
Page 161

☐ **5 'Pied Beauty'**
This short poem again celebrates the diverse delights of nature and human nature, all of which owe their existence to a changeless Creator. **Page 165**

☐ **6 'Felix Randal'**
An engaging narrative poem about the life and death of one of Hopkins's parishioners. At a deeper level, it celebrates the significance of living a good Christian life.
Page 168

☐ **7 'Inversnaid' (OL)**
Another nature poem rejoicing in the unspoiled beauty of the remote Scottish landscape. It concludes with the poet's heartfelt appeal to preserve the wilderness.
Page 172

☐ **8 'I Wake and Feel the Fell of Dark, Not Day'**
One of the 'terrible sonnets' in which Hopkins reveals his personal torment, self-disgust and despair. Some critics argue that the poet is attempting to renew his own religious faith. **Page 175**

☐ **9 'No Worst, There is None'**
Hopkins explores the experience of unbearable depression, guilt and the awful sense of feeling abandoned by God. Only sleep or death offer any relief. **Page 179**

☐ **10 'Thou Art Indeed Just, Lord, if I Contend'**
In this intensely personal poem, Hopkins wonders why good people suffer while the wicked seem to prosper. He ends by pleading with God to strengthen his own faith. **Page 183**

(OL) indicates poems that are also prescribed for the Ordinary Level course.

GERARD MANLEY HOPKINS

1 God's Grandeur

The world is charged with the grandeur of God.
   It will flame out, like shining from shook foil;
   It gathers to a greatness, like the ooze of oil
Crushed. Why do men then now not reck his rod?
Generations have trod, have trod, have trod;   5
   And all is seared with trade; bleared, smeared with toil;
   And wears man's smudge and shares man's smell: the soil
Is bare now, nor can foot feel, being shod.

And for all this, nature is never spent;
   There lives the dearest freshness deep down things;   10
And though the last lights off the black West went
   Oh, morning, at the brown brink eastward, springs –
Because the Holy Ghost over the bent
   World broods with warm breast and with ah! bright wings.

charged: powered; made responsible.
foil: shimmering gold or silver.
Crushed: compressed from olives or linseed.
reck his rod: pay heed to God's power.
seared: scorched; ruined.
bleared: blurred.
toil: industrialisation.
shod: covered; protected.

spent: exhausted.

last lights: the setting sun.

Note: Hopkins's philosophy emphasised the uniqueness of every natural thing, which he called inscape. He believed that there was a special connection between the world of nature and an individual's consciousness. Hopkins viewed the world as an integrated network created by God. The sensation of inscape (which the poet termed 'instress') is the appreciation that everything has its own unique identity. The concept is similar to that of epiphanies in James Joyce's writing.

'nature is never spent'

👤 Personal Response

1. Describe Hopkins's tone in the first four lines of this poem. Refer closely to the text in your answer.
2. How are human beings portrayed in the poem? Support your response with reference to the text.
3. Select two unusual images the poet uses. Comment on the effectiveness of each.

👁 Critical Literacy

Hopkins wrote many Italian (or Petrarchan) sonnets (consisting of an octave and a sestet). The form suited the stages in the argumentative direction of his themes. Like many other Christian poets, he 'found' God in nature. His poetry is also notable for its use of sprung rhythm (an irregular movement or pace which echoed ordinary conversation). 'God's Grandeur' is typical of Hopkins in both its subject matter and style. The condensed language, elaborate wordplay and unusual syntax – sometimes like a tongue-twister – can be challenging.

The poem's opening quatrain (four-line section) is characteristically dynamic. The **metaphor ('charged') compares God's greatness to electric power**, brilliant but hazardous. The visual effect of 'flame out' and 'shook foil' develops this representation of God's constant presence in the world. The image of oozing oil signifies a natural richness. The reference to electricity makes a subtle reappearance in line 4, where the 'rod' of an angry Creator is likened to a lightning bolt. The tone is one of energised celebration, but there is also a growing frustration: 'Why do men then now not reck his rod?' Hopkins seems mystified at human indifference to God's greatness.

The second quatrain is much more critical. We can sense the poet's own weariness with the numberless generations who have abandoned their spiritual salvation for the flawed material benefits of 'trade' and 'toil'. Hopkins's laboured repetition of 'have trod' is purposely heavy-handed. The internal rhymes of the negative verbs ('seared', 'bleared' and 'smeared') in line 6 convey his deep sense of disgust at a world blighted by industry and urbanisation. **Humankind's neglect of the natural environment is closely linked to the drift away from God**. Hopkins symbolises this spiritual alienation through the image of the 'shod' foot out of touch with nature and its Creator.

However, in response to his depression, the mood changes in the sestet (the final six lines of the sonnet). Hopkins's tone softens considerably, aided by the gentle, sibilant effect in line 10: 'There lives the dearest freshness deep down things'. As in many of his religious poems, he takes comfort in conventional Christian belief. For him, 'nature is never spent'. The world is filled with 'freshness' that confirms God's presence. This **power of renewal** is exemplified in the way morning never fails to follow the 'last lights' of dark night.

The reassuring image in the last line is of God guarding the world and promising rebirth and salvation. The source of this constant regeneration is 'the Holy Ghost' (God's grace) who 'broods' over a dependent world with the patient devotion of a bird protecting its young. In expressing his faith and surrendering himself to divine will, the poet can truly appreciate the grandeur of God. The final exclamations ('Oh, morning' and 'ah! bright wings') echo Hopkins's **sense of euphoria**.

Writing About the Poem

'Hopkins's original voice explores God's presence in this weary world.' Discuss this statement, with particular reference to the poem 'God's Grandeur'.

Sample Paragraph

Hopkins uses the sonnet form to examine man's lack of awareness of the beauty of God's world. A dynamic alliterative metaphor dramatically opens the poem, 'The world is charged with the grandeur of God'. His power and brilliance are conveyed through references to electricity, 'It will flame out, like shining from shook foil'. Yet man remains unconcerned at God's lightning bolt and does 'not reck his rod'. The tone in the second quatrain suggests the drudgery of man's mechanical world. Industrialisation has 'smeared' God's glorious creation. The repetition of 'have trod' coupled with the verbs ('seared' and 'bleared') show the horrendous effects of urbanisation on both man and landscape. Hopkins suggests that man is no longer in touch with his natural environment. A gentler tone emerges in the sestet. Hopkins realises the power of nature to regenerate itself, 'nature is never spent'.

EXAMINER'S COMMENT

A solid discussion on Hopkins's twin themes of God's power and man's indifference. There is a keen awareness of Hopkins's innovative use of language: 'A dynamic alliterative metaphor dramatically opens the poem'. Varied expressive language and accurate use of quotation also contribute to this top grade.

✒ Class/Homework Exercises

1. Comment on Hopkins's use of sound in this poem. Refer closely to the text in your answer.
2. Hopkins is a poet of intense emotion. Discuss this view, tracing how the poet expresses intense emotions throughout 'God's Grandeur'.

◉ Points to Consider

- Combination of conflicting emotions, ecstasy and distress.
- Natural world enlivened by God's presence.
- Assonance and alliteration emphasise despondency, humankind's neglect of natural environment associated with drift away from God.
- Belief in nature's ability to regenerate.
- Sonnet concludes with a benevolent image of Holy Ghost as benevolent mother bird.
- Tone becomes more reassuring in the sestet.

2 Spring

Nothing is so beautiful as Spring –
    When weeds, in wheels, shoot long and lovely and lush;
    Thrush's eggs look little low heavens, and thrush
Through the echoing timber does so rinse and wring
The ear, it strikes like lightnings to hear him sing;   5
    The glassy peartree leaves and blooms, they brush
    The descending blue; that blue is all in a rush
With richness; the racing lambs too have fair their fling.

What is all this juice and all this joy?
    A strain of the earth's sweet being in the beginning   10
In Eden garden. – Have, get, before it cloy,
    Before it cloud, Christ, lord, and sour with sinning,
Innocent mind and Mayday in girl and boy,
    Most, O maid's child, thy choice and worthy the winning.

---

in wheels: radiating out like spokes; rampant; pivoting movement.
lush: growing thickly, luxuriantly.
Thrush's eggs: songbird's eggs, which are light blue.
rinse: wash out with fresh water.
wring: to twist or squeeze; drain off excess water.
have fair their fling: the lambs are enjoying their freedom.
strain: a trace; streak; a segment of melody.
cloud: darken; depress.
Mayday: innocence of the young.
Most: the best choice.
maid's child: Jesus, son of Mary.

'Nothing is so beautiful as Spring'

👤 Personal Response

1. Describe Hopkins's tone in the first eight lines of the poem. Refer to the text in your response.
2. What is the mood in the second section of the poem? What reasons would you give for this change in the sestet? Use reference to support your point of view.
3. Write your own personal response to this poem, commenting on both the subject matter and style.

👁 Critical Literacy

'Spring' was written in May 1877. Hopkins had a special devotion to Mary, Queen of Heaven, and May is the month that is devoted to her. The poem was written after a holiday spent walking and writing poetry in Wales. Hopkins's emphatic language captures the exuberance of nature bursting into life.

The simple **opening sentence** in the first section, 'Nothing is so beautiful as Spring', is a deliberately exaggerated statement (hyperbole) used to emphasise a feeling. This Petrarchan sonnet's **octet** starts with an **ecstatic account of the blooming of nature in spring**. As we examine the poet's use of language, we can understand why it should be heard rather than read. Here in the second line – 'When weeds, in wheels, shoot long and lovely and lush' – the alliteration of 'w' and 'l', the assonance of 'ee' and the slow, broad vowels 'o' and 'u' add to this description of abundant growth. We can easily imagine the wild flowers growing before our eyes, as if caught by a slow-motion camera, uncurling and straightening to reach the heavens.

The **energy of the new plants** is contained in the verb 'shoot'. Just as the plants are shooting from the fertile earth, so one word seems to sprout out of another in the poem, e.g. 'thrush' springing from 'lush'. Now we are looking down, carefully examining a delicately beautiful sight among the long grasses: 'Thrush's eggs look little low heavens'. Note the speckled appearance of the eggs, similar to the dappling of blue and white in the sky. The oval shape is like the dome of the heavens.

The poet's **breathless excitement** at the sight of Heaven on earth is caught by the omission of the word 'like'. We hear the song of the bird as the assonance of 'rinse' and 'wring' fills our ears with strikingly rich sounds. It has a powerful effect, like a bolt of lightning. The focus shifts to the gleam on the leaves of the pear tree, as its 'glassy' appearance is observed. Hopkins looked closely at objects to try to capture their essence (inscape).

Hopkins **pushes language** to its boundaries as nouns become verbs ('leaves' and 'blooms'). The sky seems to bend down to reach the growing trees: 'they brush/The descending blue'. The blueness of the sky is captured in the alliteration of 'all in a rush/With richness'. Meanwhile, newborn lambs are frolicking happily, 'fair their fling'. This octet is a joyous exploration of a kaleidoscope of the colours, sounds and movement of spring. The poet's imagination soars as he strains language to convey the immediacy of the moment.

In the sestet, **the mood becomes reflective** as the poet considers the significance of nature: 'What is all this juice and all this joy?' As he meditates, he decides it is 'A strain of the earth's sweet being', a fleeting glimpse of a perfect world 'In Eden garden', before it was sullied with sin. Hopkins **had a deep love of God**, especially as the Creator. His tone becomes insistent as he urges God to grasp the world in order to preserve it in its perfect state. The hard 'c' sound of 'cloy' and 'cloud' shows how the beauty will become stained and imperfect if Christ does not act swiftly. Hopkins desires virtue and purity: 'innocence', 'Mayday in girl and boy'. He refers to Christ as Mary's child ('O maid's child') as he attempts to persuade God that this world is worth the effort ('worthy the winning').

The regular rhyme scheme adds to the music of the poem as well as emphasising key words: 'joy', 'cloy', 'boy', 'beginning', 'Sinning', 'winning'. The poet was influenced by reading the medieval theologian Duns Scotus, who said that the material world was an incarnation of God. Thus Hopkins felt justified in his preoccupation with the material world, as it had a sacramental value.

Writing About the Poem

'Hopkins uses poetry to speak of the glory of God.' Discuss this statement, with reference to the poem 'Spring'.

Sample Paragraph

Hopkins had felt uneasy loving the natural world in case it distracted him from loving God. But after reading the theologian Duns Scotus, who maintained that the material world was a representation of God, Hopkins felt if he loved nature, he was loving its creator. So in giving us the glorious octet of this poem 'Spring', with the weeds 'long and lovely and lush', the thrush's eggs like 'little low heavens', Hopkins is worshipping God.

In the sestet he becomes more reflective. He links the poem to the glory of God as he meditates on the meaning of all this 'juice' and 'joy'. He asks God to preserve the world in its sinless state. We also see his devotion to the Mother of God, Our Lady in this poem. The references to 'O maid's child' and 'Mayday' confirm this. May is the month associated with Mary, Queen of Heaven.

EXAMINER'S COMMENT

This confident answer has noted one of the key influences on Hopkins (Duns Scotus) in his decision to glorify God in his poetry. Personal engagement with the poem is evident in the lively language, e.g. 'in giving us the glorious octet of this poem'. Expression throughout is clear: 'He asks God to preserve the world in its sinless state.' The effective use of accurate quotation is central to this successful top-grade response.

Class/Homework Exercises

1. Hopkins uses language in an energetic, intense and religious way. Do you agree? Refer to the poem 'Spring' in your answer.
2. Hopkins is fascinated by the uniqueness of things. How does he convey the wonder of the individuality of an object through his use of language in this poem?

Points to Consider

- **Euphoric declaration of beauty of nature.**
- **Jubilant tone, rush of energy, one word sprouts from another.**
- **Rich visual detail and stunning sound effects.**
- **Religious impulse, reflection on innocence, God's beauty in nature and man.**
- **Sonnet form – descriptive octet and reflective sestet.**

3 As Kingfishers Catch Fire, Dragonflies Draw Flame

As kingfishers catch fire, dragonflies draw flame;
    As tumbled over rim in roundy wells
    Stones ring; like each tucked string tells, each hung bell's
Bow swung finds tongue to fling out broad its name;
Each mortal thing does one thing and the same: 5
    Deals out that being indoors each one dwells;
    Selves – goes itself; myself it speaks and spells,
Crying *What I do is me: for that I came.*

I say more: the just man justices;
    Keeps grace: that keeps all his goings graces;   10
Acts in God's eye what in God's eye he is –
    Christ. For Christ plays in ten thousand places,
Lovely in limbs, and lovely in eyes not his
    To the Father through the features of men's faces.

kingfishers: brilliantly coloured birds that hunt small fish.
dragonflies: brightly coloured insects with transparent wings.
tucked: plucked.
Bow: rim of bell that makes a sound when struck.

Selves: (used as a verb) defines or expresses its distinctiveness.

justices: (as a verb) acts justly.
Keeps grace: obeys God's will.

'dragonflies draw flame'

👤 Personal Response

1. Comment on the nature images in the poem's opening line.
2. Select two interesting sound effects from the poem and briefly explain the effectiveness of each.
3. 'Celebration is the central theme in this poem.' Write your response to this statement, supporting your answer with reference to the text.

👁 Critical Literacy

This sonnet is often cited as an example of Hopkins's theory of inscape, the uniqueness of every created thing as a reflection of God's glory. The poet believed that human beings have the unique ability to recognise the divine presence in everything around us. The poem is written in an irregular ('sprung') rhythm that gives it a more concentrated quality.

The poem begins with two strikingly vivid images as Hopkins describes some of nature's most dazzling creatures. In **line 1**, he observes their vivid colour and dynamic movement (note the sharp alliteration and fast-paced rhythm) in the brilliant sunlight. The poet associates both the kingfisher and the dragonflies with fire. Aural images dominate **lines 2–4**. He takes **great delight in the uniqueness of existence** by listing a variety of everyday sounds: the tinkling noise of pebbles ('Stones ring') tossed down wells, the plucking of a stringed instrument and the loud ringing of a bell are all defined through their own distinctive sounds.

Hopkins is certain that the same quality applies to humans – 'Each mortal thing'. **We all express our unique inner selves**. Every individual does the same by presenting their inner essence (that dwells 'indoors'). The poet invents his own verb to convey how each of us 'Selves', or expresses our individual identity. The didactic tone of **lines 7–8** clearly reflects his depth of feeling, summed up by his emphatic illustration about our God-given purpose on earth: 'What I do is me: for that I came'.

Hopkins's enthusiasm ('I say more') intensifies at the start of the **sestet**. His central argument is that **people should fulfil their destiny by being themselves**. Again, he invents a new verb to illustrate his point: 'the just man justices' (good people behave in a godly way). Acting 'in God's eye' and availing of God's grace is our purpose on earth. The poet focuses on his belief that human beings are made in God's image and have the capacity to become like the omnipresent Christ.

Hopkins's **final lines** are filled with the devout Christian faith that **God will redeem everyone who 'Keeps grace'**. The poet repeatedly reminds us of the 'Lovely' personal relationship between God and mankind. It is Christ's presence within every human being that makes 'the features of men's faces' lovely in God's sight. Typically, Hopkins is fully convinced of the reality of Christ and the existence of the spirit world. He sees his own role as a 'kingfisher' catching fire – reeling in souls with his mystical poems of hope and spirituality.

Some critics have commented that the poem is too instructive and that Hopkins was overly concerned with getting his message across at the expense of method. The poet himself did not consider it a success. Yet there is no denying the poetic language of feeling and excitement in every line of the poem.

✍ Writing About the Poem

What aspects of this poem are typical of Hopkins's distinctive poetic style? Refer closely to the text in your answer.

Sample Paragraph

Hopkins the priest is the key speaker in 'As Kingfishers Catch Fire'. To me, the poem is not as typical as 'God's Grandeur' or 'Spring'. However, his writing is full of unusual language. It starts with lively images drawn from nature – 'As kingfishers catch fire, dragonflies draw flame'. There is an immediacy about his images that demands attention. The alliteration of 'f' and 'd' sounds suggest flashes of colour, darting flames and dramatic movements – exactly what fish and insects do in their natural habitats. Hopkins uses personification to show the vitality of the natural world – 'Stones ring'. He makes up new words of his own, such as 'justices'. Again, this is typical of his vibrant style. Hopkins reduces sentences to childlike phrases to show his joy in being aware of creation – 'For Christ plays in ten thousand places'. Even here, the alliteration adds energy to the language. This is typical of so much of his poetry.

> **EXAMINER'S COMMENT**
>
> This is a reflective top-grade response that shows a good understanding of the poem. Points address Hopkins's distinctive writing style. There is a good focus on visual imagery, sound effects and personification. Supportive quotations are also integrated into the commentary throughout.

Class/Homework Exercises

1. Hopkins admitted that his poetry had an 'oddness' about it. Comment on his management of language in this poem. Refer closely to the text in your answer.
2. Hopkins uses the Petrarchan sonnet form of an octet (eight lines) and sestet (six lines) in this poem. How does the poet's treatment of his theme of wonder change in these two sections? Develop your answer with close reference to the text.

Points to Consider

- **Distinctive quality of everything in the natural world.**
- **Invents verb, 'selves', to suggest unique quality of nature and man.**
- **Aural imagery, onomatopoeia, use of everyday sounds, sprung rhythm.**
- **Emphasises the importance of acceptance of God's will.**

4 The Windhover

GERARD MANLEY HOPKINS

Windhover: a kestrel or small falcon; resembles a cross in flight.

To Christ our Lord

I caught this morning morning's minion, king-
   dom of daylight's dauphin, dapple-dawn-drawn Falcon, in his riding
   Of the rolling level underneath him steady air, and striding
High there, how he rung upon the rein of a wimpling wing
In his ecstasy! then off, off forth on swing,   5
   As a skate's heel sweeps smooth on a bow-bend: the hurl
    and gliding
   Rebuffed the big wind. My heart in hiding
Stirred for a bird, – the achieve of, the mastery of the thing!

Brute beauty and valour and act, oh air, pride, plume here
   Buckle! AND the fire that breaks from thee then, a billion   10
Times told lovelier, more dangerous, O my chevalier!

   No wonder of it: sheer plod makes plough down sillion
Shine, and blue-bleak embers, ah my dear,
   Fall, gall themselves, and gash gold-vermilion.

---

minion: favourite; darling.
dauphin: prince, heir to French throne.
dapple-dawn-drawn: the bird is outlined in patches of colour by the dawn light, an example of Hopkins's use of compression.
rung upon the rein: circling movement of a horse at the end of a long rein held by a trainer; the sound of the bird pealing like a bell as it wheels in the sky.
wimpling: pleated.
bow-bend: a wide arc.
Rebuffed: pushed back; mastered.
My heart in hiding: the poet is afraid, unlike the bird.
Buckle: pull together; clasp; fall apart.
chevalier: medieval knight; Hopkins regards God as a knight who will defend him.
sheer plod: back-breaking drudgery of hard work, similar to Hopkins's work as a priest.
sillion: track, furrow.
ah my dear: intimate address to God.
Fall, gall … gash: a reference to the crucifixion of Christ as he fell on the way to Cavalry, was offered vinegar and gashed by a spear on the cross.
gold-vermilion: gold and red, the colours of Christ the Saviour and also of the Eucharist, the body and blood of Christ, which offers redemption.

'how he rung upon the rein of a wimpling wing'

👤 Personal Response

1. In your opinion, has the poet been as daring in his use of language as the bird has been in its flight? Support your view by referring closely to the poem.
2. The sonnet moves from description to reflection. What does the poet meditate on in the sestet? Refer to the poem in your answer.
3. Write your own personal response to the poem, referring closely to the text in your answer.

👁 Critical Literacy

'The Windhover' was Hopkins's favourite poem, 'the best thing I ever wrote'. It is dedicated to Christ – Hopkins wrote it in 1877, when he was thirty-three years old, the same age as Christ when he died. The poet celebrates the uniqueness of the bird and his own deep relationship with God the Creator.

The name of the bird comes from its custom of hovering in the air, facing the wind, as it scans the ground for its prey. The opening lines of the octet are **joyful and celebratory** as Hopkins rejoices in the sight of the bird, 'daylight's dauphin'. The verb 'caught' suggests not just that the poet caught sight of the bird, but also that he 'caught' the essence of the bird on the page with words. This is an example of Hopkins's compression of language where he edges two meanings into one word or phrase. Hopkins shaped language by omitting articles, conjunctions and verbs to express the energy of the bird, 'off forth on swing'. **Movement fascinated the poet**. The bird is sketched by the phrase 'dapple-dawn-drawn'. A vivid image of the flecks of colour on his wings (as the dawn light catches him) is graphically drawn here.

The **momentary freshness** is conveyed by 'this morning', with the bird in flight beautifully captured by the simile 'As a skate's heel sweeps smooth on a bow-bend'. The 's' sound mimics the swish of the skater as a large arc is traced on the ice. This curve is similar to the strong but graceful bend of a bow stretched to loose its arrow, with all its connotations of beauty of line and deadly strength.

In the octet, there is typical **energetic language**: 'how he rung upon the rein of a wimpling wing/In his ecstasy!' This carries us along in its breathless description. The word 'wimpling' refers to the beautiful, seemingly pleated pattern of the arrangement of the outstretched wings of the bird. The capital 'F' used for 'Falcon' hints at its symbolism for Christ. This very personal poem uses 'I' in the octet and 'my' in the sestet. Hopkins lavishes praise on the bird: 'dauphin' (young prince, heir) and 'minion' (darling). Run-on lines add to the poet's excitement. He acknowledges that the bird has what he himself does not possess: power, self-belief and grace ('My heart in hiding'). The lively rhyme, such as 'riding'/'striding', never becomes repetitive because of the varying line breaks. The octet concludes with Hopkins's admiration of 'the thing', which broadens the focus from the particular to the general. All of creation is magnificent.

This leads to the sestet, where **God the Creator becomes central to the poem**. The essence (inscape) of the bird is highlighted: 'air, pride, plume here'. The bird is strong, brave, predatory, graceful and beautiful. The word 'Buckle' is paradoxical, as it contains two contradictory meanings: clasp together and fall apart. The bird is holding the line when it rides the rolling wind and falls apart as it swoops down on its prey. Capital letters for the conjunction 'AND' signal a moment of insight: 'the fire that breaks from thee'. The pronoun refers to God, whose magnificence is shown by 'fire'. The Holy Spirit is often depicted as a bird descending with tongues of flame. A soft tone of intimacy emerges: 'O my chevalier!' It is as if Hopkins wants God to act as the honourable knight of old, to take up his cause and fight on his behalf against his enemy. God will be Hopkins's defender against evil.

The sestet concludes with **two exceptional images**, both breaking apart to release their hidden brilliance. The ploughed furrow and the 'blue-bleak embers' of coal both reveal their beauty in destruction: 'sillion/Shine', 'gash gold-vermilion'. Christ endured Calvary and crucifixion, 'Fall, gall ... gash', and through his sacrifice, the 'Fall', achieved redemption for us. So too the priest embracing the drudgery of his service embraces his destiny by submitting to the will of God. In doing so, he reflects the greatness of God. Earthly glory is crushed to release heavenly glory. The phrase 'ah my dear' makes known the dominant force of Hopkins's life: to love God. The colours of gold and red are those of Christ the Saviour as well as the colours associated with the Eucharist, the body and blood of Christ. When Christians receive the sacrament of Holy Communion, they are redeemed. So, as the poem begins, 'dapple-dawn-drawn Falcon', it ends with 'gold-vermilion' in a triumph of glorious colour.

Writing About the Poem

'Hopkins's intense reflections on Christ in his poetry are always conveyed with visual energy.' Discuss this statement, with particular reference to 'The Windhover'.

Sample Paragraph

In 'The Windhover', Hopkins uses the image of the falcon as a symbol of Christ. Using strong images, the poet describes the bird's magnificent beauty, 'dapple-dawn-drawn', and its strength, 'rebuffed the big wind'. In the sestet, Hopkins calls God 'O my chevalier'. This gives a vivid picture of a highly moral individual. The verb 'Buckle' reminds me of the knight putting on his armour and stumbling in battle. Hopkins felt it was right to focus on nature as evidence of the power and beauty of God. In glorifying Him through the dramatic emblem of the windhover, he is glorifying divine creation, and therefore God Himself. The flash of red and gold, with which this visually powerful poem ends, 'gash gold-vermilion', reminds me that the priest carrying out his ordinary duties is also revealing the beauty of God's creation. I think Hopkins's reflections on Christ add a real spiritual quality to his poetry.

> **EXAMINER'S COMMENT**
>
> Close reading of the poem is evident in this top-grade personal response: 'The verb "Buckle" reminds me of the knight putting on his armour'. Quotations are very well used here to highlight Hopkins's commitment to his Christian faith, 'The flash of red and gold, with which this visually powerful poem ends, "gash gold-vermilion", reminds me that the priest carrying out his ordinary duties is also revealing the beauty of God's creation.' Well-controlled language use throughout.

✒ Class/Homework Exercises

1. Would you agree that 'The Windhover' illustrates much that is both spiritual and Christian in Hopkins's poetry? Give reasons for your response.
2. Hopkins creates a powerful sense of drama throughout 'The Windhover'. Discuss this view, using reference to the poem.

◉ Points to Consider

- **Deeply personal poem, engaging opening.**
- **Relationship with God accentuated by poet's ability to see the divine in nature.**
- **Medieval chivalric imagery.**
- **Bird's movement depicted by alliteration and assonance.**
- **Optimistic ending, illustrated by 'blue-black' becoming 'gold-vermilion'.**

5 Pied Beauty

GERARD MANLEY HOPKINS

Pied: varied.

Glory be to God for dappled things –
    For skies of couple-colour as a brinded cow;
        For rose-moles all in stipple upon trout that swim;
Fresh-firecoal chestnut-falls; finches' wings;
    Landscape plotted and pieced – fold, fallow, and plough;   5
        And all trades, their gear and tackle and trim.

All things counter, original, spare, strange;
    Whatever is fickle, freckled (who knows how?)
        With swift, slow; sweet, sour; adazzle, dim;
He fathers-forth whose beauty is past change: 10
                Praise him.

dappled: speckled, spotted.
brinded: streaked.
rose-moles: red-pink spots.
stipple: dotted.
Fresh-firecoal chestnut-falls: open chestnuts bright as burning coals.
pieced: enclosed.
fold: sheep enclosure.
fallow: unused.
trades: farmwork.
gear: equipment.
tackle: implements.
trim: fittings.
counter: contrasting.
spare: special.
fickle: changeable.
He: God.
fathers-forth: creates.

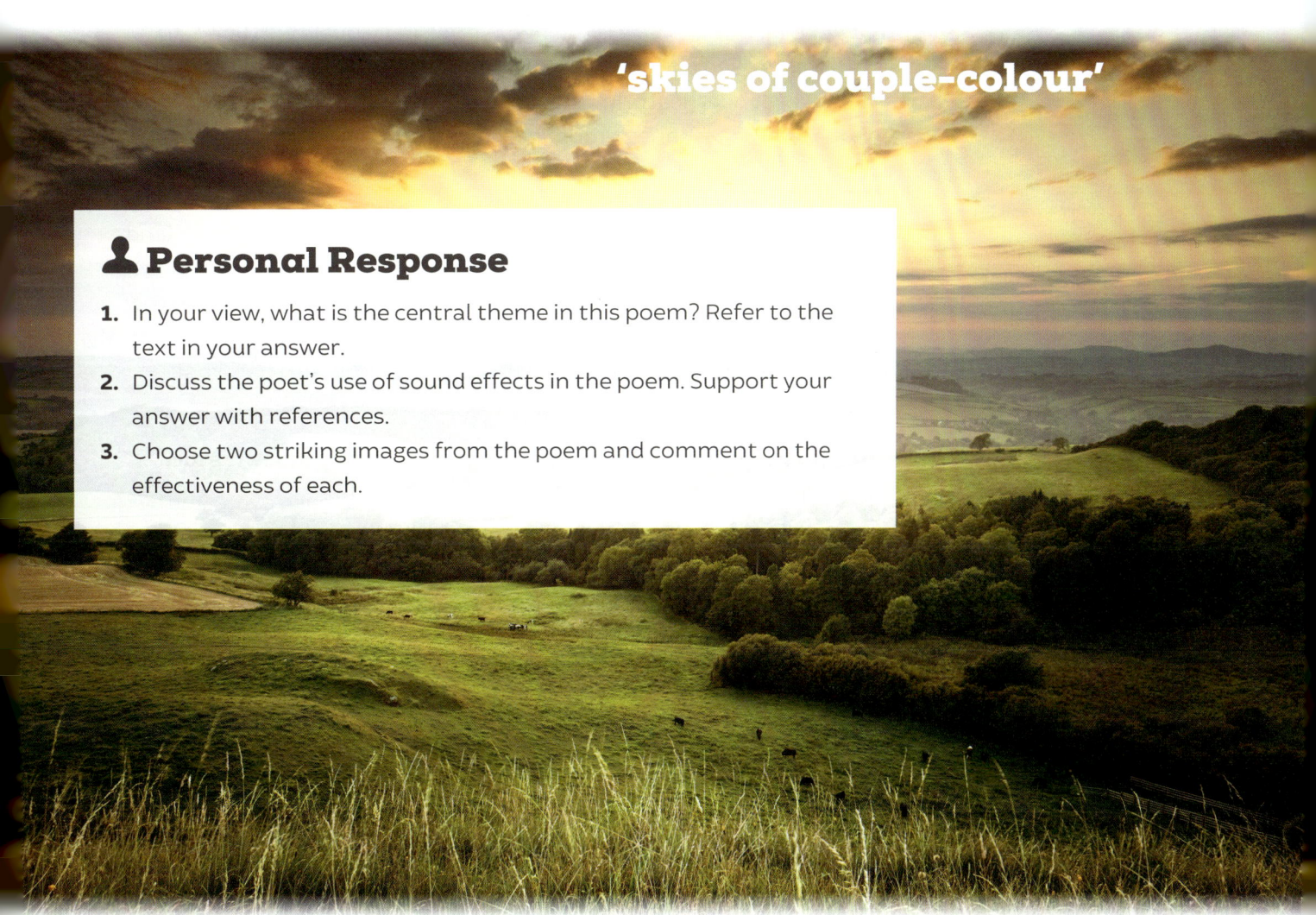

'skies of couple-colour'

👤 Personal Response

1. In your view, what is the central theme in this poem? Refer to the text in your answer.
2. Discuss the poet's use of sound effects in the poem. Support your answer with references.
3. Choose two striking images from the poem and comment on the effectiveness of each.

👁 Critical Literacy

'Pied Beauty' is one of Hopkins's 'curtal' (or curtailed) sonnets, in which he condenses the traditional sonnet form. It was written in the so-called sprung rhythm that he developed, based on the irregular rhythms of traditional Welsh verse. The poem's energetic language – particularly its sound effects – reflects Hopkins's view of the rich, abundant diversity evident within God's creation.

The simplicity of the prayer-like **opening line** ('Glory be to God') is reminiscent of biblical language and sets the poem's devotional tone. From the start, Hopkins displays a **childlike wonder** for all the 'dappled things' around him, illustrating his central belief with a series of vivid examples from the natural world.

Included in his panoramic sweep of nature's vibrant delights are the dominant blues and whites of the sky, which he compares to the streaked ('brinded') patterns of cowhide. The world is teeming with contrasting colours and textures, captured in **detailed images**, such as 'rose-moles all in stipple upon trout' and 'Fresh-firecoal chestnut-falls'.

For the exhilarated poet, everything in nature is linked. It is ironic, of course, that what all things share is their god-given individuality. In **line 4**, he associates broken chestnuts with burning coals in a fire, black on the outside and glowing underneath. In turn, the wings of finches have similar colours. Condensed imagery and compound words add even greater energy to the description.

Hopkins turns his attention to human nature in **lines 5–6.** The farmland features he describes reflect hard work and efficiency: 'Landscape plotted and pieced – fold, fallow, and plough'. The range of man's impact on the natural world is also worth celebrating, and this is reinforced by the **orderly syntax and insistent rhythm**. Human activity in tune with nature also glorifies God.

Hopkins's **final four lines** focus on the **unexpected beauty of creation** and further reveal the poet's passionate Christianity. As though overcome by the scale and variety of God's works – 'who knows how?' – the poet meditates on a range of contrasting adjectives ('swift, slow; sweet, sour; adazzle, dim'), all of which indicate the wonderful diversity of creation. As always, the alliteration gives an increased dynamism to this image of abundance and variety in nature.

The poem ends as it began – with a shortened version of the two mottoes of St Ignatius of Loyola, founder of the Jesuits: *Ad majorem Dei gloriam* (to the greater glory of God) and *Laus Deo semper* (praise be to God always). For Hopkins, **God is beyond change**. The Creator ('He fathers-forth') and all the 'dappled' opposites that enrich our ever-changing world inspire us all to 'Praise him'.

✒ Writing About the Poem

'Hopkins's appreciation of the energy present in the world is vividly expressed in his unique poetry.' Discuss this statement, with particular reference to 'Pied Beauty'.

Sample Paragraph

'Pied Beauty' is more like a prayer than an ordinary poem. It begins with 'Glory be to God' and continues to the final words 'Praise him'. In between, Hopkins lists examples of the variety of the natural environment, the 'landscape plotted and pieced'. The pace of the poem is rapid, as though he is in a rush to explain his astonishment: 'Fresh-firecoal chestnut-falls'. There is an overwhelming sense of God's mystery and greatness. This is partly due to the compound phrases, such as 'couple-colour' and 'rose-moles' which make us more aware of the varied appearances of natural things. The energetic rhythm builds to a climax in the last line. This is almost breathless – just one simple phrase that sums up Hopkins's awareness of God's creation: 'Praise him'.

> **EXAMINER'S COMMENT**
>
> A short, focused response that ranges over a number of interesting features of Hopkins's style, particularly his description of nature's energy: 'The pace of the poem is rapid, as though he is in a rush to explain his astonishment'. The rapidity of Hopkins's verse is effectively explored, particularly in the reference to the lead-up to the climax in the poem's final line. A top-grade answer.

✏ Class/Homework Exercises

1. In your opinion, what is Hopkins's attitude towards God in this poem? Refer to his use of imagery and pay particular attention to the concluding four lines.
2. Compare and contrast the views expressed in 'Pied Beauty' with any other 'religious' poem by Hopkins from your course. Develop your answer with reference to both poems.

◎ Points to Consider

- Condensed version (ten and a half lines) of traditional sonnet form (fourteen lines).
- Anthem of praise to God for nature's variety.
- Catalogue of vibrant examples of 'dappled beauty'. Effective use of compound words.
- Alliteration conveys how man's activities are in harmony with God's design.

6 Felix Randal

Felix Randal: the parishioner's name was Felix Spenser. 'Felix' in Latin means 'happy'. Randal can also mean a lowly, humble thing or trodden on.

Felix Randal the farrier, O he is dead then? my duty all ended,
Who have watched his mould of man, big-boned and hardy-handsome
Pining, pining, till time when reason rambled in it, and some
Fatal four disorders, fleshed there, all contended?

Sickness broke him. Impatient he cursed at first, but mended   5
Being anointed and all; though a heavenlier heart began some
Months earlier, since I had our sweet reprieve and ransom
Tendered to him. Ah well, God rest him all road ever he offended!

This seeing the sick endears them to us, us too it endears.
My tongue had taught thee comfort, touch had quenched thy tears   10
Thy tears that touched my heart, child, Felix, poor Felix Randal;

How far from then forethought of, all thy more boisterous years,
When thou at the random grim forge, powerful amidst peers,
Didst fettle for the great grey drayhorse his bright and battering sandal!

farrier: blacksmith.
O he is dead then?: reaction of priest at Felix's death.
hardy-handsome: compound word describing the fine physical appearance of the blacksmith.
disorders: diseases.
contended: competitively fought over Felix.
anointed: sacraments administered to the sick by a priest.
reprieve and ransom: the sacraments of confession and communion through which Christians are redeemed from sin.
Tendered: offered.
all road ever: in whatever way (local dialect).
random: casual; irregular.
fettle: prepare.
drayhorse: big horse used to pull heavy carts.
sandal: type of horseshoe.

'at the random grim forge'

👤 Personal Response

1. 'Hopkins is a poet who celebrates ordinary life and simple religious faith in his poem "Felix Randal".' Discuss this statement with reference to the poem.
2. How does the octet differ from the sestet in this Petrarchan sonnet? Refer to theme and style in your response. Use quotations in support of your views.
3. Choose two aural images that you found interesting and briefly explain their effectiveness.

👁 Critical Literacy

'Felix Randal' was written in Liverpool in 1880. The poem contrasts with others such as 'Spring'. Hopkins had been placed as a curate to the city slums of Liverpool, 'a most unhappy and miserable spot', in his opinion. He didn't communicate successfully with his parishioners and he didn't write much poetry, except this one poem about the blacksmith who died of tuberculosis, aged thirty-one.

The opening of the octet identifies the man with his name and occupation, 'Felix Randal the farrier'. Then the poet shocks us with the priest's reaction: 'O he is dead then? my duty all ended'. On first reading, this sounds both dismissive and cold. However, when we consider that the death was expected and that the priest had seen all this many times, we realise that the line rings with authenticity. For Hopkins, 'duty' was a sacred office. **The farrier is recalled in his physical prime**, using the alliteration of 'm', 'b' and 'h' in the phrase 'mould of man, big-boned and hardy-handsome'. The repetition of 'Pining, pining' marks his decline in health. His illness is graphically conveyed as his mental health deteriorated ('reason rambled') and the diseases attacked his body ('Fatal four disorders, fleshed there, all contended'). **The illnesses took possession of the body** and waged a horrific battle to win supremacy, eventually killing Felix.

The word 'broke' is suitable in this context, as in the world of horses it refers to being trained. Is Felix trained ('broke') through suffering? His realistic reaction to the news – 'he cursed' – changes when he receives the sacraments ('being anointed'). Felix was broken but is now restored by 'our sweet reprieve and ransom', the healing sacraments. **The tone changes** with the personal pronoun. The priest–patient relationship is acknowledged: we, both priest and layperson, are saved by God. A note of resigned acceptance, almost an anti-climax, is evident in the line 'Ah well, God rest him all road ever he offended!' The use of the Lancashire dialect ('all road') by the priest shows a developing relationship between the two men.

The detached priest's voice resurfaces in the ==sestet==: 'seeing the sick'. This section of the sonnet focuses on the **reality of sickness** and its effects. Both Felix and the priest received something from the experience. We respond to the sick with sympathy ('This seeing the sick endears them to us'), but we also appreciate ourselves and our own health more ('us too it endears') as we face another's mortality. The priest comforted the dying man with words ('My tongue') and the last sacraments, anointing by 'touch' and becoming a father figure to 'child' Felix. Is there a suggestion that one must become like an innocent child to enter the kingdom of Heaven? The ==tercet== (three-line segment) is intimate: 'thee', 'thy', 'Thy tears', 'my heart'. The ==last tercet== explodes in a **dramatic flashback** to the energy of the young blacksmith in his prime, when there was little thought of death: 'How far from then forethought'. Onomatopoeia and alliteration convey the lifeforce (inscapes) of the young Felix, 'boisterous' and 'powerful amidst peers'.

Sprung rhythm adds to the force of the poem as the six main stresses are interspersed with an irregular number of unstressed syllables. Felix did a man's job at the 'grim forge' when he made the 'bright and battering sandal' for the powerful carthorse, powerfully conveyed in the assonance of 'great grey drayhorse'. The poem ends not with Felix in heavenly glory, but in his former earthly glory: 'thou … Didst fettle'. God has fashioned Felix through his suffering just as Felix had fashioned the horseshoe. Both required force and effort to bend them to the shape in which they can function properly. The poem is a celebration of God's creation of the man.

Writing About the Poem

'Hopkins is a poet who celebrates unique identities and individual experiences, exploring their meaning and worth.' Discuss this statement in relation to one or more of the poems on your course, using reference to the text.

Sample Paragraph

In 'Felix Randal', Hopkins captures the unique essence of a strong man struck down by illness. He was 'big-boned and hardy-handsome', and the alliteration emphasises his physique. His reaction to his own misfortune is evident in 'he cursed at first', the assonance echoing the deep voice. Hopkins gives us the dismissive voice of the priest: 'O he is dead then? my duty all ended'. Here is a man who has seen too much suffering. His use of the expression 'all road' shows how he has tried to enter the world of his parishioners, but he quickly reverts back to his professional capacity. He has a strong belief that the sacraments will help: 'sweet reprieve and ransom'. The poem leaves us feeling that the priest has received as much from the sick man as the sick man has received from the priest: 'Thy tears that touched my heart'.

EXAMINER'S COMMENT

This paragraph dealt comprehensively with the various elements of the question. The close attention to the poet's use of language, assonance and alliteration, enhances the answer. Real personal engagement is evident in the discussion of the priest's transition from tiredness to his regained 'professional capacity'. A successful answer that deserves the top grade.

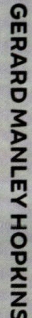

GERARD MANLEY HOPKINS

✒ Class/Homework Exercises

1. Hopkins deals with suffering in his poetry. Has this any relevance to the modern reader? Use reference to 'Felix Randal' in your answer.
2. Hopkins gives a vivid portrait of the farrier. Discuss how his changing tone conveys his view of Felix Randal. Support your answer with close reference to the text.

◉ Points to Consider

- Inscape (essence captured) of blacksmith in this Petrarchan sonnet.
- Focus on man's insignificance; glory only achieved through Christian faith.
- Sprung rhythm (many unstressed syllables) add to poem's energy.
- Simple everyday speech and colloquialisms root poem firmly in north of England.
- Final image is positive; 'b' sound accentuates energy.

7 Inversnaid

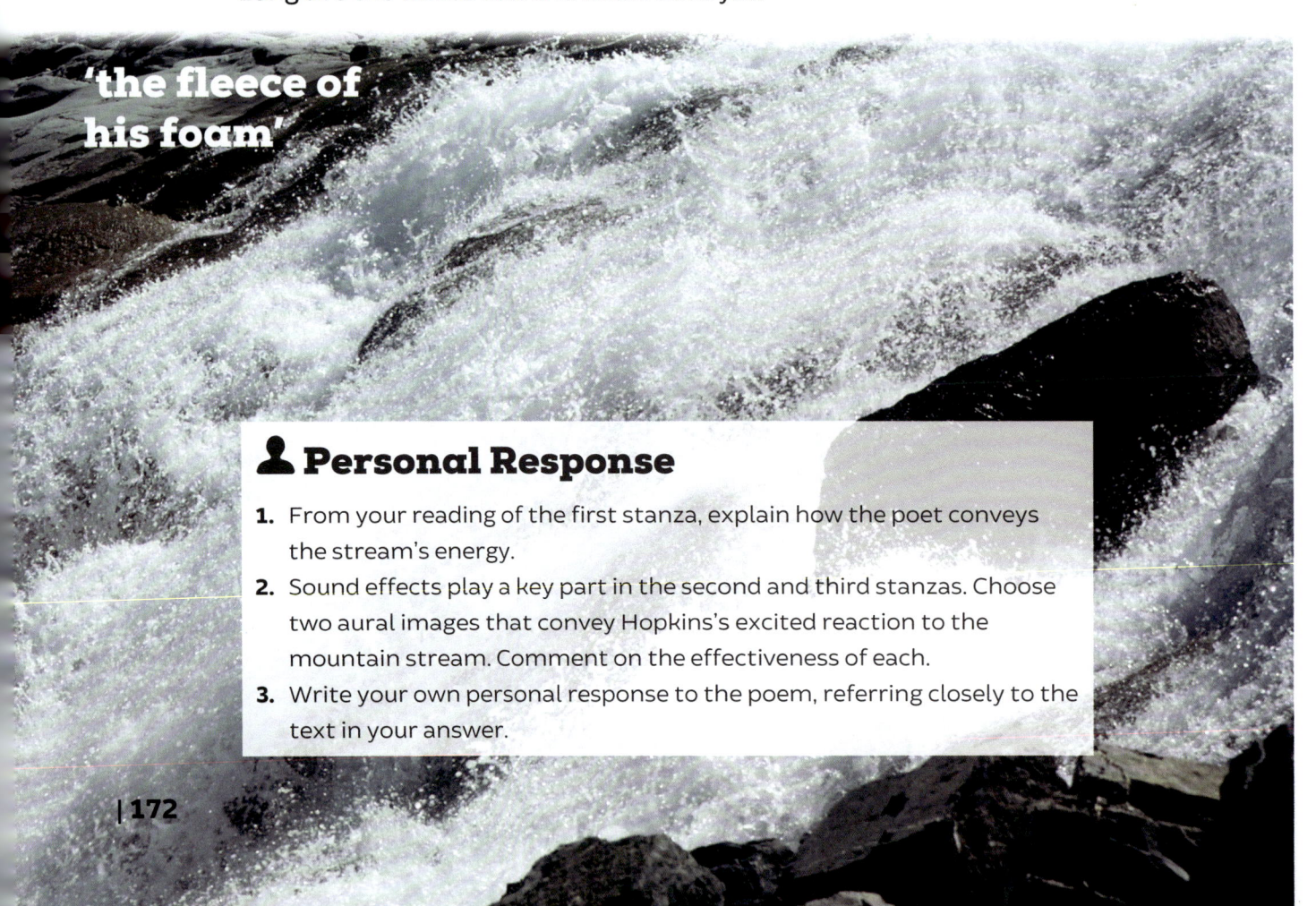

Title: Inversnaid is a remote area located near Loch Lomond in the Scottish Highlands.

This darksome burn, horseback brown,
His rollrock highroad roaring down,
In coop and in comb the fleece of his foam
Flutes and low to the lake falls home.

A windpuff-bonnet of fawn-froth 5
Turns and twindles over the broth
Of a pool so pitchblack, fell-frowning,
It rounds and rounds Despair to drowning.

Degged with dew, dappled with dew
Are the groins of the braes that the brook treads through, 10
Wiry heathpacks, flitches of fern,
And the beadbonny ash that sits over the burn.

What would the world be, once bereft
Of wet and of wildness? Let them be left,
O let them be left, wildness and wet; 15
Long live the weeds and the wilderness yet.

burn: stream.

coop: hollow.
comb: moving freely.
Flutes: grooves; whistles.

twindles: spins.
fell: fiercely.

Degged: sprinkled about.
groins of the braes: sides of hills.
heathpacks: heather outcrops.
flitches: ragged tufts.
beadbonny: mountain ash tree with bright berries.
bereft: deprived.

'the fleece of his foam'

👤 Personal Response

1. From your reading of the first stanza, explain how the poet conveys the stream's energy.
2. Sound effects play a key part in the second and third stanzas. Choose two aural images that convey Hopkins's excited reaction to the mountain stream. Comment on the effectiveness of each.
3. Write your own personal response to the poem, referring closely to the text in your answer.

◉ Critical Literacy

'Inversnaid' was written in 1881 after Hopkins visited the remote hillsides around Loch Lomond. He disliked being in cities and much preferred the sights and sounds of the wilderness. The poem is unusual for Hopkins in that there is no direct mention of God as the source of all this natural beauty.

The **opening lines** of **stanza one** are dramatic. Hopkins compares the brown, rippling stream ('This darksome burn') to a wild horse's back. The forceful alliteration – 'rollrock highroad roaring' – emphasises the power of this small stream as it rushes downhill, its course directed by confining rocks. A sense of immediacy and energy is echoed in the **onomatopoeic effects**, including end rhyme ('brown', 'down'), repetition and internal rhyme ('comb', 'foam'). This is characteristic of Hopkins, as is his use of descriptive details, likening the foamy 'fleece' of the water to the fluted surface ('Flutes') of a Greek or Roman column.

Stanza two begins with another effective metaphor. The poet compares the yellow-brown froth to a windblown bonnet (hat) as the water swirls into a dark pool on the riverbed. The **atmosphere is light and airy**. Run-on lines reflect the lively pace of the noisy stream. However, the tone suddenly darkens with the disturbing image of the 'pitchblack' whirlpool which Hopkins sees as capable of drowning all in 'Despair'. The sluggish rhythm in **lines 7–8** reinforces this menacing mood.

Nature seems much more benign in **stanza three**. The language is softer sounding – 'Degged with dew, dappled with dew' – as Hopkins describes the **steady movement of the water** through 'the groins of the braes'. Enclosed by the sharp banks, the stream sprinkles nearby branches of mountain ash, aflame with their vivid scarlet berries. As always, Hopkins delights in the unspoiled landscape: 'Wiry heathpacks, flitches of fern,/And the beadbonny ash'. Throughout the poem, he has also used traditional Scottish expressions ('burn', 'braes') to reflect the vigorous sounds of the Highlands.

The language in **stanza four** is rhetorical. Hopkins wonders what the world would be like without its wild qualities. The tone is personal and plaintive: 'O let them be left, wildness and wet'. While repetition and the use of exclamation add a sense of urgency, his plea is simple: let nature remain as it is. The final appeal – 'Long live the weeds and the wilderness yet' – is reminiscent of his poem 'Spring'. Once again, there is no doubting Hopkins's **enthusiasm for the natural beauty of remote places** and the sentiments he expresses are clearly heartfelt. Although written in 1881, the poem has obvious relevance for today's generation.

Writing About the Poem

'Hopkins's deep appreciation of nature is a central feature of his striking poetry.' Discuss this statement, with particular reference to 'Inversnaid'.

Sample Paragraph

The immediate thing that emerges about Hopkins is his closeness to nature. He seems to have a heightened awareness of the sights and sounds of the remote mountain 'burn' in 'Inversnaid'. He details the colours of the water. It is 'darksome', 'horseback brown'. Hopkins is always excited by his natural environment. To him, the river is alive. It is 'roaring down'. In the last section of the poem, Hopkins openly states his fears for nature. He begs us to preserve the 'wildness and wet'. For him, all of nature deserves respect. He ends the poem with his own slogan, 'Long live the weeds and the wilderness'. He repeats the words 'wet' and 'wildness' a number of times in the final lines, leaving us in no doubt about how much the natural landscape meant to him.

EXAMINER'S COMMENT

Hopkins's awareness of the unruly aspects of nature is effectively explored: 'He details the colours of the water. It is "darksome"'. There is a convincing sense of close engagement with the poem: 'Hopkins is always excited by his natural environment.' Accurate textual references and impressive, fluent expression ensure the top grade.

Class/Homework Exercises

1. In your opinion, does the poem 'Inversnaid' have relevance to our modern world? Support the points you make with reference to the text.
2. How does Hopkins reveal his intense love of nature in this poem? Refer to his subject matter and writing style in your response.

Points to Consider

- Celebration of nature's unruly beauty; unusually no reference to God.
- Colloquial Scots-English language locates poem in Scottish Highlands.
- Steady movement of water conveyed through onomatopoeic effects.
- Plea on behalf of unspoilt natural scenes.

8 I Wake and Feel the Fell of Dark, Not Day

GERARD MANLEY HOPKINS

I wake and feel the fell of dark, not day.
What hours, O what black hours we have spent
This night! what sights you, heart, saw; ways you went!
And more must, in yet longer light's delay.
    With witness I speak this. But where I say   5
Hours I mean years, mean life. And my lament
Is cries countless, cries like dead letters sent
To dearest him that lives alas! away.

I am gall. I am heartburn. God's most deep decree
Bitter would have me taste: my taste was me;   10
Bones built in me, flesh filled, blood brimmed the curse.
    Selfyeast of spirit a dull dough sours. I see
The lost are like this, and their scourge to be
As I am mine, their sweating selves; but worse.

---

fell: threat; blow; knocked down; past tense of fall (fall of Adam and Eve cast into darkness); also refers to a mountain.

dead letters sent/To dearest him: communication which is of no use, didn't elicit a response.

gall: bitterness; anger; acidity; vinegar.
deep decree: command that cannot easily be understood.
Bones built in me, flesh filled, blood brimmed the curse: the passive tense of the verb might suggest how God created man, yet man has sinned.
Selfyeast of spirit a dull dough sours: yeast makes bread rise; Hopkins feels he cannot become good or wholesome.
The lost: those condemned to serve eternity in Hell with no hope of redemption, unlike the poet.

'I wake and feel the fell of dark, not day'

👤 Personal Response

1. How is the oppressive atmosphere conveyed in this sonnet? Support your response with reference to the poem.
2. How does the poem conclude, on a note of hope or despair? Develop your answer by referring closely to the text.
3. Comment on the use of alliteration to convey Hopkins's sense of dejection. Mention at least two examples.

👁 Critical Literacy

'I Wake and Feel the Fell of Dark, Not Day' was written in Dublin, where Hopkins was teaching at UCD and was burdened by a massive workload of examination papers. After a long silence, he wrote the 'terrible sonnets'. Hopkins said of these, 'If ever anything was written in blood, these were.' This sonnet was discovered among his papers after his death.

The last three sonnets on the course are called the 'terrible sonnets'. Here Hopkins reaches the **darkest depths of despair.** The sonnet opens in darkness and the only mention of light in the whole poem is 'light's delay' in line 4, as it is postponed. He wakes to the oppressive blow of the dark ('the fell of dark'), not to the brightness of daylight. The heaviness of depression is being described, the oppressive darkness which Adam woke to after his expulsion from the Garden of Eden. Hopkins and his soul have shared these 'black hours' and they will experience 'more'. It is not just hours they have spent in darkness, but 'years', 'life'.

The formal, almost biblical phrase 'With witness I speak this' emphasises that what he has said is true. The hard 'c' sounds in 'cries countless' and the repetition of 'cries' keenly describe the **fruitless attempts at communication** ('dead letters'). There is no response: he 'lives alas! away'. We can imagine the poet in the deep dark of the night attempting to gain solace from his prayers to God ('dearest him'), but they go unanswered.

Hopkins feels this deep depression intensely. **Note the repetition of 'I':** 'I wake', 'I speak', 'I am gall', 'I am heartburn', 'I see', 'I am'. He is in physical pain, bitter and burning. The language might well refer to Christ's crucifixion, when he was offered a sponge soaked in vinegar to drink, and pierced through his side. However, the poet recognises that it is God's unfathomable decision that this is the way it should be: 'God's most deep decree'. **The poet is reviled by himself** in line 10: 'my taste was me'. He describes how he was fashioned: 'Bones built in me, flesh filled, blood brimmed'. The alliteration shows the careful construction of the body by the Creator, but Hopkins is full of 'the curse'.

Could this sense of revulsion be related to original sin emanating from the fall of Adam and Eve? The deadening 'd' sound of 'dull dough' shows that there is no hope of rising. The body is tainted, soured. It does not have the capacity to 'Selfyeast', to resurrect or renew. Is it being suggested that Hopkins needs divine intervention? Is there an overtone of the bread of communion, the wholesome Body of Christ? The scope of the poem broadens out at the end as the poet gains an **insight into the plight of others**. All those condemned to Hell are like this and in fact are worse off: 'but worse'. The horrific atmosphere of Hell is conveyed in the phrase 'sweating selves'. For those 'lost', it is permanent. For Hopkins, perhaps it is just 'longer light's delay'. Some day **he will be redeemed**.

✒ Writing About the Poem

'Hopkins's poetry displays a deeply personal and passionate response to the human condition.' Discuss with reference to 'I Wake and Feel the Fell of Dark, Not Day', developing your answer with relevant quotations.

Sample Paragraph

Many people can identify with Hopkins suffering from depression. This is evident in 'I Wake and Feel the Fell of Dark, Not Day'. To me he is describing waking over and over again at night. The long vowel sounds in 'O what black hours' give an idea of the man tossing and turning, trying to sleep. Hopkins's personal relationship with God was the focus of his life. His passionate pleas to God, 'To dearest him', are useless, 'dead letters'. So he is devastated. He despises himself: 'the curse', 'dull dough'. The poem is filled with self-disgust. The only slight glimmer for the poet is that those condemned to Hell are in a worse situation 'and their scourge to be … their sweating selves; but worse'. Hopkins writes passionately about being human and the feeling of unworthiness.

EXAMINER'S COMMENT

This is a mature response to the assertion that Hopkins reacts deeply and passionately to the human condition: 'The poem is filled with self-disgust.' There is also in-depth exploration of the poem's sound effects: 'The long vowel sounds in "O what black hours" give an idea of the man tossing and turning'. Vocabulary and expression are impressive, adding to a successful, top-grade paragraph.

✒ Class/Homework Exercises

1. 'Hopkins charts an extraordinary mental journey in "I Wake and Feel the Fell of Dark, Not Day".' Write a short personal response to this statement, using reference to the text.
2. Hopkins graphically explores his deep feeling of despair through light and dark imagery in 'I Wake and Feel the Fell of Dark, Not Day'. Pick one image of brightness and one of darkness which you considered effective and explain your choice.

◉ Points to Consider

- **Feeling of abandonment by God; spiritual suffering.**
- **Depressive's experience of waking into night vividly conveyed by imagery.**
- **Long vowel sounds and dragging repetition emphasise the prevailing darkness.**
- **Sense of self-disgust balanced by the poet's concluding empathy.**

9 No Worst, There is None

GERARD MANLEY HOPKINS

No worst, there is none. Pitched past pitch of grief,
More pangs will, schooled at forepangs, wilder wring.
Comforter, where, where is your comforting?
Mary, mother of us, where is your relief?
My cries heave, herds-long; huddle in a main, a chief   5
Woe, world-sorrow; on an age-old anvil wince and sing –
Then lull, then leave off. Fury had shrieked 'No ling-
ering! Let me be fell: force I must be brief.'

   O the mind, mind has mountains; cliffs of fall
Frightful, sheer, no-man-fathomed. Hold them cheap   10
May who ne'er hung there. Nor does long our small
Durance deal with that steep or deep. Here! creep,
Wretch, under a comfort serves in a whirlwind: all
Life death does end and each day dies with sleep.

Pitched past pitch: pushed beyond
pangs: sudden pains.
schooled at forepangs: prepared by earlier sorrows.
Comforter: the Holy Spirit.

main: crowd.

fell: harsh; cruel.
force: perforce; therefore.

Durance: endurance; determination.
whirlwind: turmoil.

'frightful, sheer, no-man-fathomed'

👤 Personal Response

1. Comment on how Hopkins creates a sense of suffering and pessimism in the first four lines of the poem.
2. Discuss the effectiveness of the mountain images in lines 9–12.
3. In your opinion, is this a completely negative poem? Support your response by referring closely to the text.

👁 Critical Literacy

This Petrarchan sonnet was written in Hopkins's final years, at a time when he suffered increasingly from ill health and depression. It was one of a short series of sonnets of desolation, now known as the 'terrible sonnets' or 'dark sonnets'. In 'No Worst, There is None', we see a man experiencing deep psychological suffering and struggling with his religious faith. The poem reveals a raw honesty from someone close to despair.

The opening is curt and dramatic, revealing the intensity of Hopkins's suffering: 'No worst, there is none'. He is unable to imagine any greater agony. The emphatic use of monosyllables in line 1 reflects his **angry frustration**. Having reached what seems the threshold of torment, 'Pitched past pitch of grief', the poet dreads what lies ahead and the horrifying possibility that his pain ('schooled at forepangs') is likely to increase. The explosive force of the verb 'Pitched', combined with the harsh onomatopoeic and alliterative effects, heighten the sense of uncontrollable anguish. Both 'pitch' and 'pangs' are repeated, suggesting darkness and violent movement.

The rhythm changes in line 3. The three syllables of 'Comforter' slow the pace considerably. This is also a much softer word (in contrast to the harshness of the earlier sounds) and is echoed at the end of the line by 'comforting'. Hopkins's desolate plea to the Holy Spirit and the Virgin Mary emphasises **his hopelessness**: 'where, where is your comforting?' The tone, reminiscent of Christ's words on the Cross ('My God, why hast thou forsaken me?'), is both desperate and accusatory.

The poet likens his hollow cries for help to a herd of cattle in line 5. The metaphor highlights his lack of self-worth – his hopeless prayers 'heave' and 'huddle in a main'. He feels that his own suffering is part of a **wider universal 'world-sorrow'**. There is an indication here that Hopkins recognises that experiencing a crisis of faith can affect any Christian from time to time. This possibility is supported by the memorable image of the anvil being struck in line 6. He realises that the Christian experience involves suffering the guilt of sin and doubt to achieve spiritual happiness: 'on an age-old anvil wince and sing'.

But for the poet, any relief ('lull') from suffering is short-lived. His unavoidable feelings of shame and the pain of remorse are hauntingly personified: 'Fury had shrieked'. Once again, the severe sounds and the stretching of the phrase 'No lingering!' over two lines reinforce the relentlessness of Hopkins's troubled conscience.

This tormented tone is replaced by a more reflective one in the opening lines of the **sestet**, where Hopkins moves from the physical world of his 'cries' into the metaphorical landscape of towering mountains, with their dark, unknown depths. This **dramatic wasteland**, with its 'no-man-fathomed' cliffs, is terrifyingly portrayed. The poet reminds us that the terror of depression and separation from God cannot be appreciated by those 'who ne'er hung there'. The terror of being stranded on the 'steep or deep' rock face cannot be endured for long.

In the **last two lines**, Hopkins resigns himself to the **grim consolation** that all the depression and pain of this world will end with death, just as everyday troubles are eased by sleep. The final, chilling image of the wretched individual taking refuge from the exhausting whirlwind is less than optimistic. There is no relief from the terrible desolation and Hopkins's distracted prayers have yet to be answered.

✒ Writing About the Poem

'Hopkins's deep despair is evident in the 'terrible sonnets'. Discuss this statement, with particular reference to 'No Worst, There is None'.

Sample Paragraph

At the start of 'No Worst, There is None', the tone is totally despondent. The first sentence is short and snappy, emphasising that Hopkins has reached rock bottom. In many ways he was caught between his role as a priest and his human desires. Rhetorical questions emphasise his dependence on his religious faith – 'Comforter, where, where is your comforting?' This gives a heartfelt tone. Hopkins uses effective images which always make us feel sympathy for him, for example 'My cries heave, herds-long'. His tone is sorrowful and this is emphasised by comparisons. The prayers he offers to Heaven are just words: 'My cries heave, herds-long'.

EXAMINER'S COMMENT

This response includes a number of relevant examples of the varying tones throughout. Accurate quotations are effectively used in support and there is some good engagement with the poem. The expression was slightly awkward in places: 'This gives a heartfelt tone', and there is overuse of the verb 'emphasises'. Overall, a solid high-grade standard.

The end of the poem is even more negative. He uses a tone of despair as he compares himself to a wanderer finding shelter from a 'whirlwind'. His only comfort is sleep and eventually death, which will silence his inner pain.

✒ Class/Homework Exercises

1. The poet feels utterly abandoned by God in this poem. Trace the development of thought in 'No Worst, There is None' and discuss how Hopkins uses vivid description to explore his negative feelings. Develop your answer with close reference to the text.
2. Write your own personal response to 'No Worst, There is None'. Refer closely to the text in your answer.

⊙ Points to Consider

- **Most despairing and bleakest of 'terrible sonnets'.**
- **Alarming metaphors and powerful sound effects reveal inner suffering.**
- **Ups and downs of man's spiritual journey suggested by mountain imagery.**
- **Slightly optimistic end, death brings end to suffering for man.**

10 Thou Art Indeed Just, Lord, if I Contend

GERARD MANLEY HOPKINS

Justus quidem tu es, Domine, si disputem tecum: verumtamen justa loquar ad te: Quare via imporium prosperatur? &c.

Thou art indeed just, Lord, if I contend
With thee; but, sir, so what I plead is just.
Why do sinners' ways prosper? And why must
Disappointment all I endeavour end?
    Wert thou my enemy, O thou my friend,   5
How wouldst thou worse, I wonder, than thou dost
Defeat, thwart me? Oh, the sots and thralls of lust
Do in spare hours more thrive than I that spend,
Sir, life upon thy cause. See, banks and brakes
Now leaved how thick! laced they are again   10
With fretty chervil, look, and fresh wind shakes
Them; birds build – but not I build; no, but strain,
Time's eunuch, and not breed one work that wakes.
Mine, O thou lord of life, send my roots rain.

Latin quotation: Indeed you are just, O Lord, if I dispute with you; yet I would plead my case before you. Why do the wicked prosper? The first lines of the poem are a version of a Latin quotation that is taken from the Bible.
contend: dispute; argue; challenge.
sots: drunkards.
thralls: slaves.
brakes: thickets; groves of trees.
fretty: fretted; interlaced; the herb chervil has lacy leaves.
chervil: garden herb; the 'rejoicing leaf'.
eunuch: a castrated male, incapable of reproducing.

'laced they are again/ With fretty chervil, look'

👤 Personal Response

1. List the questions put to God. What tone is evident in each – anger, rebelliousness, reverence, trust, despair, etc.?
2. Is there a real sense of pain in the poem? At what point is it most deeply felt? Refer to the text in your response.
3. Is the image of God in the poem stern or not? Do you think that Hopkins had a good or bad relationship with God? Develop your answer with reference to this poem.

👁 Critical Literacy

'Thou Art Indeed Just, Lord, if I Contend' was written in 1889 at a time of great unhappiness for Hopkins in Dublin. He had written in a letter that 'all my undertakings miscarry'. This poem is a pessimistic yet powerful plea for help from God. It was written just three months before he died.

This sonnet opens with the **formal language of the courtroom** as the poet, in clipped tones, poses three questions in the octet. With growing frustration, he asks God to explain why sinners seem to prosper. Why is he, the poet, continually disappointed? If God was his enemy instead of his friend, how could he be any worse off? God, he allows, is just, but he contends that his own cause is also just. The language is that of a coherent, measured argument: 'sir', 'I plead'.

However, in lines 3–4, 'and why must/Disappointment all I endeavour end?', the inversion of the natural order makes the reader concentrate on the notable point that 'Disappointment' is the 'end' result of all the work the poet has done. But **the tone remains rational**, as Hopkins points out to 'sir' that the worst doing their worst 'more thrive' than he does. But his frustration at his plight makes the line of the octet spill over into the sestet, as the poet complains that he has spent his life doing God's will ('life upon thy cause').

The sestet has the ring of the real voice breaking through as Hopkins urgently requests God to 'See', 'look'. Here is **nature busily thriving**, producing, building, breeding, growing. The movement and pace of continuing growth and regrowth is caught in the line 'Now leaved how thick! laced they are again'. The **alliteration** of 'banks and brakes', 'birds build' vividly portrays the abundance of nature, as does the **assonance** of 'fretty' and 'fresh'. **Flowing run-on lines** describe the surge of growing nature. Hopkins is the exception in this fertile scene. The negatives 'not', 'no', the punctuation of semi-colon and comma and the inversion of the phrase 'but not I build; no, but strain' depict the **fruitless efforts of the poet to create**. The dramatic, sterile image of 'Time's eunuch', the castrated male, contrasts the poet's unhappy state of unsuccessful effort with the ease of fruitful nature. Time is kind to nature, enabling it to renew, but the poet cannot create one work: 'not breed one work that wakes'.

The last line of the poem pleads for help and rescue. An image of a drought-stricken plant looking for life-giving water is used to describe the poet's plight of unsuccessful poetic creativity. **He looks to the 'lord of life'** for release. Hopkins had written in one of his final letters, 'If I could produce work … but it kills me to be time's eunuch and never to beget'. It is intriguing that someone of such great faith can argue ('contend') so vehemently with God. Hopkins stretches the disciplined structure of the sonnet form to echo his frustration as he strains to create.

✒ Writing About the Poem

'Hopkins's poetry deals with the theme that God's will is a mystery to us.' Discuss this statement, developing your response with relevant quotation from 'Thou Art Indeed Just, Lord, if I Contend'.

Sample Paragraph

In 'Thou Art Indeed Just, Lord', Hopkins asks God several questions: 'Why do sinners' ways prosper? And why must/Disappointment all I endeavour end?' The poet is frustrated that God's will is such a mystery and that so much suffering is allowed to happen in the world. This mood of puzzlement continues as he urgently points out how nature is thriving ('fretty chervil', 'birds build'). But he, in contrast, is far from happy. He concludes with the striking image of himself as 'Time's eunuch', a castrated slave unable to reproduce. Hopkins makes one final plea to God to nourish his infertile 'roots' with 'rain'. The alliteration associates him closely with the fertile world of nature, 'banks and brakes'. In the end, he accepts that God is the 'lord of life', his divine plan a mystery to us, but we can still trust in his love and forgiveness.

> **EXAMINER'S COMMENT**
>
> *Close reading of the text is evident in this insightful paragraph - particularly in the developed discussion on the theme of doubting God's will. Effective use is made of Hopkins's imagery and alliteration. Expression is assured and there is supportive quotation throughout. An impressive top-grade standard.*

✒ Class/Homework Exercises

1. Hopkins's innovative poetic style makes his work accessible to the modern reader. How true is this of 'Thou Art Indeed Just, Lord, if I Contend'? Use reference to the poem in your answer.
2. Hopkins complains and questions throughout this poem. What conclusion does he reach in the end? Did you find this ending satisfactory or not? Give reasons for your opinion.

◉ Points to Consider

- **Deeply personal and direct address to God.**
- **Hurt and frustration as poet wrestles with his religious faith.**
- **Struggle to control anger and frustration.**
- **Effective use of alliteration and vivid imagery.**
- **Contrast between abundance of nature and man's infertility.**
- **Concluding prayer to enable creativity to blossom.**

Sample Leaving Cert Questions on Hopkin's Poetry

1. Discuss how Hopkins's unique approach to language conveys a sense of his intense spiritual awareness. Develop your response with reference to the poems by Gerard Manley Hopkins on your course.
2. 'Gerard Manley Hopkins celebrates the wonder and beauty of nature through the effective use of evocative visual and aural imagery.' Discuss this view, developing your answer with reference to the poems by Hopkins on your course.
3. 'Hopkins's distinctive poetic style highlights his struggle with what he believes to be important truths.' Discuss this statement, developing your response with reference to the themes and language evident in the poems by Gerard Manley Hopkins on your course.

How do I organise my answer?

(Sample question 1)

Discuss how Hopkins's unique approach to language conveys a sense of his intense spiritual awareness. Develop your response with reference to the poems by Gerard Manley Hopkins on your course.

Sample Plan 1

Intro: *(Stance: agree with viewpoint in the question)* Hopkins's poems highlight his personal religious vision. His innovative poetry uses rich imagery and stunning sound effects. While celebrating God's creation, he also acknowledges man's suffering and weakness.

Point 1: *(Celebration of uniqueness – vivid imagery, alliteration)* 'The Windhover' celebrates the distinctive bird as a symbol of Christ the Saviour. Rich alliteration describes its special appearance ('wimpling wing').

Point 2: *(Prayerful praise – striking sound effects)* 'Pied Beauty', another powerful hymn of praise to God ('Glory be to God') for the dazzling variety of nature ('dappled things'). Emphatic language shows man and nature in harmony ('Landscape plotted and pieced – fold, fallow, and plough'). Simple confident conclusion ('Praise him').

Understanding the Prescribed Poetry Question

Marks are awarded using the PCLM Marking Scheme:
P = 15; C = 15; L = 15; M = 5
Total = 50

- **P** (Purpose = 15 marks) refers to the set question and is the launch pad for the answer. This involves engaging with all aspects of the question. Both theme and language must be addressed, although not necessarily equally.
- **C** (Coherence = 15 marks) refers to the organisation of the developed response and the use of accurate, relevant quotation. Paragraphing is essential.
- **L** (Language = 15 marks) refers to the student's skill in controlling language throughout the answer.
- **M** (Mechanics = 5 marks) refers to spelling and grammar.
- Although no specific number of poems is required, students usually discuss at least 3 or 4 in their written responses.
- Aim for at least 800 words, to be completed within 45–50 minutes.

POETRY FOCUS

NOTE
In keeping with the PCLM approach, the student has to take a stance by agreeing, disagreeing or partially agreeing that Hopkins's:
- **unique approach to language** (experimental expression, vibrant imagery, lively sound effects, emphatic tones, sprung rhythm, inscape, etc.)

... conveys:
- **a powerful sense of his intense spiritual awareness** (finding God's presence in the world, reflections on suffering and destruction, belief in prayer and redemption, etc.)

Point 3: *(Despair/optimism – startling opening)* In contrast 'No Worst, There is None' shows the negative impact of suffering in this imperfect world. Poem concludes with a glimmer of hope that each day's suffering is eased by sleep ('each day dies with sleep'). Troubles do end.

Point 4: *(Delight in/concern for wilderness – colloquialism, onomatopoeia, run-on lines)* 'Inversnaid' located in the wilds of the Scottish Highlands. An earnest plea is made for man to stop destroying the natural beauty of wild places ('Let them be left').

Conclusion: Hopkins creates dynamic poetry celebrating nature as God's wonderful creation. He acknowledges the sin, suffering and destruction of this world but believes a merciful God will save it. Stunning visual imagery and sound effects involve the reader in Hopkins's intense vision.

Sample Paragraph: Point 1

Hopkins celebrates an extraordinary bird in 'The Windhover'. It soars on the wind in a cross shape, a dramatic symbol of Christianity. The poem's sub-title, 'To Christ our Lord', shows Hopkins's own deep religious faith. The bird reflects God's glory. Its appearance is highlighted through the alliterative description of its outstretched 'wimpling wing'. Hopkins believed Christ was crucified to save the world. The verb 'Buckle' has two opposite meanings – fall apart and pull together. It describes the mysterious movement of the bird as it breaks from its gliding motion to swoop down on its prey. This verb also refers to God descending to earth to save mankind with tongues of flame, 'the fire that breaks from thee'. To the poet, the bird is a magnificent symbol of Christ who will be his defender ('chevalier') against the evil of this world. The poem concludes in a riot of Christ's colours, 'gold-vermilion'.

EXAMINER'S COMMENT
A focused and analytical paragraph. Effective use of selected text references supports discussion points about the poet's central theme of spiritual awareness and his distinctive language use. Quotes are skilfully interwoven into the main commentary. Confident, varied expression throughout adds to the top-grade quality.

(Sample question 2)

'Gerard Manley Hopkins celebrates the wonder and beauty of nature through the effective use of evocative visual and aural imagery.' Discuss this view, developing your answer with reference to the poems by Hopkins on your course.

Sample Plan 2

Intro: *(Stance: agree with viewpoint in the question)* Hopkins creates inspired visions of nature's abundant variety. He also contrasts nature's ability to renew itself with humanity's destructive actions.

Point 1: *(Appreciation of natural world – elaborate wordplay)* 'God's Grandeur' reveals poet's wonder at nature's power to grow again in contrast to his dismay at human destruction ('wears man's smudge'). Yet God's reassuring presence in nature guards like the bird protecting its young ('broods with warm breast').

Point 2: *(Admiration of nature's/humans' beauty/diversity – striking imagery)* 'As Kingfishers Catch Fire, Dragonflies Draw Flame' captures two of nature's most brilliant creatures, the kingfisher and dragonfly in powerful images ('catch fire', 'draw flame'). Aural effects echo a variety of sounds ('ring', 'tells', 'fling').

Point 3: *(Exuberant reflection on the natural world – aural music, inscape)* 'Spring' uses imaginative sound effects to express joy – alliteration ('long and lovely and lush'), assonance ('weeds', 'wheels'), onomatopoeia ('wring'). Close observation results in inscape, capturing the essence of an object, such as the shine on leaves ('glassy').

Point 4: *(Contrast fertile nature/sterile man – legal language, unusual syntax)* 'Thou Art Indeed Just, Lord, if I Contend' directs accusatory questions at God ('Why do sinners' ways prosper?') Sharp contrast in imagery between nature's fertility and humanity's sterility.

Conclusion: Hopkins explores the wonder of nature through exuberant description and stunning aural effects. This leads him to consider humans' destruction of nature as well as our inability to constantly create.

> **NOTE**
> In keeping with the PCLM approach, the student has to take a stance by agreeing, disagreeing or partially agreeing that Hopkins:
> - **celebrates the wonder and beauty of nature** (excited appreciation of nature's richness and diversity, its regenerative power, God's astonishing creation, etc.)
>
> ... through the effective use of:
> - **evocative visual and aural imagery** (energetic language, vivid visual images and sounds, intense rhythms, run-on lines, inscape, etc.)

Sample Paragraph: Point 4

'Thou Art Indeed Just' opens with Hopkins asking God challenging questions, 'Why do sinners' ways prosper?' The awkward order of words highlights the poet's frustration at his own useless efforts, 'why must/Disappointment all I endeavour end?' Meanwhile, nature is thriving. This is suggested in run-on lines and vivid visual imagery, 'laced they are again/With fretty chervil'. Hopkins describes the wild beauty of the natural scene around him. The wind shakes the 'banks and brakes' but they still remain intact. It is here that 'birds build' – unlike the poet who is unable to

> **EXAMINER'S COMMENT**
> *As part of a full essay, this is a solid high-grade paragraph that shows some insightful engagement with the poem. The commentary on the effectiveness of Hopkins's imagery is very good – although the rejuvenating power of nature deserves a little more development. Supportive and accurate quotations are used well and expression is controlled throughout.*

build anything. The sterile image, 'Time's eunuch', describes his hopeless attempts to produce work. At the end of the poem, Hopkins's reflections on the wonder of nature widen out to include the many different emotions experienced by human beings when we observe nature's beauty and mystery.

> **EXAM FOCUS**
> - As you may not be familiar with some of the poems referred to in the sample plans, substitute poems that you have studied closely.
> - Key points about a particular poem can be developed over more than one paragraph.
> - Paragraphs may also include cross-referencing and discussion of more than one poem.
> - Remember that there is no single 'correct' answer to poetry questions, so always be confident in expressing your own considered response.

Leaving Cert Sample Essay

'Hopkins's distinctive poetic style highlights his struggle with what he believes to be important truths.' Discuss this statement, developing your response with reference to the themes and language evident in the poems by Gerard Manley Hopkins on your course.

> **INDICATIVE MATERIAL**
>
> - **Hopkins's distinctive style** (experimental language – sound, imagery, symbolism, repetition, sprung rhythm, dramatic effects, range of tones and poetic forms, etc.)
>
> … highlights:
>
> - **his struggle** (conflicting feelings, intense sense of delight and dejection, self-doubt, etc.)
>
> … with:
>
> - **important truths** (deeply held beliefs – God as Creator, celebration of nature, as source of salvation, etc.)

Sample Essay

1. Hopkins is known for his unusual writing style. His use of language is odd and unexpected. He often omits words and includes vivid visual images and dramatic sound effects. Two key themes in his poetry are the beauty of nature and his deep belief in God. Hopkins engages readers in his personal struggle with religious faith in several of his poems.

2. In 'Spring', Hopkins expresses great delight in the mystery and beauty of the season. He believed that loving nature was almost like loving God, its creator. This is seen in the dynamic description of common weeds, 'long and lovely and lush'. He draws attention to the intense blue of the sky, a 'rush with richness'. Hopkins links all this 'juice' and 'joy'. It's all evidence of God's work. As a Jesuit priest, he believes this is a glimpse of the earth like it was before Adam and Eve were expelled from the Garden of Eden. This idea of innocent purity is further highlighted by references to Mary, the mother of God, 'O maid's child' and 'Mayday'. May is a special month. It is traditionally associated with the worship of Mary, to whom Hopkins had a special devotion.

3. Hopkins uses language in various ways to express spiritual beliefs through sensuous imagery. He is fascinated by the sounds of nature. The high-pitched piercing cry of the thrush is described using slender vowel assonance, 'rinse and wring'. The deep blue sky sweeps down to meet the tree branches overhead – which is suggested in the sibilance of 'brush'. Throughout the poem, he uses language to capture the excitement of the moment. In some cases, Hopkins uses nouns as verbs, for example, 'leaves' and 'blooms'. Run-on lines re-create the growth and activity happening at springtime. In pushing language beyond the usual limits, Hopkins successfully captures the spirit of the magical spring season, created by God.

4. 'Felix Randal' was written during a very unhappy period of the poet's life when he cared for sick people in a slum area of Liverpool. Man replaces nature here as the main subject of the poem. The young blacksmith is first described in his prime at the height of his powers. This is done through alliteration and compound adjectives, 'big-boned' and 'hardy-handsome'. Felix used metal for horses' shoes by beating out iron. But his health has now failed and he has suffered terrible sickness, 'Fatal four disorders, fleshed there, all contended'. The unusual order of words is typical of Hopkins. In a way, he is trying to draw attention to how life can be cruel and that nobody can ever fully understand why there is suffering in the world.

5. However, the poet's deep faith consoles him. He sees Felix as a man who has to become a 'child' to enter heaven. Hopkins's earlier attitude seemed detached, 'O he is dead then?' – but this is now replaced by deep compassion for another human being. He uses the local dialect, 'all road ever he offended'. He hopes that God will forgive Felix for whatever sins he has committed and will welcome him into heaven. Hopkins ends the poem by celebrating the gift of life while it lasts. He remembers when Felix Randal was in full health and had little 'forethought' of his death, standing at the forge when he worked hard, making a 'bright and battering sandal' or horseshoe for a great drayhorse.

6. 'I Wake and Feel the Fell of Dark, Not Day' is one of the so-called 'terrible sonnets' written during the poet's unhappy time working in Dublin. He draws attention to the personal pain of sleepless nights by using emphatic alliteration, 'I wake and feel the fell of dark, not day'. The unsuccessful prayers for relief from this torment are suggested by the harsh phrase, 'cries countless'. Hopkins uses first person pronouns to stress his pain, 'I am gall. I am heartburn'. While he acknowledges God's love, he complains that he is trapped in an endless cycle. All he can taste is his own 'bitter' self and he seems to be cursed. The only glimmer of hope is his realisation that he has a possibility of salvation unlike those souls cast down to the fires of Hell, their suffering vividly described as 'sweating selves'.

7. Hopkins writes passionately about the beauty of nature which to him is the physical symbol of God's glory. But he also writes about the darker aspects of life, sickness, suffering and feelings of abandonment. Whether celebrating God's presence in beauty or struggling with pessimism, Hopkins's innovative use of language allows readers to engage with his deeply-held conviction that God, not man, is the creator of the universe.

(770 words)

> **EXAMINER'S COMMENT**
>
> Good solid response that explores the main aspects of the question (Hopkins's style, his struggle and personal truths). The poet's effective use of visual and aural imagery is a particular strength of the essay. While some points could be developed in greater detail (e.g. regarding the acceptance of God's will in paragraph 5), discussion is generally sustained and supported with suitable reference. Apart from notelike commentary (paragraph 2) and some repetition ('draw attention to'), overall expression is good.

GRADE: H1
P = 15/15
C = 13/15
L = 12/15
M = 5/5
Total = 45/50

👓 Revision Overview

'God's Grandeur'
In this dramatic sonnet, Hopkins explores how God's reassuring presence is infused in the world of nature.

'Spring' (OL)
A beautifully crafted reflection on the beauty, innocence and spiritual significance of nature.

'As Kingfishers Catch Fire, Dragonflies Draw Flame'
Central themes include nature's beauty, variety and uniqueness. Hopkins relates mankind's ultimate spiritual purpose to the natural world.

'The Windhover'
The sense of religious wonder is a key feature of this striking sonnet in which Hopkins presents the beauty of nature as a compelling metaphor for Christ's beauty.

'Pied Beauty'
Another hymn to creation. Hopkins praises the variety and beauty of the world, glorifying the infinite power of God and the hope that can be found in faith.

'Felix Randal'
Italian sonnet tracing the relationship between a spiritual healer and the sufferer. Both complement each other in the act of attaining eternal salvation.

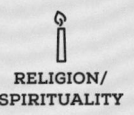

'Inversnaid' (OL)
Hopkins wonders what would become of the world without unspoiled remote landscapes and he urges people to retain such beautiful places.

'I Wake and Feel the Fell of Dark, Not Day'
In this 'dark sonnet', Hopkins explores the theme of exile from God, the personal doubt that many believers feel at times.

'No Worst, There is None'
Another of the 'terrible sonnets'. As a Christian, Hopkins is intensely aware of the spiritual torment of feeling alienated from God.

'Thou Art Indeed Just, Lord, if I Contend'
Another powerful examination of the mystery of faith. Hopkins questions the existence of evil in the world but concludes by placing his own trust in God.

💬 Last Words

'What you look hard at seems to look hard at you.'
G. M. Hopkins

'Hopkins is more concerned with putting across his perceptions than with fulfilling customary expectations of grammar.'
Robert Bernard Martin

'Design, pattern, or what I am in the habit of calling inscape is what I above all aim at in poetry.'
G. M. Hopkins

GERARD MANLEY HOPKINS

NATURE | MEANING OF LIFE | SUFFERING | RELIGION/SPIRITUALITY | TRANSIENCE

POETRY FOCUS

Patrick Kavanagh
1904–1967

'What does matter is that if you have anything worthwhile in you, any talent, you should deliver it.'

Born in 1904 near Inniskeen, Co. Monaghan, in the shadow of Ulster's 'hungry hills', Patrick Kavanagh left school at the age of 13, apparently destined to plough the 'stony-grey soil' rather than write about it. But his interest in literature won out – 'I dabbled in verse,' he said, 'and it became my life.' Many of his poems celebrate the simple beauty and mystery of nature. In 1936, his first book, *Ploughman and Other Poems*, was published, and in 1938 he followed this up with the autobiographical *The Green Fool*. For over 20 years, Kavanagh worked on the small family farm before moving to Dublin in 1939 to try to establish himself as a writer. His epic poem, 'The Great Hunger', was published in 1942. Kavanagh's reputation as a poet is based largely on the lyrical quality of his work, his mastery of language and form and his ability to transform the ordinary into something of significance. He is widely regarded as one of the most influential Irish poets, whose main achievement was to give an authentic voice to rural Ireland during the 1940s and 1950s.

Investigate Further

To find out more about Patrick Kavanagh, or to hear readings of his poems, you could do a search of some useful websites, such as YouTube, BBC Poetry, poetryfoundation.org, or access additional material on this page of your eBook.

Prescribed Poems

○ **1 'Inniskeen Road: July Evening'**
This well-known sonnet focuses on Kavanagh's role as a poet and his relationship with the local rural community in Co. Monaghan.
Page 196

○ **2 'Shancoduff' (OL)**
One of Kavanagh's favourite poems, it illustrates his poetic appreciation of ordinary life in the Monaghan countryside.
Page 200

○ **3 from 'The Great Hunger'**
This long, powerful piece traces the life and times of Patrick Maguire, an elderly bachelor farmer. Kavanagh's critical view of Irish rural society is grim and disturbing.
Page 204

○ **4 'Advent'**
Originally titled 'Renewal', the poem uses a two-sonnet structure to explore Kavanagh's religious experience of the Advent season.
Page 210

○ **5 'A Christmas Childhood' (OL)**
Kavanagh describes a memorable Christmas when he was six years old and recalls how his 'child poet' associated the occasion with the birth of Christ in Bethlehem.
Page 214

○ **6 'Epic'**
Based on an actual dispute over a small area of land in Co. Monaghan, the poem addresses wider aspects of conflict and the theme of poetic inspiration.
Page 219

○ **7 'Canal Bank Walk'**
Written after a lengthy stay in hospital, in this poem Kavanagh is keen to enjoy the wonderful gifts of nature, poetry and the overwhelming experience of being alive.
Page 222

○ **8 'Lines Written on a Seat on the Grand Canal, Dublin'**
Another sonnet expressing Kavanagh's wish to be commemorated in one of his favourite places. Characteristically, he celebrates the wonder and greatness of ordinary things.
Page 226

○ **9 'The Hospital'**
After recovering from a serious illness, the poet considers his new-found appreciation of natural beauty and the mystery of life itself while time allows.
Page 230

○ **10 'On Raglan Road'**
Set on the streets of Dublin, this bittersweet ballad of unrequited love reveals much that is of interest about Kavanagh's own personality.
Page 233

(OL) indicates poems that are also prescribed for the Ordinary Level course.

1 Inniskeen Road: July Evening

The bicycles go by in twos and threes –
There's a dance in Billy Brennan's barn tonight,
And there's the half-talk code of mysteries
And the wink-and-elbow language of delight.
Half-past eight and there is not a spot　　　　　5
Upon a mile of road, no shadow thrown
That might turn out a man or woman, not
A footfall tapping secrecies of stone.

I have what every poet hates in spite
Of all the solemn talk of contemplation.　　　　10
Oh, Alexander Selkirk knew the plight
Of being king and government and nation.
A road, a mile of kingdom, I am king
Of banks and stones and every blooming thing.

Title: the townland of Mucker near Inniskeen, Co. Monaghan was Kavanagh's birthplace. He lived there on the small family farm until the late 1930s.

Billy Brennan's barn: a local farmhouse where country dances took place.

solemn talk of contemplation: poets are often said to be deep thinkers.
Alexander Selkirk: famous Scottish sailor (1676–1721) marooned on an uninhabited Pacific island for five years. His experience was the model for Daniel Defoe's novel *Robinson Crusoe*.
blooming: flowering; also a colloquial expletive expressing impatience.

'a mile of kingdom'

👤 Personal Response

1. There is a mood of excitement in the poem's opening four lines. How does Kavanagh's use of language achieve this effect?
2. Comment on the effectiveness of the comparison with Alexander Selkirk.
3. In your opinion, what are the thoughts and feelings expressed by Kavanagh in the last two lines of the poem?

👁 Critical Literacy

Taken from Kavanagh's first collection, *Ploughman and Other Poems*, this sonnet provides an interesting presentation of the poet's relationship with nature and the local community as well as giving a glimpse of Irish rural life in the 1930s. Kavanagh's dual role – as both a member of his local community and a commentator on society – is succinctly dramatised. The octave (first eight lines) focuses on the local environment, while the sestet (final six lines) sums up Kavanagh's own reflections on his life as a poet.

Lines 1–2 set the scene as young people from Kavanagh's parish make their way to the local dance. **Colloquial language and energetic rhythms echo everyday speech**: 'There's a dance in Billy Brennan's barn tonight'. The alliterative 'b' sound and use of the present tense add to the mood of lively anticipation. Kavanagh's diction becomes more poetic in lines 3–4 as he makes a sceptical observation about 'the half-talk code of mysteries/ And the wink-and-elbow language of delight'. In distancing himself from the young people cycling to the dance, the poet emphasises his own sense of exclusion. Examine the tone Kavanagh uses. Is it ironic, cynical, superior, self-pitying? It's difficult to know if he is enjoying the excited gestures of the carefree passers-by or if he is envious of them – or both.

The social atmosphere and relaxed mood of the opening quatrain is followed by a more **reflective commentary** in lines 5–8. Left alone on the roadside, Kavanagh is drawn by the intense solitude ('no shadow thrown') of his surroundings. There is a certain poignancy to his loneliness, especially since he seems all too aware of the nature of his isolation. But although the poet is detached from human company ('man or woman'), he has the comfort of being close to nature – the 'secrecies of stone'. Of course, the secrets are never disclosed. Is Kavanagh thinking about the wonders of the natural world or the secret lives of the young dance-goers? Or even of his own poetic imagination? We can only guess. At any rate, the slower pace of this second quatrain, combined with the broad vowel assonance, contribute much to the pensive tone and mood of bittersweet alienation.

The sestet offers the poet's own explanation for most of the questions raised in the opening eight lines. Addressing the reader directly, Kavanagh outlines the reality of what it means to be a poet – and for him it is a **double-edged sword**. He 'hates' the popular perception that poets are introspective philosophers constantly immersed in serious 'contemplation'. In line 11, he compares himself to the marooned sailor Alexander Selkirk. While the reference seems to be only half-serious, it serves to highlight the artist's role and relationship with society. Writing is a solitary occupation (a 'plight'), but it also guarantees the freedom and independence 'Of being king and government and nation'.

The ironic tone of lines 13–14 reminds readers of the **contradictions of the poet's life**. As the self-styled 'king' of 'every blooming thing', Kavanagh illustrates the conflicting aspects of a literary life. The pun on 'blooming' underlines both the positive and negative sides of being a writer. Kavanagh may be somewhat removed from his own community, but he is gifted with a creative imagination which allows him to appreciate the wonders of nature.

✒ Writing About the Poem

From your reading of 'Inniskeen Road: July Evening', what do you learn about Kavanagh himself? Refer to the text in your answer.

Sample Paragraph

Kavanagh understands he is different to the other young men in his area. I think Kavanagh knows he is different and he admits that he is cut off from what he calls 'the wink-and-elbow language of delight'. But he acknowledges that this is the price a poet must pay. He is an observer and seems to almost enjoy being unlike the others. At the same time, he is honest enough to admit that it is a lonely life. The ending of the poem tells me most about Kavanagh. He seems resigned to his 'plight' because he is at one with nature. In fact he jokes that he is 'king/Of banks and stones and every blooming thing'. I find the tone good-humoured and proof that he was happy with the simple joys of Inniskeen. He has come to terms with loneliness and is making the most of life.

EXAMINER'S COMMENT

This is a clear, well-sustained response that ranges over the text in search of appropriate evidence about the poet's personality. There is some good personal engagement and a lively style throughout. Identifes several aspects of Kavanagh's character, including his role as observer, his loneliness and closeness to nature. Good mid-grade standard.

✏ Class/Homework Exercises

1. One literary critic described 'Inniskeen Road: July Evening' as 'a love poem to a place, written towards the end of the affair'. Write your response to this comment, using close reference to the text of the poem.
2. In your opinion, what is the dominant mood in the poem? Is it happy, sad, reflective or bittersweet? Develop your answer with reference to the text.

◉ Points to Consider

- Key themes include the poet's relationship with society and rural life.
- Beauty and mystery of the natural world.
- Evocative moods: alienation, self-pity, joy, pride.
- Sonnet form, colloquial language and rhythms.
- Sensuous visual details and aural imagery.

2 Shancoduff

Title: meaning Old Black Hollow, from the Irish words 'sean' (old) and 'dubh' (black).

My black hills have never seen the sun rising,
Eternally they look north towards Armagh.
Lot's wife would not be salt if she had been
Incurious as my black hills that are happy
When dawn whitens Glassdrummond chapel.   5

My hills hoard the bright shillings of March
While the sun searches in every pocket.
They are my Alps and I have climbed the Matterhorn
With a sheaf of hay for three perishing calves
In the field under the Big Forth of Rocksavage.   10

The sleety winds fondle the rushy beards of Shancoduff
While the cattle-drovers sheltering in the Featherna Bush
Look up and say: 'Who owns them hungry hills
That the water-hen and snipe must have forsaken?
A poet? Then by heavens he must be poor.'   15
I hear and is my heart not badly shaken?

Lot's wife: reference to the Bible story where the wife of Lot was turned into a pillar of salt for disobeying God.

shillings: small silver coins from old Irish currency.

Matterhorn: the highest peak of the Alps, a mountain range in Switzerland.

sleety: icy rain.

snipe: marshland bird.

'My black hills have never seen the sun rising'

👤 Personal Response

1. Choose one interesting image from the poem that you find appealing. Briefly explain your choice.
2. What effect does the naming of local places tell you about Kavanagh and his relationship with the area in which he grew up?
3. What evidence is there of Kavanagh's self-deprecating humour in this poem? Why do you think he uses this?

👁 Critical Literacy

Kavanagh had a love–hate relationship with the place he grew up in, Inniskeen. Shancoduff, a north-facing hill, is shown in winter. Kavanagh's family had bought a small farm there, not far from his home. His brother, Peter, said Kavanagh regarded it as 'wonderland'. The view stretched fifteen miles to the Mourne Mountains.

Like an indulgent lover, Kavanagh turns the negatives of this hostile place into positives, just as a lover refuses to see any faults in his loved one. The hills may be drab and 'Incurious' and mean (they 'hoard'), but they are his. The ownership is stressed in the protective, possessive adjective 'My': 'My black hills', 'My hills', 'my Alps'. He recognises that the land will remain 'Eternally' while the people come and go.

He personifies this land with carefully chosen verbs and adjectives: 'look', 'Incurious', 'happy', 'hoard'. Kavanagh loves the local. He sees magic here as he describes sunrise over the little country church in line 5: 'dawn whitens Glassdrummond chapel'. The place becomes luminous and radiant. These hills can't be bothered to look at the sun; 'they look north'. The poet turns their lack of curiosity into a positive, saying look at what happened to Lot's wife for her curiosity – she gazed at a forbidden sight, the destruction of the sinning cities Sodom and Gomorrah, and was turned into a pillar of salt. Kavanagh, like his hills, also turned his face, refusing to accept the literary scene in Dublin.

The **litany of place names** is a feature of Kavanagh's poetry, and points to the pride he had in Shancoduff. To him, these hills were as important and as impressive as the Alps, the famous mountain range in Switzerland. The polysyllabic sounds of these place names are masculine, threatening, full of the fierce pride of a border place as they stand surveying all before them. An ordinary act of feeding the calves becomes a heroic feat in this place in line 8: 'I have climbed the Matterhorn'. This is an example of Kavanagh's use of **hyperbole**. These hills are rebellious; they won't follow the rhythm of nature, they don't change in tune with the seasons. Like misers, they 'hoard' the bright pockets of ice and snow while the springtime sunshine desperately tries to thaw the land. The exasperation of the sun's effort is vividly caught in the description of the sun searching the pockets of the hills. These miserly hills won't give up their 'shillings', yet Kavanagh praises their thriftiness.

The tenderness of the lover is conveyed in the verb 'fondle', as Kavanagh again personifies this bleak place in line 11: the 'rushy beards of Shancoduff'. But **a negative note is struck as the drovers and farmers sneer** at 'them hungry hills'. They look dispassionately at this place, as the land is so unproductive. The use of direct speech brings the conflict to life, as they criticise not only the land but the profession of the owner, 'a poet'. To these men, he must be mad. **The rhetorical question at the end shows Kavanagh's devastation at this criticism**, rather like a lover being made to face the reality that his loved one is ugly.

Reality, like the biting winds, is piercing the poet's illusions: 'I hear and is my heart not badly shaken?' Is it the lack of potential for farming or the fear that these hills will not provide sufficient creative stimulus that leaves the poet 'badly shaken'? Whatever the answer, **these places pushed Irish poetry into a new direction**, showing that an emphasis on the ordinary is a worthwhile subject for poetry.

Writing About the Poem

'The relationship between place and person is central to the poetry of Patrick Kavanagh.' Discuss this statement in relation to the poem 'Shancoduff'.

Sample Paragraph

Although Kavanagh has a love–hate relationship with his birthplace, it is this very conflict that inspired him to write. At this time, in the 1930s, the poet was looked at as someone odd. We hear this in the direct speech of the cattle-drovers, as they looked disparagingly at Shancoduff and its owner. 'Who owns them hungry hills … A poet?' They speak as if he wouldn't know what to do with the land. This criticism hurt Kavanagh: 'I hear and is my heart not badly shaken?' This protective attitude is evident in the repetition of the adjective 'my'. He thinks it is good that the hills are 'Incurious'. He feels they are happy once they see the chapel of Glassdrummond shining in the dawn light. The love he has for the place is evident as we see the importance he places on the poor little hill, 'my Alps'. Shancoduff is not beautiful, with its 'rushy beards', but to the poet, it is. This poem is rooted in the harsh countryside of Monaghan, and this place is firmly rooted in Kavanagh's heart.

EXAMINER'S COMMENT

A sensitive reading of the poem. Well-written top-grade standard, strongly supported throughout with relevant quotations. The candidate has discussed the importance of this place to the poet, and has therefore fulfilled the required task.

✒ Class/Homework Exercises

1. Would you consider the poetry of Kavanagh to be the poetry of 'rediscovery and celebration'? Discuss this claim in relation to the poem 'Shancoduff'.
2. In your opinion, does Kavanagh present an appealing picture of the rural landscape in this poem? Explain your response, using reference to the text.

⊙ Points to Consider

- The poet's life as an outsider and the essential value of nature are central themes.
- Kavanagh's visionary experience transcends the ordinary.
- Effective use of direct language, contrasts, personification, descriptive visual imagery and rich sound effects.
- Range of references: place names, biblical allusions.
- Initial dark tone develops into defiance and celebration.

3 from The Great Hunger

Clay is the word and clay is the flesh
Where the potato-gatherers like mechanized scare-crows move
Along the side-fall of the hill – Maguire and his men.
If we watch them an hour is there anything we can prove
Of life as it is broken-backed over the Book   5
Of Death? Here crows gabble over worms and frogs
And the gulls like old newspapers are blown clear of the hedges, luckily.
Is there some light of imagination in these wet clods?
Or why do we stand here shivering?
                          Which of these men   10
Loved the light and the queen
Too long virgin? Yesterday was summer. Who was it promised marriage to himself
Before apples were hung from the ceilings for Hallowe'en?
We will wait and watch the tragedy to the last curtain,
Till the last soul passively like a bag of wet clay   15
Rolls down the side of the hill, diverted by the angles
Where the plough missed or a spade stands, straitening the way.

A dog lying on a torn jacket under a heeled-up cart,
A horse nosing along the posied headland, trailing
A rusty plough. Three heads hanging between wide-apart   20
Legs. October playing a symphony on a slack wire paling.
Maguire watches the drills flattened out
And the flints that lit a candle for him on a June altar
Flameless. The drills slipped by and the days slipped by
And he trembled his head away and ran free from the world's halter,   25
And thought himself wiser than any man in the townland
When he laughed over pints of porter
Of how he came free from every net spread
In the gaps of experience. He shook a knowing head
And pretended to his soul   30
That children are tedious in hurrying fields of April
Where men are spanging across wide furrows,
Lost in the passion that never needs a wife –
The pricks that pricked were the pointed pins of harrows.

Children scream so loud that the crows could bring 35
The seed of an acre away with crow-rude jeers.
Patrick Maguire, he called his dog and he flung a stone in the air
And hallooed the birds away that were the birds of the years.
Turn over the weedy clods and tease out the tangled skeins.
What is he looking for there? 40
He thinks it is a potato, but we know better
Than his mud-gloved fingers probe in this insensitive hair.

'Move forward the basket and balance it steady
In this hollow. Pull down the shafts of that cart, Joe,
And straddle the horse,' Maguire calls. 45
'The wind's over Brannagan's, now that means rain.
Graip up some withered stalks and see that no potato falls
Over the tail-board going down the ruckety pass –
And *that's* a job we'll have to do in December,
Gravel it and build a kerb on the bog-side. Is that Cassidy's ass 50
Out in my clover? Curse o' God –
Where is that dog?
Never where he's wanted.' Maguire grunts and spits
Through a clay-wattled moustache and stares about him from the height.
His dream changes like the cloud-swung wind 55
And he is not so sure now if his mother was right
When she praised the man who made a field his bride.

Watch him, watch him, that man on a hill whose spirit
Is a wet sack flapping about the knees of time.
He lives that his little fields may stay fertile when his own body 60
Is spread in the bottom of a ditch under two coulters crossed in Christ's Name.

He was suspicious in his youth as a rat near strange bread
When girls laughed; when they screamed he knew that meant
The cry of fillies in season. He could not walk
The easy road to his destiny. He dreamt 65
The innocence of young brambles to hooked treachery.
O the grip. O the grip of irregular fields! No man escapes.
It could not be that back of the hills love was free
And ditches straight.
No monster hand lifted up children and put down apes 70
As here.
      'O God if I had been wiser!'
That was his sigh like the brown breeze in the thistles.
He looks towards his house and haggard. 'O God if I had been wiser!'

skeins: root strands.

Graip: dig with a small fork.
ruckety: uneven.

clay-wattled: soiled; unclean.

a wet sack: used by farmers to keep their clothes dry.
coulters: plough blades.

haggard: storage area for fodder.

But now a crumpled leaf from the whitethorn bushes 75
Darts like a frightened robin, and the fence
Shows the green of after-grass through a little window,
And he knows that his own heart is calling his mother a liar.
God's truth is life – even the grotesque shapes of its foulest fire.

The horse lifts its head and cranes 80
Through the whins and stones
To lip late passion in the crawling clover.
In the gap there's a bush weighted with boulders like morality,
The fools of life bleed if they climb over.

The wind leans from Brady's, and the coltsfoot leaves are holed with rust, 85
Rain fills the cart-tracks and the sole-plate grooves;
A yellow sun reflects in Donaghmoyne
The poignant light in puddles shaped by hooves.

Come with me, Imagination, into this iron house
And we will watch from the doorway the years run back, 90
And we will know what a peasant's left hand wrote on the page.
Be easy, October. No cackle hen, horse neigh, tree sough, duck quack.

coltsfoot: creeping yellow weed.

sole-plate: horseshoe; underside of farm implement.
Donaghmoyne: parish near Inniskeen.

what a peasant's left hand wrote: probably refers to Kavanagh himself as the authentic voice of rural Ireland.
sough: sigh.

'The drills slipped by and the days slipped by'

👤 Personal Response

1. What impression of Maguire and his men do you get from lines 1–9 of the poem? Refer to the text in your answer.
2. Describe the mood in the last eight lines of the poem. How does Kavanagh create this mood?
3. Comment on the meaning and significance of the poem's title, 'The Great Hunger'.

👁 Critical Literacy

'The Great Hunger' was written in 1942 when Kavanagh was living in Dublin. This epic narrative reveals the harsh realities of rural Irish life and focuses primarily on one character's relationship with the land. The poem also explores the effects of grinding poverty and sexual inhibition. It challenges the romantic notion of the happy-go-lucky peasant that had been promoted elsewhere in Ireland's literary tradition. Throughout the poem, Kavanagh uses a narrator to present Patrick Maguire and to link key scenes in the character's unfulfilled life.

The extract's opening section (lines 1–17) portrays Patrick Maguire and his farm labourers in their natural element – 'Along the side-fall of the hill'. The sluggish rhythm and mock-serious biblical tone ('Clay is the word and clay is the flesh') reflect the helplessness of these men who are, in every sense, stuck in the mud. They are depicted as less than human, 'like mechanized scare-crows', in a **relentlessly desolate setting**. This hostile environment of 'wet clods' has left them 'broken-backed'. Kavanagh's imagery suggests a primitive world where 'crows gabble over worms and frogs'. The narrative voice informs us of the emptiness of life here and invites us to observe Maguire's 'tragedy to the last curtain'. Particular emphasis is placed on loneliness and sexual longing ('Who was it promised marriage to himself'). Forlorn rhetorical questions echo the men's deep feelings of regret. Their despair is succinctly expressed in the evocative sentence 'Yesterday was summer', a devastatingly bleak acceptance of lost opportunity.

Immediately following this prologue to Maguire's story, lines 18–38 include several **images of failure**: 'a torn jacket', a 'rusty plough', a 'Flameless' candle. Although the sexual allusions are somewhat overstated, Maguire's frustration is still as pitiful as it is easy to mock. Kavanagh's extended lines, delivered largely at a plodding pace, suggest a monotonous existence: 'The drills slipped by and the days slipped by'. Yet despite being tied down like a tethered horse, Maguire deludes himself that he is happy and considers himself 'wiser than any man in the townland'. He even sneers at family life ('children are tedious'), but it is all pretence, as much an empty act of bravado as his vain gesture when he 'flung a stone in the air' to scare away 'the birds of the years'.

The narrator's attitude to Maguire is somewhat ambivalent: it is seemingly sympathetic and yet highly critical at times. Consider, for instance, the tone of line 41: 'He thinks it is a potato, but we know better'. Is the voice superior and patronising, or sincere and understanding? Maguire speaks for himself in lines 43–57 and confirms our initial impressions of a boorish man whose entire life revolves around farming. His curt utterances reflect the realistic rhythms of country life: 'Pull down the shafts of that cart'. This picture of a rough, hard-working farmer who 'grunts and spits' is convincingly constructed. But **Kavanagh also explores Maguire's secret life**. Deep down, the ageing bachelor is plagued by doubts about the sacrifices he has made for the sake of the land and 'is not so sure now if his mother was right/When she praised the man who made a field his bride'. While the brooding introspection is not completely unexpected, it is nonetheless a compelling expression of the human tragedy that affected an entire generation of men like Patrick Maguire.

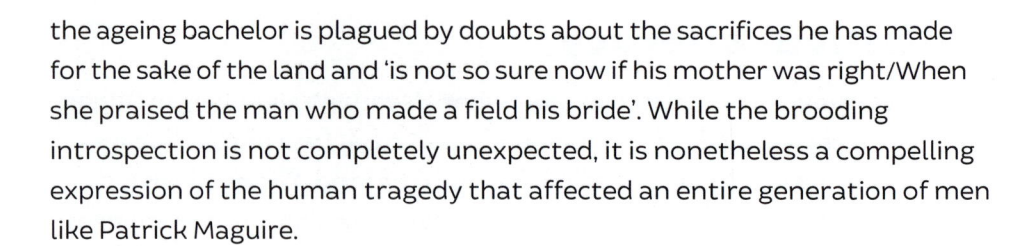

The softer tone of narrative comment in lines 58–61 is in keeping with Kavanagh's essential sympathy for **people whose emotional, sexual and spiritual needs were being stifled**. Maguire's depressed spirit is compared to 'a wet sack flapping about the knees of time'. The metaphor conveys a disconcerting sense of the ageing farmer's futile struggle. Ironically, he will give up his own happiness so that 'his little fields may stay fertile'. Such a sacrifice is hardly glorious. The image of Maguire's corpse buried 'under two coulters crossed in Christ's Name' provides a final symbol of depression. Throughout much of this section, Kavanagh controls the rhythm carefully, maintaining a funereal pace in line with the poem's sombre atmosphere.

Lines 62–79 take us back to Maguire's youthful years, a time of embarrassment and confusion which he has come to regret: 'O God if I had been wiser!' The poet's negative language ('suspicious', 'treachery', 'irregular', 'frightened') underlines a scathing **tone of bitter recrimination**. Repetition and the use of exclamations add to the feeling of resentment towards an earlier culture of ignorance and insensitivity: 'O the grip. O the grip of irregular fields!' Images of 'a crumpled leaf' and 'a frightened robin' symbolise the powerlessness of young people growing up in a narrow-minded era of deprivation.

Maguire again singles out one person for particular attention: 'And he knows that his own heart is calling his mother a liar'. **Kavanagh is probably using the figure of the Irish mother to represent powerful institutions of official Ireland that he was critical of**, such as the Catholic Church, the family and the country's education system. The poet's message could not be more lucid. For Kavanagh, Irish society's traditional repression of human sexuality was a denial that 'God's truth is life – even the grotesque shapes of its foulest fire'.

Lines 80–88 include a number of natural images from the familiar Irish landscape. **The poet's cinematic technique is atmospheric**, creating a mood of yearning and endurance, evoked by glimpses of the 'poignant light' of a 'yellow sun'. Despite the pervading sense of despondency, there is a recognition of the timeless beauty that typifies Kavanagh's sense of place. In lines 89–92, readers are asked to use their imagination to watch 'the years run back' on Patrick Maguire's sullen life. The final hushed tone is reassuringly lyrical, echoing the voice of an elderly man at work on his farm: 'Be easy, October. No cackle hen, horse neigh'. The scene is set for the rest of Maguire's tragic story.

✏ Writing About the Poem

Based on your reading of this extract from 'The Great Hunger', what impact did Kavanagh's portrayal of Irish rural life make on you? Refer to the text of the poem in your answer.

Sample Paragraph

Of the Kavanagh poems I studied, 'The Great Hunger' gave the best insight into Irish rural life during the early 20th century. The first word in the poem is 'Clay'. It sets the downbeat tone. 'Clay is the word and clay is the flesh' told me that Kavanagh saw farm work almost as a type of religion. His central character is Patrick Maguire, a farmer who has never married. I imagined him as a grumpy workaholic. He puts on an act that he is content with his lonely life. The fact that I took Maguire seriously is proof of how convincing a portrait Kavanagh created. Maguire laughs 'over pints of porter'. But it's all false. Kavanagh lets us hear Maguire's sad voice, 'O God if I had been wiser'. By the end, it's clear that he is filled with anger. Kavanagh presents powerful images of decay: 'weedy clods', a 'rusty plough'. To me these create an atmosphere of a rural Ireland that was failing. It is a negative picture, but a compelling one.

> **EXAMINER'S COMMENT**
>
> This is a successful individual response that shows clear engagement with the poem. The answer remains focused on the question throughout. Discussion points are well supported with references and short quotations. The paragraph is also rounded off very well. Top-grade standard.

✒ Class/Homework Exercises

1. In your view, does the poet feel sympathy for Maguire? Refer closely to the text of the poem in your answer.
2. Kavanagh's imagery often evokes a haunting sense of place. To what extent is this true of 'The Great Hunger'? Develop your answer with reference to the poem.

◉ Points to Consider

- Key themes: traditional rural life, nature, loneliness and sexual repression.
- Restrictive impact of conservative values, family and religion.
- Both a lyrical and realistic portrayal of the bleak, beautiful environment.
- Narrative voices, atmospheric cinematic scenes, dramatic sketches.
- Colloquial speech, contrasting images and tones.

4 Advent

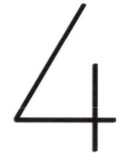

Title: the four weeks before Christmas, which in Kavanagh's time was a period of penance and fasting in preparation for the coming of Christ.

We have tested and tasted too much, lover—
Through a chink too wide there comes in no wonder.
But here in this Advent-darkened room
Where the dry black bread and the sugarless tea
Of penance will charm back the luxury   5
Of a child's soul, we'll return to Doom
The knowledge we stole but could not use.

And the newness that was in every stale thing
When we looked at it as children: the spirit-shocking
Wonder in a black slanting Ulster hill,   10
Or the prophetic astonishment in the tedious talking
Of an old fool will awake for us and bring
You and me to the yard gate to watch the whins
And the bog-holes, cart-tracks, old stables where Time begins.

O after Christmas we'll have no need to go searching   15
For the difference that sets an old phrase burning —
We'll hear it in the whispered argument of a churning
Or in the streets where the village boys are lurching.
And we'll hear it among simple decent men, too,
Who barrow dung in gardens under trees,   20
Wherever life pours ordinary plenty.
Won't we be rich, my love and I, and please
God we shall not ask for reason's payment,
The why of heart-breaking strangeness in dreeping hedges,
Nor analyse God's breath in common statement.   25
We have thrown into the dust-bin the clay-minted wages
Of pleasure, knowledge and the conscious hour —
And Christ comes with a January flower.

lover: soul; spiritual self.

dry black bread: eaten during Advent penance.

we'll return to Doom: we will discard as useless.

whins: furze/gorse bushes.

Time begins: after the birth of Christ, the calendar was changed and BC became AD.

difference … burning: allows us to see wisdom in an old saying.
churning: cream is stirred and turned until butter is made.

reason's payment: rational explanation.
dreeping: dripping.

clay-minted wages: useless payment.

January flower: symbol of the return of innocence.

'heart-breaking strangeness in dreeping hedges'

👤 Personal Response

1. In the first stanza, the poet wishes to leave the world of adult experience and return to a world of childhood innocence. How do you interpret the phrase 'the luxury/Of a child's soul'?
2. Why does Kavanagh consider 'wonder' and 'astonishment' to be so important? What is the opposite of these? Why does he dislike the opposite?
3. Which vivid detail strikes you most in the second sonnet, lines 15–28? Why does this detail appeal to you?

👁 Critical Literacy

This poem was first published on Christmas Eve 1942 in *The Irish Times* and was originally called 'Renewal'. It concerns Kavanagh's early years in Dublin. He was a man of little formal education, as he had left school at 13 to work the land, and here he is remaking his soul and announcing, in these two sonnets, that he is a poet of wonder. He finds that in order to go on, he must go back.

The sound of **world-weary, jaded senses** are vividly caught in the opening lines: 'We have tested and tasted too much'. The hard repetitive 't' sound and the use of the past tense capture the empty round of excess partying and too much drink. The reference to 'lover' suggests an intimate presence in the poet's life, whether a friend or his spiritual self. He has done too much, seen too much. He longs for the simple life. The poem is set in Advent, the four weeks prior to Christmas. This was a time of self-denial when people fasted and did penance to purify themselves in readiness for the coming of Christ at Christmas. They denied themselves sugar and butter as a penance ('dry black bread and the sugarless tea'). The short, gloomy evenings of winter are shown in the phrase 'Advent-darkened room'.

Kavanagh has written that 'revelations come as an aside'. Here, the 'chink' offers a tantalising glimpse into another mysterious world. He is saying that when everything is laid out in front of you, there is no desire for it. **This is what he doesn't want**. What he does want is the 'luxury/Of a child's soul'. The ability to look at things with breathless curiosity and awestruck wonder is what he desires now. He has experienced much, but like Adam and Eve in the Garden of Eden, he has knowledge that he cannot use. He wants to return it 'to Doom'. Innocence has gone and knowing is worthless.

In line 8, the poet uses a striking paradox: 'the newness that was in every stale thing'. **He wants to look again at the world through the eyes of a child** so that his soul can be shocked by the 'Wonder in a black slanting Ulster hill'. As a child, he could see the menacing threat in the dark hill silhouetted against the dying light of the sky. Paradoxes graphically show this poetic rebirth so that listening to a repetitive old man becomes a source of childish surprise. The sonnet concludes with a wonderful image of 'You and me' leaning over a gate, waiting, observing and realising that in the most ordinary things lies the extraordinary.

In the second sonnet, the present tense moves to the future as he imagines with the expressive, heartfelt 'O' what will happen if he opens himself up to experiencing the **'ordinary plenty'**. He will understand the wisdom in an old saying, 'the difference that sets an old phrase burning'. The onomatopoeia allows us to hear it, along with the poet, in the line 'We'll hear it in the whispered argument of a churning'. The simple sights of corner boys and men tending their gardens are all shown to be where life is pouring out its riches. The intimate tone of the poet continues in the phrase 'Won't we be rich, my love and I' as he asks us **not to over-analyse, but rather experience**.

The beauty of a damp December evening on a remote Irish road is depicted vividly in the 'heart-breaking strangeness of dreeping hedges'. Kavanagh makes up a new word, 'dreeping', to convey the saturated weight of water on the hedgerow. But we are not to ask 'The why'. Our language ('common statement') is not adequate to comprehend 'God's breath'. Instead, we will discard what is useless, 'the clay-minted wages' of the senses, 'pleasure, knowledge'. We will leave aside knowingness, 'the conscious hour'. The second sonnet concludes in the present tense with the birth of Christ: 'And Christ comes with a January flower'. The innocence of childhood and purity has been regained and the creative impulse is in full bloom.

✍ Writing About the Poem

The original title of this poem was 'Renewal'. What type of renewal was Kavanagh seeking and why? Develop your response with suitable reference and quotation from the poem.

Sample Paragraph

This poem begins with its tired phrase 'We have tested too much, lover'. Kavanagh needed to recapture childhood, so that he could experience the world without asking for 'reason's payment'. He wants to be moved, 'spirit-shocking', 'astonished'. He looks forward to a rebirth, just as the people of his time purified themselves so that they were worthy to receive the sacraments on Christmas Day. The simplicity of the line, 'Christ comes with a January flower', suggests that Kavanagh has realised this rebirth, from the excesses of pleasures of the flesh and intellect, to the more mysterious gifts of the imagination and creative impulse. Kavanagh allows us to see what he saw, the 'dreeping' hedges, and hear what he heard, 'whispered arguments of churning'.

EXAMINER'S COMMENT

Solid high-grade standard. Responded clearly to the task of exploring what renewal meant to the poet. However, there could have been greater focus on why renewal was important to Kavanagh. There were also some slight misquotes.

A water-hen screeched in the bog,
Mass-going feet
Crunched the wafer-ice on the pot-holes,
Somebody wistfully twisted the bellows wheel.

My child poet picked out the letters
On the grey stone,
In silver the wonder of a Christmas townland,
The winking glitter of a frosty dawn.

Cassiopeia was over
Cassidy's hanging hill,
I looked and three whin bushes rode across
The horizon — the Three Wise Kings.

An old man passing said:
'Can't he make it talk' —
The melodion. I hid in the doorway
And tightened the belt of my box-pleated coat.

I nicked six nicks on the door-post
With my penknife's big blade —
There was a little one for cutting tobacco.
And I was six Christmases of age.

My father played the melodion,
My mother milked the cows,
And I had a prayer like a white rose pinned
On the Virgin Mary's blouse.

Mass-going feet: the sound of the poet's Catholic neighbours on their way to Mass.
wistfully: quietly and sadly.
bellows wheel: used to keep traditional turf and coal fires alight.

Cassiopeia: 'W'-shaped group of stars.

'the wonder of a Christmas townland'

👤 Personal Response

1. To what extent is 'A Christmas Childhood' a religious poem? Refer to the text in your answer.
2. Select any two images from the poem that you find particularly interesting. Briefly explain your choice in each case.
3. From your reading of the poem, what evidence can you find in Kavanagh's childhood that suggests he would become a poet in later life?

👁 Critical Literacy

Originally published as two separate poems, 'A Christmas Childhood' recreates Kavanagh's memories of a magical occasion when he was six years old. While he celebrates the intense feelings he had as a child for his parents, nature and his Christian faith, the poet is also aware of the passing of time and the loss of innocence.

Part I opens with a vivid image from Kavanagh's childhood: 'One side of the potato-pits was white with frost'. This enduring memory is followed immediately by the adult poet's **nostalgic reflection**: 'How wonderful that was, how wonderful!' This pattern of commenting on early experiences continues throughout the poem. The mysterious beauty of nature is central to Kavanagh's time as a child on the family farm and his most enduring memories are of colours, light and music.

For the innocent six-year-old boy, reverberating sounds from the wires between paling-posts created 'magical' music. A gap of sky between the high hay ricks became 'a hole in Heaven's gable'. He imagined an ordinary apple tree as the Tree of Knowledge which led to Adam and Eve's original sin and their expulsion from the Garden of Eden. The adult voice that dominates lines 9–16 is filled with **regret at the loss of innocence**. He seems to resent adulthood, contrasting it with the 'Garden that was childhood's'. Part I ends with two 'common' recollections – the 'tracks of cattle' and a 'green stone lying sideways in a ditch' – both fixed in his memory as timeless images of 'a beauty that the world did not touch'.

Kavanagh's adult voice is almost entirely absent from Part II of the poem. Instead, we experience the excitement of Christmas through the child's eyes: 'I knew some strange thing had happened'. In particular, **he recalls people and music**, often together: 'My father played the melodion', 'my mother/ Made the music of milking'. Simple language and vivid images convey a clear sense of eager anticipation. Kavanagh remembers that even the stars in the sky 'danced'. The special atmosphere of the festive occasion affected every family ('Lennons and Callans') in the close-knit parish.

Religious imagery becomes increasingly prominent as the young narrator makes connections between his own Christmas in Co. Monaghan and Christ's Nativity. The lamp in the farm outhouse becomes 'a star/And the frost of Bethlehem made it twinkle'. The **rich onomatopoeia** in lines 29–32 is characteristic of Kavanagh's musical effects. Carefully chosen verbs, such as 'screeched' and 'Crunched', are especially evocative. The gentle sibilance of 'Somebody wistfully twisted the bellows wheel' gives us a quiet sense of Irish country life a century ago.

The final stanzas continue to dramatise 'the wonder of a Christmas townland'. In retrospect, the poet recognises the first indications of his poetic imagination, his 'child poet', picking out the shapes of letters on frosted stones. **The mystery of creation always absorbed Kavanagh** and he can never forget the fascination of the night sky in winter: 'Cassiopeia was over/Cassidy's hanging hill'.

The poem concludes with a remarkable self-portrait of a wide-eyed child, 'six Christmases of age', a young boy who is intensely aware of the sensation of each moment of being alive. We see him gazing out at the great big world ('I hid in the doorway') as he tests his new penknife: 'I nicked six nicks on the door-post'. The colloquial language and flowing rhythm of lines 45–48 echo the child's newfound sense of his place in life. The last stanza provides an impressive overview of **the poet's closeness to his family**, especially his mother: 'And I had a prayer like a white rose pinned/On the Virgin Mary's blouse'. The clarity and simplicity of the image (white roses are rare and very beautiful), together with the poet's reverential tone, leave us with a memorable sense of Kavanagh's tender feelings.

✒ Writing About the Poem

It has been said that Kavanagh's poetry has been primarily concerned with a sense of loss. To what extent is this true of 'A Christmas Childhood'?

Sample Paragraph

I agree that feelings of loss are central to Kavanagh poems. The title of 'Christmas Childhood' is nostalgic. The poet has been shaped by his youthful experiences. He always seems to be yearning for a return to those happy times, the innocent experiences of 'the gay garden of childhood'. Growing up in the countryside, Kavanagh's life was very simple, dominated by his Catholic religion. It is clear that he was full of wonder. This is what he misses

EXAMINER'S COMMENT

Reveals a reasonably good understanding of the poem. Quotations are slightly inaccurate, but help to support key points well. A little more analysis of the poet's tone would have improved the answer. Solid high-grade standard.

most – the innocence he experienced. The poem is filled with memories which were once great mysteries to him – the unexplained 'music' from the paling-posts and images of the first Christmas story, such as the three whin bushes (the 'Wise Kings'). The poem is written in a nostalgic tone, suggesting loss. He compares his mother to Christ's mother in a metaphor which shows his love and loss – 'I had a prayer like a white rose on the Virgin Mary's blouse'. This suggests yearning for an innocent time.

✒ Class/Homework Exercises

1. What differences can you find between the two sections of the poem? Refer to both theme and style of writing in your answer.
2. In your view, is 'A Christmas Childhood' a sentimental poem? Does Kavanagh wallow in the past or are his feelings sincere? Refer closely to the text in your answer.

⊙ Points to Consider

- **Nostalgic autobiographical poem about a magical and mysterious Christmas.**
- **Themes include childhood innocence, beauty of nature, poetic inspiration.**
- **Ordinary becomes extraordinary.**
- **Stylistic features: vivid imagery and sound effects, dramatic vignettes and rural colloquialisms.**

6 Epic

PATRICK KAVANAGH

Title: (noun) long poem about heroic events; (adj.) ambitious; impressive.

I have lived in important places, times
When great events were decided: who owned
That half a rood of rock, a no-man's land
Surrounded by our pitchfork-armed claims.
I heard the Duffys shouting 'Damn your soul'   5
And old McCabe, stripped to the waist, seen
Step the plot defying blue cast-steel —
'Here is the march along these iron stones.'
That was the year of the Munich bother. Which
Was more important? I inclined   10
To lose my faith in Ballyrush and Gortin
Till Homer's ghost came whispering to my mind.
He said: I made the *Iliad* from such
A local row. Gods make their own importance.

half a rood: small portion of land – a rood is a quarter of an acre.

Step the plot: traditional method of measuring the land by walking it.
march: boundary.
Munich bother: the poet's wry description of a crisis just before the outbreak of World War II.
more important: Kavanagh is hesitating between the importance of the local or international row.
Ballyrush and Gortin: townlands near Inniskeen, Co. Monaghan.
Homer: Greek epic poet who wrote the *Iliad* about a dispute between the Greeks and the Trojans which led to the long, bloody Trojan Wars.

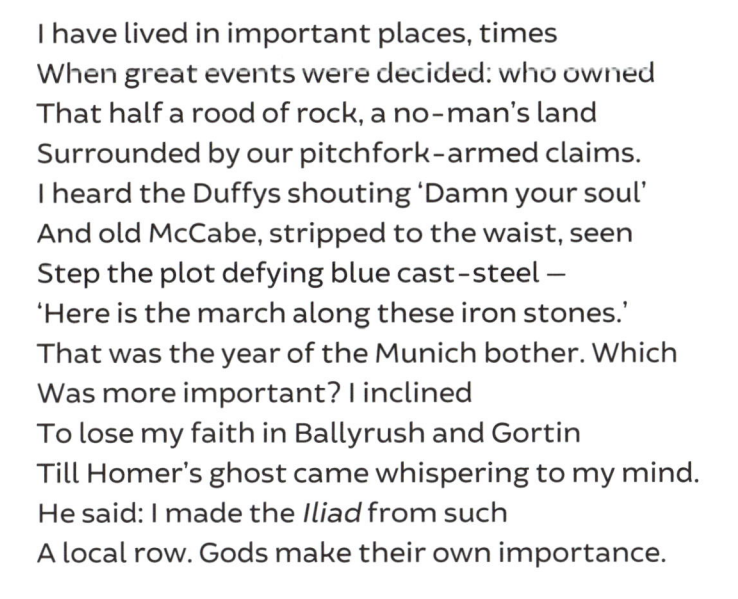

'I made the Iliad from such/ A local row'

👤 Personal Response

1. Do you think the title of the poem is misleading or mischievous? What leads you to that opinion?
2. Choose one war image from the poem that you found particularly interesting and effective. Briefly explain your choice.
3. In your opinion, what is Kavanagh's main point or message in this poem?

👁 Critical Literacy

This poem was written about a local dispute between two Co. Monaghan farmers. Kavanagh's brother, Peter, recalls 'the row over half-a-rood of rock in 1938'. This poem was set before the poet made the decision to move to Dublin, and just before the outbreak of World War II. Kavanagh believed in the importance of the local.

Epic poetry is usually very long, telling of great heroic exploits over a vast area and involving thousands of people. This small sonnet opens on a grand, authoritative scale, declaring that the poet had 'lived in important places' (line 1) and had been witness to great decisions. **Wryly humorous**, the poet then describes an argument between two Irish farmers over an eighth of an acre of stony ground. Yet all the fire and passion of a real conflict is there, as McCabe defiantly steps out the land, shouting, 'Here is the march'.

The use of real names for the people and the places adds **a sense of immediacy and authenticity** to this event. They almost take on a magical significance. The quoted outbursts, such as 'Damn your soul' (line 5), add drama and excitement as we feel that we are really hearing the bitterness overflow in this parochial quarrel. However, the use of the phrases 'no-man's land' and 'armed claims' broaden the scope of the poem, showing it to be a microcosm of what is being played out on a European scale ('the Munich bother'). This careless, casual remark referring to the row over international boundaries which led to World War II also leads to the central question of the sonnet: 'Which/Was more important?' The poet begins to hesitate, and the assured tone of the opening starts to waver: 'I inclined/To lose my faith' in the importance of this minor dispute between two farmers at a time of international crisis.

Suddenly, the ghost of Homer appears to reassure the poet that great works such as the *Iliad* were made from 'such/A local row'. The onomatopoeia of the word 'whispering' suggests a hidden secret being passed between two poets. Kavanagh regains his former confidence and realises that **it is the poet who decides on the significance of the event**: 'Gods make their own importance' (line 14). The use of the run-on lines in this poem shows the literal spilling over of boundaries and also cleverly hides the normal rhyme of the sonnet form. In times of war, all boundaries fluctuate.

✎ Writing About the Poem

The poet Michael Longley has declared that Patrick Kavanagh is a 'mythologist of the ordinary'. How does Kavanagh link the ordinary and myth in this poem? How effective is it? Develop your response with reference to and quotation from the poem.

Sample Paragraph

Kavanagh takes an ordinary local row and explores it in such a way that the parochial becomes universal. The poem begins in a self-important way as the speaker announces that he has 'lived in important places' and also at times when 'great events were decided'. So the reader assumes that the speaker is someone who has travelled widely and knows about world affairs. The immediacy of the scene is captured by the real names of people, 'Duffys' and 'McCabe', and places, 'Ballyrush and Gortin'. However, we are then brought into an international context with 'the Munich bother', referring to events which led to the outbreak of war. He wonders is the local or the international row more important? Both were about boundaries. Kavanagh's confidence is restored in the right of the poet to determine the great value of an event. 'Gods make their own importance.'

> **EXAMINER'S COMMENT**
>
> *The weaving together of the ordinary and the mythic are ably examined in this response. A little more attention might have been given to the 'effective' element of the question. Overall, a very good, high-grade answer underpinned by succinct quotations and impressive expression.*

PATRICK KAVANAGH

Class/Homework Exercises

1. In your opinion, is the mood of this poem confident and assertive, or hesitant and diffident? Refer closely to the text in your answer.
2. Sonnets often move from description to reflection. To what extent is this the case in 'Epic'? Refer to the poem in your response.

Points to Consider

- Poet compares a shouting match over Monaghan farmland to the outbreak of World War II and the Trojan War.
- Central theme: poetry itself has a political function in connecting the personal and the political.
- Effective use of sonnet form, battle imagery and conversational speech rhythms.
- Contrasting tones: personal, ironic, comic, didactic and formal.

Canal Bank Walk

Leafy-with-love banks and the green waters of the canal
Pouring redemption for me, that I do
The will of God, wallow in the habitual, the banal,
Grow with nature again as before I grew.
The bright stick trapped, the breeze adding a third   5
Party to the couple kissing on an old seat,
And a bird gathering materials for the nest for the Word,
Eloquently new and abandoned to its delirious beat.
O unworn world enrapture me, encapture me in a web
Of fabulous grass and eternal voices by a beech,   10
Feed the gaping need of my senses, give me ad lib
To pray unselfconsciously with overflowing speech,
For this soul needs to be honoured with a new dress woven
From green and blue things and arguments that cannot be proven.

the canal: the Grand Canal, Dublin.
Pouring redemption: the poet feels cleansed and renewed, like a baptised child.
wallow: relish; surrender to.
the banal: everyday or mundane things.
Grow with nature again: after recovering from ill health, the poet feels reborn.
the Word: biblical reference to the will of God, the Creator.

ad lib: spontaneity.

a new dress: freshness; simplicity.
green and blue things: nature; earth, sky and water.
arguments: beliefs; religious faith.

'Leafy-with-love banks and the green waters'

👤 Personal Response

1. In your own words, explain what you understand by the 'redemption' Kavanagh mentions in line 2.
2. Select one image from the poem that you found particularly interesting and effective. Justify your choice.
3. Comment on the effectiveness of the poet's use of verbs in the sestet.

👁 Critical Literacy

This sonnet was written in the mid-1950s after Kavanagh had been seriously ill. He spent much of his time convalescing by the banks of Dublin's Grand Canal. It was a time of spiritual and poetic renewal for the poet and he began to celebrate all the wonders of creation. As he wrote in his *Self-Portrait* (1964), 'as a poet, I was born in or about 1955, the place of my birth being the banks of the Grand Canal'. He added that this period of time marked a return to the simplicity of his earliest poems.

The poem begins on an enthusiastic note: 'Leafy-with-love'. This innovative phrase has a vivid, child-like quality that sets the upbeat mood of the sonnet. Throughout the first quatrain, **Kavanagh finds a sense of redemption** in 'the green waters of the canal' and feels inspired to do the 'will of God'. Water is used in both a literal and metaphorical way. It is free and fast-flowing, but it also purifies the poet's soul and restores his spirit, like the sacramental water of baptism. Along with the present tense, the energetic pace and run-through lines (enjambment) work to produce an exuberant atmosphere. The poet is eager to share his desire to 'wallow' in the canal's miraculous surroundings so that he can 'Grow with nature again'. Sensing that he has been given a second chance at life, he is determined to appreciate every moment.

The second quatrain focuses even more closely on Kavanagh's immediate environment and illustrates **the poet's observational skill**. Everything around him takes on an astonishing freshness, almost as though he is conscious of the world for the first time: 'Eloquently new and abandoned to its delirious beat'. He seems spellbound by the most common sights in nature (the 'bright stick') and in human nature ('the couple kissing'). His avid mood is explained by the crucial reference to divine creation: 'the Word'. Like other 'nature poets', Kavanagh intuitively recognises God's presence in the natural world. This is expressed in the invigorating image of the small bird in its element, 'gathering materials for the nest'.

The **sestet** is more obviously reverential in tone: 'O unworn world enrapture me, encapture me'. The emphasis comes from a combination of the exclamatory 'O', internal rhyme and repetition. Urgent verbs add further intensity to the **sincerity of feeling** in lines 9–14. The poet is anxious to retain his heightened awareness of nature, with its 'fabulous grass and eternal voices by a beech'. But he has another hope – that he can 'pray unselfconsciously', using language in the same simple way as the overflowing canal water.

The sonnet ends confidently. Lines 13–14 are extended, the rhythm relaxed and leisurely. In imagining his own rebirth, Kavanagh returns to the earlier baptism image: 'this soul needs to be honoured with a new dress'. In his case, the baptismal clothes will be made 'From green and blue things and arguments that cannot be proven'. The language has a refreshing quality that echoes his rediscovered passion for life. He is finally **content to accept the mysteries of nature and God's will** without question. From now on, Kavanagh's poetry will celebrate the beauty and wonder of creation through innocent eyes.

Writing About the Poem

To what extent do you agree that 'Canal Bank Walk' celebrates ordinary life through the use of everyday language? Refer to the poem in your response.

Sample Paragraph

To some extent this is a very true statement. Kavanagh had just come out of hospital after a very serious operation. He started to see life as precious, something to live one day at a time. To him, it was like a religious experience. The language is very simple especially when he is talking about the canal water. Colour images are important, e.g. 'green waters of the canal'. He also uses childish expressions e.g. 'green and blue things'. The language a young child would come out with. He also becomes very aware of God as the Creator of all the world. Kavanagh describes everyday objects and then finds the ordinary to be extraordinary, e.g. the 'bright stick'. An old stick is not exactly a thing of beauty. Everything is part of God's work. Not all of his language is colloquial, e.g. 'enrapture me' but many descriptions, e.g. the 'couple kissing' are very ordinary and add realism to the poem.

> **EXAMINER'S COMMENT**
>
> *A reasonable attempt at addressing the question, using some good examples of the poet's simple language. The expression is functional, but flawed by repetition (both 'very' and 'e.g.' are overused). Some analysis of the upbeat tone and energetic rhythm would have improved this mid-grade response.*

✒ Class/Homework Exercises

1. Comment on Kavanagh's use of imagery, rhythm and sound in 'Canal Bank Walk'. Refer closely to the text in your answer.
2. What aspects of 'Canal Bank Walk' are typical of Kavanagh's poetry? Consider both the poet's themes and his language in your response.

⊙ Points to Consider

- Beautiful reflective sonnet about the poet's experience of nature as spiritually enriching.
- Other themes include a sense of wonder and the importance of the imagination.
- Use of highly descriptive language, lyrical intensity, vivid colourful imagery and forceful rhythms.
- Sustained tone of enthusiasm throughout.

8 Lines Written on a Seat on the Grand Canal, Dublin

'Erected to the Memory of Mrs Dermot O'Brien'

O commemorate me where there is water,
Canal water preferably, so stilly
Greeny at the heart of summer. Brother
Commemorate me thus beautifully
Where by a lock Niagarously roars   5
The falls for those who sit in the tremendous silence
Of mid-July. No one will speak in prose
Who finds his way to these Parnassian islands.
A swan goes by head low with many apologies,
Fantastic light looks through the eyes of bridges –   10
And look! a barge comes bringing from Athy
And other far-flung towns mythologies.
O commemorate me with no hero-courageous
Tomb – just a canal-bank seat for the passer-by.

Title: the memorial seat to Mrs Dermot O'Brien still stands on the canal bank. After Kavanagh's death, his friends erected a canal bank seat in memory of him, as he had wished.

stilly/Greeny: new words made up by Kavanagh, a stylistic feature of his poetry.

Niagarously: Kavanagh often invented words. This refers to the famous Niagara Falls waterfall.

Parnassian: Mount Parnassus, near Delphi in Greece, was sacred to the god Apollo and the Muses, and is seen as the source of poetry and music.

mythologies: stories of people and events that are out of the ordinary.

O commemorate me: Kavanagh wished to be remembered beside canal water.

'just a canal bank seat for the passer-by'

👤 Personal Response

1. In your opinion, what is Kavanagh's central message or theme in this poem? Briefly explain your answer.
2. Choose one interesting and effective image from the poem. Give a reason for your choice.
3. Do you consider the tone of this poem to be solemn or celebratory? Support your answer with relevant reference.

👁 Critical Literacy

This poem was written while Kavanagh was convalescing from lung cancer, contracted in 1955. The poet, in a new mood of serenity and calm, admired the idea of having a seat as a symbol of remembrance. This poem is often viewed as the conclusion of his poetic journey.

Kavanagh **wishes that his memory should be honoured beside the canal**. The Grand Canal in Dublin was a place of contentment and acceptance of life for the poet. He believed that water purifies, just as it does in the sacrament of baptism, causing a rebirth so that the child may come to a state of grace. The colour green recalls the natural world. The phrase 'stilly/Greeny' seems childish and almost silly at first, but the poet wanted to **view things as he had as a child**, with wonder and amazement. He also wanted us to share this view with him. The poem is set in the 'heart of summer' (line 3). The canal bank occupies a special place in the heart of the poet. The old bitterness of the early poems has gone; now he is filled with love towards his fellow man. He humorously imagines the roar of the lock on the canal as having the force of Niagara Falls. This is typical of Kavanagh's wry use of hyperbole. The onomatopoeia of 'roars' coupled with the newly coined polysyllabic word 'Niagorously' effectively communicates the powerful *whoosh* of the water through the lock gate. All this movement and noise is contrasted with the great stillness of midsummer: 'the tremendous silence'.

Kavanagh's wish to be commemorated is not an act of pride, but one of generosity. He wants others to share this positive experience of rebirth, which he had the privilege of undergoing beside the canal. The poet feels that they, too, will be inspired: 'No one will speak in prose' (line 7). He likens the stretch of canal to Parnassus, the famous Greek mountain, a source of inspiration to all those involved in the arts. There are wonderful pleasures to be experienced on the canal, such as the 'bridges', the 'swan' and the 'barge', but these simple sights are transformed by the power of the poet's creativity. 'Fantastic light' is seen spilling from the personified bridges: 'through the eyes of bridges'. We, too, can see the sharp, shooting light searing through the arches. The graceful curve of the swan's neck is highlighted by the phrase 'head low with many apologies'. The simple barge incorporates the heroic deeds and strange tales of the past: 'far-flung towns mythologies' (line 12).

Kavanagh did not want future generations to look at his memorial, the seat, but rather at the view from the seat. Then **the viewer could see the same stretch of water** which had brought him spiritual redemption. He has no desire for anything grand or heroic. Instead, he wishes others to appreciate the joys of nature just as he had done. The opening and ending of the sonnet forms what seems like the black edge of the memorial card for the dead, 'O commemorate me' (line 13). This sense of place is very important to Gaelic poets. Kavanagh is paying tribute not to a place in the past, but to one in the present on the Grand Canal of Dublin.

Writing About the Poem

'The Canal Bank sonnets mark the fulfilment of Kavanagh's wonderful poetic journey'. Discuss this view with reference to the poem 'Lines Written on a Seat', using quotations to back up your opinion.

Sample Paragraph

Kavanagh sat in the 'tremendous silence' of 'mid-July' and let the sounds and sights of the canal bank make him feel born again. He learns to look with a child's eye at nature. His phrase, 'stilly/Greeny' water, masks a deeper meaning. We must learn to look with the innocent eye of a child if we wish to be fulfilled in our lives. He makes us hear the lock 'roar' as he uses his new word, 'Niagorously'. All the power of the great Niagara Falls is likened to the water gushing through the lock gate in Dublin. Here, he has regained his poetic inspiration: 'No one will speak in prose'. He is able to appreciate the beauty in ordinary things, such as the swan with its 'head low with many apologies'. The poet is at one with nature and is happily fulfilled. He also makes us look with wonder at the 'Fantastic light'. The poetic journey for Kavanagh ends here.

EXAMINER'S COMMENT

A very well-expressed response which focuses clearly on the assigned task to discuss the poetic journey of Kavanagh. Short quotations are used effectively. Clear and to the point throughout. Top-grade standard.

✏ Class/Homework Exercises

1. Kavanagh felt one should not take oneself too 'sickly seriously', so he uses 'outrageous rhyming' such as 'bridges' and 'courageous'. Comment on Kavanagh's use of unusual words elsewhere in this sonnet, explaining the impact they make on you.
2. 'Kavanagh's heartfelt poems can often make a powerful impact on the reader.' To what extent is this true of 'Lines Written on a Seat'? Refer closely to the text in your answer.

◉ Points to Consider

- Sonnet form provides an apt structure for the intense emotion in the poem.
- The spiritual significance of nature is a central theme.
- Child-like language reflects poet's sense of delight in the natural world.
- Use of hyperbole, emphatic repetition, exclamations, visual energy.
- Range of tones: euphoric, reverential and resigned.

The Hospital

A year ago I fell in love with the functional ward
Of a chest hospital: square cubicles in a row,
Plain concrete, wash basins – an art lover's woe,
Not counting how the fellow in the next bed snored.
But nothing whatever is by love debarred,   5
The common and banal her heat can know.
The corridor led to a stairway and below
Was the inexhaustible adventure of a gravelled yard.

This is what love does to things: the Rialto Bridge,
The main gate that was bent by a heavy lorry,   10
The seat at the back of a shed that was a suntrap.
Naming these things is the love-act and its pledge;
For we must record love's mystery without claptrap,
Snatch out of time the passionate transitory.

a chest hospital: the Rialto Hospital, Dublin, where Kavanagh was a patient for two months in 1955.

debarred: forbidden, excluded.
banal: common, mundane.

claptrap: foolishness, insincerity.
the passionate transitory: fiery short-lived period of time.

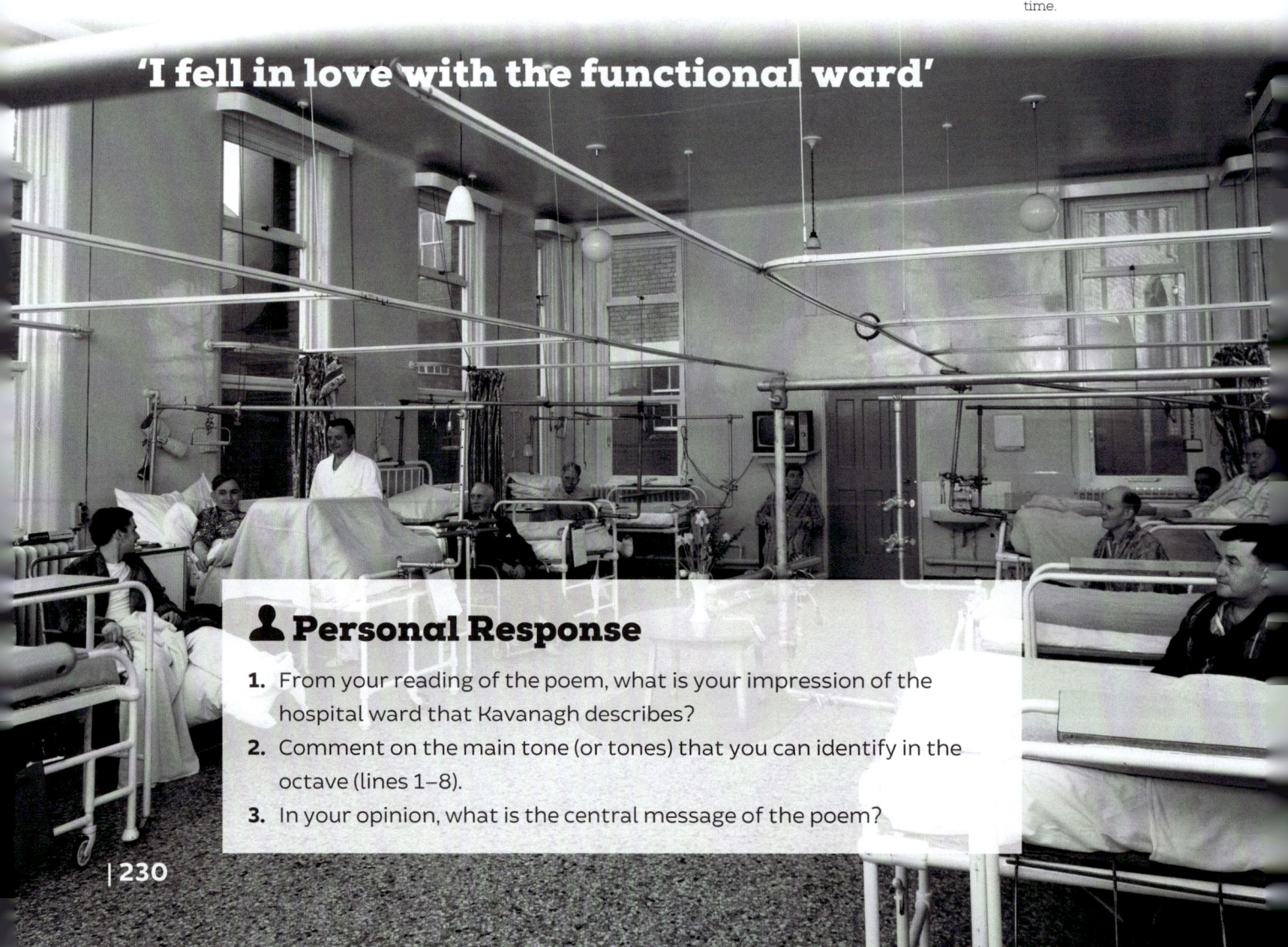

'I fell in love with the functional ward'

Personal Response

1. From your reading of the poem, what is your impression of the hospital ward that Kavanagh describes?
2. Comment on the main tone (or tones) that you can identify in the octave (lines 1–8).
3. In your opinion, what is the central message of the poem?

👁 Critical Literacy

'The Hospital' is an unusual love poem. Dull, drab hospital wards are unexpected subjects of affection. Kavanagh wrote the sonnet in 1956 while recovering from a lengthy stay in Dublin's Rialto Hospital. His experience as a patient had a deep effect on him. He became more positive about life and regained some of the innocent wonder of his childhood. The poem is about himself and his attitude to writing poetry.

Kavanagh's **opening lines** are clearly meant to surprise. He casually announces his latest romance: 'A year ago I fell in love with the functional ward/Of a chest hospital'. The picture he paints, however, could hardly be less passionate: 'Plain concrete, wash basins – an art lover's woe'. This **mock serious attitude** is also evident in his announcement that 'the fellow in the next bed snored'.

In **lines 5–8**, the poet's true voice emerges and his previous casualness is replaced with a more focused tone: 'But nothing whatever is by love debarred'. Kavanagh wants us to know that love transcends all expectations and has no limits. He personifies the emotion – 'The common and banal her heat can know' – to highlight the intensity of love. What is important to Kavanagh is the experience of love as an expression of **appreciating the world in a fresh and positive way**. The seemingly unremarkable hospital itself is just one of countless wonders around him, such as 'the inexhaustible adventure of a gravelled yard'.

In the **sestet**, Kavanagh considers the far-reaching effects of love. He lists some of the ordinary things that would not be immediately seen as suitable subjects for love poetry – the Rialto Bridge, a damaged gate, a secluded garden seat. The poet's own beliefs are summed up in **line 12**: 'Naming these things is the love-act and its pledge'. By creating poems out of ordinary life, **Kavanagh can express his own appreciation of the world's simple wonders**. Poetry even gives them a certain immortality.

The tone of **lines 13–14**, in which Kavanagh speaks on behalf of other writers, is more forceful and instructive: 'we must record love's mystery without claptrap'. For the poet, **love is a sense of natural integration with all of creation**. In turn, love poems should be realistic and sincere, written in direct, straightforward language ('without claptrap'). He illustrates this in the **final line**, where he recognises that because love is subject to time, love poetry (which registers such intense feelings) is all the more important. The poet's most important function, therefore, is to 'Snatch out of time the passionate transitory'.

Writing About the Poem

In your view, is 'The Hospital' a love poem? Refer closely to the text in your answer.

Sample Paragraph

Kavanagh includes the word 'love' at least five times in 'The Hospital'. He starts by shocking us slightly with his claim that he has fallen 'in love with the functional ward/Of a chest hospital'. What soon becomes clear, though, is that it isn't the actual building he's in love with at all. He is actually in love with life. So even the most ordinary things – what he calls 'common and banal' – are suddenly worthy of love. I find his tone to be sincere when he says that 'nothing whatever is by love debarred'. He now fully understands the magic of ordinary, everyday things – buildings, bridges, an old gravel yard. He talks about the 'inexhaustible adventure' of such things. As a poet, his duty is to write about commonplace subjects without any 'claptrap'. Kavanagh has written an interesting love poem, but his tone is passionate – especially where he advises poets like himself to follow their hearts and celebrate 'love's mystery'.

EXAMINER'S COMMENT
Engaging, clear answer succinctly addresses the question. Effective use of accurate quotation to support opinion. Well-written top-grade response.

Class/Homework Exercises

1. 'Nature and human nature are central to much of Kavanagh's poetry.' To what extent is this true of 'The Hospital'? Develop the points you make by close reference to the poem.
2. 'Kavanagh's attitude and tone changes sharply in this love sonnet from scorn to serious reflection.' Discuss this statement, developing your views with relevant quotation.

Points to Consider

- Sonnet form: descriptive octet, reflective sestet.
- Key themes: transience, love, wonder, duty, immortality.
- Simple direct language expresses moment of epiphany – 'This is what love does to things'.
- Poetic techniques include detailed description, colloquialisms, variety of tones – rueful, humorous, serious, urgent.

10 On Raglan Road

PATRICK KAVANAGH

Title: Raglan Road is a tree-lined street off Pembroke Road where Kavanagh lived for a time.

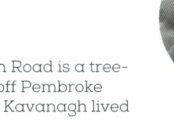

(Air: 'The Dawning of the Day')

On Raglan Road on an autumn day I met her first and knew
That her dark hair would weave a snare that I might one day rue;
I saw the danger, yet I walked along the enchanted way,
And I said, let grief be a fallen leaf at the dawning of the day.

On Grafton Street in November we tripped lightly along the ledge   5
Of the deep ravine where can be seen the worth of passion's pledge,
The Queen of Hearts still making tarts and I not making hay –
O I loved too much and by such, by such, is happiness thrown away.

I gave her gifts of the mind, I gave her the secret sign that's known
To the artists who have known the true gods of sound and stone   10
And word and tint. I did not stint for I gave her poems to say
With her own name there and her own dark hair like clouds over fields of May.

On a quiet street where old ghosts meet I see her walking now
Away from me so hurriedly my reason must allow
That I had wooed not as I should a creature made of clay –   15
When the angel woos the clay he'd lose his wings at the dawn of day.

snare: trap with a noose.
rue: feel regret for.

ravine: narrow, steep-sided valley gouged out by a stream.
pledge: solemn promise.
Queen of Hearts: reference to a nursery rhyme character; also the name of a playing card.

sound and stone/And word and tint: art forms; music, sculpture, literature, painting.
not stint: was not miserly with.

my reason must allow: thinking logically.

'On a quiet street where old ghosts meet'

Personal Response

1. In your opinion, what is Kavanagh's attitude to love in the opening lines of 'On Raglan Road'? Support your answer with reference to the poem.
2. Kavanagh is proud of his profession as a poet. Do you agree or disagree? Give evidence from the poem to support your view.
3. In your view, what is the poet's mood at the end of the poem: resigned, distraught, bitter, angry, nostalgic, etc.? Give reasons for your response, using reference to the text.

Critical Literacy

This popular love poem of Kavanagh's, with its bittersweet lament for unrequited or lost love, was first published on 3 October 1946 in *The Irish Press*. It was inspired by a beautiful young medical student, Hilda Moriarty. The poem has been recorded by many artists as a ballad sung to the tune of 'The Dawning of the Day'.

The poet's **disappointment in love** leads him to warn against placing trust in love and against loving too much. One of the strengths of this poem is its firm rooting in time and place, which adds to the authenticity of the experience. The action takes place on an autumn day in Dublin on Raglan Road. This is where he first saw and fell in love with a dark-haired beauty. Throughout the first stanza, he presents himself as unsophisticated; he knew it was dangerous, but he continued and was willing to accept 'grief'. He seems helpless, lured by beauty and the possibility of love: 'the enchanted way'. He is resigned to the possibility of sorrow, representing it as a natural outcome, as real as a 'fallen leaf' in autumn at dawn: 'let grief be a fallen leaf at the dawning of the day'.

The second stanza moves to winter. The couple seem oblivious to the dangers ('tripped lightly') as they walk along Grafton Street. The assonance of the slender vowel sound 'i' and the repetition of the 'l' in 'lightly along the ledge' capture the carefree spirit of early love. However, this is a dangerous balancing act – someone could get hurt and go hurtling into 'the deep ravine' if 'passion's pledge' proves to be worthless. Is it wise to worship a loved one? 'The Queen of Hearts' refers to the nursery rhyme and also to the card from a deck of cards which inflicts a penalty on the player. This is a successful woman who is in control of her destiny, whereas the poet, blinded by love, is not attending to his business: 'not making hay'. Kavanagh has gambled heavily on love ('O I loved too much') and lost ('and by such, by such, is happiness thrown away'). The **ballad form of four-line stanzas** with its regular rhyme, in this case *aabb*, is suited to this simple yet universal tale of lost love. The rhythm is taken from the song 'The Dawning of the Day'. The long, winding lines captivate the reader/listener as effectively as Kavanagh was ensnared all those years before. The use of internal rhyme ('hair'/'snare', 'grief'/'leaf') comes from the old bardic tradition of Gaelic poetry.

This poem is written entirely from the poet's perspective, and in stanza three, Kavanagh proudly declares all the gifts he gave her: 'gifts of the mind'. He gave her something very precious, 'the secret sign', which is known only to artists, those who have been in communication with the gods of music, sculpture, literature and painting: 'the artists who have known the true gods of sound and stone/And word and tint'. She was allowed into this special community. The frequent use of the first person 'I' indicates Kavanagh's great pride in his position as poet. The broad-vowelled simile, 'her own dark hair like clouds over fields of May', captures not only billowing dark clouds sailing over bright fields in early summer but also the cascading beauty of his loved one's hair. Suddenly, our sympathy returns to the awkward countryman hopelessly in love.

The closing stanza returns to the present. The relationship has ended and now Kavanagh sees her walking quickly away from him. With regret, he has to conclude that he did not love her as an ordinary human being, but as a being to be worshipped. He decides that she did not deserve this. He dismissively calls her 'a creature made of clay'. He adopts a much grander persona for himself, regarding himself as an angel, someone not entirely of this world. **Kavanagh had a great sense of the importance of the poet's place in society.** He concludes the poem by saying that the poet loses his special gifts ('lose his wings') if he courts the woman in this way. Are we still sympathetic to the poet's plight at the end of the poem?

Writing About the Poem

'Patrick Kavanagh often gives a universal significance to the local and ordinary.' Discuss this view with reference to 'On Raglan Road'.

Sample Paragraph

In Kavanagh's love poem, 'On Raglan Road', four short stanzas record a particular place and time, the 'local and the ordinary', when an awkward 40-year old Monaghan man fell madly in love with a beautiful medical student. Vivid personification evocatively captures the universal spell of female beauty, 'her dark hair would weave a snare'. Like so many before him, the love-struck poet blindly pursues,'I saw the danger, yet I walked the enchanted way'. All lovers offer beautiful gifts on their beloved. Kavanagh

EXAMINER'S COMMENT

This well-written top-grade response clearly addresses the question and shows an appreciation of the poet's skill in widening the perspective of the local to the universal. Good range of references and accurate quotations support the critical commentary.

gives her 'poems to say'. But as often happens, love is lost. Readers are brought to the sad realisation that love lost is as natural as 'a fallen leaf' in autumn.

✒ Class/Homework Exercises

1. 'Kavanagh's poetry is pervaded by a deep sense of loss.' Do you agree or disagree with this statement? Support the points you make with reference to the text.
2. 'Kavanagh's rich visual imagery captures the bitter-sweet experience of lost love.' To what extent is this true of 'On Raglan Road'? Develop your answer with reference to the poem.

⊙ Points to Consider

- **Themes include love, loss, pride, transience, etc.**
- **Simple ballad form: four-line stanzas, regular rhyme scheme, aabb – suitable for universal story of lost love.**
- **Poetic techniques include striking visual imagery and musical sound effects, particularly internal rhyme ('tint'/'stint') from the Gaelic bardic tradition.**
- **Variety of tones: joyful, regretful, nostalgic, proud and resigned.**

Sample Leaving Cert Questions on Kavanagh's Poetry

1. Discuss how Kavanagh's imaginative use of particular places and characters helps reveal the essential compassion in his work. Develop your response with reference to the poems by Patrick Kavanagh on your course.

2. 'Patrick Kavanagh uses deceptively simple language to create poetry that transforms the ordinary into something extraordinary.' Discuss this view, developing your answer with reference to both the themes and language found in the poetry of Kavanagh on your course.

3. 'The beauty and mystery of nature are central to Kavanagh's plain-speaking poetry.' To what extent do you agree with this statement? Develop your response with reference to the poems by Patrick Kavanagh on your course.

Understanding the Prescribed Poetry Question

Marks are awarded using the PCLM Marking Scheme:
P = 15; C = 15; L = 15; M = 5
Total = 50

- **P** (Purpose = 15 marks) refers to the set question and is the launch pad for the answer. This involves engaging with all of the question. Both theme and language must be addressed, although not necessarily equally.
- **C** (Coherence = 15 marks) refers to the organisation of the developed response and the use of accurate, relevant quotation. Paragraphing is essential.
- **L** (Language = 15 marks) refers to the student's skill in controlling language throughout the answer.
- **M** (Mechanics = 5 marks) refers to spelling and grammar.
- Although no specific number of poems is required, students usually discuss at least 3 or 4 in their written responses.
- Aim for at least 800 words, to be completed within 45–50 minutes.

How do I organise my answer?

(Sample question 1)

Discuss how Kavanagh's imaginative use of particular places and characters helps to reveal the essential compassion in his work. Develop your response with reference to the poems by Patrick Kavanagh on your course.

Sample Plan 1

Intro: (*Stance: agree with viewpoint in question*) Poems of a claustrophobic, spiritually impoverished Ireland produce not only repressed individuals but also 'spirit-shocking wonder' at nature's beauty. Tone varies from affectionate lover to proud poet as he shines a light on ordinary life.

Point 1: (*Inspired reference to rural location – poet's persona as tender lover*) 'Shancoduff' – a specific rural area with all its flaws and wonder – is recreated through incandescent visual imagery, rich aural effects and wide-ranging allusions.

Point 2: (*Tragedy of old bachelor farmer – persona of empathetic observer*) 'The Great Hunger' – evocative use of language ('broken-backed', 'rusty plough') and vivid simile. Lonely voice of Maguire, 'O God if I had been wiser', conveys his tragedy.

POETRY FOCUS

NOTE

In keeping with the PCLM approach, the student has to respond by agreeing, disagreeing or partially agreeing that Kavanagh's:

- **imaginative use of particular places and characters** (creative and visionary references to specific locations and people in Monaghan and Dublin transfigure the local into the universal through rich imagery, personification, comparisons, colloquial speech, etc.)

... reveals:

- **the essential compassion in his work** (awareness of the loneliness and suffering of others, close affinity with nature, alternating emotive tones of nostalgia, empathy, frustration, etc.)

Point 3: *(Beauty of place and person – persona of resigned, rejected lover)* 'On Raglan Road' – through distilled reflection of the beauty and danger of all-consuming love, conveyed by assonance and alliteration ('we tripped lightly along the ledge/Of the deep ravine').

Point 4: *(Beauty of place and community – nostalgic recollection)* 'A Christmas Childhood'– through intense visual detail ('One side of the potato-pits was white with frost'), evocative sound effects ('the music of milking'), the mystery and beauty of creation is reinterpreted.

Conclusion: By reimagining and revaluing people in specific locations, both natural and urban, Kavanagh makes them important. His empathetic poetry memorialises the local while pointing out its greater significance.

Sample Paragraph: Point 1

Kavanagh thinks of Shancoduff as a lover. The repetition of 'my' suggests his protective attitude. A vivid image reveals his pride in protecting his 'black hills … When dawn whitens Glassdrummond chapel'. Kavanagh lists a series of placenames, 'Armagh', 'Rocksavage', and his tender tone reflects his love for this landscape. Even during winter, the language lovers use is applied to the boggy land, 'sleety winds fondle the rushy beards'. Kavanagh also makes reference to a biblical figure, 'Lot's wife' and to one of Europe's great mountains, 'the Matterhorn', both of which imply the importance of Shancoduff to the poet who treats the area like someone he wishes to protect. I get the impression that Kavanagh wants to protect his native countryside and he feels compassion for everything around him – including the 'perishing calves'.

EXAMINER'S COMMENT

As part of a full essay, this solid high-grade paragraph is generally focused on the question (places and compassion). Well-supported references to the 'language lovers use' and the 'tender tone' provide the basis for relevant analysis of the poem. Overall, good clear expression – apart from the overuse of 'protect'.

(Sample question 2)

'Patrick Kavanagh uses deceptively simple language to create poetry that transforms the ordinary into something extraordinary.' Discuss this view, developing your answer with reference to both the themes and language found in the poetry of Kavanagh on your course.

> **NOTE**
> In keeping with the PCLM approach, the student has to explore poems of Kavanagh's on the course that include:
> - **deceptively simple language** (familiar colloquialisms, exaggeration, everyday speech rhythms, child-like expressions, striking visual imagery, accessible description of rural life and the natural world, thought-provoking comparisons and allusions, etc.)
> … that transforms:
> - **the ordinary into something extraordinary** (insightful, creative outlook produces visionary moments, reveals hidden significance of local places and events, discovers spiritual meaning in the beauty of nature, etc.)

Sample Plan 2

Intro: *(Stance: agree with viewpoint in question)* Kavanagh's intricately crafted poetry uses the rhythm of the vernacular to change the ordinary into the extraordinary. A local row, a hospital stay, childhood memories and rural scenes gain wider significance through the poet's innovative language.

Point 1: *(Local row becomes heroic event through ordinary language, humorous tone)* 'Epic' – authentic use of colloquial language, wide-ranging allusions and run-on lines. These blur the sonnet's structure, echoing the poem's theme and turning the farmers' feud into an impressive occurrence.

Point 2: *(Poet's illness leads to insight – through humour, visual detail and sound effects)* 'The Hospital' – series of vivid memories reveal poet's redemption through shrewd use of juxtaposition ('love'/ 'hospital ward'), precise detail, sibilant peace ('seat at the back of a shed that was a suntrap').

Point 3: *(Childhood memory transformed into religious experience – through vivid description and aural effects)* 'A Christmas Childhood' – nursery rhyme tongue twister ('I nicked six nicks') evokes innocence. Onomatopoeia creates the beauty of Christmas ('Mass-going feet/ Crunched the wafer-thin ice').

Point 4: *(Recollection converted into spiritual reawakening – ingenious use of vernacular and double perspective)* 'Advent' – adult/child view evoked through alliteration and run-on line ('tedious talking/ Of an old fool' – adult view) and comment ('prophetic astonishment' – child's view). Vernacular expressions expose the beauty in the ordinary through onomatopoeia ('village boys are lurching').

Conclusion: Kavanagh's poetic vision provides moments of epiphany through simply naming things in such an imaginative way that this 'love-act' transforms the ordinary into something precious – enabling the local to become the universal.

Sample Paragraph: Point 1

In 'Epic', Kavanagh transforms a local disagreement over 'half a rood of rock' into something larger-than-life. Kavanagh's colloquial language vividly describes the defiance of 'McCabe stripped to the waist', stepping out the land to define the boundary, 'march'. The poem itself reflects the theme of the importance of boundaries. At the end, the ghost of the Greek poet, Homer, whispers that his epic poem 'Iliad' was also based on a local dispute. Homer, shares the secret that it is the role of the poet to mythologise, 'Gods make their own importance'. Kavanagh experiences a moment of epiphany about the wider significance of local people and events. In 'Epic', he highlights the importance of the local and argues that myths can be made out of these insignificant little disputes.

> **EXAMINER'S COMMENT**
>
> *Focused commentary engages effectively with a challenging question. As part of a full essay, this informed paragraph clearly illustrates Kavanagh's vision of ordinary life. Supportive references and accurate quotations range through the poem. The final sentence rounds off the discussion impressively. Expression is varied and well controlled. An assured top-grade standard.*

EXAM FOCUS

- As you may not be familiar with some of the poems referred to in the sample plans, substitute other prescribed poems that you have studied closely.
- Key points about a particular poem can be developed over more than one paragraph.
- Paragraphs may also include cross-referencing and discussion of more than one poem.
- Remember that there is no single 'correct' answer to poetry questions, so always be confident in expressing your own considered response.

Leaving Cert Sample Essay

'Patrick Kavanagh's carefully crafted poems range from intense longing to sheer delight.' Discuss the extent to which you agree or disagree with the above statement. Develop your response with reference to the poems by Kavanagh on your course.

Sample Essay

1. Patrick Kavanagh's lyrical poems 'Inniskeen Road', 'Advent', 'A Christmas Childhood' and the Canal Bank sonnets reveal desire and enchantment with local detail, but which is of worldwide significance. Kavanagh tells universal truths about love and life in vigorous, colloquial language.

2. Feelings of longing and joy are found in 'Inniskeen Road'. A compound phrase, 'wink-and-elbow language of delight', captures the pleasure of a shared joke among friends who are on the way to a local dance. Kavanagh is not really part of that scene and, in one sense, he longs to be accepted. His status as lonely outsider is graphically detailed, 'there is not a spot

upon a mile of road, no shadow thrown'. Onomatopoeia and alliteration recreate the deserted scene, 'not a footfall tapping secrecies of stone'. Yet, in the reflective sestet, the poet delights in his solitary role, 'I am king of banks and stones and every blooming thing'. The colloquialism, 'blooming', suggests both the growth of nature and also the poet's resentment at being excluded from the community.

3. 'Advent' recalls the religious period before Christmas when people fasted. A harsh alliterative phrase dismisses overindulgence in sensual pleasure, 'We have tested and tasted too much, lover'. The poet longs for a state of childhood innocence when the world was viewed with wonder, seeing 'the newness that was in every stale thing'. Kavanagh reconstructs what it is like to look at the world through the unspoilt eyes of a child, full of 'spirit-shocking wonder' when observing 'a black slanting Ulster hill'. His invented word, 'dreeping', reveals the 'heart-breaking strangeness' of wet saturated hedges. He wants readers to relive the exhilarating spiritual experience of the coming of Christ 'with a January flower'.

4. Longing for innocence is also found in 'A Christmas Childhood' where Kavanagh recalls memories of Christmas Eve when he was just six years old. Everything excited him then as he watched his parents working on the family farm and associated them with the Bethlehem Bible story of the first Christmas. He 'knew some strange thing had happened'. Once again, ordinary things became transformed, as his 'father played the melodion'. It seems Kavanagh is yearning to experience such happiness when he felt so close to his mother who made 'the music of milking'. Everyday language and vivid imagery bring the rural farmyard to life. He longs for the past and his innocent imagination when wild whin bushes reminded him of the 'Three Wise Kings'.

5. Kavanagh wants to be close to nature again as he remembers the 'child poet' in himself, fascinated by what looked like writing on frost-covered stones. He again longs to be 'six Christmases of age', an innocent little boy who 'hid in the doorway' and playing with his penknife, 'I nicked six nicks on the door-post'. The tone is nostalgic throughout and Kavanagh uses everyday colloquial language to express his love for his parents and the natural world.

6. The sonnet, 'Canal Bank Walk', uses more compound imagery, 'Leafy-with-love', to capture the pleasure Kavanagh experiences in nature while he recuperates after a serious operation. Sitting on the bank of the canal he glories in 'the green waters of the canal pouring redemption for me'. He is now enjoying what he previously longed for, the awareness of the extraordinary in the ordinary such as 'The bright stick trapped'. Internal rhyme, 'enrapture me', encapture me', creates a

INDICATIVE MATERIAL

- **Kavanagh's carefully crafted poems** (sonnet, ballad, rich visual/aural imagery, onomatopoeia, alliteration, personification, local and global allusions, striking comparisons, colloquialism, end rhyme/internal rhyme, innovative use of compound words, etc.)

… range from:

- **intense longing to sheer delight** (through bittersweet nostalgic memories, joy and sorrow of romantic love, transience and loss, enchantment with nature, pride in role as poet, etc.)

hypnotic rhythm. Rustling sounds of 'eternal voices by a beech' suggest an ecstatic summer mood. The poet longs to enjoy the moment, 'give me ad lib'. He longs to be 'honoured with a new dress woven' from nature's 'green and blue things'.

7. 'Lines Written on a Seat' humorously invents a new word, 'niagarously', to describe the water flowing through the Grand Canal as if it were imitating the great Canadian waterfall, Niagara Falls. Personification transforms the bridges. 'Fantastic light' spills through their 'eyes'. The graceful curve of a swan's neck is highlighted, 'head low with many apologies'. He is not interested in a showy 'hero-courageous tomb', but 'a canal seat for the passer-by'. The poet is happy with the mysterious joys of nature, a place to sit and appreciate the insignificant little things in life.

8. Kavanagh's poems are often full of longing, acceptance and joy. They invite readers to share in the fun of the crowd going to a local rural dance, and to experience the pain and loneliness of the creative artist. They also allow us to see through the clear eyes of a little child the wonders of the world, and to appreciate the beauty of the natural world.

(770 words)

> **EXAMINER'S COMMENT**
>
> *A good direct response that shows close personal engagement with Kavanagh's poetry. While the introduction emphasises the universality of the poet's themes, the main body of the essay is well focused on both elements of the question (craft and feelings). Paragraphs 2 and 6 are particularly thorough on Kavanagh's imaginative writing style (such as aural effects, colloquial language and imagery). Relevant accurate quotes are very well worked into the critical discussion throughout. Expression is clear and assured – although a little repetitive (the verb 'longs' is overused). Overall, a well-supported top-grade standard.*

GRADE: H1
P = 14/15
C = 14/15
L = 13/15
M = 5/5
Total = 46/50

👀 Revision Overview

'Inniskeen Road: July Evening'
This dramatic sonnet presents Kavanagh's relationship with nature and his community. A reflective sestet considers the contradictions of a poet's life.

'Shancoduff' (OL)
Kavanagh's conflicted attitude to his rural homeland is evident in this darkly humorous poem. Yet he is clearly devastated when any criticism is levelled at this special place.

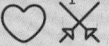

from 'The Great Hunger'
Dramatic scenes from a bachelor farmer's life explore his ambivalent relationship with the land, the devastating consequences of poverty and the repression of sexuality. The poet's alternative view of traditional Irish rural living provides a moving insight into human frustration.

'Advent'
Kavanagh's dissatisfaction with the material world and his longing for spiritual renewal is explored in the opening sonnet. The second sonnet imagines the heartening experience of a poetic rebirth.

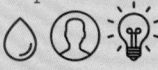

'A Christmas Childhood' (OL)
An idyllic memory poem celebrating his childhood experience of Christmas, a special time of magic and mystery for Kavanagh. As an adult, he is keenly aware of passing time and the loss of innocence.

'Epic'
This ironic account of a small-scale land dispute between local farmers widens into a consideration of international conflicts. The poem also reflects on the poet's function in society.

'Canal Bank Walk'
Popular sonnet celebrating the natural world and the poet's spiritual renewal following a life-threatening illness. A sense of God's creation is central to many of Kavanagh's later poems.

'Lines written on a Seat on the Grand Canal, Dublin'
Another Dublin sonnet declaring the poet's wholehearted desire to be honoured humbly with a simple seat in one of his favourite places.

'The Hospital'
Another unusual love sonnet expressing the poet's spiritual and poetic renewal. Kavanagh encourages readers to appreciate life's mundane and everyday joys.

'On Raglan Road'
Kavanagh's deep pride in his role as poet is unapologetically stated in this poignant love song set on 'a quiet street' in Dublin.

💬 Last Words

'Kavanagh gave you permission to dwell without cultural anxiety among the usual landmarks of your life. He brought us back to where we came from.'
Seamus Heaney

'At his memorial seat on the Grand Canal, visitors are asked to sit with their backs to the memorial description, reading instead the scene before them.'
Antoinette Quinn

'I've often wondered if I'd be different if I had been brought up to love better things.'
Patrick Kavanagh

NATURE | IDENTITY | CREATIVITY | MEANING OF LIFE | LOSS | HISTORY/MEMORY | LOVE | CONFLICT/HATE | CHILDHOOD

Derek Mahon
1941–2020

'I suppose the function of poetry for me is the celebration of the English language.'

Derek Mahon was born in Belfast and educated at Trinity College Dublin and Paris-Sorbonne. He worked as a journalist in London and in New York, where he also taught at NYU. His poetry expresses the feelings of exile and the oppressiveness of history that characterise much of modern life. His is a pessimism that discovers great beauty in mundane locations (an abandoned shed filled with decomposing mushrooms, a lively fishing village, an offshore island) but despairs at their impermanence and eventual meaninglessness. Mahon's poems often project into a devastating future. Recurring settings in his work include desolate landscapes, deserted beaches and other closely observed scenes of immense isolation. This reflects his complex attitude to his own middle-class Ulster background. Despite its emergence from the turmoil of Northern Ireland, his poetic voice is formal, moderate and even restrained. Although he self-consciously distanced himself from Ireland, Derek Mahon still managed to address this alienation from homeland. Part of his impressive skill was to apply exceptional technical ability and light humour to such serious themes as the past, identity, place, conflict, loneliness and modern culture.

Investigate Further

To find out more about Derek Mahon, or to hear readings of his poems not available in your eBook, you could search some websites, such as YouTube.

Note: The poet made some slight revisions to several poems before his death. These are included in *Poetry Focus 2025*. However, several years earlier, he recorded a previous version of the poems for the audio eBook edition.

Prescribed Poems

1 'Grandfather' (OL)
In this personal sonnet about his grandfather, Mahon presents a fascinating image of an old man who seems to have difficulty coming to terms with his retirement. The grandfather's character remains a mystery throughout: 'Nothing escapes him; he escapes us all'.
Page 246

2 'Day Trip to Donegal'
Mahon's visit to a coastal village in Donegal turns out to be an unsettling experience. On returning to his familiar Belfast home, he feels suddenly troubled and forsaken. He is haunted by a vivid nightmare and imagines himself 'alone far out at sea'.
Page 250

3 'Ecclesiastes'
Using the language of a fundamentalist Christian preacher, the poet describes Belfast as a bleak, oppressive city. But he is unable to deny his roots and – almost against his will – feels at home there.
Page 254

4 'After the *Titanic*' (OL)
This powerfully moving monologue allows us to hear the voice of Bruce Ismay in his response to one of history's great sea tragedies. Ismay defends his actions on the night of the disaster and appeals for understanding: 'Include me in your commemorations'.
Page 258

5 'As It Should Be'
This highly ironic poem explores aspects of fanaticism and the cycle of violence in Irish history. A Free State officer gives his version of shooting a rebel soldier ('gunned him down in a blind yard'). Mahon satirises the arrogant officer's self-serving attempts to justify the killing.
Page 263

6 'A Disused Shed in Co. Wexford'
Mahon's most famous evocation of the downtrodden and forgotten. He describes the 'thousand mushrooms' in the abandoned shed, finally exposed to daylight. Rich symbolism and sensuous images highlight the anguish of suffering people, begging us to 'speak on their behalf'.
Page 267

7 'Rathlin'
Ireland's violent history – and the continuing cycle of conflict – is a recurring theme in Mahon's poetry. On a visit to Rathlin Island he recalls a late 16th-century massacre and discovers ghostly presences from the past. In the end, the poet wonders whether 'the future lies before us or behind'.
Page 272

8 'The Chinese Restaurant in Portrush'
This beautiful and delicate poem, set in a small Chinese restaurant, reflects on a number of interesting themes: identity and home; loss and separation; and the Troubles.
Page 276

9 'Kinsale'
This short poem deals with another of Mahon's favourite themes: the tension between Ireland's past and its present. While the poet hints at the country's troubled history, he sees some reason for optimism in modern-day Kinsale.
Page 280

10 'Antarctica' (OL)
This poem is based on Scott's ill-fated expedition to the South Pole in 1912. One of the team members, Lawrence Oates, gave up his life so that his companions might have a better chance of survival. Mahon sums up this futile act of heroism: 'At the heart of the ridiculous, the sublime'.
Page 283

(OL) indicates poems that are also prescribed for the Ordinary Level course.

1. Grandfather

They brought him in on a stretcher from the world,
wounded but humorous, and he soon recovered.
Boiler-rooms, row upon row of gantries rolled
away to reveal the landscape of a childhood
only he can recapture. Even on cold   5
mornings he is up at six with a block of wood
or a box of nails, discreetly up to no good
or banging round the house like a four-year-old –

never there when you call. But after dark
you hear his great boots thumping in the hall   10
and in he comes, as cute as they come. Each night
his shrewd eyes bolt the door and wind the clock
against the future, then his light goes out.
Nothing escapes him; he escapes us all.

Boiler-rooms: engine rooms in ships.
gantries: bridge-like scaffolds that support cranes, usually in a shipyard.
discreetly: carefully, circumspectly.
cute: sly, cunning.
shrewd: clever, perceptive.

'row upon row of gantries'

👤 Personal Response

1. What was your impression of the poet's grandfather? Is he a happy man?
2. Derek Mahon uses colloquial language throughout this poem. Choose two examples and comment briefly on the effectiveness of each.
3. Write a short personal response to this poem. Refer to the text in your answer.

👁 Critical Literacy

'Grandfather' comes from Derek Mahon's first poetry collection, *Night Crossing* (1968). The poet's grandfather was a foreman boiler-maker in the famous Belfast shipyard Harland and Wolff, where the *Titanic* was built. Mahon gives 'a voice to those who are marginalised in society' and instead of a picture of a faceless retired man, a wonderful character – eccentric, liberated and elusive – emerges from this compact sonnet. We hear the admiration and slight exasperation of the poet as he observes the noisy presence of his grandfather in the house. Mahon uses an amended sonnet form to comment imaginatively on a rather rebellious, 'cute' individual.

Derek Mahon is very conscious of his roots. He has said that 'the shipyards of Belfast are no less part' of the Irish experience 'than a country town in the Gaeltacht'. In a sense, he is celebrating industrialised, urban Belfast. Many of the **stereotypical characteristics of Northern Irish people** (tenacity, rebelliousness, self-reliance and a wry sense of humour) are evident in the description of Mahon's grandfather, who had to retire from the Belfast shipyards after a work-related accident. The prepositions 'in', 'on' and 'from' in the first line contain and confine the storyline of the poem. Mahon's grandfather is now away from the world of work, and forced to spend his time in the house.

His **indomitable spirit** is conveyed in the sparse second line: 'wounded but humorous, and he soon recovered'. His good-humoured battle for health is captured in these few words. The harsh, masculine world of the shipyard is vividly depicted by images of 'Boiler-rooms' and 'gantries'. This tough environment now recedes, almost like a cartoon sequence: 'row upon row … rolled/away'. The strict, ordered world of physical work is replaced by the magical 'landscape of a childhood'. Freedom and relaxation beckon, but only to him, as 'only he can recapture' it. Although he has been released from the obligations and burdens of the working world, he seems to be uncomfortable with the transition to retirement. Is there a sense that he feels redundant and ill at ease?

The grandfather's individuality is brilliantly captured by Mahon's adaptation of the sonnet form, mixing elements from the Petrarchan and Shakespearean tradition. The grandfather is not someone who conforms to the conventional notion of a 'normal' elderly person. The rhymes mirror this, as they slip and slide like the elusive grandfather ('world'/'rolled'; 'childhood'/'recovered'). Line 5 paints a picture of **an old man who is still energetic, secretive and liberated**. He endures hardship without complaint ('Even on cold/mornings'). An early riser ('up at six'), he is industrious and noisily goes about doing little jobs with his 'block of wood/or a box of nails'. While there is more than a hint of frustration, he still enjoys a child-like freedom ('like a four-year-old').

The **run-on line that bridges the octet and sestet** illustrates the old man's lively personality. The poet's mild exasperation is evident when he remarks that his grandfather is 'never there when you call'. The poem turns on the word 'But' and we see the grandfather at night. The colloquial phrase 'as cute as they come' firmly roots him in Belfast, referring both to **the charm and cunning of this eccentric character**. He performs the night duties of the house, securing it against harm, as he goes to 'bolt the door' and 'wind the clock'. He is aware of the dangers 'after dark'. Finally he rests: 'then his light goes out'. The phrase refers not only to the switching off of his bedroom light, but also to the extinguishing of his energy. His earlier presence – captured in the percussive musical sounds of 'banging' and 'thumping' – is at last still and silent.

The final line is enigmatic and places the grandfather centre stage: 'Nothing escapes him; he escapes us all'. This old man is aware of everything, yet **he retains his mystery, his uniqueness**. Throughout this personal reflection, Mahon's tone is both nostalgic and affectionate. His technical expertise is clearly evident in this sonnet. He plays with its form as 'discreetly' as his grandfather moves around the house.

✒ Writing About the Poem

'Derek Mahon's acute eye and precise ear are notable features of his poetry.' Discuss this view with particular reference to 'Grandfather'. Support your points with reference to the text.

Sample Paragraph

I was surprised by the poem 'Grandfather'. The onomatopoeia in the verbs 'thumping' and 'banging', with their explosive letters 'p' and 'b', made us hear this noisy man as he went about 'like a four-year-old'. Yet, he was 'fixing things' with his 'block of wood/or a box of nails'. I could also hear the slightly irritated voice of the poet. The grandfather was 'up at six'; he was 'never there when you call'. The twanging tones of Northern Ireland are heard in the colloquial phrases 'up to no good' and 'as cute as they come'. Wonderfully detailed images are also presented.

This man still retains traces of his former life as his 'great boots' can be heard around the house. 'Each night' he is careful to 'bolt the door' and 'wind the clock'. I really liked the last line, as I could see this clever, mischievous old man whom 'Nothing escapes' and I could sense that he was answerable to no one ('he escapes us all').

> **EXAMINER'S COMMENT**
> A clear treatment of the two aspects of the question: Mahon's 'acute eye' and 'precise ear'. Focused points throughout – particularly effective sound effects, showing very good understanding of the poem. There was also real engagement and the response was ably supported by relevant quotation. Well-sustained top-grade personal response.

✒ Class/Homework Exercises

1. 'Derek Mahon is a poet who is more interested in people than places.' To what extent do you agree with this statement in relation to 'Grandfather'? Refer closely to the text in your response.
2. 'Mahon often explores unsettling themes of isolation and loneliness in his poetry.' To what extent is this evident in 'Grandfather'? Refer to the poem in your answer.

◉ Points to Consider

- Subtle portrait of a thought-provoking character.
- Nostalgic glimpse of poet's Belfast working-class family.
- Petrarchan sonnet, gentle rhythm, affectionate tone.
- Effective aural and visual images add authenticity.
- Evocative sense of time, old age and mortality.

2 Day Trip to Donegal

We reached the sea in early afternoon,
climbed stiffly out; there were things to be done,
clothes to be picked up, friends to be seen.
As ever, the nearby hills were a deeper green
than anywhere in the world, and the grave 5
grey of the sea the grimmer in that enclave.

Down at the pier the boats gave up their catch,
a squirming glimmer of gills. They fetch
ten times as much in the city as there,
and still the fish come in year after year – 10
herring and mackerel, flopping about the deck
in attitudes of agony and heartbreak.

We left at eight, drove back the way we came,
the sea receding down each muddy lane.
Around midnight we changed down into suburbs 15
sunk in a sleep no gale-force wind disturbs.
The time of year had left its mark
on frosty pavements glistening in the dark.

Give me a ring, goodnight, and so to bed …
That night the slow sea washed against my head, 20
performing its immeasurable erosions –
spilling into the skull, marbling the stones
that spine the very harbour wall,
muttering its threat to villages of landfall.

At dawn I was alone far out at sea 25
without skill or reassurance – nobody
to show me how, no promise of rescue –
cursing my constant failure to take due
forethought for this; contriving vain
overtures to the vindictive wind and rain. 30

grave: sombre, ominous.
enclave: enclosed area.

squirming: twisting.

receding: retreating, withdrawing.

marbling: polishing, staining.
spine: run along.
landfall: the coastline.

forethought: preparation.
vain: pointless.
overtures: advances, proposals.
vindictive: bitter, vengeful.

'I was alone far out at sea'

👤 Personal Response

1. Based on your reading of the first two stanzas, describe the poet's initial impressions of Donegal. Support the points you make with reference to the text.
2. Choose one image (or phrase) from the poem that you thought was particularly striking. Briefly explain your choice.
3. In your opinion, what is the central theme of this poem? Refer to the text in your answer.

👁 Critical Literacy

This poem appeared in Mahon's first poetry collection, *Night Crossing* (1968). On a first reading, it appears to be a typical nature poem based on a simple account of an excursion to the windswept coast of Donegal. Many poems feature a journey motif, usually symbolic of the search for self-discovery, insight or meaning. In this case, more attention is given to the return trip and the dream that dominates the poem's final two stanzas.

In the <mark>opening stanza</mark>, Mahon wastes little time in setting the scene and providing atmosphere, as he describes his arrival in Donegal. Characteristically, **the language has a conversational quality** ('there were things to be done'). He and his friends are uncomfortable after the long journey ('climbed stiffly out'). But their mood lightens a little as they begin to take in the beauty of their surroundings, the rural seaside scene and the impressive landscape: 'a deeper green/than anywhere in the world'. There is, however, something unappealing about the place and the ocean is described in dubious terms: 'the grave/grey of the sea the grimmer in that enclave'. The gentle alliteration of 'gr' emphasises the sound of nearby waves. Interestingly, Mahon paints the sea's greyness in terms of mood rather than colour; its distant, menacing nature is emphasised.

<mark>Stanza two</mark> focuses on details of the harbour, where local fishermen are at work. The poet observes 'herring and mackerel, flopping about the deck'. Precise, vivid description personifies the 'squirming glimmer of gills'. His **sympathies are drawn to their suffering** ('in attitudes of agony and heartbreak'). By reminding us of distressing emotional experiences, Mahon makes us consider the systematic mass slaughter of powerless animals, something most of us take for granted. The image of the dead and dying fish can also be seen as a symbol of human suffering throughout history.

Much of <mark>stanza three</mark> describes the return journey to Belfast. The account reads like a diary: 'We left at eight, drove back the way we came'. Mahon's sibilant effects capture the fading sound of the 'sea receding' in the distance. By midnight, he reaches his familiar home on the outskirts of the city. It is 'sunk in a sleep no gale-force wind disturbs'. The descent into **this secure,**

inviting world – in contrast to the more threatening Donegal coast – is emphasised by the reference to the vehicle's gears: 'we changed down into suburbs'. However, the evidence of nature's mysterious beauty is still apparent 'on frosty pavements glistening in the dark'.

Stanza four marks a **noticeable turning point** for the poet. Having left his friends, he is exhausted by the journey and retires for the night: 'and so to bed'. Immediately, **the poem becomes intensely introspective**, as his thoughts are haunted by vivid memories of the day trip: 'the slow sea washed against my head'. Once again, the prominent sibilance suggests the insistent sound of the waves. In a nightmarish blend of actual events and his own heightened imagination, Mahon uses the powerfully eroding sea as a metaphor for his growing sense of disquiet. Somewhere between sleep and waking, the relentless ocean is 'spilling into the skull'. Disturbing references to the 'immeasurable' destruction of the coastline 'muttering its threat' add to this increasingly uneasy mood of fear and discomfort.

After a restless night, Mahon wakes early. He feels isolated and alone ('far out at sea'). He is acutely aware that he has been cast adrift with 'no promise of rescue'. Stanza five is dominated by frustration and despair. **Repetition and broad vowel sounds echo the depth of desolation he feels**: 'cursing my constant failure'. Run-on lines and an unrestrained rhythm also reflect the poet's edgy stream of consciousness. As a final futile gesture, he resorts to imploring 'the vindictive wind and rain' to save him. In associating his alienation with being lost at sea, the poet might well be suggesting other universal human fears, perhaps the fear of facing death alone. This dark ending illustrates how Derek Mahon can take a relatively simple subject (a day trip to the coast) and turn it into a nightmare full of terrifying images.

Writing About the Poem

'Mahon's poetry is memorable for its striking images, but he is primarily a poet who makes us think.' Discuss this view in relation to 'Day Trip to Donegal'. Refer closely to the poem in your answer.

Sample Paragraph

On first reading, 'Day Trip to Donegal' appears straightforward. The poet and his friends arrive at the coast. His vivid description seems exaggerated – the hills of Donegal are 'a deeper green/than anywhere in the world'. I thought he painted a disturbing picture of the grey sea and grim atmosphere. His image of the dying fish, flopping about in 'agony and heartbreak', makes us think of human suffering. On his return to Belfast, Mahon has troubled dreams: 'slow sea washed against my head'.

The metaphor is extraordinary, reminding me of how affected he has been by the Donegal coast. Mahon comes across as a vulnerable figure 'alone far out at sea'. There is a suggestion that he is suddenly aware of his own desperate state – uncertain and lonely.

> **EXAMINER'S COMMENT**
> A well-focused top-grade response, addressing both elements of the question. There is also good personal engagement. Accurate and appropriate quotations are skilfully used as a basis for insightful discussion throughout. The expression is varied and controlled.

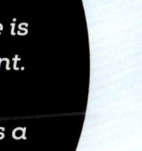

Class/Homework Exercises

1. In your opinion, how was Derek Mahon affected by his visit to Donegal? Refer closely to the poem in your answer.
2. Based on your reading of 'Day Trip to Donegal', what point do you think Mahon is making about humankind's relationship with nature? Refer to the text in your answer.

Points to Consider

- Uncertainty, alienation and estrangement are central themes.
- Sustained mood of unease pervades the poem.
- Graphic imagery highlights humans' harmful intrusion in the natural world.
- Effective use of personification, assonance and sibilance.
- Range of tones: reticent, reflective, pessimistic, fatalistic.

3. Ecclesiastes

Title: Ecclesiastes is the name of an Old Testament book in the Bible; much of the philosophy in the book argued that life is essentially meaningless and should therefore be enjoyed.

God, you could grow to love it, God-fearing, God-
    chosen purist little puritan that,
for all your wiles and smiles, you are (the
    dank churches, the empty streets,
the shipyard silence, the tied-up swings) and   5
    shelter your cold heart from the heat
of the world, from woman-inquisition, from the
    bright eyes of children. Yes, you could
wear black, drink water, nourish a fierce zeal
    with locusts and wild honey, and not   10
feel called upon to understand and forgive
    but only to speak with a bleak
afflatus, and love the January rains when they
    darken the dark doors and sink hard
into the Antrim hills, the shore, the heaped   15
    graves of your fathers. Bury that red
bandana and stick, that banjo; this is your
    country, close one eye and be king.
Your people await you, their heavy washing
    flaps for you in the housing estates –   20
a credulous people. God, you could do it, God
    help you, stand on a corner stiff
with rhetoric, promising nothing under the sun.

purist: extremist.
puritan: highly moral person.
wiles: tricks.
dank: damp.
tied-up swings: playgrounds were closed on Sundays by Protestant-controlled local councils.
inquisition: questioning, opposition.
zeal: fanaticism, fervour.
locusts and wild honey: the simple food of biblical prophets and sinners doing penance.
afflatus: divine guidance.
bandana and stick, that banjo: symbols of rebellion and creativity.
credulous: unsuspecting, naive.
rhetoric: oratory; exaggeration.

'the empty streets'

👤 Personal Response

1. In your opinion, what is Mahon's attitude to traditional Belfast Protestantism? Is he contemptuous or sympathetic towards it?
2. Choose one example of irony from the poem and comment on its effectiveness.
3. In your view, does the poem end on an optimistic or pessimistic note? Briefly explain your answer, using reference to the text.

👁 Critical Literacy

'Ecclesiastes' is set in Derek Mahon's home town of Belfast. The poem was first published in 1972, when sectarian violence was on the rise in Northern Ireland; it is as close as the poet gets to writing directly about the Ulster Protestant tradition. In the course of this satirical poem, Mahon reveals mixed feelings towards his roots and condemns the fanatical preaching that exploits 'credulous people'. Ironically, just like Bible-thumping preachers, poets also use the power of language to communicate with others.

The **opening lines** of the poem have the sense of an interior monologue, with Mahon (seemingly in an ironic mood) reflecting on some familiar features of Ulster Protestantism: 'dank churches, the empty streets' (**line 4**). His portrayal of Northern Protestants is highly critical. They are 'God-fearing' but self-satisfied ('chosen') believers whose strict form of worship is strait-laced and cheerless. Sharp consonant sounds and the abrupt repetition of 'God' echo **the violent oratory of the more extreme religious preaching** heard in Belfast during the early 1970s. Nevertheless, the poet retains a close affiliation with his uncompromising heritage, despite all its austerity: 'God, you could grow to love it'. The colloquial language adds an authentic touch, as Mahon delves deeper into the reality of strict patriarchal Protestantism. A salvation of sorts is offered, but it involves sacrificing human warmth and family life: 'the/bright eyes of children' (**line 8**).

This deeply sombre mood continues in **lines 9–10**, where the poet focuses on the 'fierce zeal' of some Protestant clergymen who 'wear black, drink water' and imagine themselves as ancient biblical holy men living on 'locusts and wild honey'. The **scathing tone** satirises hard-line fanatics who are out of touch and lack compassion. Mahon's imagery becomes increasingly bleak; he sets this grim, doctrinal religion in its local context of 'January rains' and 'dark doors'. There is no disguising his deep distaste for the rigid inhumanity of die-hard puritans who never 'feel called upon to understand and forgive'. But while the presence of this extreme Protestant tradition is highlighted in the reference to 'the heaped/graves of your fathers', there is also a possibility that such intolerant attitudes might be dying out.

However, such change seems unlikely in the immediate future and the poet echoes the conservative voice of dull Ulster Protestant culture, which continues to oppose any signs of freedom or adventure: 'Bury that red/ bandana and stick, that banjo' (lines 16–17). As far as Mahon is concerned, Northern Ireland remains blinded by the past; it is still a place where powerful traditionalists can 'close one eye and be king'. This ironic observation recalls the old proverb: 'In the land of the blind, the one-eyed man is king.' **The tone – equally regretful and resentful – is typically ambivalent**, reflecting the poet's apparent love–hate relationship with his homeland.

In the poem's final lines, Mahon accepts that his own roots will always lie within the Ulster Protestant tradition: 'Your people await you'. Almost against his will, he is drawn to Belfast's ordinary working-class areas ('the housing estates') with 'a credulous people' who are easily led. The poet feels sympathy for his fellow Protestants, while rejecting their religious bigotry. Mahon leaves us with a **dramatic image of a street preacher** ('stiff/with rhetoric') ranting at passers-by and 'promising nothing under the sun'. This ridiculous figure seems to sum up all the intransigence and absurdity of small-minded religious teaching. There is little doubt that Mahon's preacher warns of a dark and dismal future for Northern Ireland.

Writing About the Poem

'Derek Mahon's Protestant culture provides the basis for much of his poetry.' Discuss this statement, with particular reference to 'Ecclesiastes'. Support the points you make with reference to the poem.

Sample Paragraph

'Ecclesiastes' refers to a book of the Bible and would be familiar to many Belfast Protestants. Mahon grew up in Belfast and religion has always played an important role there – sometimes it has caused more harm than good. Mahon uses the strident voice of a preacher to express his criticism of the puritanical religion, based on fear and penance. He describes it as 'God-fearing'. Images of Belfast are bleak: 'dank churches', and 'preachers wear black'. At the same time, the poet's tone is one of affection. He thinks of Protestant generations who have settled in Co. Antrim: 'the heaped graves of fathers'. Although Mahon mocks the conservative aspects of his own Protestant culture, he still has a regard for it. To him, these 'credulous people' are hardworking and sincere.

EXAMINER'S COMMENT

This is a solid response, which addresses the question throughout. There is evidence of good engagement with the poem – especially with the poet's ambivalent attitude to the Protestant tradition. While references are used well, some of the quotes are inaccurate. A high-grade response, overall.

✒ Class/Homework Exercises

1. 'Tensions and conflict are prominent themes in the poetry of Derek Mahon.' Discuss this view, with reference to 'Ecclesiastes'.
2. 'Mahon makes effective use of vivid visual images throughout the poem to symbolise the harsh reality of Belfast life.' Discuss this view, developing your answer with reference to the text.

⊙ Points to Consider

- Insightful commentary on traditional Northern Protestantism.
- Poet captures the essence of strict evangelism while subtly mocking it.
- Colloquial language echoes Belfast working-class speech.
- Other style features include repetition, irony, evocative visual and aural imagery.
- Range of tones: satirical, nostalgic, affectionate, fearful.

4 After the *Titanic*

They said I got away in a boat
and humbled me at the inquiry. I swear
   I sank as far that night as any
hero. As I sat shivering on the dark water
   I turned to ice to hear my costly 5
life go thundering down in a pandemonium of
   prams, pianos, sideboards, winches,
boilers bursting and shredded ragtime. Now I hide
   in a lonely house behind the sea
where the tide leaves broken toys and hatboxes 10
   silently at my door. The showers of
April, flowers of May mean nothing to me, nor the
   late light of June, when my gardener
describes to strangers how the old man stays in bed
   on seaward mornings after nights of 15
wind, takes his morphine and will see no one. Then it is
   I drown again with all those dim
lost faces I never understood, my poor soul
   screams out in the starlight, heart
breaks loose and rolls down like a stone. 20
   include me in your commemorations.

'and humbled me at the inquiry'

Titanic: Huge ship built in Belfast, which sank on its maiden voyage in 1912. Over 1,500 people were killed in the greatest loss of lives in maritime history.

I: Bruce Ismay, managing director of the White Star Line, which owned the *Titanic*. He was one of the few male survivors of the tragedy.
inquiry: investigation.

pandemonium: turmoil, uproar.
winches: machines for hauling or lifting.
ragtime: early form of jazz, sometimes called 'ragged rhythm'; a reference to the bravery of the orchestra which continued to play as the ship sank.

seaward: looking towards the sea.
morphine: addictive drug.

commemorations: memorial ceremonies.

👤 Personal Response

1. From your initial reading of 'After the *Titanic*', do you feel any sympathy for Bruce Ismay? Support your response with reference to the poem.
2. Comment on the poet's use of sound effects in lines 7–8.
3. Mahon is often praised for his powerfully vivid imagery. Choose two visual images that appeal to you in the poem. Comment on the effectiveness of each.

👁 Critical Literacy

'After the *Titanic*' comes from Derek Mahon's second collection, *Lives* (1975). It charts the journey of Joseph Bruce Ismay, managing director of the White Star Line, the shipping company that owned the *Titanic*. Ismay was strongly criticised for his alleged failure to help drowning passengers and he was one of only a handful of men to escape the sinking ship. Mahon has a gift for entering into the lives of others, particularly lone, abandoned individuals like Bruce Ismay.

In this dramatic monologue, Derek Mahon **adopts the persona Bruce Ismay, manager of the White Star Line, the company responsible for the *Titanic*. This despondent man** attempts to refute the accusations of cowardice levelled at him: 'They said I got away in a boat' (line 1). However, we quickly become aware of Ismay's self-absorption when we note the overuse of 'I', 'me' and 'my'. All the sentences in this poem relate to his life after the sinking of the *Titanic*. Ismay complains about how he has been viewed by the public. The finger of accusation has been pointed directly at him ('humbled me at the inquiry'), but he emphatically pleads his case ('I swear'), insisting that he 'sank as far that night as any/hero'.

But we cannot help wondering if Ismay protests too much. Other men had given their lives so that women and children could be saved. Mahon's **visual effects graphically illustrate the bitterly cold night** ('shivering on the dark water') as well as Ismay's own fear: 'I turned to ice'. This phrase in line 5 is ironic, as readers are all too aware that the ship sank because it hit an iceberg. There is also the implication that Ismay's own life halted – froze – on the night of 14 April 1912. He spent the next 25 years reliving over and over again the horrifying events of that terrible disaster. Since that moment, he has been as cold as death.

Mahon is a solitary observer. He **invites us to witness the turmoil of the awful tragedy** through striking images in lines 6–7. The consonants in 'pandemonium', 'prams' and 'pianos' are scattered by the dissonance of random items thrown together chaotically by the sinking ship: 'sideboards, winches'. The band played on boldly as the vessel sank and this is remembered in the phrase 'shredded ragtime'. Mahon's choice of the adjective 'shredded' presents a sad picture of the musicians' torn sheet music floating on the surface of the dark Atlantic water. The poet asks us to reflect not only on the dreadful suffering of the ship's passengers on that fateful night, but also on Bruce Ismay's character ('my costly/life'). This wealthy man is shown to be totally self-serving, in stark contrast to the stoical, brave musicians on the ship.

Line 8 brings the scene to the present: 'Now I hide'. Ismay has retired and taken refuge from the hostile world in a 'lonely house behind the sea'. **Mahon asks us to reflect sympathetically on his shame and isolation.** For Ismay, there is no escaping the past. The sea itself brings constant, silent reminders of the women ('hatboxes') and children ('broken toys') who have drowned, possibly because of his selfish actions. Nonetheless, it is clear that he is now a broken man who has no interest in nature's seasonal changes: 'The showers of/April, flowers of May mean nothing to me'. The harmony of the natural world is beautifully suggested by the rhyme of 'flowers' and 'showers'. Ismay is acutely aware of the judgement of others. He recounts how his 'gardener/describes to strangers' the reclusive routine of his day. Although the sun rises in spite of everything, Ismay spends his time in a drug-fuelled half-existence.

Towards the end of the poem, Mahon focuses on Ismay's increasing desolation. We are haunted by his stark admission: 'I drown again with all those dim/lost faces' (lines 17–18). Surprisingly, Ismay also admits he 'never understood' them. Does this mean that he did not recognise the worth and dignity of the *Titanic* victims? Or did he see himself as superior to them? The **poem concludes with a hysterical outburst**, as Ismay expresses his anguish. Mahon's powerful verbs ('screams', 'breaks', 'rolls') dramatically capture the suffering of this guilt-ridden man. Broad vowel sounds ('loose', 'down', 'stone') haul the line downwards. It is as if Ismay is drowning in his own despair. The poet has created an atmosphere of lonely torment in which Ismay's tortured soul is collapsing.

The poem's final line could be seen as a misguided demand from a self-serving man: 'Include me in your commemorations'. Even though Ismay survived the tragedy, he would like to be acknowledged in memorial ceremonies for all those who lost their lives on the *Titanic*. But this line could also be read as a plea for mercy for a wretched man who 'dies' every night. **Is it possible to view Bruce Ismay as a victim?** The poet leaves readers to make up their own minds.

Derek Mahon has always been interested in form and structure, in 'purposefulness, instead of randomness'. He has stated: 'It's important to me what a poem looks like on a page.' **This poem has an irregular left-hand pattern, suggesting all is out of order: the sinking ship, the lost lives, the**

anguished Ismay. The untidy right-hand pattern is reminiscent of the debris carried by the waves, which appears to Ismay as silent reminders of his 'crime'. Run-on lines also suggest the sea's ebb and flow. Whether or not we sympathise with Bruce Ismay, there is no denying that Mahon has created a memorable poem from one of history's greatest maritime tragedies.

Writing About the Poem

'In his poetry, Derek Mahon often allows troubled characters to reveal their true inner selves.' Discuss this statement with reference to 'After the *Titanic*'. Use suitable reference in support of your answer.

Sample Paragraph

Mahon is drawn to people on the edge of society. In 'After the *Titanic*', Mahon speaks with the self-pitying voice of Ismay. He made a decision to take a place on a lifeboat, against the long-standing tradition of women and children first. We realise he may have physically saved himself, but his soul died that night and he is forced to live as an outcast ('takes his morphine and will see no-one'). Mahon shows us the dark side of Ismay – the arrogant man concerned with his 'costly/ Life'. The first person pronoun ('I') is used many times: 'I turned to ice', 'I drown again', showing this man's self-absorption. Mahon's dramatic verbs ('screams out', 'breaks loose', etc.) suggests the horror of Ismay's personal hell. The poet lets us hear this unhappy man demand to be remembered in the outpouring of grief for the victims.

EXAMINER'S COMMENT

This is a well-developed top-grade answer, which shows considered engagement with the poem. Interesting discussion points about how Mahon explores Ismay's conflicted personality are well supported by the careful use of suitable quotation.

Class/Homework Exercises

1. Several tones are evident throughout this poem. Select two which you found interesting and comment briefly on their effectiveness.
2. What is your overall impression of Bruce Ismay? Is he a villain? Or victim? Or both? Refer to the text in your answer.

⊙ Points to Consider

- The poet portrays the different personality traits of a broken man.
- Themes include personal responsibility, cowardice, guilt, victimhood, effects of public criticism.
- Varying tones and moods: sorrow, horror, guilt, pleading.
- Vivid details, dramatic imagery, striking aural effects.

5 🔊 As It Should Be

DEREK MAHON

We hunted the mad bastard
through bog, moorland, rock, to the starlit west
and gunned him down in a blind yard
between ten sleeping lorries
and an electricity generator.   5

Let us hear no idle talk
of the moon in the Yellow River;
the air blows softer since his departure.

Since his tide-burial during school hours
our children have known no bad dreams.   10
Their cries echo lightly along the coast.

This is as it should be.
They will thank us for it when they grow up
to a world with method in it.

blind: enclosed.

electricity generator: machine for producing electric current.

the moon in the Yellow River: reference to Denis Johnston's 1931 play, *The Moon in the Yellow River*, which is set in the Irish Free State. A new hydro-electric generator is being built; a revolutionary tries to blow it up and is later shot.
tide-burial: the carrying of a body out to sea by the tide.

method: law and order.

'through bog, moorland, rock'

👤 Personal Response

1. Mahon is a poet who is known for his sense of compassion. How is this evident in the description of the murdered man? Support your response with reference to the poem.
2. Select one image in the poem that you found particularly interesting and comment on its effectiveness.
3. Write a short personal response to the poem, highlighting the impact it made on you. Refer to the text in your answer.

👁 Critical Literacy

Derek Mahon's *Lives* (1975) contains this frightening defence of violence. Once again, the poet enters into the mindset of an outsider – a murderer who states the truth 'as it should be'. Mahon lets us hear this man speak and invites us to form our own opinion about his beliefs and actions. The poet has said that he experienced 'contempt for what I felt was the barbarism on both sides' during the Northern Troubles. 'As It Should Be' has a very important message to the world today, which is torn apart by violent fundamentalism.

Mahon assumes the persona of the killer and the poem's dramatic opening stanza refers to the collective personal pronoun ('We'). This gives the killer the status of belonging to a group. He acted with their approval: 'We hunted the mad bastard'. The victim is dehumanised by the use of the word 'bastard', rather than his actual name. In the speaker's opinion, this man is 'mad', a lunatic. The desperate chase over barren land is described with economy and precision in the list: 'bog, moorland, rock'. We can imagine the frantic flight of this hunted man, desperately slipping and falling as he tries to escape his pursuers. Then the mood changes as the romantic, magical setting of the 'starlit west' is reached – a suitable location, perhaps, for a dreamy idealist.

Mahon's poem is based on a play by Denis Johnston, *The Moon in the Yellow River* (1931). In this drama set in the Irish Free State, a rebel character attempts to blow up a new hydro-electric generator. For the Free State, the building of Ardnacrusha Station was an important symbol of progress and independence. In the play, the rebel is shot by an officer of the Free State forces, which condone the killing. The new setting of the 'starlit west' reflects the idealistic notions of the 'mad bastard'. The harsh setting of industrial power and progress ('sleeping lorries/and an electricity generator') is where the fugitive rebel is eventually murdered, 'in a blind yard'. The **matter-of-fact reporting of the killing is shocking**. The yard is a walled-up, secret place where terrible things can happen unremarked, unpunished. It is a place from which there is no escape. Is the speaker 'blind' also, only aware of his own narrow fanatical viewpoint? We are led to realise that freedom comes at a terrible price; the birth of a nation is not without pain.

The curt dismissal in the ==second stanza== ('Let us hear no idle talk') is typical of the colloquial idiom used by extremists when they discount opposing points of view. Mahon's choice of the adjective 'idle' shows the contempt of the killer for any opinion except his own. It suggests a foolish action, like trying to catch the moon's reflection in a river. Short lines hint at the speaker's cynical sense of confidence. Despite the brutality of the victim's death, there is a glib attempt to justify the killing: 'the air blows softer since his departure'. **The tone is highly complacent.** Instead of acknowledging the vicious act for what it was, a less offensive term is used: 'departure'. Is the speaker deluding himself or his audience? Through subtle irony, Mahon is slowly making us aware of where his own sympathies lie.

The euphemistic self-justification continues in the ==third stanza==, with a reference to the victim's 'tide-burial'. Mahon shows us that the victim did not even have the dignity of being buried, but was dumped at sea in broad daylight ('during school hours'). **The certain voice of the murderer** is evident when he states that 'our children have known no bad dreams'. With this act, the younger generation is out of danger; it was all done for the children's good. Who could argue with that? The carefree innocence of youth is captured in this lyrical line: 'Their cries echo lightly along the coast'. This is what the killer says he has defended. But has he? Surely a man's blood now stains this coast? Although the poet does not comment directly, he is presenting an alternative perspective and inviting us to form our own opinions.

The ==fourth stanza== echoes the self-righteous in the tones of the Old Testament: 'This is as it should be'. The unwavering, headstrong voice shows no repentance. Now we start to question why it should be this way. Will the children 'thank' the killers for such atrocities 'when they grow up'? Will these violent events ensure or damage the children's happiness? **Mahon awakens our critical faculties.** The chilling concluding image of a 'world with method in it' leaves us wondering exactly whose order has been established in the world. The confident voice of the speaker has a decidedly hollow ring, as the morality of fanaticism is held up for scrutiny. Characteristically, Derek Mahon has given a localised conflict a much greater universal significance.

✒ Writing About the Poem

'Derek Mahon uses polite, refined mockery to examine serious subject matter.' Discuss this statement in relation to the poem 'As It Should Be', developing the points you make with reference to the text.

Sample Paragraph

In 'As It Should Be', Mahon takes on the voice of an extremist to examine the issue of fundamentalism, the belief that one point of view matters to the exclusion of all others. The poet's excellence with language enables him to avoid direct commentary on the event, but through 'polite, refined mockery' of the murderer's own words, he shows the message to be seriously flawed. Bigotry is heard in the phrase 'Let us hear no idle talk'. A lack of compassion for the victim is shown in the speaker's description of him as a 'mad bastard'. The self-delusional denial of callous murder is shown by his use of 'departure' to describe the brutal killing. Mahon's awareness of the truth is contrasted with the murderer's lack of self-awareness in the line: 'This is as it should be'. Mahon's precise observation of the detached murderer allows us to be clearly aware of the man's human inadequacy.

> **EXAMINER'S COMMENT**
>
> A sound understanding of the poem and a clear sense of engagement is evident throughout. The answer carefully explores how Mahon's skill allows readers to see the real truth of the speaker's words. A more focused discussion of tone and irony would have been welcome. Overall, there is effective use of succinct quotation. A high-grade standard.

Class/Homework Exercises

1. 'Although Derek Mahon's poetry is often set in one place only, the emotions aroused by the poems have a much wider resonance.' Discuss this view of Mahon's work, with particular reference to the poem 'As It Should Be'. Refer closely to the text in your response.
2. The poem includes a range of tones – satirical, ruthless, ironic, didactic, etc. In your opinion, what is the dominant tone? Explain your answer using reference to the text.

⊙ Points to Consider

- **Perceptive commentary on paramilitary conflict.**
- **Poet conveys the essence of self-justifying violence while subtly condemning it.**
- **Precise description, evocative visual imagery and colloquial expression.**
- **Variety of tones: ironic, brutal, self-delusional, didactic, etc.**

A Disused Shed in Co. Wexford

Let them not forget us, the weak souls among the asphodels.
– Seferis, Mythistorema
(for J. G. Farrell)

Even now there are places where a thought might grow –
Peruvian mines, worked out and abandoned
to a slow clock of condensation,
an echo trapped for ever, and a flutter
of wildflowers in the lift-shaft,   5
Indian compounds where the winds dance
and a door bangs with diminished confidence,
lime crevices behind rippling rain barrels,
dog corners for bone burials;
and in a disused shed in Co. Wexford,   10

deep in the grounds of a burnt-out hotel,
among the bathtubs and the washbasins
a thousand mushrooms crowd to a keyhole.
This is the one star in their firmament
or frames a star within a star.   15
What should they do there but desire?
So many days beyond the rhododendrons
with the world revolving in its bowl of cloud,
they have learnt patience and silence
listening to the rooks querulous in the high wood.   20

They have been waiting for us in a foetor
of vegetable sweat since civil war days,
since the gravel-crunching, interminable departure
of the expropriated mycologist.
He never came back, and light since then   25
is a keyhole rusting gently after rain.
Spiders have spun, flies dusted to mildew
and once a day, perhaps, they have heard something –
a trickle of masonry, a shout from the blue
or a lorry changing gear at the end of the lane.   30

There have been deaths, the pale flesh flaking
into the earth that nourished it;
and nightmares, born of these and the grim
dominion of stale air and rank moisture.
Those nearest the door grow strong –   35
'Elbow room! Elbow room!'
the rest, dim in a twilight of crumbling
utensils and broken pitchers, groaning
for their deliverance, have been so long
expectant that there is left only the posture.   40

A half century, without visitors, in the dark –
poor preparation for the cracking lock
and creak of hinges; magi, moonmen,
powdery prisoners of the old regime,
web-throated, stalked like triffids, racked by drought   45
and insomnia, only the ghost of a scream
at the flash-bulb firing squad we wake them with
shows there is life yet in their feverish forms.
Grown beyond nature now, soft food for worms,
they lift frail heads in gravity and good faith.   50

They're begging us, you see, in their wordless way,
to do something, to speak on their behalf
or at least not to close the door again.
Lost people of Treblinka and Pompeii!
'Save us, save us,' they seem to say,   55
'let the god not abandon us
who have come so far in darkness and in pain.
We too had our lives to live.
You with your light meter and relaxed itinerary,
let not our naive labours have been in vain!'   60

rank: rotten.

pitchers: pots.

magi: wise men.
moonmen: astronauts (mycologists resemble astronauts in spacesuits).
triffids: fictional plants that threaten the world (from John Wyndham's science fiction novel *The Day of the Triffids*).
racked: tortured.
insomnia: restlessness.

Treblinka: notorious Nazi death camp in Poland.
Pompeii: Italian city destroyed in AD 79 when Mount Vesuvius erupted.

light meter: photographic device to measure brightness.
itinerary: tourist route.
naive: foolish, innocent.

'stale air and rank moisture'

👤 Personal Response

1. Based on your reading of stanza two, what are your initial impressions of the disused shed? Refer to the poem in your answer.
2. Comment briefly on Mahon's use of metaphorical language in the poem.
3. In your opinion, what is the central theme of this poem? Refer to the text in your response.

👁 Critical Literacy

The epigraph of the poem establishes Mahon's deep concern about history's forgotten victims. 'Let them not forget us, the weak souls among the asphodels' is a compelling plea from the powerless. Just like 'After the *Titanic*' and 'As It Should Be', this poem – widely regarded as one of Mahon's finest – illustrates the poet's ability to give a voice to the silenced. 'A Disused Shed in Co. Wexford' is also a poem of great scope, inviting readers to reflect on the tragic lives of others.

Stanza one opens on a meditative note: 'Even now there are places where a thought might grow'. Mahon's preoccupation with seeking meaning is reflected in the intensely dramatic language. He manages to convey a **sense of time passing as well as a feeling of abandonment** in the 'Peruvian mines' and 'Indian compounds'. 'An echo trapped for ever' suggests silent spaces, long since deserted by forgotten generations. As he considers the lives of others and the mystery of time, Mahon seems acutely aware of the shared human experience that transcends the 'slow clock'. He associates the disused shed with other desolate places where confined people might have been exploited or oppressed.

This theme is developed in stanza two, which personifies the 'thousand mushrooms' trapped in the darkness: 'What should they do there but desire?' Their overwhelming sense of longing is all the more poignant since they are resigned to their claustrophobic isolation and 'have learnt patience'. The poet recognises that they are hidden away from the outside 'world revolving in its bowl of cloud', a powerful image evoking both the joy and mystique of creation. For Mahon, **the mushrooms are symbols of all those who have been marginalised over the centuries**. History has no shortage of abandoned communities. In Ireland alone, the poet might be thinking of Anglo-Irish Protestants in the Republic or of disaffected communities in Northern Ireland. At any rate, there is no doubt about the sympathetic mood in these lines and the compassionate tone for all who have suffered.

In stanza three, **the decaying mushrooms are associated with the stagnant period following Irish independence**: 'waiting for us in a foetor/of vegetable sweat since civil war days'. Mahon uses another metaphor (the mycologist's departure) to illustrate how many people felt disowned and forsaken at this time. Images of waste and disintegration ('a keyhole rusting gently', 'flies dusted to mildew') contribute to an understanding of 'interminable' time. The poet also leaves us with a sense of desperate people's awareness of diminishing hope ('a shout from the blue') when faced with the harsh reality of irrevocable loss.

This feeling of anguish dominates stanza four. Mahon's continuing personification of the festering mushrooms vividly evokes the wretched endeavours of all those who experience oppression. References to 'pale flesh flaking', 'nightmares' and the 'dominion of stale air' signify the deadly legacy of human suffering. The derelict shed is filled with 'rank moisture'. **Mahon's rich, sensuous language gives way to a more melodramatic, nightmarish scene** as he envisages the more resistant mushrooms forcing themselves ('Elbow room!') towards the light at the expense of those left 'groaning/for their deliverance'. But they are condemned to captivity for ever and are forced to accept that 'there is left only the posture' of escape.

The poet assumes the role of a tourist in stanza five. The visitor – the first in 'A half century' – is intrigued by the discovery of these hideously distorted mushrooms. To the outsider, they now resemble something from another weird world: 'magi, moonmen'. There is even a sense of menace about these grotesque 'powdery prisoners', which begin to resemble man-eating 'triffids'. **Mahon creates an increasingly surreal and hysterical atmosphere**, dramatising the suffering of the mushrooms, 'racked by drought/and insomnia', when confronted by the intruding sightseer with his camera. The scene is chaotic and confrontational as 'their feverish forms' face 'the flash-bulb firing-squad'. The inevitable presence of death is also evident in the sensuous account of how the decaying fungi have become 'soft food for worms'. In their final failure, all they can do is 'lift frail heads in gravity and good faith'.

Mahon combines the twin themes of history and separation in the highly charged final stanza. On behalf of the world's downtrodden and forgotten, the mushrooms are 'begging us, you see, in their wordless way,/to do something'. The poet refers to **specific victims**: both of the Holocaust and of a great natural disaster ('Lost people of Treblinka and Pompeii'). In a powerful, pleading tone, the mushrooms now speak directly for the voiceless dead: 'let the god not abandon us'.

The poem ends as it began, with a final impassioned plea to the tourist ('with your light meter') to at least set the record straight. **Is Mahon also asking us to acknowledge the suffering ('darkness and pain') and all the other shameful events of history?** The last line echoes the plaintive epigraph: 'let not our naive labours have been in vain!' Once again, this strange and iconic poem can be read in many different ways. As always, readers must come to their own understanding and have the confidence to make their own personal responses.

✒ Writing About the Poem

'In many of his most compelling poems, Derek Mahon addresses issues concerning the world's marginalised and oppressed peoples.' Discuss how 'A Disused Shed in Co. Wexford' reflects this statement, using close reference to the text.

Sample Paragraph

'A Disused Shed in Wexford' was a powerful protest which encouraged me to relate to the suffering of other people. Inside the mushroom shed, Mahon imagines those who have been badly treated in history. The images of the 'Peruvian mines' and 'Indian compounds' made me think of countries where 'lost people' have endured terrible experiences. Mahon uses the decayed mushrooms as a symbol of corruption. He hints at voiceless groups, including those who suffered after the Irish Civil War. His tone is sympathetic to those – 'groaning for deliverance'. I could sympathise with their troubles when he mentioned the death camps 'of Treblinka' and the victims of Pompeii. He personified the mushrooms – 'their pale looking flesh' struggling for freedom – 'Elbow room!' The fact the shed is disused suggested that oppressed people are easily forgotten.

EXAMINER'S COMMENT

This is a well-focused paragraph, which explores Mahon's sympathies for oppressed groups. There is a sense of engaging personal response throughout. Quotations are apt – although slightly inaccurate. Expression is generally clear and well controlled. Overall, a high-grade standard.

✒ Class/Homework Exercises

1. 'Although Mahon's poems can be challenging at times, they are essentially thought-provoking and meaningful.' To what extent is this true of 'A Disused Shed in Co. Wexford'? Develop the points you make with reference to the poem.
2. 'Images of abandonment, suffering and decay make a powerful impact in Mahon's poems.' Discuss this view, with reference to 'A Disused Shed in Co. Wexford'.

⊙ Points to Consider

- Extended metaphor of the long-abandoned mushrooms.
- Themes include exploitation, destruction and the sadness of human loss.
- Historical references offer a powerful global perspective.
- Significance of what the mushrooms symbolise revealed through their surreal 'voices'.
- Atmospheric language evokes the silence and emptiness in deserted locations.
- Effective use of personification and striking imagery.

7 Rathlin

A long time since the last scream cut short –
then an unnatural silence; and then
a natural silence, slowly broken
by the shearwater, by the sporadic
conversation of crickets, the bleak   5
reminder of a metaphysical wind.
Ages of this, till the report
of an outboard motor at the pier
shatters the dream-time, and we land
as if we were the first visitors here.   10

The whole island a sanctuary where amazed
oneiric species whistle and chatter,
evacuating rock-face and cliff-top.
Cerulean distance, an oceanic haze –
nothing but sea-smoke to the ice-cap   15
and the odd somnolent freighter.
Bombs doze in the housing estates
but here they are through with history –
custodians of a lone light which repeats
one simple statement to the turbulent sea.   20

A long time since the unspeakable violence –
since Somhairle Buí, powerless on the mainland,
heard the screams of the Rathlin women
borne, seconds later, on a north-east wind.
Only the cry of the shearwater   25
and the roar of the outboard motor
disturb the singular peace. Spray-blind,
we leave here the infancy of the race,
unsure among the pitching surfaces
whether the future lies before us or behind.   30

Title: Rathlin is a small island located off the coast of Co. Antrim. In the late 16th century, the island's entire population (estimated at over 600 people) was massacred by English invaders. Rathlin is now a well-known bird sanctuary and nature reserve.

shearwater: type of long-winged seabird.
sporadic: occasional.
metaphysical: mystical, supernatural.
report: echo.
dream-time: bliss; in Aboriginal mythology, dream-time is also called the alcheringa, the golden age when the first ancestors were created.
sanctuary: holy place of refuge; nature reserve.
oneiric: dreamlike.
Cerulean: sky-blue.
somnolent: lifeless, drowsy.
freighter: cargo boat.
custodians: guardians, protectors.
turbulent: stormy.
Somhairle Buí: Irish chieftain (Sorley Boy MacDonald) whose family and supporters were killed on Rathlin in the 1575 atrocity.
singular: unusual.
pitching: tossing.

'as if we were the first visitors here'

👤 Personal Response

1. Based on your reading of stanza one, describe the poet's initial response to Rathlin Island. Refer to the text in your answer.
2. Choose one visual image that you found particularly effective in the poem. Briefly explain why you chose it.
3. In your opinion, do the last three lines of the poem suggest hope or fear or both? Briefly explain your response.

👁 Critical Literacy

Like several other poems by Derek Mahon, 'Rathlin' describes a journey and its significance. Ireland's violent past is a recurring theme throughout his work. In this case, he touches on Rathlin's infamous massacres during the late 16th century and the island's present importance as a wildlife sanctuary. The poet contrasts the tranquillity he experiences on his visit with the horrendous events 400 years earlier, when Rathlin's population was killed by invaders. Reports claimed that the cries of the victims were carried to the mainland by the wind and that a local Irish chieftain, Somhairle Buí, heard them but was unable to help.

In the opening stanza, Mahon reflects on the unspeakable violence of a 16th-century bloodbath, which left an unnatural silence on Rathlin. In crafting a truly harrowing image – 'the last scream' of a dying islander – **the poet dramatises the slaughter and its traumatic aftermath**. His description is dominated by contrasting sounds. An eerie calm ('natural silence') is replaced by 'the sporadic/conversation of crickets' – the sharp 'r' and 'c' onomatopoeic effects echoing their nocturnal chirping. Considering the island's disturbing past, it is grimly ironic that Rathlin has become a sanctuary for beautiful seabirds, such as the shearwater. Mahon senses that his own intrusive arrival in a noisy motorboat 'shatters the dream-time'. But he remains acutely aware of how nothing can erase the brutality of history; 'the bleak/reminder of a metaphysical wind'.

This deeply sombre mood continues in stanza two. The poet focuses on the island's serene beauty and its 'amazed' birdlife, unaccustomed to human visitors. There is an underlying sense that the birds' fearful response ('evacuating rock-face and cliff-top') mirrors the reaction of the 16th-century inhabitants when faced with invaders. Mahon suggests the **subtle association between past and present** through vague images: 'Cerulean distance, an oceanic haze'. Here, sibilant and assonant sounds accentuate the gentle mood. This lethargic atmosphere is emphasised by random details, such as occasional 'sea-smoke' and 'the odd somnolent freighter'. But the tranquil security is shattered by an unexpected reference to Northern Ireland's continuing conflict: 'Bombs doze in the housing estates'. Although Rathlin may be 'through with history', sectarian violence is never far beneath the surface in the North. Even the 'lone' lighthouse that warns against 'the turbulent sea' seems to expose the vulnerability of this peaceful place.

Stanza three returns to the massacre. Mahon imagines the distraught chieftain, Somhairle Buí, standing on the mainland listening to the terrible 'screams of the Rathlin women' as they are butchered. This image reflects the desperate frustration of 'powerless' people everywhere to secure peace in times of conflict. Again, there is a contrast between that horrific past and the stillness of the present, where only the noises of the shearwater and the boat engine disturb the unusual calm. **The poem ends ambiguously**, as Mahon and his fellow travellers leave Rathlin, not knowing whether 'the future lies before us or behind'.

On the return journey over rough seas, the poet is 'Spray-blind' – perhaps another metaphor for his uncertainty. Is he distancing himself from violence? Or heading towards greater conflict on the mainland? In his own mind, he is leaving 'the infancy of the race'. The phrase is open to several interpretations. Innocent children were murdered in the 16th-century atrocities. Yet **Rathlin's newfound natural harmony might signal the start of a peaceful era when people can be more cautiously optimistic**. Some critics have stated that the metaphor of Rathlin's lighthouse sending its message to the restless sea suggests that the lessons of the past can be learned in the difficult times of the present. Perhaps the island symbolises the world at large in all its inconsolable tragedy. As always, readers must find their own meaning and decide for themselves.

Writing About the Poem

'The notion of history repeating itself is an important theme in Derek Mahon's poetry.' Discuss this view, with particular reference to 'Rathlin'.

Sample Paragraph

The first line of 'Rathlin' is a reference to an atrocity from the 1500s when innocent women and children were killed. Mahon remembers 'the last scream cut short' before silence descended. Although Rathlin is a bird sanctuary nowadays, Mahon is realistic, 'Bombs doze in the housing estates'. To me, he is simply saying that sectarian violence has not gone away. In the final stanza, he returns to the 16th-century slaughter. It is a mirror image of what continues in his homeland, where ordinary people are 'powerless' to influence the conflict. The disturbing ending suggests that violence is likely

EXAMINER'S COMMENT

This paragraph addresses the question directly and traces the progress of Mahon's theme through the poem. There is evidence of personal engagement and clear appreciation of the way images from the past are linked to the present. Apt quotations and fluent expression throughout. A top-grade standard.

to continue. Mahon wonders 'whether the future lies before us or behind'. In my opinion, he believes history repeats itself and peace is always temporary.

> ### ✒ Class/Homework Exercises
>
> 1. 'Derek Mahon's poetry explores the mystery and significance that is hidden beyond appearances.' Discuss this view, with particular reference to 'Rathlin'. Support the points you make with reference to the poem.
> 2. 'Mahon's imaginative use of sound effects helps to create contrasting atmospheres and moods throughout the poem.' Discuss this view, using close reference to the text.

◉ Points to Consider

- Poem links Ireland's violent past with present-day peace.
- Poet questions whether barbarity can ever be eradicated.
- Detailed language evokes the island's timeless atmosphere.
- Suggestion that violence is still a part of the Irish experience.
- Contrasting tones, uncertain open-ended conclusion.

8 The Chinese Restaurant in Portrush

Before the first visitor comes the spring
softening the sharp air of the coast
in time for the first seasonal 'invasion'.
Today the place is as it might have been,
gentle and almost hospitable. A girl   5
strides past the Northern Counties Hotel,
light-footed, swinging a book bag,
and the doors that were shut all winter
against the north wind and the sea mist
lie open to the street, where one   10
by one the gulls go window-shopping
and an old wolfhound dozes in the sun.

While I sit with my paper and prawn chow mein
under a framed photograph of Hong Kong
the proprietor of the Chinese restaurant   15
stands at the door as if the world were young,
watching the first yacht hoist a sail –
an ideogram on sea-cloud – and the light
of heaven upon the hills of Donegal;
and whistles a little tune, dreaming of home.   20

Title: Portrush is a predominantly Protestant seaside town in north Co. Antrim.

'invasion': intrusion; arrival of a large number of people who do not belong to the region.
hospitable: friendly, welcoming to strangers.

wolfhound: oblique reference to Ulster conflicts and the legend of Cú Chulainn, who was known as the hound of Ulster. The sleeping hound suggests that rivalries have been laid aside, if only temporarily.
prawn chow mein: Chinese dish of fried noodles, seafood and vegetables.
proprietor: owner of a business.
ideogram: a character or symbol in writing that stands not for a word or sound but for a concept, idea or the thing itself; here the sail could be the character that paints the idea of home for the emigrant.

'dreaming of home'

👤 Personal Response

1. In your opinion, what is the dominant tone in the first three lines of the poem? Is it relaxed and welcoming? Or irritated and resentful? Briefly explain your answer.
2. Choose two details from the poem that suggest that the town of Portrush is 'gentle and almost hospitable'. Briefly explain each choice.
3. Write a short personal response to the poem, in which you highlight the impact it made on you. Refer to the text in your answer.

👁 Critical Literacy

'The Chinese Restaurant in Portrush' examines the concept of home and belonging. Once again, the poet is the wry, solitary observer. This leisurely poem moves gracefully from a view of an off-season seaside town to a casual sketch of Mahon himself and the proprietor of the Chinese restaurant. What connects everyone and everything – both distant and local – is the illusory word 'home'.

Derek Mahon is well-known for his **characteristically keen sense of place**. This poem **opens** on a spring day in a small resort in Northern Ireland. Soft sibilant sounds ('spring', 'softening', 'coast') convey **the relaxing atmosphere of the new season in the quiet town of Portrush**. The expected influx of holidaymakers is regarded by both poet and residents as an 'invasion'. The arrival of tourist groups is seen as an intrusion. Over the centuries, Irish history has been marked by violent invasions and Mahon now seems relieved that he is living in relatively peaceful times, when 'the place is as it might have been'. However, prior to the holiday season, Portrush is 'gentle'; it belongs to Mahon and the residents. Indeed, the town is 'almost hospitable'. The qualification clearly suggests that the small resort – and perhaps Ireland itself – gives a hesitant welcome to its visitors. Overall, there is an underlying reticence – and even resentment – in these opening lines.

The mood changes abruptly with the **dynamic image of a modern, purposeful girl** who 'strides past'. The lively monosyllabic verb suggests her 'light-footed' determination. She appears to belong here, as she confidently twirls her book-bag. To the poet, everything is unfolding as it should, signalling a new year and new experiences: 'the doors … open'. Are the references to books and unlocked doors a suggestion that open minds are also needed here? The mood of expectation and hope increases as a droll note of humour creeps in with the allusion to gulls who 'go window-shopping' (line 11). But the inevitable, harsh reality of sectarian conflict in Northern Ireland is hinted at in the image of the 'old wolfhound' (line 12).

This is a land where bitter rivalries lie deep, indicated by the mention of 'sharp air' and 'invasion'. For the present, however, the old **mythical conflicts**

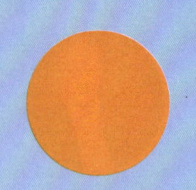

have been almost forgotten and there is peace: the hound 'dozes in the sun'. Mahon rarely deals directly with the sectarian Troubles of Northern Ireland. He has written, 'I felt very far from home in those years. In fact for a large part of my life I've been terrified of home.' Nevertheless, he does not feel like an outsider in Portrush and he distances himself instinctively from 'the first visitor'.

The second section of the poem is set in the quiet interior of the restaurant. **The mood becomes more personal and Mahon's tone is restrained** as he sketches a charming illustration of himself with his newspaper and prawn chow mein (line 13). The restaurant owner stands nearby, looking out 'as if the world were young'. Is there a hint that the world is now cynical and disappointed? The mood of optimism returns, however, as the boats in the distance take to the sea again after the harsh winter. The restaurant owner watches 'the first yacht hoist a sail'. Now the poet imagines how a Chinese person might think. The sail becomes an ideogram, perhaps for place of birth. The owner is 'dreaming of home'. Did the sail remind him of this? The **relaxed atmosphere** is conveyed particularly in the phrase 'whistles a little tune'. The proprietor continues to dream as he admires the beautiful, idyllic countryside 'and the light/of heaven upon the hills of Donegal'. As in much of the poem, run-on lines contribute to the gentle rhythm and enhance the wistful mood.

In the final lines, the view has moved from streetscape to horizon and beyond. Mahon challenges us by **placing a poem that celebrates home in the transient**. He is being gently sardonic by locating the poem in a tourist town, a place of coming and going. By contrast, the image of Hong Kong in its 'framed photograph' shows a fixed, idealised place. The city was then a British colony. Interestingly, like Northern Ireland, Hong Kong was displaced and was not part of its natural homeland. The poet seems to be suggesting that home is a place where one lives, where nurturing takes place. But in this poem, home seems an illusion, an unattainable dream. There is a sense of yearning as the Chinese man stands 'dreaming of home' (line 20). Does Mahon also share this yearning for that instinctive sense of belonging? Are Portrush, Hong Kong or Donegal really home for anyone in the poem? Or is there a more positive sense that home is never entirely out of reach?

Writing About the Poem

'A sense of separation is central to the poetry of Derek Mahon.' Discuss the statement with particular reference to 'The Chinese Restaurant in Portrush'. Develop your views with close reference to the text.

Sample Paragraph

'The Chinese Restaurant in Portrush' describes a detached figure who tries to make sense of what home means. He is visiting an Irish holiday resort. It is off-season, which adds to the isolation. He cuts himself off from contact with others as he sits on his own in a foreign restaurant. He is not in harmony with his environment. Deep sadness is found throughout this poem as hints of what might have happened come to the surface: 'as if the world was young'. Mahon is like the inward-looking residents in the town, he resents the day trippers. He feels different to these outsiders. Both the Chinese immigrant and the local poet feel separated from where they feel they belong.

EXAMINER'S COMMENT

While this answer was on track some of the time, it drifted from the question. The repetitive style at the start (where too many sentences began with 'He') and the slightly inaccurate quotations were offset by some good critical discussion in the second half of the paragraph. Overall, a note-like response. A solid middle-grade standard.

DEREK MAHON

Class/Homework Exercises

1. 'While Mahon makes readers face up to life's realities, he is never sentimental or self-pitying.' Discuss this view of Derek Mahon's poetry, with particular reference to 'The Chinese Restaurant in Portrush'. Refer closely to the text in your response.
2. 'Mahon's use of cinematic imagery adds drama and interest throughout the poem.' Discuss this view, with reference to the text.

◉ Points to Consider

- **Central themes include identity and belonging.**
- **Underlying sense of Ireland's troubled history.**
- **Concrete visual imagery, cinematic quality, interesting metaphors.**
- **Leisurely rhythms convey ease as spring rejuvenates the world.**
- **Effective use of sound and range of tones.**

9 Kinsale

Title: The small town of Kinsale in Co. Cork is now a lively fishing port and tourist centre. Its historic importance goes back to the Battle of Kinsale in 1601 when English forces overcame the armies of the Ulster chieftains Hugh O'Neill and Hugh O'Donnell. To a large extent, this marked the end of Gaelic rule in Ireland.

The kind of rain we knew is a thing of the past –
deep-delving, dark, deliberate you would say,
browsing on spire and bogland; but today
our sky-blue slates are steaming in the sun,
our yachts tinkling and dancing in the bay 5
like racehorses. We contemplate at last
shining windows, a future forbidden to no one.

deep-delving: exploring the past.

browsing on: considering; surviving on.

spire and bogland: religion and land are traditional symbols of power in Irish history.

'our yachts tinkling and dancing in the bay'

Personal Response

1. In your view, what impact has the casual conversational opening line? Is the speaker simply chatting about the weather? Or is there a deeper meaning?
2. Select one interesting image from the poem and comment briefly on its effectiveness.
3. In your opinion, does the poem end on a positive or negative note? Give reasons for your answer.

👁 Critical Literacy

In 'Kinsale' the poet returns to the theme of Irish identity and imagines a future that is 'forbidden to no one'. Mahon lived in the Co. Cork seaside town and would be well aware of its significance in the historical conflict between Ireland and England. Although he does not refer directly to the past in this short, celebratory poem, he makes effective use of symbols to suggest the contrast between modern Ireland and its turbulent history.

The opening lines are conversational. Mahon reflects on an earlier time, which he associates with wet, gloomy weather: 'The kind of rain we knew is a thing of the past'. **There is a sense of relief that the worst is over.** Alliteration emphasises the harsh conditions of the past: 'deep-delving, dark, deliberate'. From the outset, readers are quietly encouraged to agree with the poet's view ('you would say').

A sombre tone is created by slow rhythm, intrusive punctuation and a polysyllabic adjective ('deliberate'). It is likely that the rain symbolises Mahon's view of Kinsale – and of Ireland – in the past. He may well be imagining a time of relative poverty, prior to the sudden prosperity of the late 20th century. He could also be reflecting on times of violence and failed rebellion, such as the Battle of Kinsale in 1601. The underlying **mood of haunting oppression** is enhanced by further alliteration and broad vowel assonant sounds: 'browsing on spire and bogland'. The mention of church spires and native bogland suggests the powerful influences of religion and land in Irish history.

Line 3 marks a turning point in the poem. Mahon distances himself from the past and focuses on modern times. The metaphor of sunshine following rain is an obvious symbol of celebration and optimism. However, the colourful images of present-day Kinsale are fresh and vibrant. A pulsating sibilance contributes to the changing atmosphere, as though the dreary past is evaporating before our eyes: 'sky-blue slates are steaming in the sun'. Mahon's **dynamic description reflects the feeling of renewed energy and prosperity** that is evident around Kinsale, where yachts are now 'tinkling and dancing in the bay/like racehorses'. The light, musical effects of the onomatopoeic verbs and the unusual simile suggest much about affluent lifestyles during Ireland's economic boom in the 1990s. Repetition of the inclusive pronoun 'our' also conveys a sense of communal confidence.

In contrast to the 'deep-delving' rain, refreshing light and cheerfulness dominate the poem's final lines. Mahon adopts the role of observer, looking at the new Ireland through 'shining windows'. It appears that Ireland's future will be a bright one, filled with hope and opportunity: 'forbidden to no one'. The poet has a cautious optimism regarding the years ahead. However, **readers might also 'contemplate' a more sceptical undertone**. Is Mahon warning against the complacency of newfound wealth? Perhaps he is suggesting that just as Irish people would be unwise to take the temporary sunshine for granted, we should never lose sight of Kinsale's darker history.

✒ Writing About the Poem

'The importance of place and identity are central themes in Derek Mahon's poetry.' Discuss this view with reference to 'Kinsale'.

Sample Paragraph

'Kinsale' reminded me of Mahon's poem 'Rathlin'. Each place has a violent history that has impacted on Irish people. I thought it was interesting that the poet takes a broad view of Ireland – North and South – reminding us of the defeats suffered by the native Irish over centuries. As a people, we have moved from 'deep-delving, dark' rain to sunny days and 'shining windows'. Although the poem is seven lines long, it gives a concise history lesson of how far the Irish nation has come from the times of colonisation. This suggests an independent people who have survived a difficult history. Mahon hints at the historical power of the Catholic Church, and at peasant farmers in his phrase 'spire and bogland'. He is also cynical of the more recent Celtic Tiger boom with its short-lived wealth: 'yachts tinkling and dancing'. 'Kinsale' made me think about the way Irish people sometimes lose touch with reality.

> **EXAMINER'S COMMENT**
>
> A good response that takes a clear approach to the question. The opening comparison with 'Rathlin' provided an interesting context for exploring Mahon's themes of place and identity. Expression was controlled throughout and suitable quotations were used to support discussion points. Top-grade personal response.

✎ Class/Homework Exercises

1. 'Many of Derek Mahon's poems reaffirm positive values, such as hope, open-mindedness and sympathy for others.' Comment on this statement, with particular reference to 'Kinsale'.
2. 'Mahon's effective use of visual and aural imagery brings to life the differences between modern and historical Ireland.' Discuss this view, with close reference to his poem 'Kinsale'.

⊙ Points to Consider

- **Key themes of identity and place.**
- **Subtle use of contrasting symbols to stress dark past and promising future.**
- **Compound words and personification add richness.**
- **Effective alliteration, sibilance, assonance add musicality.**
- **Variety of tones: casual, sombre, cheerful, optimistic.**

10. Antarctica

For Richard Ryan

'I am just going outside and may be some time.'
The others nod, pretending not to know.
At the heart of the ridiculous, the sublime.

He leaves them reading and begins to climb,
goading his ghost into the howling snow;   5
he is just going outside and may be some time.

The tent recedes beneath its crust of grime
and frostbite is replaced by vertigo:
at the heart of the ridiculous, the sublime.

Need we consider it some sort of crime,   10
this numb self-sacrifice of the weakest? No,
he is just going outside and may be some time –

in fact, for ever. Solitary enzyme,
though the night yield no glimmer there will glow,
at the heart of the ridiculous, the sublime.   15

He takes leave of the earthly pantomime
quietly, knowing it is time to go.
'I am just going outside and may be some time.'
At the heart of the ridiculous, the sublime.

DEREK MAHON

Title: Antarctica: region surrounding the South Pole.

Dedication: Irish poet.

'I am just going outside and may be some time': words of Lawrence Oates, a team member on Captain Scott's ill-fated expedition to the South Pole in 1912. Oates deliberately sacrificed his life so that his companions might have a better chance of survival.
ridiculous: absurd, foolish, illogical.
sublime: majestic, noble, inspiring, heavenly.
goading: urging, encouraging.
recedes: sinks, fades.
grime: dirt-ingrained frost.
frostbite: skin and body tissue numbed and damaged because of freezing conditions.
vertigo: dizziness, usually caused by looking down from a height.

enzyme: substance that acts as a trigger to promote a particular reaction; metaphor for Lawrence Oates.

earthly pantomime: life seen as an absurd show; a slapstick comedy.

'quietly, knowing'

Personal Response

1. Choose two phrases that convey the freezing environment of the Antarctic in this poem. Comment briefly on the effectiveness of each.
2. The actual words spoken by Lawrence Oates before he went to his certain death are used repeatedly in the poem. In your opinion, what effect does this have on the reader?
3. Do you think that the poet has given a positive or negative picture of Oates? Refer to the text in your answer.

Critical Literacy

'Antarctica' is based on a true incident that took place during Captain Scott's famous expedition to the South Pole (1911–12), when he was narrowly beaten to the finish by the Norwegian Roald Amundsen. Captain Lawrence Oates, a member of Scott's team, developed gangrene as a result of severe frostbite in his feet. He asked to be left behind, but his companions refused. Believing that he was holding back the team, Oates knowingly went to his death. His sacrifice, sadly, did not prevent the others dying. This adds another layer of poignancy to the poem. Mahon is interested in ghostly voices from the past. The poem is written in the form of a villanelle, with five tercets (three-line verses) and a final quatrain (four-line stanza).

This poem is set in the hostile, empty space of the South Pole. **A dignified man, Lawrence Oates decides his tragic fate alone.** In the first tercet (three-line stanza), Oates's own words are used: 'I am just going outside and may be some time'. This heart-rending statement has the distant tone of a lost voice echoing down the generations. Readers are aware that Oates's sacrifice ultimately proved futile. The first and third lines form two refrains, which are woven effortlessly throughout the poem and are combined in the concluding couplet. The reaction of Oates's team members is now shown: 'The others nod'. Respecting his decision, they are aware of what he is about to do, although they are 'pretending not to know'. In the third line, we hear Mahon's voice: 'At the heart of the ridiculous, the sublime'. The poet is quietly meditating on the fact that even though a gesture appears foolish ('ridiculous'), nevertheless it can contain heroic elements ('the sublime').

In the second stanza, the poet paints a picture of a selfless man pushing himself against the extremes of winter weather: 'goading his ghost into the howling snow'. The alliteration of the hard 'g' emphasises the physical effort of this courageous man. Mahon's use of the present tense makes the scene realistically dramatic. The assonance of the broad 'o' vowel vividly impersonates the screaming snowstorm. This is the **hostile environment** into which Oates has chosen to go.

The third tercet shows the scene from the perspective of Captain Oates: the tent disappears, 'recedes' with a crusting of hoar frost. Everything is dissolved into a whirlpool of white. The numbing pain of his frostbite is now replaced by the giddy sensation of vertigo as he loses his sense of balance in the spiralling storm.

Mahon **questions whether this act is a 'crime'** in the fourth tercet. Suicide was once regarded as the greatest sin a person could commit, the ultimate act of despair. But an emphatic 'No' from the poet dispels any critical questioning of 'this numb self-sacrifice of the weakest'.

The poet's use of a dash and run-on lines points deliberately into the grim fifth stanza. He emphasises the fact that Oates is gone 'for ever'. Although the men in this tragic story are not named directly, they symbolise the greater good of humanity. The resolute rhythm mirrors the slow, decisive trudging of the disappearing man. He presents a harrowing image of this man as a 'Solitary enzyme'. Oates is seen as an example of humanity's capacity for noble self-sacrifice, a **lone force capable of altering states**. He has become a catalyst for good. Humanity is ennobled by the supreme generosity of a man giving his life for the sake of others.

In the final quatrain Oates's quiet, dignified departure is described: 'He takes leave of the earthly pantomime'. **The absurdity of life** is stressed by use of the word 'pantomime', with its connotations of slapstick comedy and children's laughter. The poem concludes with the two refrains: Oates's **self-effacing, courageous words** ('I am just going outside and may be some time') and the poet's thoughtful comment ('At the heart of the ridiculous, the sublime').

The **formal structure** of the poem is in keeping with the stiff-upper-lip personality of Captain Oates and it also **graces his act with ritual and ceremony**. Mahon has chosen a villanelle form. The tightly controlled rhyme scheme (*aba*) echoes the self-determination of Oates ('He takes leave', 'time to go'). There is a significant contrast in the poem: between the words 'sublime' and 'ridiculous', which appear four times each. They represent the two views of Oates's behaviour. However, 'sublime' is given emphasis – it is rhymed throughout ('time', 'climb', 'grime', 'crime', 'enzyme', 'pantomime'). Indeed, Mahon concludes with the adjective ('sublime'), as a final tribute to the remarkable dignity and extraordinary courage of Lawrence Oates.

Writing About the Poem

'Derek Mahon's dramatic poetry arouses emotions of deep pity and sorrow in the reader.' Comment on this view of the poet's work, referring to the poem 'Antarctica'. Support your comments with reference to the text.

Sample Paragraph

Lawrence Oates, in his act of self-sacrifice, epitomises greatness. I was filled with admiration for this man when he calmly says: 'I am just going outside and may be some time'. The tone resonates quietly, yet forcefully; and the phrase is more powerful as these are Oates's actual last words. The phrase 'Solitary enzyme' captures one man's struggle against nature. The small, determined figure ('goading his ghost into the howling snow') shows the endurance of a man who just keeps going, 'though the night yield no glimmer'. I felt pity for this man when 'frostbite is replaced by vertigo'. The sacrifice was in vain, since the other explorers perished. But our feelings are aroused by the self-control of Oates. The 'sublime' act, giving one's life for the others, fills us with pity, but also with great pride in the human race.

> **EXAMINER'S COMMENT**
>
> *A well-illustrated answer focusing on the task – although the dramatic aspect needs to be addressed more. Quotes are integrated effectively into critical comments. There is also a strong sense of personal engagement with the poem. The expression is mature throughout. Varied vocabulary enlivens the response. Top-grade standard.*

Class/Homework Exercises

1. Compare and contrast the character of Captain Oates with another loner from Mahon's poetry on your course. Which character appeals to you more? Explain your response, with reference to the poem.
2. 'Antarctica' has been described as a poem that is both gloomy and uplifting at the same time. To what extent do you agree with this view? Refer to the text in your answer.

Points to Consider

- **Themes of loss, stoicism and heroism.**
- **Effective repetition of direct speech.**
- **Striking visual and aural imagery.**
- **Controlled use of villanelle form complements self-control of central character.**

Sample Leaving Cert Questions on Mahon's Poetry

1. 'Mahon often presents fresh, subtle perspectives on historical events through his innovative and skilful use of language.' Discuss this view, developing your answer with reference to the poetry of Derek Mahon on your course.
2. 'Discuss how effectively Derek Mahon makes use of language and imagery to address recurring themes of identity and belonging.' Develop your answer with reference to the poetry of Mahon on your course.
3. 'Derek Mahon's restrained poetic voice offers understanding and sympathy to the lives of outcasts.' To what extent do you agree or disagree with this view? Develop your answer with reference to the poetry of Mahon on your course.

How do I organise my answer?

(Sample question 1)

'Mahon often presents fresh, subtle perspectives on historical events through his innovative and skilful use of language.' Discuss this view, developing your answer with reference to the poetry of Derek Mahon on your course.

Sample Plan 1

Intro: *(Stance: agree with viewpoint in question)* Mahon's intense poetry honestly presents multiple angles on history through energetic yet finely drawn visual and aural imagery. Employs satire but also compassion, encouraging readers to reflect on events.

Point 1: *(Ambivalent perspective using satire, visual imagery and compound words)* 'Ecclesiastes' – interior monologue reveals poet's love/hate relationship with Ulster Protestant tradition of 1970s Belfast. Eloquent condemnation of preacher's fanatical rhetoric. Striking imagery ('dank churches, the empty streets') reflects hard-line religion.

Point 2: *(Mockery, curt lines and euphemism expose killer's self-deceptive perspective)* 'As It Should Be' – dramatic mockery exposes cynicism of fundamentalist killer involved in barbaric events in Northern Ireland Troubles. Euphemism, 'tide-burial', uncovers brutal reality of killer's inhumane perspective. Chilling revelation of killer's mindset.

Understanding the Prescribed Poetry Question

Marks are awarded using the PCLM Marking Scheme:
P = 15; C = 15; L = 15; M = 5
Total = 50

- **P** (Purpose = 15 marks) refers to the set question and is the launch pad for the answer. This involves engaging with all of the question. Both theme and language must be addressed, although not necessarily equally.
- **C** (Coherence = 15 marks) refers to the organisation of the developed response and the use of accurate, relevant quotation. Paragraphing is essential.
- **L** (Language = 15 marks) refers to the student's skill in controlling language throughout the answer.
- **M** (Mechanics = 5 marks) refers to spelling and grammar.
- Although no specific number of poems is required, students usually discuss at least 3 or 4 in their written responses.
- Aim for at least 800 words, to be completed within 45–50 minutes.

DEREK MAHON

POETRY FOCUS

> **NOTE**
> In keeping with the PCLM approach, the student has to take a stance by agreeing, disagreeing or partially agreeing that Mahon presents:
> - **fresh, subtle perspectives on historical events** (nuanced, provocative, ambivalent viewpoints on past events, particularly 1970s Northern Ireland, etc.)
> ... through:
> - **innovative and skilful language** (original, carefully structured poetic forms, stunning visual images and sound patterns, personification, adoption of different personas, sensual evocation of specific places and times, etc.)

Point 3: *(Contrasting images disclose different viewpoints on Ireland past and present)* 'Kinsale' – visual contrasts ('shining windows'/'rain … deep-delving, dark') reveal startling disparity between the turbulent times of Ireland's historic past and the optimistic future which beckons. Metaphor of rain symbolises past poverty and oppression resulting from colonial suppression and religious dominance.

Point 4: *(Shocking symbolism and a compassionate tone combine to reveal poet's stance on suffering)* – 'A Disused Shed in Co. Wexford' – decaying mushrooms graphically evoke history's forgotten victims ('foetor/of vegetable sweat'). Damning personification ('pale flesh flaking') adds to the shocking picture of suffering.

Conclusion: Mahon's keen eye for detail, honest approach and technical ability produces poetry which has many unusual, complex positions aimed at disturbing and provoking the reader to gaze intently on historical events and, where appropriate, to take action.

Sample Paragraph: Point 1

Mahon's original outlook on an historical event is evident in his monologue 'Ecclesiastes'. Here, he not only condemns the fanatical Protestant preaching in 1970s Northern Ireland, but he also reveals his affection for Belfast. A colloquial exclamation opens the poem, describing his attitude to his bleak hometown, 'God you could grow to love it'. But the strait-laced authorities have clamped down, there are 'empty streets' and 'tied-up swings'. Their self-importance and small mindedness are exposed through repetition, 'God-fearing, God-chosen purist'. Yet Mahon is in love with the North. He regards them as 'credulous', because they are so easily deceived by the preacher's empty rhetoric, 'promising nothing under the sun'. Beneath the criticism of the poem's surface lies a tender affection for the 'Antrim hills'.

> **EXAMINER'S COMMENT**
> As part of a full essay, this paragraph makes consistently clear links back to the task. Some focused discussion on the poet's conflicted attitudes towards Belfast. Good range of references and supportive quotations throughout reflects close engagement with the text. Overall, expression is controlled and the effective concluding sentence rounds off this solid top-grade response.

(Sample question 2)

'Discuss how effectively Derek Mahon makes use of language and imagery to address recurring themes of identity and belonging.' Develop your answer with reference to the poetry of Mahon on your course.

DEREK MAHON

Sample Plan 2

Intro: *(Stance: agree with viewpoint in question)* Mahon lurks on the perimeter, watching, reflecting. Filled with uncertainty after a day trip, subtly challenging self-justifying paramilitary conflict, attempting to connect with Ireland's violent past, realising the significance of 'home'. Uses interesting imagery, aural effects and a variety of tones.

Point 1: *(Unsettling experience conveyed through colloquialism, personification, aural effects)* 'Day Trip to Donegal' – disturbing experience of outing conveyed through colloquial expression ('climbed stiffly out'). Uneasy introspection, sibilant personification ('the slow sea washed against my head'). Nightmarish sense of estrangement ('no promise of rescue').

Point 2: *(Adopted persona of detached killer masks complacent fanatical beliefs)* 'As It Should Be' – murderer's matter-of-fact reporting of killing unsettles reader ('gunned him down in a blind yard'). Hollow ring of certainty. Unsettling final image ('world with method in it') – whose order prevails?

Point 3: *(Establishing sense of identity through history of place using sound effects)* 'Rathlin' – onomatopoeic verb ('screams') evokes horrific 16th-century massacre. Past brutality linked with underlying violence of contemporary North ('troubled sea'). Ambiguous conclusion – does history repeat itself?

Point 4: *(Home and belonging explored through precise observation)* 'The Chinese Restaurant in Portrush' – contrasting pictures of confident, modern local girl and displaced Chinese man 'dreaming of home'. Unhurried rhythm and sibilance establish relaxed ambience. But does anyone really belong here?

Conclusion: Mahon's poetry explores the difficulty of finding identity and a place to call home not only for the poet, but for the characters in his poetry and even the reader who is dislocated and disturbed. Thought-provoking and complex poems of clarity and mystery.

> **NOTE**
>
> In keeping with the PCLM approach, the student has to explore poems of Mahon's on the course that include:
> - **effective use of language and imagery** (powerful imagery, cinematic quality, colloquial speech, personification, aural effects, contrasts, rhythmic control, varied tones – reflective, fatalistic, ironic, brutal, didactic, relaxed, etc.)
> … to address themes:
> - **of identity and belonging** (individuality, home, separation, uncertainty, importance of past, etc.)

Sample Paragraph: Point 1

'Day Trip to Donegal' raises disturbing questions about personal identity. Colloquial expressions recall the relaxed company of friends, 'Give me a ring, goodnight, and so to bed …' But the poet's sleep is haunted by nightmares of the trip, 'spilling into the skull'. Sibilant personification and assonance, 'the slow sea washed against my head', vividly convey the insistent rhythm of the sea as it performs its natural function of eroding the land. The underlying tone is restless. Mahon feels strangely displaced, 'alone far out at sea'. He has no community to call on for help, 'no promise of rescue'. Terrifying images conclude the poem. The poet is on his own in a hostile environment, 'the vindictive wind and rain', which actively is conspiring against him. Mahon feels displaced.

> **EXAMINER'S COMMENT**
>
> Top-grade standard addresses both aspects of the question directly, engaging well with the poem. Excellent use of apt reference and accurate quotation illustrate the poet's technical skill at evoking atmosphere through unnerving tones, rhythm, vivid imagery and sound effects. Expression is clear and varied throughout.

> **EXAM FOCUS**
>
> - As you may not be familiar with some of the poems referred to in the sample plans, substitute poems that you have studied closely.
> - Key points about a particular poem can be developed over more than one paragraph.
> - Paragraphs may also include cross-referencing and discussion of more than one poem.
> - Remember that there is no single 'correct' answer to poetry questions, so always be confident in expressing your own considered response.

Leaving Cert Sample Essay

'Derek Mahon's restrained poetic voice offers understanding and sympathy to the lives of outcasts.' To what extent do you agree or disagree with this view? Develop your answer with reference to the poetry of Mahon on your course.

Sample Essay

1. Derek Mahon is fascinated by those on the edge of society: a retired grandfather, innocent victims of tragedy, troubled survivors, unassuming heroes. This compassionate poet enters their persona and lets readers observe and hear the outcasts. Mahon's refined awareness of the world is expressed in a restrained poetic voice that conveys his empathy.

2. In 'Grandfather', he observes and comments on a recently retired Belfast shipyard worker. Half-rhymes, 'world'/'rolled', 'recovered'/'childhood', suggest the elusive old man who is 'discretely up to no good'. Mahon's

exasperation is cleverly revealed by the description, 'like a four-year-old – never there when you call'. The grandfather refuses to submit to the family's set rules and expectations. Boisterous onomatopoeia, 'banging', 'thumping', recreates the noisy persona of the old man disrupting the peace of the house.

3. Yet the poet's affection and admiration for his independent relative is evident in the Northern Irish colloquialism, 'as cute as they come'. Mahon appreciates how difficult it must be for this former craftsman to be confined to the limited space of the house. His previous workplace in the shipyard is vividly conveyed through detailed imagery, 'Boiler-rooms, row upon row of gantries'. The poet is sympathetic to the former foreman boiler-maker who has had to leave behind the organised world of work, but who still refuses to leave behind his industrious ways. Run-on lines capture his vigorous daily activity, 'Even on cold/mornings he is up at six'. Mahon's sonnet captures the original outsider with deep affection.

4. 'After the *Titanic*' explores not only the harrowing experiences of the terrified passengers on the *Titanic*, but also recalls Bruce Ismay's unhappy life after he survived the harrowing tragedy of the sinking. The horror of the innocent victims' experiences on the night of the sinking of the famous ship is graphically created by the thunderous sounds, 'pandemonium of prams, pianos, sideboards, winches, boilers bursting'. The phrase, 'shredded ragtime' references the courage of the ship's band who kept playing bravely while the ship went down. This display of bravery is in direct contrast to the questionable behaviour of the shipping company's director, Ismay, who in direct breach of law, took a place in the scarce lifeboats while lower-class women and children were excluded. Mahon's controlled use of visual and aural imagery heightens the reader's sense of his empathy for the victims.

5. But Mahon provides another perspective through the voice of Ismay himself who selfishly chose to survive, 'They said I got away in a boat and humbled me at the inquiry'. Mahon shows that although Ismay survived physically, he drowned emotionally and mentally. He lives in anguished isolation, 'takes his morphine and will see no-one'. Mahon exposes the self-pity and anguish of Ismay who selfishly demands that he be included in the prayers for the unfortunate victims of the sinking of the historic ship, 'Include me in your commemorations'. The poet's calm presentation of multiple perspectives encourages the reader to consider all victims, innocent or guilty.

6. 'Antarctica' uses the precise words of Captain Lawrence Oates when he went to his death to try to save his comrades on the failed expedition to reach the South Pole in 1912, 'I am just going outside and may be some

INDICATIVE MATERIAL

- **Mahon's restrained poetic voice** (controlled, subtle use of traditional poetic forms, fair-minded treatment of themes, refined visual and aural imagery, tactful tones, tasteful use of direct speech and colloquialisms, etc.)

... offers:

- **understanding and sympathy to the lives of outcasts** (empathy with lonely marginalised people, compelling insights into Irish history and culture, acknowledgement of victims, emphasis on the importance of belonging and identity, etc.)

DEREK MAHON

time'. The adverb 'just' shows the lack of melodrama in this generous man's act of sacrifice. 'Solitary enzyme' captures Oates's heroic self-sacrifice in the hostile South Pole. The alliterative 'goading his ghost' describes the man's fierce determination and broad vowels echo the menacing taunts of the region, 'howling snow'. A pitiful sight of the disappearing tent is emphasised by the repeated slender vowel 'e': 'The tent recedes beneath its crust of grime'. Mahon's admiration for Captain Oates – another outsider – is shown in the careful rhyming of 'sublime' with 'time', 'climb', 'enzyme'. The poem concludes with the awe-inspiring 'sublime'.

7. In 'Chinese Restaurant in Portrush', the poet helps us to visualise places where people can get on with their ordinary lives. Springtime in the small northern seaside town contributes to the positive atmosphere. Although there is a sense that both the Chinese restaurant manager and Mahon himself are dreaming of a home elsewhere, the mood in the poem is generally upbeat. The two men admire 'the hills of Donegal', Mahon enjoys watching the street where 'the gulls go window-shopping' and the restaurant owner 'whistles a little tune'. The poet understands the manager's sense of loneliness and has sympathy with him. They share feelings of not belonging.

8. Derek Mahon's carefully controlled voice expresses understanding and sympathy to those who exist on the margins of society through his effective use of multiple perspectives, amended poetic forms, clever use of rhyme, measured direct speech and colloquialisms, and restrained visual and aural imagery.

(780 words)

EXAMINER'S COMMENT

Impressive overall engagement with both the question and Mahon's poems – particularly 'Grandfather' and 'After the Titanic'. Excellent use of supportive quotations shows close knowledge of the texts. A little of the discussion on style is slightly general, however, and lacks firm focus on the 'restrained voice' element of the question. Expression is generally very good throughout this detailed essay.

GRADE: H1
P = 14/15
C = 14/15
L = 13/15
M = 5/5
Total = 46/50

Revision Overview

'Grandfather' (OL)
Evocative, subjective sonnet celebrating the poet's grandfather. Mahon's nostalgic portrait expresses both exasperation and admiration for this unpredictable character.

'Day Trip to Donegal'
Dramatic poem recalling the poet's visit to coastal Donegal. The outing sparks uneasy feelings of alienation and estrangement.

'Ecclesiastes'
Scathing commentary on the negative consequences of strict traditional Northern Protestantism coupled with tender affectionate for Mahon's people and his place, Belfast.

'After the *Titanic*' (OL)
Dramatic glimpse of how Mahon perceives Bruce Ismay to see himself. His revealing thoughts offer an alternative provocative image of the disgraced company director.

'As It Should Be'
Telling dramatic monologue of fundamentalist paramilitary killer attempting to justify his violent actions.

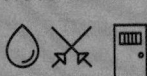

'A Disused Shed in Co. Wexford'
Mahon's visionary view of an abandoned shed results in troubling, graphic reflections about the silenced victims of oppression and violence.

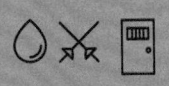

'Rathlin'
Evocative description of a journey evoking the memory of past brutality on Rathlin Island is contrasted with the present-day peace of this newly established bird sanctuary.

'The Chinese Restaurant in Portrush'
This wry commentary on the meaning of home references both Ireland's troubled past and today's displaced people.

'Kinsale'
Using contrast to portray the difference between past and present, this brief lyric acknowledges Ireland's dark history while celebrating renewed hope for the future.

'Antarctica' (OL)
The poem details Lawrence Oates's act of self-sacrifice on the fateful polar expedition. Mahon views this as an expression of the 'sublime' qualities of honourable individuals.

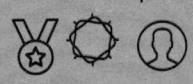

Last Words

'Our bravest and most stylish wielder of the singing line.'
Michael Longley

'He (Mahon) has been reported as saying that much of the best of contemporary American poetry has been written by rap artists: "At least it rhymes".'
Patrick Cotter

'I lie here in a riot of sunlight watching the day break and the clouds flying. Everything is going to be all right.'
Derek Mahon

HISTORY/MEMORY · IDENTITY · SPIRITUALITY · ALIENATION · BELONGING · WORK · LOSS

GUILT · DESTRUCTION · PEACE · JOY/HOPE · SACRIFICE · COURAGE

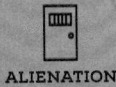

POETRY FOCUS

Sylvia Plath
1932–1963

'Out of the ash
I rise with my red hair
And I eat men like air.'

Born in Boston, Massachusetts in 1932, Sylvia Plath was a writer whose best-known poems are noted for their intense focus and vibrant, personal imagery. Her writing talent – and ambition to succeed – was evident from an early age. She kept a journal during childhood and published her early poems in literary magazines and newspapers. After studying Art and English at college, Plath moved to Cambridge, England in the mid-1950s. Here she met and later married the poet Ted Hughes. The couple had two children, Frieda and Nicholas, but the marriage was not to last. Plath continued to write through the late 1950s and early 1960s. During the final years of her life, she produced numerous confessional poems of stark revelation, channelling her long-standing anxiety and doubt into poetic verses of great power and pathos. At her creative peak, Sylvia Plath took her own life on 11 February 1963.

Investigate Further

To find out more about Sylvia Plath, or to hear readings of her poems, you could search some useful websites, such as YouTube, BBC poetry, poetryfoundation.org and poetryarchive.org, or access additional material on this page of your eBook.

Prescribed Poems

Note that Plath uses American spellings in her work.

○ **1 'Black Rook in Rainy Weather'**
Plath uses the description of the rook to explore poetic inspiration and her joy when creative 'miracles' occur. **Page 296**

○ **2 'The Times Are Tidy'**
Disillusioned with the blandness of her times, this bitter social commentary contrasts the uneventful 1950s with the idealistic fairytale world of the past. **Page 300**

○ **3 'Morning Song'**
The poem records Plath's feelings after the birth of her daughter and focuses on the wonder of the mother–child relationship. **Page 303**

○ **4 'Finisterre'**
A highly descriptive poem dominated by disturbing themes of decay and death. Plath and her husband visited Finisterre on the north-west coast of France in 1960. **Page 307**

○ **5 'Mirror'**
The central themes are self-knowledge and ageing. In the first stanza, the poet is the mirror; in the second, she is the woman looking into it. **Page 311**

○ **6 'Pheasant'**
Another personal poem about humans' relationship with nature. Plath believed that respect for life's natural order was vital. **Page 315**

○ **7 'Elm'**
An intensely introspective poem, rich in dark imagery and symbolism. The poet personifies the elm tree, giving it a voice. **Page 319**

○ **8 'Poppies in July' (OL)**
One of Plath's bleakest poems, contrasting the vitality of the poppies with her own exhausted longing to escape a world of pain. **Page 323**

○ **9 'The Arrival of the Bee Box'**
This narrative addresses several key themes, including power, freedom and oppression. **Page 327**

○ **10 'Child' (OL)**
In this short poem, Plath observes the innocence of childhood, but is overcome by personal feelings of failure and hopelessness. **Page 332**

(OL) indicates poems that are also prescribed for the Ordinary Level course.

1 Black Rook in Rainy Weather

On the stiff twig up there
Hunches a wet black rook
Arranging and rearranging its feathers in the rain.
I do not expect a miracle
Or an accident   5

To set the sight on fire
In my eye, nor seek
Any more in the desultory weather some design,   **desultory:** unexceptional, oppressive.
But let spotted leaves fall as they fall,
Without ceremony, or portent.   10   **portent:** omen.

Although, I admit, I desire,
Occasionally, some backtalk
From the mute sky, I can't honestly complain:
A certain minor light may still
Lean incandescent   15   **incandescent:** glowing.

Out of kitchen table or chair
As if a celestial burning took
Possession of the most obtuse objects now and then –
Thus hallowing an interval   **hallowing:** making holy.
Otherwise inconsequent   20   **inconsequent:** of no importance.

By bestowing largesse, honor,   **largesse:** generous, giving.
One might say love. At any rate, I now walk
Wary (for it could happen
Even in this dull ruinous landscape); skeptical,   **skeptical:** wary, suspicious.
Yet politic; ignorant   25   **politic:** wise and likely to prove advantageous.

Of whatever angel may choose to flare
Suddenly at my elbow. I only know that a rook
Ordering its black feathers can so shine
As to seize my senses, haul
My eyelids up, and grant   30

A brief respite from fear
Of total neutrality. With luck,
Trekking stubborn through this season
Of fatigue, I shall
Patch together a content   35

Of sorts. Miracles occur,
If you care to call those spasmodic
Tricks of radiance miracles. The wait's begun again,
The long wait for the angel,
For that rare, random descent.   40

spasmodic: occurring in bursts.

'Hunches a wet black rook'

👤 Personal Response

1. What is the mood of the poet? How does the weather described in the poem reflect this mood?
2. Select one image from the poem that you find particularly striking or dramatic. Briefly explain your choice.
3. What do you think the final stanza means? Consider the phrase 'The wait's begun again'. What is the poet waiting for?

👁 Critical Literacy

'Black Rook in Rainy Weather' was written while Plath was studying in Cambridge in 1956. It contains many of her trademarks, including the exploration of emotions, the use of weather, colour and natural objects as symbols, and the dreamlike world. She explores a number of themes: fear of the future, lack of identity and poetic inspiration.

Stanza one begins with the straightforward description of a bird grooming itself, which the poet observes on a rainy day. But on closer inspection, the mood of the poem is set with the words 'stiff' and 'Hunches'. The bird is at the mercy of the elements ('wet') and there is no easy movement. **This atmospheric opening is dull and low key.** The black rook is a bird of ill omen. But the bird is presenting its best image to the world as it sits 'Arranging and rearranging its feathers'. Plath longed to excel in both life and art. If she were inspired by poetry, the rook would take on a new light as if on fire. Yet she doesn't see this happening. Even the weather is 'desultory' in the fading season of autumn. Poetic inspiration is miraculous; it is not ordinary. The world is experienced in a heightened way. Notice the long line, which seems out of proportion with the rest as she declares that she doesn't expect any order or 'design' in the haphazard weather. The decaying leaves will fall with no ritual, without any organisation. **This is a chaotic world**, a random place with no design, just as poetic inspiration happens by chance. It is also accidental, like the falling leaves.

After this low-key opening, the poem starts to take flight in stanzas three and four when the poet states: 'I desire'. Plath employs a witty metaphor as she looks for 'some backtalk' from the 'mute sky'. **She would like to connect with it.** It could happen on her walk, or even at home if she were to experience a 'certain minor light' shining from an ordinary, everyday object like a chair. The association of fire and light makes an ordinary moment special. It is 'hallowing'; it is giving generously ('largesse'). She is hoping against hope. Plath may be sceptical, but she is going forward carefully in case she misses the magic moment. **She must stay alert and watchful.** She must also be 'politic', wise.

Stanzas six, seven and eight explore poetic inspiration. Plath doesn't know if it will happen to her or how it will happen. Two contrasting attitudes are at loggerheads: hope and despair. The rook might inspire her: '**Miracles occur**'. If she were motivated, it would relieve 'total neutrality', this nothingness she feels when living uninspired. Although she is tired, she is insistent, 'stubborn'. The poet will have to 'Patch' something together. She shows human vulnerability, but she is trying. This new-found determination is a very different tone from the negative one at the beginning.

Literature was as important to Plath as friends and family. What she can't live without, therefore, is inspiration – her life would be a dark, passionless existence. **Depression** is an empty state with no feeling or direction, yet her view of creativity is romantic. It is miraculous, available only to a chosen few. 'The long wait for the angel' has begun. Notice the constant use of the personal pronoun 'I'. This is a poet who is very aware of self and her own personal responses to events and feelings. The outside world becomes a metaphor for her own interior world.

Plath uses both archaic language and slang, as if reinforcing the randomness of the world. This is also mirrored in the run-on lines. All is haphazard, but carefully arranged, so even the extended final sentence stretches out as it waits for the 'random descent' of inspiration. Throughout the poem's **carefully arranged disorder**, two worlds are seen. One is negative: 'desultory', 'mute', 'dull', 'stubborn', 'fatigue'. This is indicative of Plath's own bleak mood. The other world is positive: 'light', 'celestial', 'largesse', 'love', 'shine'. This offers the possibility of radiance.

✒ Writing About the Poem

'Plath's poems are carefully composed and beautifully phrased.' Write a paragraph in response to this statement, developing your answer with close reference to the poem 'Black Rook in Rainy Weather'.

Sample Paragraph

Just like the rook in 'Black Rook in Rainy Weather', Plath 'arranges and rearranges' her words with precision and care to communicate the dull life of 'total neutrality' which occurs when she is not inspired, when nothing sets 'the sight on fire'. I particularly admire how she arranges disorder in the poem. This mirrors the chance of poetic inspiration. Long lines poke untidily out of the first three stanzas, seeking the 'minor light' to 'Lean incandescent' upon them. I also like how the lines run in a seemingly untidy way into each other, as do some stanzas. Stanza three goes into four, as it describes the chance of a light coming from an ordinary object, such as a kitchen chair, which is seen only if the poet is inspired. The alliteration of 'rare, random' in the last line echoes the gift of poetic technique which will be given to the poet if she can receive the blessing of poetic inspiration: 'Miracles occur'.

> **EXAMINER'S COMMENT**
>
> *Close reading of the poem is evident in this top-grade original response to Plath's poetic technique. Quotations are very well used here to highlight the poet's ability to create anarchic order.*

✎ Class/Homework Exercises

1. Plath criticised the poem, 'Black Rook in Rainy Weather' for its 'glassy brittleness'. In your opinion, what does she mean? Refer to both the content and style of the poem, supporting your answer with reference to the text.
2. In your opinion, has the poet given up hope of being inspired? Use reference to the poem in your answer.

◉ Points to Consider

- Waiting for poetic inspiration, the hope for something better.
- Despondency – negative adjectives, harsh verbs.
- Miracle of inspiration, contrasting imagery of fire and light.
- Careful rhyme patterns echo design of the rook's plumage.
- Language – colloquial and formal, slang and religious terminology.

2 The Times Are Tidy

Unlucky the hero born
In this province of the stuck record
Where the most watchful cooks go jobless
And the mayor's rôtisserie turns
Round of its own accord.   5

There's no career in the venture
Of riding against the lizard,
Himself withered these latter-days
To leaf-size from lack of action:
History's beaten the hazard.   10

The last crone got burnt up
More than eight decades back
With the love-hot herb, the talking cat,
But the children are better for it,
The cow milks cream an inch thick.   15

province: a remote place.
stuck record: the needle would sometimes get jammed on a vinyl music album.
rôtisserie: meat on a rotating skewer.
lizard: dragon.
crone: old witch.

'riding against the lizard'

Personal Response

1. What is suggested by the poem's title? Is Plath being cynical about modern life? Develop your response in a short paragraph.
2. Select one image from the poem which suggests that the past was much more dangerous and exciting than the present. Comment on its effectiveness.
3. Do you agree or disagree with the speaker's view of modern life? Give reasons for your answer.

👁 Critical Literacy

'The Times Are Tidy' was written in 1958. In this short poem, Plath casts a cold eye on contemporary life and culture, which she sees as bland and unadventurous. The poem's ironic title clearly suggests Plath's dissatisfaction with the over-regulated society of her day. Do you think you are living in a heroic age or do you believe that most people have lost their sense of wonder? Is there anyone in public life whom you really admire?

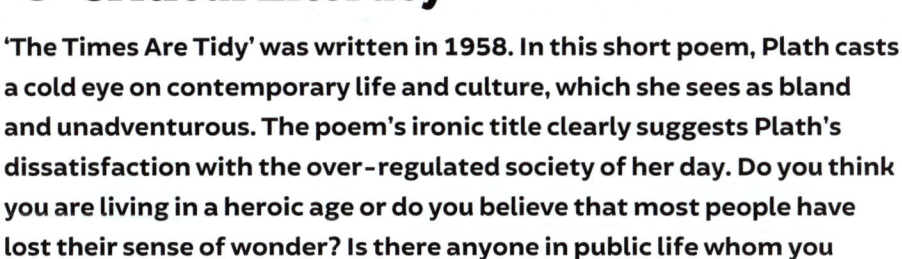

Stanza one is dominated by hard-hitting images reflecting how the world of fairytale excitement has disappeared. From the outset, **the tone is scornful and dismissive**. Plath believes that any hero would be totally out of place amid the mediocrity of our times. True talent ('the most watchful cooks') is largely unrewarded. The unexpected imagery of the 'stuck record' and the mayor's rotating spit symbolise complacent monotony and lack of progress, particularly during the late 1950s, when Plath wrote the poem. Both images convey a sense of purposeless circling, of people going nowhere. It seems as though the poet is seething with frustration at the inertia and conformity of her own times.

Plath's **darkly embittered sense of humour** becomes evident in stanza two. She laments the current lack of honour and courage – something which once existed in the world of fairytales. Unlike the past, contemporary society is compromised. There are no idealistic dragon-slayers any more. The worker who dares to stand up and criticise ('riding against the lizard') is risking demotion. The modern dragon – a metaphor for the challenges we face – has even been reduced to a mere lizard. Despite this, we are afraid of confrontation and prefer to retreat. The verb 'withered' suggests the weakness and decay of our safe, modern world. The poet openly complains that 'History's beaten the hazard'. Over time, we have somehow defeated all sense of adventure and daring. These qualities belong in the distant past.

In stanza three, Plath continues to contrast past and present. Witches are no longer burned at the stake. This might well suggest that superstition has disappeared, and with it, all imagination. The last two lines are ironic in tone, reflecting the poet's deep **disenchantment with the excesses of our consumer society**. The final image – 'the cow milks cream an inch thick' – signifies overindulgence.

The poet clearly accepts that **society has changed for the worse**. Children may have everything they want nowadays, but they have lost their sense of wonder and excitement. Plath laments the loss of legendary heroism. Medieval dragons and wicked witches (complete with magic potions and talking cats) no longer exist. Her conclusion is that life today is unquestionably less interesting than it used to be. Unlike so much of Plath's work, the personal pronoun 'I' is not used in this poem. However, the highly contemptuous views and weary, frustrated tone clearly suggest that Plath feels unfulfilled.

✍ Writing About the Poem

Write a paragraph in which you comment on Plath's critical tone in 'The Times Are Tidy'.

Sample Paragraph

The tone of voice in 'The Times Are Tidy' is extremely critical of modern life. Plath has nothing good to say about today's world as she sees it. The poem's title is self-satisfied, just like the neatly organised society that Plath seems to despise. The opening comment – 'Unlucky the hero born/In this province' – emphasises this negative tone. The poet's mocking attitude becomes increasingly disparaging as she rages against the unproductive images of easy living – 'the stuck record' and 'the mayor's rôtisserie'. Plath goes on to contrast today's apathetic society with the medieval era, when knights in armour existed. The poet omits all the positive aspects of modern life and chooses to give a very one-sided view. Plath ends on a sarcastic note, sneering at the advances of our world of plenty – 'cream an inch thick'. The voice here is both critical and superior.

EXAMINER'S COMMENT

This top-grade paragraph demonstrates strong analytical skills and is firmly focused on Plath's judgmental tone. The supporting references range widely and effectively illustrate the poet's critical attitude. Quotations are particularly well integrated and the management of language is assured throughout.

✒ Class/Homework Exercises

1. Outline the main theme in 'The Times Are Tidy'. In your answer, trace the way the poet develops her ideas during the course of the poem.
2. Trace the changing tones in the poem 'The Times Are Tidy'. Support your answer with close reference to the text.

◉ Points to Consider

- **Poet's distaste for pursuit of materialism prevalent in 1950s American society.**
- **Collapse of moral standards in public life.**
- **Death of the spirit of adventure, no challenge to society's smugness.**
- **Humour and irony, derisive tone, entertaining images and sound effects.**
- **Contrast between modern 'tidy' times and 'untidy' times of legend.**

3 Morning Song

SYLVIA PLATH

Love set you going like a fat gold watch.
The midwife slapped your footsoles, and your bald cry
Took its place among the elements.

Our voices echo, magnifying your arrival. New statue.
In a drafty museum, your nakedness   5
Shadows our safety. We stand round blankly as walls.

I'm no more your mother
Than the cloud that distils a mirror to reflect its own slow
Effacement at the wind's hand.

All night your moth-breath   10
Flickers among the flat pink roses. I wake to listen:
A far sea moves in my ear.

One cry, and I stumble from bed, cow-heavy and floral
In my Victorian nightgown.
Your mouth opens clean as a cat's. The window square   15

Whitens and swallows its dull stars. And now you try
Your handful of notes;
The clear vowels rise like balloons.

---

midwife: a person trained to assist at childbirth.
elements: primitive, natural, atmospheric forces.
Effacement: gradual disappearance.
pink roses: images on the wallpaper.
vowels: speech sounds made without stopping the flow of the breath.

'clear vowels rise'

👤 Personal Response

1. Comment on the suitability and effectiveness of the simile in line 1.
2. What is the attitude of the mother to the new arrival? Does her attitude change in the course of the poem? Refer to the text in your answer.
3. A metaphor links two things so that one idea explains or gives a new viewpoint about the other. Choose one interesting metaphor from the poem and comment on its effectiveness.

👁 Critical Literacy

'Morning Song' was written in 1961. Plath explores the complex issues of the relationship between a mother and her child, celebrating the birth of the infant but also touching on deep feelings of loss and separation.

Do all mothers immediately welcome and fall in love with a new baby? Are some of them overwhelmed or even depressed after giving birth? Are parents often anxious about the new responsibilities a baby brings? Plath wrote this poem after two intensely personal experiences, celebrating the birth of her daughter, Frieda, who was 10 months old, and shortly after a miscarriage. The poem is realistic and never strays into sentimentality or cliché. The title 'Morning' suggests a new beginning and 'Song' a celebration.

==Stanza one== describes the arrival of the child into the world in a confident, rhythmic sentence announcing the act of creation: 'Love set you going'. The simile comparing the child to a 'fat gold watch' suggests a plump baby, a rich and precious object. Broad vowel effects emphasise the physical presence of the infant. The 'ticking' sound conveys action and dynamism, but also the passage of time. Plath's child is now part of the mortal world where change and death are inevitable. At this moment of birth, the baby is the centre of attention as the midwife and parents surround her. But this is a cruel world, as we see from the words 'slapped' and 'bald'. The infant is part of the universe as she takes her place among the 'elements'. The verbs in this stanza are in the past tense – **the mother is looking back at the event**. The rest of the poem is written in the present tense, which adds to the immediacy of the experience.

==Stanza two== has a feeling of disorientation, as if the mother feels separated from the child now that she has left the womb. There is a nightmarish, surreal quality to the lines 'Our voices echo, magnifying your arrival'. Plath sees the child as a new exhibit ('New statue') in a museum. Commas and full stops break up the flow of the lines and **the tone becomes more stilted and detached**. The child as a work of art is special and unique, but the museum is 'drafty', again a reference to the harshness of the world. The baby's vulnerability is stressed by its 'nakedness'. The midwife's and parents' frozen response is caught in the phrase 'blankly as walls'. They anxiously observe, unsure about their ability to protect. This baby also represents a threat to the parents' relationship as she 'Shadows' their safety. The child is perceived as having a negative impact on them, perhaps driving them apart rather than uniting them.

Stanza three focuses on the **complex relationship between child and mother**. Plath feels she can't be maternal ('no more your mother'). This is vividly shown in the image of the cloud that rains, creating a puddle. **But in the act of creation, it destroys itself and its destruction is reflected in the pool of water.** Throughout her life, the poet was haunted by a fear of her own personal failure. Does she see a conflict between becoming a mother and remaining a writer? She also realises that as the child grows and matures she will age, moving closer to death, and this will be reflected in the child's gaze. The mood of this stanza is one of estrangement and powerlessness. Notice how the three lines of the stanza run into each other as the cloud disappears.

In stanza four, the tone changes to one of intimate, maternal love as the caring mother becomes alert to her child's needs. The situation described is warm and homely – the 'flat pink roses' are very different from the chill 'museum' of a previous stanza. The fragile breathing of the little child is beautifully described as 'your moth-breath/Flickers'. **Onomatopoeia in 'Flickers' mimics the tiny breathing noises of the child.** The mother is anticipating her baby's needs as she wakes ('listen'). The breathing child evokes happy memories of Plath's seaside childhood ('A far sea moves in my ear').

The infant cries and the attentive mother springs into action. She laughs at herself as she describes the comical figure she makes, 'cow-heavy and floral' in stanza five. She feels awkward as she 'stumble[s]' to tend her child, whose eager mouth is shown by a startling image ('clean as a cat's') when it opens wide to receive the night feed of milk. **The stanza flows smoothly** over into stanza six, just as nature flows to its own rhythm and does not obey clocks or any other man-made rules. Night becomes morning as the child swallows the milk and the window swallows the stars.

Children demand a parent's time and energy. **This child now defines herself** with her unique collection of sounds ('Your handful of notes'). This poem opened with the instinctive, elemental 'bald' cry of a newborn, but closes on a lovely, happy image of music and colour, as the baby's song's notes 'rise like balloons'.

✒ Writing About the Poem

'Morning Song' begins with the word 'Love'. How does Plath treat the theme of love over the course of the poem? Develop your answer with reference to the text.

Sample Paragraph

'Morning Song' opens with a tender statement that the poet's daughter was conceived in love – 'Love set you going'. This warm tone changes, however, to the curiously disengaged voice of the second stanza where the parents 'stand round blankly as walls'. The birth of their child into a harsh world, 'drafty museum', seems to overwhelm them. In the third stanza, the sense of separation deepens and Plath admits that she does not really feel like the child's mother at all. Instead, she explores her feelings of worthlessness through the complex image of the disintegrating cloud, which creates only to be destroyed in the act of creation. The poem ends on a more affectionate and genuinely loving note as the attentive mother feeds her child while listening to her baby's song 'rise like balloons'. For me, the gentle effect of this image suggests the innocence of the infant.

EXAMINER'S COMMENT

A focused and well-supported response showing good personal engagement with the poem. The central point about Plath's conflicting emotions is clearly stated and the development of thought is traced throughout the poem. Excellent language control and impressive vocabulary (e.g. 'curiously disengaged voice', 'complex image of the disintegrating cloud') are in keeping with the top-grade standard.

Class/Homework Exercises

1. 'The sense of alienation is often agonisingly evoked in Plath's poetry.' To what extent is this true of 'Morning Song'? Support your answer with reference to the poem.
2. 'Sylvia Plath makes effective use of unusual and startling imagery to explore deeply personal themes.' Discuss this view with particular reference to the poem 'Morning Song'.

Points to Consider

- Poet's ambivalent attitude to motherhood: loss of individual identity conflicting with deep love.
- Striking, unexpected imagery: contrasts between the child's delicacy and the mother's clumsiness.
- Development from inanimate objects (the watch, statue, mirror, cloud) to animate objects (moth, cow, cat, singer).
- Varying tones: tender, anxious, alienated, reflective, caring, fulfilled.
- Intense feelings of dislocation replaced by increasing sense of inter-connectedness.

4 Finisterre

This was the land's end: the last fingers, knuckled and rheumatic,
Cramped on nothing. Black
Admonitory cliffs, and the sea exploding
With no bottom, or anything on the other side of it,
Whitened by the faces of the drowned. 5
Now it is only gloomy, a dump of rocks –
Leftover soldiers from old, messy wars.
The sea cannons into their ear, but they don't budge.
Other rocks hide their grudges under the water.

The cliffs are edged with trefoils, stars and bells 10
Such as fingers might embroider, close to death,
Almost too small for the mists to bother with.
The mists are part of the ancient paraphernalia –
Souls, rolled in the doom-noise of the sea.
They bruise the rocks out of existence, then resurrect them. 15
They go up without hope, like sighs.
I walk among them, and they stuff my mouth with cotton.
When they free me, I am beaded with tears.

Our Lady of the Shipwrecked is striding toward the horizon,
Her marble skirts blown back in two pink wings. 20
A marble sailor kneels at her foot distractedly, and at his foot
A peasant woman in black
Is praying to the monument of the sailor praying.
Our Lady of the Shipwrecked is three times life size,
Her lips sweet with divinity. 25
She does not hear what the sailor or the peasant is saying –
She is in love with the beautiful formlessness of the sea.

Gull-colored laces flap in the sea drafts
Beside the postcard stalls.
The peasants anchor them with conches. One is told: 30
'These are the pretty trinkets the sea hides,
Little shells made up into necklaces and toy ladies.
They do not come from the Bay of the Dead down there,
But from another place, tropical and blue,
We have never been to. 35
These are our crêpes. Eat them before they blow cold.'

land's end: literally 'Finisterre'; the western tip of Brittany.

Admonitory: warning.

trefoils: three-leaved plants.

paraphernalia: discarded items.
doom-noise: hopeless sounds.

Our Lady of the Shipwrecked: the mother of Christ prayed for sailors.

conches: shells.
trinkets: cheap jewellery.

crêpes: light pancakes.

SYLVIA PLATH

'and the sea exploding'

👤 Personal Response

1. Would you agree that this is a disquieting poem that is likely to disturb readers? Refer to the text in your answer.
2. There are several changes of tone in this poem. Describe two contrasting tones, using close reference to the text.
3. What does the poem reveal to you about Sylvia Plath's own state of mind? Use reference to the text in your response.

👁 Critical Literacy

'Finisterre' was written in 1960 following Plath's visit to Brittany, France. As with many of her poems, the description of the place can be interpreted both literally and metaphorically.

The sea has always inspired poets and artists. It is at times welcoming, menacing, beautiful, peaceful and mysterious. Throughout her short life, Sylvia Plath loved the ocean. She spent her childhood years on the Atlantic coast just north of Boston. This setting provides a source for many of her poetic ideas. Terror and death loom large in her descriptive poem 'Finisterre', in which the pounding rhythm of storm waves off the Breton coast represents **Plath's inner turmoil**.

Stanza one opens dramatically and immediately creates a disturbing atmosphere. Plath describes the rocky headland as being 'knuckled and rheumatic'. In a series of powerful images ('Black/Admonitory cliffs', 'the sea exploding'), the poet recreates the uproar and commotion of the scene. The **grisly personification** is startling, linking the shoreline with suffering and decay. There is a real sense of conflict between sea and land. Both are closely associated with death ('the faces of the drowned'). The jagged rocks are compared to 'Leftover soldiers' who 'hide their grudges under the water'. There is a noticeable tone of regret and protest against the futility of conflict, which is denounced as 'old, messy wars'.

Plath's **negative imagery** is relentless, with harsh consonant sounds ('knuckled', 'Cramped') emphasising the force of raging storm waves. The use of contrasting colours intensifies the imagery. As the 'sea cannons' against the headland, the atmosphere is 'only gloomy'. It is hard not to see the bleak seascape as a reflection of Plath's own unhappy state of mind.

In stanza two, the poet turns away from the cruel sea and focuses momentarily on the small plants clinging to the cliff edge. However, these 'trefoils, stars and bells' are also 'close to death'. If anything, they reinforce the **unsettling mood** and draw the poet back to the ocean mists, which she thinks of as symbolising the souls of the dead, lost in 'the doom-noise of the sea'. Plath imagines the heavy mists transforming the rocks, destroying them 'out of existence' before managing to 'resurrect them' again. In a **surreal sequence**, the poet enters the water ('I walk among them') and joins the wretched souls who lie there. Her growing sense of panic is suggested by the stark admission: 'they stuff my mouth with cotton'. The experience is agonising and leaves her 'beaded with tears'.

Plath's thoughts turn to a marble statue of 'Our Lady of the Shipwrecked' in stanza three. Once again, in her imagination, she creates a **dramatic narrative** around the religious figure. This monument to the patron saint of the ocean should offer some consolation to the kneeling sailor and a grieving peasant woman who pray to the mother of God. Ironically, their pleas are completely ignored – 'She does not hear' their prayers because 'She is in love with the beautiful formlessness of the sea'. Is the poet expressing her own **feelings of failure and despondency here**? Or is she also attacking the ineffectiveness of religion? The description of the statue is certainly unflattering. The figure is flighty and self-centred: 'Her marble skirts blown back in two pink wings'. In contrast, the powerful ocean remains fascinating.

In the fourth stanza, Plath turns her attention to the local Bretons who sell souvenirs to tourists. Unlike the previous three stanzas, **the mood appears to be much lighter** as the poet describes the friendly stall-keepers going about their business. It is another irony that their livelihood (selling 'pretty trinkets') is dependent on the sea and its beauty. Like the statue, the locals seem unconcerned by the tragic history of the ocean. Indeed, they are keen to play down 'the Bay of the Dead' and explain that what they sell is imported 'from another place, tropical and blue'. In the final line, a stall-holder advises the poet to enjoy the pancakes she has bought: 'Eat them before they blow cold'. Although the immediate mood is untroubled, the final phrase brings us back to the earlier – and more disturbing – parts of the poem where Plath described the raging storms and the nameless lost souls who have perished at sea.

Writing About the Poem

Write a paragraph commenting on Sylvia Plath's use of detailed description in 'Finisterre'.

Sample Paragraph

In 'Finisterre', the opening images of the rocks – 'the last fingers, knuckled and rheumatic' – are of decrepit old age. The strong visual impact is a feature of Plath's writing. The first half of the poem is filled with memorable details of the windswept coastline. Plath uses broad vowels to evoke a pervading feeling of dejection. Words such as 'drowned' and 'doom' help to create this dismal effect. The dramatic aural image, 'The sea cannons', echoes the roar of turbulent waves crashing onto the rocks. Plath's close observation is also seen in her portrait of the holy statue – 'Her lips sweet with divinity'. The poem ends with a vivid sketch of the traders selling postcards and 'Little shells made up into necklaces and toy ladies'. Overall, the use of details leaves readers with a strong sense of place and community.

EXAMINER'S COMMENT

Quotations are very well used here to highlight Plath's ability to create specific scenes and moods through precise description. The examples range over much of the poem and the writing is both varied and controlled throughout. A top-grade response.

Class/Homework Exercises

1. It has been said that vivid, startling imagery gives a surreal quality to 'Finisterre'. Using reference to the poem, write a paragraph responding to this statement.
2. 'Plath's unique imagination addresses unhappiness and hopelessness.' To what extent do you agree with this statement? Develop your answer with suitable reference to 'Finisterre', referring to the poem's content and style.

Points to Consider

- **Fearful, ominous description of ordinary place.**
- **Disquieting tone of Our Lady of the Shipwrecked as aloof and self-absorbed.**
- **Ironic contrast between sweet appearance of statue and grim reality of shipwrecks in bay.**
- **Formal structure of poem contrasts with terror of situation.**
- **Striking images and sounds, personification, rich symbolism.**

5 Mirror

SYLVIA PLATH

I am silver and exact. I have no preconceptions.
Whatever I see I swallow immediately
Just as it is, unmisted by love or dislike.
I am not cruel, only truthful –
The eye of a little god, four-cornered. 5
Most of the time I meditate on the opposite wall.
It is pink, with speckles. I have looked at it so long
I think it is part of my heart. But it flickers.
Faces and darkness separate us over and over.

Now I am a lake. A woman bends over me, 10
Searching my reaches for what she really is.
Then she turns to those liars, the candles or the moon.
I see her back, and reflect it faithfully.
She rewards me with tears and an agitation of hands.
I am important to her. She comes and goes. 15
Each morning it is her face that replaces the darkness.
In me she has drowned a young girl, and in me an old woman
Rises toward her day after day, like a terrible fish.

exact: accurate, giving all details; to insist on payment.
preconceptions: thoughts already formed.

reaches: range of distance or depth.

agitation: shaking, trembling.

'The eye of a little god, four-cornered'

👤 Personal Response

1. Select two images that suggest the dark, sinister side of the mirror. Comment briefly on your two choices.
2. What, in your opinion, is the main theme or message of this poem?
3. Write your own personal response to this poem, referring closely to the text in your answer.

👁 Critical Literacy

'Mirror' was written in 1961 as Sylvia Plath approached her twenty-ninth birthday. In this dark poem, Plath views the inevitability of old age and death, our preoccupation with image and our search for an identity.

Do you think everyone looks at themselves in a mirror? Would you consider that people are fascinated, disappointed or even obsessed by what they see? Does a mirror accurately reflect the truth? Do people actually see what is reflected or is it distorted by notions and ideals which they or society have? Consider the use of mirrors in fairytales: 'Mirror, mirror on the wall, who's the fairest of them all?' Mirrors are also used in myths – like the story of Narcissus, who drowned having fallen in love with his reflection – and in children's books such as *Through the Looking Glass*. Mirrors are also used in horror films as the dividing line between fantasy and reality.

In this poem, Plath gives us a startling new angle on an everyday object. The function of a mirror is to reflect whatever is put in front of it. Stanza one opens with a ringing declaration by the mirror: 'I am silver and exact'. This **personification has a sinister effect** as the mirror describes an almost claustrophobic relationship with a particular woman. The dramatic voice of the mirror is clear and precise. It announces that it reports exactly what there is without any alteration. We have to decide if the mirror is telling the truth, as it says it has no bias ('no preconceptions'). It does not judge; it reflects the image received. The mirror adopts the position of an impartial observer, but it is active, almost ruthless ('I swallow').

Yet how truthful is a mirror image, as it flattens a three-dimensional object into two dimensions? The image sent out has no depth. The voice of the mirror becomes smug as it sees itself as the ruler of those reflected ('The eye of a little god'). Our obsession with ourselves causes us to worship at the mirror that reflects our image. In the modern world, people are often disappointed with their reflection, wishing they were thinner, younger, better looking. But **the mirror insists it tells the truth**; it doesn't flatter or hurt. The mirror explains how it spends its day gazing at the opposite wall, which is carefully described as 'pink, with speckles'. It feels as if the wall is part of itself. This reflection is disturbed by the faces of people and the dying light. The passage of time is evoked in the phrase 'over and over'.

In stanza two, the tension increases and the mirror announces that it is 'a lake'. Both are flat surfaces that reflect. However, a lake is another dimension, it has depth. **There is danger.** The image is now drawn into its murky depths. The woman is looking in and down, not just at. It is as if she is struggling to find who she really is, what her true path in life is. Plath frequently questioned who she was. Expectations for young women in the 1950s were limiting. Appearance was important, as were the roles of wife, mother and homemaker. But Plath also wanted to write: 'Will I submerge my embarrassing desires and aspirations, refuse to face myself?' (from Plath's journals). The mirror becomes irritated and jealous of the woman as she turns to the deceptive soft light of 'those liars, the candles or the moon'. **The woman is dissatisfied with her image.** In her insecurity, she weeps and wrings her hands. Plath always tried to do her best, to be a model student, almost desperate to excel and be affirmed. Is there a danger in seeking perfection? Do we need to love ourselves as we are? Again, the mirror pompously announces 'I am important to her'.

The march of time passing is emphasised by 'comes and goes', 'Each morning' and 'day after day'. The woman keeps coming back. The mirror's sense of its significance is shown by the frequent use of 'I' and the repetition of 'in me'. As time passes, the woman is facing the truth of her human condition as her reflection changes and ages in the mirror. Her youth is 'drowned', to be replaced by a monstrous vision of an old woman 'like a terrible fish'. **The lonely drama of living and dying is recorded with a nightmarish quality.** There is no comforting rhyme in the poem, only the controlled rhythm of time. The mirror does not give what a human being desires: comfort and warmth. Instead, it impersonally reminds us of our mortality.

✒ Writing About the Poem

What is your personal response to the relationship between the mirror and the woman? Support your views with reference to the poem.

Sample Paragraph

I feel the mirror is like an alter ego, coolly appraising the woman in an unforgiving way. The mirror is 'silver'. Although the mirror repeatedly states that it does not judge, 'I have no preconceptions', the woman feels judged and inadequate: 'She rewards me with tears and an agitation of hands.' I think the relationship between the woman and the mirror is dangerous. She does indeed 'drown' in the mirror, as she never feels good enough. The mirror rules her like a 'little god, four-cornered'. This relationship shows a troubled self, a lack of self-love. Who is saying that the older woman is 'like a terrible fish'? I think the mirror has become the voice of a society which values women only for their looks and youth, rather than what they are capable of achieving.

> **EXAMINER'S COMMENT**
>
> In this fluent and personal response, close analysis of the text contributes to a distinctive and well-supported, top-grade account of the uneasy relationship between the mirror and the woman.

✒ Class/Homework Exercises

1. 'Plath's use of dramatic monologue is an unsettling experience for readers.' Discuss this statement with reference to 'Mirror'.
2. 'All who share the human condition have a bright and dark side.' Discuss Plath's exploration of this theme in her poem 'Mirror'. In your response, pay particular attention to her use of imagery.

◉ Points to Consider

- Key themes include transience and mortality.
- Chilling personification of the mirror.
- Exploration of identity, duality of being.
- Startlingly shocking imagery and drama convey frightening tone.

6 Pheasant

SYLVIA PLATH

You said you would kill it this morning.
Do not kill it. It startles me still,
The jut of that odd, dark head, pacing

Through the uncut grass on the elm's hill.
It is something to own a pheasant, 5
Or just to be visited at all.

I am not mystical: it isn't
As if I thought it had a spirit.
It is simply in its element.

That gives it a kingliness, a right. 10
The print of its big foot last winter,
The tail-track, on the snow in our court –

The wonder of it, in that pallor,
Through crosshatch of sparrow and starling.
Is it its rareness, then? It is rare. 15

But a dozen would be worth having,
A hundred, on that hill – green and red,
Crossing and recrossing: a fine thing!

It is such a good shape, so vivid.
It's a little cornucopia. 20
It unclaps, brown as a leaf, and loud,

Settles in the elm, and is easy.
It was sunning in the narcissi.
I trespass stupidly. Let be, let be.

You: probably addressed to Plath's husband.

jut: extending outwards.

mystical: spiritual, supernatural.

pallor: pale colour.

crosshatch: criss-cross trail.

cornucopia: unexpected treasure.

narcissi: bright spring flowers.

'in its element'

👤 Personal Response

1. Comment on Sylvia Plath's attitude to nature based on your reading of 'Pheasant'.
2. Compile a list of the poet's arguments for not killing the pheasant.
3. Write a paragraph on the effectiveness of Plath's imagery in the poem.

👁 Critical Literacy

'Pheasant' was written in 1962 and reflects Plath's deep appreciation of the natural world. Its enthusiastic mood contrasts with much of her more disturbing work. The poem is structured in eight tercets (three-line stanzas) with a subtle, interlocking rhyming pattern (known as terza rima).

The poem opens with an urgent plea by Plath to spare the pheasant's life: 'Do not kill it'. In the first two stanzas, the tone is tense as the poet offers a variety of reasons for sparing this impressive game bird. She is both shocked and excited by the pheasant: 'It startles me still'. Plath admits to feeling honoured in the presence of the bird: 'It is something to own a pheasant'. The broken rhythm of the early lines adds an abruptness that heightens the sense of urgency. **Plath seems spellbound by the bird's beauty** ('The jut of that odd, dark head') now that it is under threat.

But the poet is also keen to play down any sentimentality in her attitude to the pheasant. Stanza three begins with a straightforward explanation of her attitude: 'it isn't/As if I thought it had a spirit'. Instead, **she values the bird for its graceful beauty and naturalness**: 'It is simply in its element.' Plath is keen to show her recognition of the pheasant's right to exist because it possesses a certain majestic quality, 'a kingliness'.

In stanza four, the poet recalls an earlier winter scene when she marvelled at the pheasant's distinctive footprint in the snow. The bird has made an even greater impression on Plath, summed up in the key phrase 'The wonder of it', at the start of stanza five. She remembers **the colourful pheasant's distinguishing marks against the pale snow**, so unlike the 'crosshatch' pattern of smaller birds, such as the sparrow and starling. This makes the pheasant particularly 'rare' and valuable in Plath's eyes.

The poet can hardly contain her regard for the pheasant and her tone becomes increasingly enthusiastic in stanza six as she dreams of having first a 'dozen' and then a 'hundred' of the birds. In a few **well-chosen details**, she highlights their colour and energy ('green and red,/Crossing and recrossing') before adding an emphatic compliment: 'a fine thing!' Her delight continues into stanza seven, where Plath proclaims her ceaseless admiration for the pheasant: 'It's a little cornucopia', an inspirational source of joy and surprise.

Throughout the poem, the poet has emphasised that the pheasant rightly belongs in its natural surroundings, and this is also true of the final lines. Stanza eight is considered and assured. From the poet's point of view, **the pheasant's right to live is beyond dispute**. While the bird is 'sunning in the narcissi', she herself has become the unwelcome intruder: 'I trespass stupidly'. Plath ends by echoing the opening appeal to spare the pheasant's life: 'Let be, let be.' The quietly insistent repetition and the underlying tone of unease are a final reminder of the need to respect nature.

It has been suggested that the pheasant symbolises Plath's insecure relationship with Ted Hughes. For various reasons, their marriage was under severe strain in 1962 and Plath feared that Hughes was intent on ending it. This interpretation adds a greater poignancy to the poem.

Writing About the Poem

There are several mood changes in 'Pheasant'. What do you consider to be the dominant mood in the poem? Refer to the text in your answer.

Sample Paragraph

The mood at the beginning of 'Pheasant' is nervous and really uptight. Plath seems to have given up hope about the pheasant. It is facing death. She repeats the word 'kill' and admits to being shocked at the very thought of what the bird is facing. But she herself seems desperate and fearful. This is shown by the sentence, 'Do not kill it'. But the outlook soon changes. Plath describes the pheasant 'pacing' and 'in its element'. But she seems less stressed as she describes the 'kingliness' of the pheasant. But the mood soon settles down as Plath celebrates the life of this really beautiful bird. The mood becomes calmer and ends in almost a whisper, 'Let be, let be'.

EXAMINER'S COMMENT

This is a reasonable middle-grade answer to the question, pointing out the change of mood following the first stanza. Some worthwhile references are used to show the poem's principal mood. The expression, however, is flawed in places (e.g. repeatedly using 'But' to start sentences). This response requires more critical analysis and development to raise the standard.

Class/Homework Exercises

1. Plath sets out to convince the reader of the pheasant's right to life in this poem. Does she succeed in her aim? Give reasons for your answer.
2. 'Sylvia Plath's deep appreciation of the harmonious order of the natural world is expressed through vivid imagery.' To what extent is this true of her poem 'Pheasant'? Develop your answer with reference to the text.

⊙ Points to Consider

- **Heartfelt plea on behalf of the rights of wild creatures.**
- **Graphic description of beauty of bird.**
- **Tension, poet as intruder.**
- **Imperatives (verbal commands) inject urgency.**
- **Subtle music, casual flow of the rhythm of normal speech.**

7 Elm

For Ruth Fainlight

I know the bottom, she says. I know it with my great tap root:
It is what you fear.
I do not fear it: I have been there.

Is it the sea you hear in me,
Its dissatisfactions?
Or the voice of nothing, that was your madness?

Love is a shadow.
How you lie and cry after it
Listen: these are its hooves: it has gone off, like a horse.

All night I shall gallop thus, impetuously,
Till your head is a stone, your pillow a little turf,
Echoing, echoing.

Or shall I bring you the sound of poisons?
This is rain now, this big hush.
And this is the fruit of it: tin-white, like arsenic.

I have suffered the atrocity of sunsets.
Scorched to the root
My red filaments burn and stand, a hand of wires.

Now I break up in pieces that fly about like clubs.
A wind of such violence
Will tolerate no bystanding: I must shriek.

The moon, also, is merciless: she would drag me
Cruelly, being barren.
Her radiance scathes me. Or perhaps I have caught her.

I let her go. I let her go
Diminished and flat, as after radical surgery.
How your bad dreams possess and endow me.

I am inhabited by a cry.
Nightly it flaps out
Looking, with its hooks, for something to love. 30

I am terrified by this dark thing
That sleeps in me;
All day I feel its soft, feathery turnings, its malignity.

malignity: evil.

Clouds pass and disperse.
Are those the faces of love, those pale irretrievables? 35
Is it for such I agitate my heart?

disperse: scatter widely.
irretrievables: things lost for ever.

I am incapable of more knowledge.
What is this, this face
So murderous in its strangle of branches? –

Its snaky acids hiss. 40
It petrifies the will. These are the isolate, slow faults
That kill, that kill, that kill.

snaky acids: deceptive poisons.
petrifies: terrifies.

'I am terrified by this dark thing'

Personal Response

1. There are many sinister nature images in this poem. Select two that you find particularly unsettling and comment on their effectiveness.
2. Briefly describe how love is presented and viewed by the poet. Support the points you make with reference to the text.
3. Write your own individual response to this poem, referring to the text in your answer.

👁 Critical Literacy

Written in April 1962, 'Elm' is one of Sylvia Plath's most intensely dramatic poems. Plath personifies the elm tree to create a surreal scene. It 'speaks' in a traumatic voice to someone else, the 'you' of line 2, the poet herself – or the reader, perhaps. The two voices interact throughout the poem, almost always expressing pain and anguish. Critics often associate these powerful emotions with the poet's own personal problems – Plath had experienced electric shock treatment for depression. However, this may well limit our understanding of what is a complex exploration of many emotions.

The opening stanza is unnerving. The poet appears to be dramatising an exchange between herself and the elm by imagining what the tree might say to her. The immediate effect is eerily surreal. From the start, **the narrative voice is obsessed with instability and despair**: 'I know the bottom'. The tree is described in both physical terms ('my great tap root' penetrating far into the ground) and also as a state of mind ('I do not fear it'). The depth of depression imagined is reinforced by the repetition of 'I know' and the stark simplicity of the chilling comment 'It is what you fear'.

The bizarre exchange between the two 'speakers' continues in stanza two. The elm questions the poet about the nature of her **mental state**. Does the wind blowing through its branches remind her of the haunting sound of the sea? Or even 'the voice of nothing' – the numbing experience of madness?

Stanzas three and four focus on the dangers and disappointments of love – 'a shadow'. The tone is fearful, emphasised by the comparison of a wild horse that has 'gone off'. The relentless sounds of the wind in the elm will be a bitter reminder, 'echoing' this loss of love 'Till your head is a stone'. **Assonance** is effectively used here to heighten the sense of hurt and abandonment. For much of the middle section of the poem (stanzas five to nine), the elm's intimidating voice continues to dramatise a series of horrifying experiences associated with insanity. The tree has endured extreme elements – rain ('the sound of poisons'), sunshine ('Scorched to the root'), wind ('of such violence') and also the moon ('Her radiance scathes me'). **The harsh imagery and frenzied language** ('burn', 'shriek', 'merciless') combine to create a sense of shocking destructiveness.

Stanzas ten and eleven mark a turning point where the voices of the tree and the poet become indistinguishable. This is achieved by the seemingly harmless image of an owl inhabiting the branches, searching for 'something to love'. The speaker is haunted by 'this dark thing'. The **poet's vulnerability** is particularly evident in her stark admission: 'I feel its soft, feathery turnings, its malignity'. Plath has come to relate her unknown demons to a deadly tumour.

In the last three stanzas, the poet's voice seems more distant and calm before the final storm. The image of the passing clouds ('the faces of love') highlight the notion of rejection as the root cause of Plath's depression. The poem ends on a visionary note when she imagines being confronted by a 'murderous' snake that appears in the branches: 'It petrifies the will'. The scene of **growing terror builds to a hideous climax** until her own mental and emotional states (her 'slow faults') end up destroying her. The intensity of the final line, 'That kill, that kill, that kill', leaves readers with a harrowing understanding of Plath's paralysis of despair.

✍ Writing About the Poem

Do you think that 'Elm' has a surreal, nightmarish quality? In your response, refer to the text to support your views.

Sample Paragraph

I agree that Plath created a disturbing mood in 'Elm'. Giving the tree a voice of its own is like something from a child's fairy story. Plath compares love to a galloping horse. The poem is mainly about depression and madness. So it's bound to be out of the ordinary. The speaker asks weird questions, such as 'Is it the sea you hear in me?' She is obsessive and totally paranoid. Everything is against her, as far as she imagines it. The weather is an enemy even, the rain is 'tin-white like arsenic'. The end is as if she is having a dream and imagines a fierce snake in the tree coming after her. This represents Plath's deepest nightmare, the fear of loneliness. Violent images – 'a hand of wires', 'snaky acids hiss' – create a surreal atmosphere. The poem is confusing – especially the images.

> **EXAMINER'S COMMENT**
> *This short mid-grade paragraph includes some worthwhile references to the poem's disturbing aspects. The points are note-like, however, and the writing style lacks control in places. Effective use of apt quotations.*

✒ Class/Homework Exercises

1. What evidence of Plath's deep depression and hypersensitivity is revealed in the poem 'Elm'? Refer closely to the text in your answer.
2. Plath said of her later poetry, 'I speak them to myself ... aloud'. In your opinion, how effective are the sound effects and use of direct speech in the poem 'Elm'? Develop your response with reference to 'Elm'.

⊙ Points to Consider

- **Inner torment, awful fear of being oneself.**
- **Terrifying personification of elm.**
- **Rich symbolism and imagery, effective sounds.**
- **Nightmare world, surreal mood, paralysis of fear, threat of madness.**
- **Simple unvarnished style, poem overflows with poet's feelings of lost love.**

8 Poppies in July

SYLVIA PLATH

Little poppies, little hell flames,
Do you do no harm?

You flicker. I cannot touch you.
I put my hands among the flames. Nothing burns.

And it exhausts me to watch you   5
Flickering like that, wrinkly and clear red, like the skin of a mouth.

A mouth just bloodied.
Little bloody skirts!

There are fumes that I cannot touch.
Where are your opiates, your nauseous capsules?   10

If I could bleed, or sleep! –
If my mouth could marry a hurt like that!

Or your liquors seep to me, in this glass capsule,
Dulling and stilling.

But colorless. Colorless.   15

hell flames: most poppies are red, flame-like.

fumes: the effects of drugs.
opiates: sleep-inducing narcotics.
nauseous: causing sickness.

liquors: drug vapours.
capsule: small container.

colorless: drained, lifeless.

'You flicker. I cannot touch you'.

👤 Personal Response

1. Comment on the title, 'Poppies in July'. Is the title misleading? Give a reason for your response.
2. What evidence can you find in 'Poppies in July' that the speaker is yearning to escape?
3. Colour imagery plays a significant role in the poem. Comment on how effectively colour is used.

👁 Critical Literacy

Like most confessional writers, Sylvia Plath's work reflects her own personal experiences, without filtering any of the painful emotions. She wrote 'Poppies in July' in the summer of 1962, during the break-up of her marriage.

The first stanza is marked by a sense of unease and foreboding. The speaker (almost certainly Plath herself) compares the blazing red poppies to 'little hell flames' before directly confronting them: 'Do you do no harm?' **Her distress is obvious** from the start. The poem's title may well have led readers to expect a more conventional nature poem. Instead, the flowers are presented as being highly treacherous, and all the more deceptive because they are 'little'.

Plath develops the fire image in lines 3–6. However, even though she places her hands 'among the flames', she finds that 'Nothing burns' and she is forced to watch them 'Flickering'. It almost seems as though she is so tired and numb that **she has transcended pain** and can experience nothing: 'it exhausts me to watch you'. Ironically, the more vivid the poppies are, the more lethargic she feels.

The uncomfortable and disturbed mood increases in the fourth stanza with two **startling images**, both personifying the flowers. Comparing the poppy to 'A mouth just bloodied' suggests recent violence and physical suffering. The 'bloody skirts' metaphor is equally harrowing. There is further evidence of the poet's overpowering weariness in the prominent use of broad vowel sounds, for example in 'exhausts', 'mouth' and 'bloodied'.

In the fifth stanza, Plath's disoriented state turns to a distracted longing for escape. Having failed to use the vibrancy of the poppies to distract her from her pain, she now craves the feeling of oblivion or unconsciousness. But although she desires the dulling effects of drugs derived from the poppies, her **tone reflects her feelings of helplessness** as she describes the 'fumes that I cannot touch'.

The mood becomes even more distraught in lines 11–12, with the poet begging for any alternative to her anguished state. 'If I could bleed, or sleep!'

is an emphatic plea for release. It is her final attempt to retain some control of her life in the face of an overwhelming sense of powerlessness. Plath's **growing alienation** seems so unbearably intense at this point that it directly draws the reader's sympathy.

The last three lines record the poet's surrender, perhaps a kind of death wish. Worn down by her inner demons and the bright colours of the poppies, Plath lets herself become resigned to a 'colorless' world of nothingness. Her **complete passivity** and vulnerability are emphasised by the dreamlike quality of the phrase 'Dulling and stilling'. As she drifts into a death-like 'colorless' private hell, there remains a terrible sense of betrayal, as if she is still being haunted by the bright red flowers. The ending of 'Poppies in July' is so dark and joyless that it is easy to understand why the poem is often seen as a desperate cry for help.

Writing About the Poem

'Poppies in July' is one of Plath's most disturbing poems. What aspects of the poem affected you most?

Sample Paragraph

'Poppies in July' was written when Plath was struggling with the fact that her husband had deserted her. This affected her deeply and it is clear that the poppies are a symbol of this difficult time. Everything about the poem is negative. The images of the poppies are nearly all associated with fire and blood. Plath's language is alarming when she compares the poppies to 'little hell flames' and also 'the skin of a mouth'. The most disturbing aspect is Plath's own unstable mind. She seems to be in a kind of trance, obsessed by the red colours of the poppies, which remind her of blood. She seems suicidal – 'If I could bleed'. For me, this is the most disturbing moment in the poem. The poet cannot stand reality and seeks a way out through drugs or death. The last image is of Plath sinking into drowsiness, unable to cope with the world around her.

EXAMINER'S COMMENT

Overall, a solid high-grade response which responds personally to the question. While some focus is placed on the disturbing thought in the poem, there could have been a more thorough exploration of Plath's style and how it enhances her theme of depression.

POETRY FOCUS

✒ Class/Homework Exercises

1. Would you agree that loneliness and pain are the central themes of 'Poppies in July'? Refer to the poem when writing your response.
2. Discuss how the poet uses vivid description in this poem to explore her negative feelings. Develop your answer with reference to the text.

⊙ Points to Consider

- Desire to escape into oblivion.
- Personal aspect, engaged in inner conflict.
- Compelling drama, upsetting imagery, intense mood of despair.
- Despairing mood conveyed in downward motion of poem.
- Contrast between dynamic, vivid flowers, a symbol of vibrancy of life, and longed-for dullness of oblivion.

9 The Arrival of the Bee Box

I ordered this, this clean wood box
Square as a chair and almost too heavy to lift.
I would say it was the coffin of a midget
Or a square baby
Were there not such a din in it.   5

The box is locked, it is dangerous.
I have to live with it overnight
And I can't keep away from it.
There are no windows, so I can't see what is in there.
There is only a little grid, no exit.   10

grid: wire network.

I put my eye to the grid.
It is dark, dark,
With the swarmy feeling of African hands
Minute and shrunk for export,
Black on black, angrily clambering.   15

swarmy: like a large group of bees.

How can I let them out?
It is the noise that appalls me most of all,
The unintelligible syllables.
It is like a Roman mob,
Small, taken one by one, but my god, together!   20

I lay my ear to furious Latin.
I am not a Caesar.
I have simply ordered a box of maniacs.
They can be sent back.
They can die, I need feed them nothing, I am the owner.   25

Caesar: famous Roman ruler.

I wonder how hungry they are.
I wonder if they would forget me
If I just undid the locks and stood back and turned into a tree.
There is the laburnum, its blond colonnades,
And the petticoats of the cherry.   30

laburnum: tree with yellow hanging flowers.
colonnades: long groups of flowers arranged in a row of columns.

SYLVIA PLATH

'It is the noise that appalls me'

They might ignore me immediately
In my moon suit and funeral veil.
I am no source of honey
So why should they turn on me?
Tomorrow I will be sweet God, I will set them free.　　　35

The box is only temporary.

moon suit: protective clothing worn by beekeepers; all-in-one suit.

👤 Personal Response

1. How would you describe the poet's reaction to the bee box – fear or fascination, or a mixture of both? Refer to the text in your response.
2. Select two surreal images from the poem and comment on the effectiveness of each.
3. Would you describe this poem as exploring and overcoming one's fears and anxieties? Is the ending optimistic or pessimistic, in your opinion?

👁 Critical Literacy

'The Arrival of the Bee Box' was written in 1962, shortly after Plath's separation from her husband. Her father, who died when she was a child, had been a bee expert and Plath had recently taken up beekeeping. She explores order, power, control, confinement and freedom in this deeply personal poem.

The poem opens with a simple statement: 'I ordered this'. Straightaway, the emphasis is on order and control. The poet's tone in stanza one seems both matter-of-fact and surprised, as if thinking: 'Yes, I was the one who ordered this' and also 'Did I really order this?' **This drama has only one character, Plath herself.** We observe her responses and reactions to the arrival of the bee box. Notice the extensive use of the personal pronoun 'I'. We both see and hear the event.

The box is described as being made of 'clean wood' and given a homely quality through the simile 'Square as a chair'. But then a surreal, dreamlike metaphor, 'the coffin of a midget/Or a square baby', brings us into a **nightmare world**. The abnormal is suggested by the use of 'midget' and 'square baby'. The coffin conveys not only death, but also entrapment and confinement, preoccupations of the poet. The box has now become a sinister object. A witty sound effect closes the first stanza, as 'din in it' mimics the sound of the bees. The noisy insects are like badly behaved children.

Stanza two explores the **poet's ambivalent attitude to the box**. She is curious to see inside ('I can't keep away from it'). Yet she is also frightened by it, as she describes the box as 'dangerous'. She peers in. The third stanza becomes claustrophobic with the repetition of 'dark' and the grotesque image of 'the swarmy feeling of African hands/Minute and shrunk for export'. The milling of the bees/slaves is vividly captured as they heave around in the heat amid an atmosphere of menace and oppression, hopelessly desperate.

We hear the bees in stanza four. The metaphor of a Roman mob is used to show how they will create **chaos and danger if they are let loose**. The assonance of 'appalls' and 'all' underlines the poet's terror. The phrase 'unintelligible syllables', with its onomatopoeia and its difficult pronunciation, lets us hear the angry buzzing. Plath is awestruck at their collective force and energy: 'but my god, together!'

In stanza five the poet tries to listen, but only hears 'furious Latin' she does not understand. She doubts her capacity to control them, stating that she is 'not a Caesar', the powerful ruler of the Romans. She regards them as 'maniacs'. Then she suddenly realises that if she has ordered them, she can return them: 'They can be sent back'. **She has some control of this situation.** Plath can even decide their fate, whether they live or die: 'I need feed them nothing'. She has now redefined the situation as she remembers that she is 'the owner'. They belong to her.

The poet's feminine, nurturing side now emerges as she wonders 'how hungry they are'. The stereotype of the pretty woman surfaces in the description of the bees' natural habitat of trees in stanza six. Plath thinks that if she releases them, they would go back to the trees, 'laburnum' and 'cherry'. She herself would then merge into the landscape and become a tree. This is a reference to a Greek myth where Daphne was being pursued by Apollo. When she begged the gods to save her, they turned her into a tree.

The poet refers to herself in her beekeeping outfit of veil and boiler suit in stanza seven. She rhetorically asks why the bees would attack her, as she can offer no sustenance ('I am no source of honey'). **She decides to be compassionate**: 'Tomorrow I will be sweet God, I will set them free'. She realises that they are imprisoned for the time being: 'The box is only temporary'.

This poem can also be read on more than one level. The box could represent the poet's attempt to be what others expect, the typical 1950s woman – pretty, compliant, nurturing. The bees could symbolise the unstable side of her personality, which both fascinated and terrified Plath. **The box is like Pandora's box**: safe when locked, but full of danger when opened. Although she finds this disturbing, she also feels she must explore it in the interests of developing as a poet. The references to the doomed character of Daphne and the 'funeral veil' echo chillingly. Would these dark thoughts, if given their freedom, drive her to suicide? The form of this poem is seven stanzas of five lines. One final line stands alone, free like the bees or her dark thoughts. If the box represents Plath's outside appearance or body, it is mortal, it is temporary.

✒ Writing About the Poem

How does this poem address and explore the themes of order and power? Write a paragraph in response. Develop your views with reference to the text.

Sample Paragraph

'The Arrival of the Bee Box' opens with a reference to order, 'I ordered this'. It is an assertion of power. Throughout the poem the repetition of 'I' suggests a person who consciously chooses to act in a certain way. 'I put my eye to the grid'. It is as if the poet wishes to confront and control her fears over the contents of the box. This box contains live bees, whose well-being lies in the hands of the poet. 'I need feed them nothing'. The box metaphor suggests control. Although she realises that she is not 'Caesar', the mighty Roman ruler, she can choose to be 'sweet God'. She alone has the power to release the bees, 'The box is only temporary'. This poem can also be read as referring to innermost fears and desires. The person can choose to accept them or confront them.

EXAMINER'S COMMENT

This is an assured top-grade response which focuses well on the central themes of order and power. Apt and accurate quotations are used effectively. The opening point on Plath's use of the personal pronoun is particularly impressive.

Class/Homework Exercises

1. How does Plath create a dramatic atmosphere in 'The Arrival of the Bee Box'?
2. Plath examines repression in 'The Arrival of the Bee Box'. Why do you think she fears a loss of control? In your response, refer to both the subject matter and style.

⊙ Points to Consider

- Central themes include power, control, freedom, self-expression.
- Innovative use of metaphor, contrasting moods.
- Unusual personification, startling images and drama.
- Clever word-play, witty sound effects, internal rhyme.
- Disconcerting ending emphasised by single stand-alone line.

10 Child

Your clear eye is the one absolutely beautiful thing.
I want to fill it with color and ducks,
The zoo of the new

Whose name you meditate –
April snowdrop, Indian pipe,   5
Little

Stalk without wrinkle,
Pool in which images
Should be grand and classical

Not this troublous   10
Wringing of hands, this dark
Ceiling without a star.

meditate: reflect.

Indian pipe: American woodland flower.

Stalk: plant stem.

classical: impressive, enduring.

troublous: disturbed.

👤 Personal Response

1. What was your own immediate reaction after reading 'Child'? Refer to the poem in your answer.
2. Which images in the poem are most effective in contrasting the world of the child and the world of the adult?
3. Plath uses various sound effects to highlight her themes in 'Child'. Comment briefly on one interesting example.

'The zoo of the new'

👁 Critical Literacy

Sylvia Plath's son was born in January 1962. A year later, not long before the poet's own death, she wrote 'Child', a short poem that reflects her intense feelings about motherhood.

The opening line of stanza one shows the **poet's emphatic appreciation of childhood innocence**: 'Your clear eye is the one absolutely beautiful thing'. The tone at first is hopeful. Her love for the new child is generous and unconditional: 'I want to fill it with color'. The childlike language is lively and playful. Plath plans to give her child the happiest of times, filled with 'color and ducks'. The vigorous rhythm and animated internal rhyme in the phrase 'The zoo of the new' are imaginative, capturing the sense of **youthful wonder**.

In stanza two, the poet continues to associate her child with all that is best about the natural world. The baby is like the most fragile of flowers, the 'April snowdrop'. The soothing broad vowel assonance in this phrase has a musical effect, like a soft lullaby. Yet her own fascination appears to mask a deeper concern. Plath feels that such a perfect childhood experience is unlikely to last very long. Despite all her positive sentiments, what she wants for **the vulnerable child** seems directly at odds with what is possible in a **flawed world**.

Run-on lines are a recurring feature of the poem and these add to the feeling of freedom and innocent intensity. Stanza three includes two **effective comparisons**, again taken from nature. Plath sees the child as an unblemished 'Stalk' that should grow perfectly. A second quality of childhood's pure innocence is found in the 'Pool' metaphor. We are reminded of the opening image – the child's 'clear eye', always trusting and sincere.

The poet would love to provide a magical future for her young child, so that the pool would reflect 'grand and classical' images. However, as a loving mother, she is trapped between her **idealism** – the joy she wants for her child – and a **distressing reality** – an awareness that the child's life will not be perfectly happy. This shocking realisation becomes clear in stanza four and overshadows her hopes completely. The final images are stark and powerful – the pathetic 'Wringing of hands' giving emphasis to her helplessness. The last line poignantly portrays the paradox of the tension between Plath's dreams for the child in the face of the despair she feels about the oppressive world: this 'Ceiling without a star'. The intensely dark mood is in sharp contrast with the rest of the poem. The early celebration has been replaced by anguish and an overwhelming sense of failure.

✒ Writing About the Poem

Do you think 'Child' is a positive or negative poem? Refer to the text in explaining your response.

Sample Paragraph

'Child' is about inadequacy. The poet wants the best for her son. Although the first half of the poem focuses on her wishes to protect him, this changes. Plath starts off by wanting to fill the boy's life with happy experiences (bright colours and toys). There are references to nature right through the poem and Plath compares her son to an 'April snowdrop'. This tender image gave me a positive feeling. Everything about the child is wonderful at first. This changes at the end. The mood turns negative. Plath talks of being confined in a darkened room that has a 'Ceiling without a star'. This is in total contrast with the images early on which were of the outdoors. The ending is 'troublous' because Plath fears her child will grow up and experience pain just as she has.

> **EXAMINER'S COMMENT**
>
> This paragraph addresses the question well and offers a clear response. There is some good personal engagement which effectively illustrates the changing mood from optimism to pessimism and uses apt quotations in support. The style of writing is a little note-like and pedestrian. Fresher expression and more development of points would have raised the standard from its present good solid middle grade.

✒ Class/Homework Exercises

1. Write a paragraph comparing 'Child' with 'Morning Song'. Refer to theme and style in both poems.
2. 'Plath explores the changing nature of parental love in her poem "Child".' Discuss this statement, developing your response by reference to the poem.

◎ Points to Consider

- One of several poems about children, moving from tenderness to anxiety.
- Lullaby, easy flowing movement, images of light and darkness.
- Contrast between love of child and poet's own depression.
- Appropriate style, clear, simple language.
- Juxtaposition of joyful, colourful world of child and dark despair of poet.

Sample Leaving Cert Questions on Plath's Poetry

1. 'Sylvia Plath makes effective use of various stylistic features to express a range of intense and compelling feelings.' Discuss this view, developing your response with reference to both the themes and poetic style of Sylvia Plath on your course.
2. 'Plath's powerful portrayal of the world of nature is conveyed through verbal energy and strikingly vivid symbolism.' To what extent do you agree or disagree with this view? Develop your response with reference to poems by Sylvia Plath on your course.
3. 'Sylvia Plath makes creative use of language and imagery to add layers of meaning to her work.' Discuss this statement, developing your response with reference to the language and themes found in the poetry of Plath on your course.

How do I organise my answer?

(Sample question 1)

'Sylvia Plath makes effective use of various stylistic features to express a range of intense and compelling feelings.' Discuss this view, developing your response with reference to both the themes and poetic style of Sylvia Plath on your course.

Sample Plan 1

Intro: *(Stance: agree with viewpoint in the question)* Plath's gripping emotional experiences are often painfully revealed through her use of startling imagery, careful choice of language.

Point 1: *(Conflicting feelings – startling imagery)* 'Morning Song' explores the conflicting emotions of new parents. Vibrant similes capture affection and pride ('Love set you going like a fat gold watch') and anxiety ('We stand round blankly as walls'). Precisely drawn images ('One cry, and I stumble from bed') show the mother embracing her new role.

Point 2: *(Mixed feelings – ranging imagery and moods)* 'Child' recreates the wonder of the simple world of a child through imaginative internal rhyme ('The zoo of the new'). Contrasting images of tenderness ('April snowdrop') and failure ('Ceiling without a star').

Understanding the Prescribed Poetry Question

Marks are awarded using the PCLM Marking Scheme:
P = 15; C = 15; L = 15; M = 5
Total = 50

- **P** (Purpose = 15 marks) refers to the set question and is the launch pad for the answer. This involves engaging with all aspects of the question. Both theme and language must be addressed, although not necessarily equally.
- **C** (Coherence = 15 marks) refers to the organisation of the developed response and the use of accurate, relevant quotation. Paragraphing is essential.
- **L** (Language = 15 marks) refers to the student's skill in controlling language throughout the answer.
- **M** (Mechanics = 5 marks) refers to spelling and grammar.
- Although no specific number of poems is required, students usually discuss at least 3 or 4 in their written responses.
- Aim for at least 800 words, to be completed within 45–50 minutes.

NOTE

In keeping with the PCLM approach, the student has to take a stance by agreeing, disagreeing or partially agreeing that Plath makes effective use of:

- **various stylistic features** (vivid visual imagery, rich symbolism, lively personification, careful rhyme, dramatic settings, evocative moods and tones, etc.)

... to express:

- **a range of intense and compelling feelings** (powerful search for personal identity, troubling attitudes, deep desire for inspiration/escape, awareness of nature, transience, etc.)

Point 3: *(Desire for inspiration – precise language structure)* 'Black Rook in Rainy Weather' shows both bird and poet carefully 'Arranging and rearranging' feathers and words. The randomness of life is created by lines and stanzas running untidily into each other.

Point 4: *(Distress – startling comparative language)* 'Poppies in July' records the poet's distress through the unlikely comparison of colourful summer flowers to 'little hell flames'. She longs to escape reality. Soft 'l' sounds ('Dulling', 'colorless') suggest her descent into nothingness.

Conclusion: Plath's inner turmoil is successfully revealed in her use of shocking imagery, telling contrasts and disturbing tones. Various poetic techniques highlight her extreme emotional struggles.

Sample Paragraph: Point 1

'Morning Song' reveals the mixed feelings a new mother can experience after the birth of a baby. Plath uses a very unexpected image to show the natural feelings of joy, 'Love set you going like a fat gold watch'. This suggests the regular sound of the little baby's heartbeat. Another surprising image reveals how anxious parents feel, 'We stand around blankly as walls'. The mother seems strangely alienated from her child. Weather images of transience, such as 'cloud' and 'wind', suggest she is worried about losing her identity as an individual. Her own personality is being gradually destroyed, 'slow effacement', by her newfound identity as a mother. But Plath also introduces precise, tender images of her baby, e.g. 'moth-breath flickers', to show the mother beginning to settle in to embracing her new role. Her pride in the baby is seen in the colourful concluding simile of her baby's cries which she imagines rising 'like balloons'.

EXAMINER'S COMMENT

Succinct and successful commentary that engages well with the poem. Focused well on how contrasting images emphasise the poet's conflicted feelings about her child. Some reference to sound effects or tone would have been welcome. Relevant supportive quotes are well integrated into the critical analysis. Expression is also controlled throughout this top-grade response.

(Sample question 2)

'Plath's powerful portrayal of the world of nature is conveyed through verbal energy and strikingly vivid symbolism.' To what extent do you agree or disagree with this view? Develop your response with reference to poems by Sylvia Plath on your course.

Sample Plan 2

Intro: *(Stance: agree with viewpoint in the question)* Plath's awareness of nature's wonders reflected in closely observed details. Poems convey her own troubled state of mind and people's complex relationship with the natural world. Vigorous language describes landscape, flora and wildlife.

Point 1: *(Description of place – personification)* 'Finisterre' uses vivid personification to dramatise the struggle between land ('Admonitory cliffs') and water ('sea exploding'). Turbulent seascape scene contrasts between the 'sweet' appearance of Our Lady's statue and the tragic reality of drowned victims ('in the doom-noise of the sea').

Point 2: *(Close observation – repetition, dramatic language)* 'Elm' is also physically and metaphorically described ('strangle of branches'). Frantic verbs ('burn', 'drag') establish a destructive mood. Emphatic repetition suggests the paralysis of despair ('That kill, that kill').

Point 3: *(Vitality of natural world – disturbing aural and visual imagery)* 'Poppies in July' shocks by presenting flowers associated with happiness as symbols of evil ('little hell flames', 'Little bloody skirts'). Energetic onomatopoeia ('Flickering', 'wrinkly') suggests the sensitive interior of a mouth ('just bloodied').

Point 4: *(Man's relationship with nature – varied tones)* 'Pheasant' explores poet's appreciation of the bird in its natural habitat ('pacing/ Through the uncut grass'). A firm verbal command ('Do not kill it') shows Plath's activism on behalf of the wild bird. Admiring tone ('kingliness', 'such a good shape') replaced by shame at human intrusion ('I trespass stupidly').

Conclusion: Plath's acute observations of nature expose a beautiful yet brutal world onto which she projects her personal feelings of doubt and obsession. Stunning visual and aural techniques leave a lasting impression on readers.

NOTE

In keeping with the PCLM approach, the student has to take a stance by agreeing, disagreeing or partially agreeing with the statement that:

- **Plath's powerful portrayal of the world of nature** (keen appreciation of nature's vitality, close observation of the impact of physical environment, deep sense of people's complex relationship with natural world, etc.)

… is conveyed through:

- **verbal energy and strikingly vivid symbolism** (rich imagery/ metaphors/ symbols, thought-provoking contrasts, startling personification, sinister dramatic language, etc.)

Sample Paragraph: Point 4

In her poem, 'Pheasant', Plath describes the world of nature very effectively using detailed description of a 'rare' bird 'in its element'. She is clearly fascinated by the bird's beauty, 'such a good shape'. To her, it is a symbol of perfection. The poet becomes its protector, begging for its life, 'Do not kill it'. Plath shows her concern by repeating her call, 'Let be, let be', and this shows the urgency of her plea to respect nature. It's obvious that she really admires this bird which is so richly coloured, 'green and red'. The use of soft sibilant sound effects create a wonderful picture of feeling at ease while she watches the pheasant 'sunning in the narcissi'. But the poet suddenly realises she is intruding on nature and she becomes ashamed. The phrase, 'I trespass stupidly', reveals her awareness that she should not be there.

> **EXAMINER'S COMMENT**
>
> As part of a full essay answer, this short top-grade paragraph shows a close understanding of the poem. Discussion points deal with both aspects of the question (the portrayal of nature as a symbol of perfection and Plath's poetic style). There is some good engagement with the text, particularly in addressing how Plath's concerns are conveyed through sounds and repetition. Supportive quotations are carefully integrated into the commentary throughout.

> **EXAM FOCUS**
> - As you may not be familiar with some of the poems referred to in the sample plans, substitute other prescribed poems that you have studied closely.
> - Key points about a particular poem can be developed over more than one paragraph.
> - Paragraphs may also include cross-referencing and discussion of more than one poem.
> - Remember that there is no single 'correct' answer to poetry questions, so always be confident in expressing your own considered response.

Leaving Cert Sample Essay

'Sylvia Plath makes creative use of language and imagery to add layers of meaning to her work.' Discuss this statement, developing your response with reference to the language and themes found in the poetry of Plath on your course.

Sample Essay

1. Plath's personal poems explore her intense feelings about many themes, such as control and oppression in 1950s American society. Her poetry is filled with thought-provoking ideas. These range from the negative impact society has on the individual to reflections on her own mental state. Throughout her poetry, striking visual imagery, personification and strong sound effects are cleverly used to express her views.

2. Plath presents the monotonous world of 1950s America in 'The Times are Tidy'. It's clear that she herself felt unfulfilled there – especially with its bland, highly organised society. This is suggested in the carefully ordered rhymes she uses – 'record'/'accord', 'lizard'/'hazard'. Plath also makes use of subtle images which suggest the dreary routine of everyday life, 'the stuck record', 'the mayor's rôtisserie'. She mocks American materialism and the excesses of this consumer society, 'cream an inch thick'. The poet sees personality being crushed, 'withered'. She regrets the loss of individual heroism, 'Unlucky the hero born/In this province'.

3. Her tone is highly ironical throughout the poem. For Plath, the 1950s was a disappointing period of time which she believed was dull and uninspiring. I get the impression she was thinking back to the Second World War when Americans did have some sense of heroism. The poem ends on a negative tone. Plath believes that the joy and excitement have gone. American children might be growing up in well-off families – 'are better for it', but their sense of adventure has been lost.

4. The dramatic experience of a woman confronting the reality of her reflected image is the main subject of 'Mirror'. Plath takes on the cold, critical voice of the mirror, 'the eye of a little god'. She describes the damaging relationship between the controlling mirror and the dependent woman. Totally dissatisfied with what is reflected back to her, she stands 'with tears and an agitation of hands'. A highly disturbing metaphor, 'I am a lake', suggests the woman's dangerous situation. The 'truthful' mirror reflects the reality that she is getting older, 'like a terrible fish'. Plath's inventive personification is used to question the pressure society puts on women to maintain a youthful appearance.

5. 'Elm' also uses personification to show how life's pressures can push a person close to insanity. In this dramatic poem, a surreal conversation takes place between the poet and the elm. The tree questions the poet about her mental wellbeing. Is she longing for love which has disappeared? This is skilfully compared to a runaway animal, 'gone off, like a horse'. The use of intense language ('burn', 'shriek') adds to the destructive mood. Unsettling images and harsh sound effects explore the theme of loss of control and madness. The poet confesses that her feelings of deep-rooted despair resemble a cancer that is silently increasing in size, 'All day I feel its soft, feathery turnings'.

6. Ironically, while Plath criticised American society for its control and order in 'The Times are Tidy', she herself now takes up this very same role in her poem, 'The Arrival of the Bee Box'. She 'ordered this', so now she is in charge of what happens to the bees. There are numerous dream-like scenes linked to history and power struggles. In referring to 'the swarmy feeling of African hands ... angrily clambering', Plath makes readers

INDICATIVE MATERIAL

- **Plath makes creative use of language and imagery** (evocative and provocative images, dramatic moments/ settings, startling personification, contrasting tones, etc.)

... to add:

- **layers of meaning to her work** (sense of emotional pain, closeness to nature, critical views of society, obsession with mortality, awareness of identity, self-expression, etc.)

SYLVIA PLATH

consider the history of slavery and the abuse of power. Onomatopoeia and repetition suggest their captivity in the shocking image of imprisoned people. The noise of the imprisoned bees is conveyed in the phrase, 'unintelligible syllables' of the 'Roman mob'.

7. The poem raises many subtle questions. Would the escape of the bees lead to destruction? Do they represent Plath's own dark thoughts of rebellion against the repressive society of her time? Once again, the poem could represent her effort to be what is expected. The perfect American stereotype. Images, such as, 'petticoats of the cherry' and 'stood back' suggest a submissive pretty woman. One who knows her place.

8. At one point, she refers to the bees as 'a box of maniacs'. This metaphor could be linked to the poet's own fears. Mainly about her own repressed emotions. And her general mental state. In the end, she decides to be kind, 'I will set them free'. The line, 'The box is only temporary', shows that the poet has chosen freedom for the bees and herself.

9. Plath's effective use of language highlights her wide-ranging thoughts on the theme of power. She opposed the social expectations where girls are thought of as inferior to males. I thought the ideas in her poetry were subtle and had many possible meanings.

(760 words)

EXAMINER'S COMMENT

A good personal response to the question, exploring interesting ideas in Plath's poetry. Focused well on the use of imagery, personification and mood, with impressive analysis of these stylistic features in paragraphs 2, 4 and 5. The critical commentary is supported by suitable quotation ranging across several key poems. Points are coherent and generally well-developed – although there is some note-like commentary in paragraphs 7 and 8. Overall, expression is clear throughout this solid top-grade essay.

GRADE: H1
P = 15/15
C = 14/15
L = 14/15
M = 5/5
Total = 48/50

👓 Revision Overview

'Black Rook in Rainy Weather'
Life-affirming poem in which Plath explores the mystery of poetic inspiration and the importance of appreciating everyday life as it is.

'The Times Are Tidy'
Focuses on political themes and the poet's personal dissatisfaction with the materialistic and unheroic era she lived in.

'Morning Song'
Feeling estranged from her own child, the poet addresses themes of motherhood, alienation and human frailty.

'Finisterre'
Dramatic seascape depicting a turbulent scene that reflects the poet's troubled state of mind and her thoughts on the futility of conflict.

'Mirror'
In this chilling poem, the personified mirror reflects Plath's own thoughts about identity and people's fixation with their inevitable mortality.

'Pheasant'
The poet is embarrassed by her unwitting intrusion into a natural scene, yet she enjoys and appreciates the beauty of the pheasant in its element.

'Elm'
Plath invents a demon in her subconscious that gives her a self-destructive vision. Shocked by this powerful, violent and uncontrolled experience, she surrenders to mental exhaustion.

'Poppies in July' (OL)
Expresses the longing to escape from deep depression. The poet is so emotionally drained that she struggles to find any feeling that connects her to reality.

'The Arrival of the Bee Box'
Plath explores various feelings of power and powerlessness associated with bee-keeping. The poet's indecisiveness seems to reflect her own chaotic state of mind.

'Child' (OL)
This dark yet beautiful poem captures Plath's personal insecurity concerning her marriage and her conflicted feelings as a mother.

💬 Last Words

'Her poems have that heart-breaking quality about them.'
Joyce Carol Oates

'Artists are a special breed. They are passionate and temperamental. Their feelings flow into the work they create.'
J. Timothy King

'I am a genius of a writer. I have it in me. I am writing the best poems of my life.'
Sylvia Plath

CREATIVITY | REGRET | NATURE | WONDER | LOVE | AGEING | IDENTITY | ESCAPE | CHILDHOOD | FREEDOM

POETRY FOCUS

Tracy K. Smith
1972–

'You want a poem to unsettle something'

Tracy K. Smith was born on 16 April 1972 in Massachusetts and grew up in California. She became interested in writing and poetry early in life, reading Emily Dickinson and Mark Twain in elementary school. Dickinson's poems in particular struck her as working like 'magic'. Smith studied at Harvard University where Seamus Heaney was one of her teachers. The work of Elizabeth Bishop and Rita Dove also became significant influences.

Her poetry is lyrical and political – combining honesty, imagination and compassion as she explores issues of desire, loss and the African-American experience. While she shows her wonder in the world, she never retreats from its injustices. Reflections on race and slavery surface throughout her poems.

Smith is the author of several prize-winning collections, including *Life on Mars*, which won the 2012 Pulitzer Prize. She also served as the 22nd Poet Laureate of the United States from 2017 to 2019.

Smith's poetry retains a close awareness of how individual lives are embedded in wider society. Her signature poetic voice, whether in elegy or praise or outrage, insists upon vibrancy and hope – particularly in moments of grief and empathy.

Investigate Further

To find out more about Tracy K. Smith, or to hear readings of her poems not already available in your eBook, you could search some useful websites, such as YouTube, BBC Poetry, poetryfoundation.org and poetryarchive.org, or access additional material on this page of your eBook.

Prescribed Poems

Note that Smith uses American spellings in her work.

○ 1 'Joy'
Smith's intimate memory poem in tribute to her late mother confronts the significance of death and asks readers to review their own beliefs about the possibility of an afterlife.
Page 344

○ 2 'Dominion over the Beasts of the Earth'
A series of vivid memories about the excitement and uncertainty of young love addresses universal themes of desire, personal choices and coming of age.
Page 349

○ 3 'The Searchers' (OL)
Based on a Hollywood movie about a white girl brought up by Native Americans, the poem reflects on issues of identity, race and belonging.
Page 356

○ 4 'Letter to a Photojournalist Going-In'
Smith describes the reality of being a war photojournalist and considers the wider impact of the photographer's work – particularly its effect on his personal relationships.
Page 361

○ 5 'The Universe is a House Party'
In this imaginative and thought-provoking exploration of modern life, the poet contrasts the limits of human comprehension with the vast, mysterious universe.
Page 366

○ 6 'The Museum of Obsolescence'
Smith imagines a public gallery in the distant future. The building displays forgotten and useless artefacts from the human species' time on planet Earth.
Page 371

○ 7 'Don't You Wonder, Sometimes?'
While processing the sorrow she feels after her father's death, the poet combines references to pop culture and science fiction to reflect on people's place in the universe.
Page 376

○ 8 'It's Not' (OL)
In this moving elegy in tribute to her father, the poet examines some of the mysteries of science and explores crucial questions about life and death.
Page 383

○ 9 'The Universe as Primal Scream'
Hearing the screams of young children leads to a meditation on the limited nature of human life, the universe, death and the hereafter.
Page 387

○ 10 'The Greatest Personal Privation' (OL)
Powerful poem in which Smith imagines the voices of two mid-19th-century African-American slaves and urges readers to question governments and challenge injustice.
Page 393

○ 11 'I am 60 odd years of age'
(*from* 'I Will Tell You the Truth About This, I Will Tell You All About It')
The compelling voices of African-American Civil War soldiers and their families challenge racism, awakening awareness of and compassion for forgotten people.
Page 399

○ 12 'Ghazal'
In declaring her support for those whose voices cry out for justice, Smith confronts both historical discrimination and ongoing inequality that have made an impact on the African-American identity.
Page 406

(OL) indicates poems that are also prescribed for the Ordinary Level course.

TRACY K. SMITH

1 Joy

In memoriam KMS 1936–1994

Imagining yourself a girl again,
You ask me to prepare a simple meal
Of dumplings and kale.

The body is memory.
You are nine years old,   5
Playing hospital with your sisters.

These will be my medicine,
You tell them, taking a handful
Of the raisins that you love.

They've made the room dark   10
And covered you with a quilt,
Though this is the South in summer.

The body is appetite.
You savor the kale,
Trusting this one need.   15

But the body is cautious,
Does not want more
Than it wants. Soon

There will be a traffic
Of transparent tubes, striking   20
Their compromise with the body.

When you close your eyes,
I know you are listening
To a dark chamber

Around a chord of light.   25
I know you are deciding
That the body's a question:

What do you believe in?

👤 Personal Response

1. Based on the evidence of the poem, briefly describe your impression of the poet's mother.
2. Throughout the poem, Smith describes the body in various ways, using metaphors and images. Choose one image or metaphor which you found particularly interesting. What did it reveal to you about the body's ability?
3. In your opinion, what is the meaning of the concluding question? Is the tone demanding or pleading? Briefly explain your response.

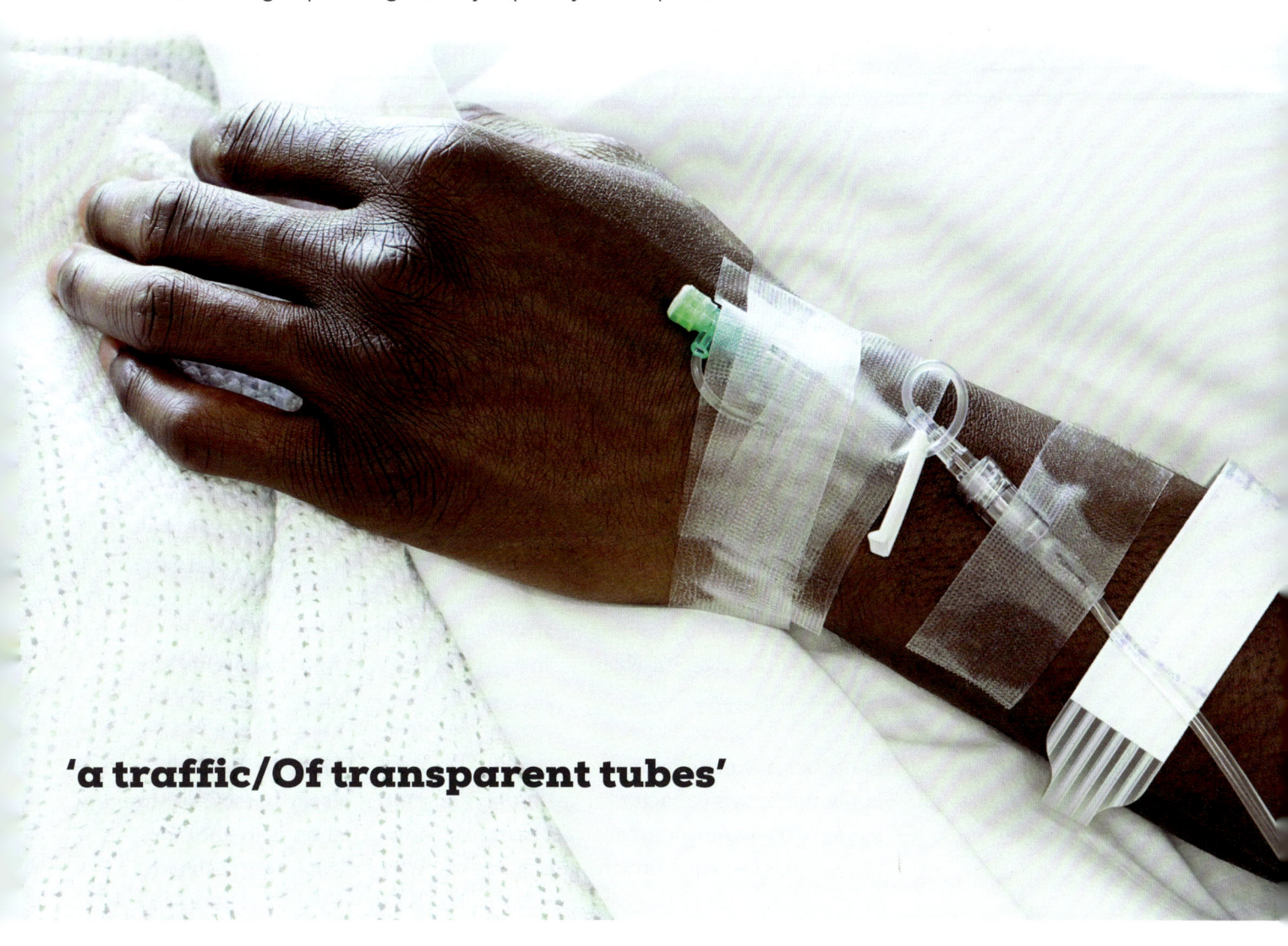

TRACY K. SMITH

'a traffic/Of transparent tubes'

👁 Critical Literacy

'Joy' forms Part III of Tracy K. Smith's debut collection, *The Body's Question*. The poem is one of several elegies written in response to her mother's death from cancer in 1994. After graduating from Harvard, the poet returned home; 'I knew I needed to go home and be with my mom because she was coming to the end'. This intimate memory poem makes Smith's mother luminous and imperishable. In this tender elegy, the body itself becomes a question and puzzle.

POETRY FOCUS

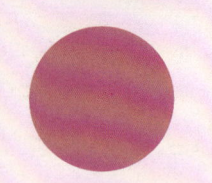

From the outset, Smith confronts the **challenging themes of loss, grief and identity** using plain-spoken, precise description. Her terminally ill mother visualises herself as a young 'girl again'. She asks her daughter to make her a 'simple meal' of filled dough and green vegetables, 'dumplings and kale' (line 3). This occasion hints at Christ's Last Supper which he shared with his disciples shortly before his death.

Smith's mother, a schoolteacher from Alabama, was **a devout Christian** who believed that God created the world and that a person can attain salvation after death through faith in Jesus Christ. Smith wrote: 'The black church was part of my parents' lives ... The role of that institution lay in erecting hope and structure and the sense that there is justice ... something larger that's watching and keeping tabs'.

The emphatic metaphor 'The body is memory' (line 4) suggests that **the human body stores a memory bank** of echoes from the past. Often, very ill people in their final days recollect and revert back to happier times, 'You are nine years old'. A cherished moment with her sisters is recalled, 'Playing hospital'. Time and identity shapeshift as the mother's confident young voice is heard, '*These will be my medicine*' (line 7), announcing that the 'raisins' would cure her. Is Smith imagining all this? Or is the mother actually recounting this precious memory to her daughter?

In line 10, the poem slips back to the present. Smith's **dispassionate description** of the grim reality of her mother's final days replaces the nostalgic memory of childhood. Carers darken the room and place a soft covering on the sick woman. Hard consonants ('c', 'k' and 'q') ominously foreshadow her impending death, vividly contrasting with the soft sibilance of the alliterative phrase describing the sultry weather, 'this is the South in summer'.

Another powerful metaphor, 'The body is appetite' (line 13), suggests not only the body's capacity for taste and hunger but also its **desire and longing**. Again, the daughter attentively watches her mother enjoying her food, 'You savor the kale'. Smith's mother is calmly and resolutely resigned to her destiny. Her faith gives her the power to believe that her illness is part of God's plan for her. The poet understands how her mother is putting her trust into a satisfaction of her senses and she also becomes aware that the body is 'cautious'. Although her mother relishes her meal, her body still warns against over-indulging, 'Does not want more/Than it wants' (lines 17–18).

Run-on lines reflect a **sudden flurry of medical activity**. The hard sound of the alliterative phrase, 'traffic/Of transparent tubes', (lines 19–20), graphically conveys the intrusive medical procedures now being carried out on the poet's dying mother, enabling her to survive a little longer, 'striking/

Their compromise with the body'. But despite this agreement, the violent verb 'striking' implies an attack on the body as well as an acceptance of a situation that is unwanted.

Line 22 poignantly notes the mother's final moments as her senses shut down and she withdraws from this world, 'When you close your eyes'. Smith's deep sense of empathy is emphasised in the repeated phrase, 'I know'. Richly nuanced metaphors fill this personal moment with **universal significance**. The private darkened bedroom hints at the oncoming final obscurity of death. Yet there is also the suggestion of greater light on the outside. Is the mother now viewing life through a clearer lens at the moment of death?

The 'chord of light' (line 25) is a reminder of the **biblical sense of redemption** sung about so often in the church which Smith's mother regularly attended. The image also pays homage to an alternative viewpoint, her father's scientific understanding of the universe. The poet wonders about her mother's level of awareness at this crucial time. Is she now experiencing things in a new way? Is she experiencing joy?

The poem closes with Smith's firm belief that her mother has decided 'the body's a question'. After nine carefully arranged three-line stanzas, a single stand-alone line emerges to ask a final question, 'What do you believe in?' – leaving readers with an open-ended conclusion. **Smith has said that 'poems live in questions'**. To whom is this particular question posed? Does the query refer to a spiritual or scientific understanding of the world? Is the mother trying to gently guide her daughter or is she challenging her? She herself did not fully share her mother's deep religious beliefs. 'I have a lot of ambivalence to it ... I like a lot of the mystery but not the language' (TKS).

Or is Smith interrogating the reader? **The poem resists closure**, weaving instead a continuous present, rejecting the notion of tying everything up neatly. 'I realised I didn't know how to solve the problem – just dwell upon it, live in it, make it present, and speak to it ... the most honest stance you can take is that of questioning' (TKS).

All through the poem, Smith **freezes time into a lyrical, light-filled memory space**, a sharp contrast to the darkened bedroom. This allows readers a period to question the significance of death and to review their own beliefs about the possibility of an afterlife.

Writing About the Poem

'Tracy K. Smith's most dramatic poetry is often written as a response to her personal doubts.' Discuss this view with reference to her poem 'Joy'.

Sample Paragraph

'Joy' is presented as an important private moment between a loving daughter and her dying mother. The scene is set in several locations, beginning with the joyful childhood setting of her mother 'Playing hospital' and a pretend happy outcome of a cure with 'raisins'. But a more harrowing setting is the darkened room from which there is no escape. The graphic image of a 'traffic of transparent tubes' invading the sick mother's body is highly dramatic. The location is a reality apart from earthly experience where Smith imagines a 'chord of light' almost like an ascension into heaven for the deeply religious mother. But Smith does not share her mother's faith. The peaceful mood is challenged by the closing question, 'What do you believe in?' Dramatically, both the poet and readers are left wondering about what happens after death.

> **EXAMINER'S COMMENT**
>
> *An assured top-grade response that includes some perceptive engagement with the poem. The consideration of relevant dramatic aspects (such as setting, imagery and tension) is impressive. Points are expressed clearly and aptly supported with reference and quotation.*

Class/Homework Exercises

1. 'Tracy K. Smith often explores issues of loss and identity'. Discuss this view with reference to her poem 'Joy'.
2. 'The effective use of powerful language and imagery is a recurring feature of Smith's poetry.' To what extent is this true of 'Joy'?

Points to Consider

- Moving elegy in tribute to the poet's mother.
- Smith uses different locations in her exploration of the mystery of life and death.
- Stylistic features include striking imagery, metaphor and interesting poetic structure.
- Effective juxtaposition of religious and scientific imagery to explore the unknowable.
- Varied tones: elegiac, nostalgic, mournful, hopeful and questioning.

2 Dominion over the Beasts of the Earth

Title: According to the Bible, God gave humans dominion or power over all other creatures.

TRACY K. SMITH

... and whatsoever Adam called every living creature, that was the name thereof.
                                    – Genesis 2:19

Last night it was Mauricio again,
At the hacienda they say
He and Veronica bought together.
Dark rooms. Floors lain
With exquisite dust. We ran   5
Back and forth, opening
All the sturdy doors, giddy
As kid goats that have learned
To dance on two hooves.
Breath after breath charging   10
In and out. Heavy, heavy,
And then weightless, moving
With the prescience of light.

Hazlo que te da
La puta gana. He said it   15
Over and over. Mauricio –
Enormous Mauricio
With the drunken legs
And hands as large
And white as magnolias –   20
What would've really happened
If we'd done it that night
In your neighborhood
At the end of the world?
What would we have changed,   25
Splayed together on that
Rotten mattress
While the buses slept
And the papers curled
Around themselves,   30
Cradling their news?

hacienda: ranch, large estate.

lain: covered.

exquisite: delicate, beautiful.

sturdy: strong, solid.

kid: young (less than one year).
hooves: hard covering of the end of a goat's feet.

prescience: foresight, insight.

Hazlo ... gana: Do whatever the hell you want.

magnolias: large white flowers.

Splayed: spread out.

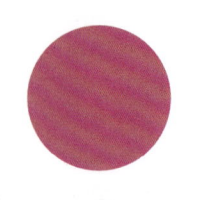

I want to speak now
To the ones I've said
Meant nothing,
And I want to call them all   35
Mauricio.

Mauricio at 13 with skin
Like sunset over the Pacific.   **Pacific:** Pacific Ocean.
Boy on the cusp, on a bicycle   **cusp:** point of transition.
On the porch my father put up.   40
Did I stare at my lap,   **lap:** knees and lower thighs.
Wishing myself someone else?
Kathy, with the wild limbs,
A fast girl with bracelets   **fast:** experienced, confident.
That made music on her wrists?   45
And the starlings perched   **starlings:** small garden birds.
In rafters – did I invent them?   **rafters:** wooden roof beams.
Tell me, Mauricio, at that age
What does a boy carry with him?

Years later you were tall,   50
A teacher, a spool
That would not stay wound.   **spool:** small reel for holding thread.
When I burned our letters,   **wound:** stored in place.
Ordinary moths swarmed my eyes.   **moths swarmed:** insects clouded.

I almost even want to speak   55
To that Mauricio
Who lay awake one whole summer,
Weak with anger, behind me.
Who finally drove off,
Windows obscured by an army   60   **obscured:** hidden, masked.
Of striped shirts, but even now
Tries to climb back
Along the frayed thread of dreams.   **frayed:** worn, unravelled.
He stood up to fight once
In a crowded room, insisting   65
I was his wife. I couldn't laugh
Until I made sure the ring
That married me to the right person
(Two sizes too loose)
Was still on my finger.   70

'the hacienda'

A Note on the Title

The title of the poem is taken from the first book of the Hebrew Bible and the Christian Old Testament. The book gives an account of the creation of the world and the early history of humanity. It states that human beings are superior to all other living creatures. God brought the animals to man, allowing him to name them, enabling man to be part of creation in a caretaking or stewardship role. But rights and power come with responsibility.

Tracy K. Smith had a devoutly Baptist religious upbringing and attended Bible classes. As a young woman, she was very aware of the Old Testament emphasis on how Christians are expected to resist uncontrolled sexual desires.

The creatures in the Bible story are symbolic of the lower animal nature within humans. God expected people to exercise dominion (or control) over themselves, over their passions and desires. In 'Dominion over the Beasts of the Earth', Smith explores adolescence and emerging adulthood.

POETRY FOCUS

👤 Personal Response

1. Briefly describe the atmosphere Smith creates in the poem's opening stanza. Is it exciting? Dreamlike? Ecstatic? Menacing? Refer to the text in your answer.
2. In your opinion, how effective is Smith at creating a vivid sense of place in this poem? Refer to the text in your response.
3. Write your own short response to the poem, focusing on the impact it made on you.

👁 Critical Literacy

'Dominion over the Beasts of the Earth' comes from Tracy K. Smith's *The Body's Question* (2003). This debut collection included many love poems and memory poems that were confessional or sensual in tone. The poet has said that these early poems allowed her 'to tell stories that weren't necessarily my own stories, and to let pieces of myself come into those other stories'.

The title of the poem (a quotation from the Book of Genesis) states that humans are superior to all other living creatures. Smith had a devoutly Baptist religious upbringing and attended Bible classes. As a young woman, she was very aware of the Old Testament emphasis on how Christians are expected to resist uncontrolled sexual desires. In 'Dominion over the Beasts of the Earth', she explores female sensuality and the sometimes turbulent transition from childhood to adulthood.

In the opening lines, Smith invites readers to share a vivid teenage memory of a warm sultry night in Mexico. The speaker recalls spending time in a run-down hacienda with Mauricio, with whom she was infatuated. While the exotic setting and staccato rhythms ('We ran/Back and forth') emphasise **a sense of daring excitement**, the reference to 'Dark rooms' suggests the unreliability of memories. The vibrant simile in lines 7–8 highlights the young couple's passionate feelings as they rushed around, feeling as 'giddy/As kid goats'.

This **atmosphere of new-found freedom** and a feeling of being almost out of control continues in line 10: 'Breath after breath charging'. The speaker imagines having a light-headed awareness of her 'weightless' body. She shifts her attention back to Mauricio, who urged her to do whatever she wanted. The focus is on her recollection of his physical attractiveness, his 'Enormous' physique and large hands, 'white as magnolias'.

She wonders about how close they were to becoming lovers at that moment – and how their lives might have been affected: 'What would we have changed' (line 25). But her **fascination with this coming-of-age moment** remains – even though she is still unsure about its true significance. The speaker recalls details of the scene where her 'world' might have been transformed. Images of the 'Rotten mattress' and discarded newspapers suggest that the encounter with Mauricio was really an unromantic, tawdry experience.

In looking back on turning points during her emerging adulthood, **the speaker broadens her approach** by wondering about all of the other boys she remembers: 'the ones I've said/Meant nothing'. In a reflective mood and with characteristic humour, she chooses to forget their individual personalities and 'call them all/Mauricio' (line 35). This might also be a subtle reference to man's 'naming' of the animals, an empowering act given to him by God. Is the poet now exercising her power over her memories, obliterating their unique identities by calling them all the same name?

In contrast to the earlier uncertainty and unresolved questions about adolescent development, the **mood becomes much more nostalgic**. The portrayal of 'Mauricio at 13' – whose skin was like 'sunset over the Pacific' – celebrates the beauty and potential of youth. In retrospect, the speaker acknowledges that he was 'on the cusp', poised on the threshold between innocence and maturity. She also recalls her awkwardness and lack of confidence during her early teenage years: 'Wishing myself someone else' (line 42).

The speaker confesses that she envied another 'fast' girl, 'Kathy, with the wild limbs', who seemed more assured and was popular with boys. But she begins to challenge her own random recollections – of Kathy's 'bracelets/ That made music on her wrists' and an image of roosting starlings. The **lingering uncertainty about memories of the past** – 'did I invent them?' (line 47) – leads her to think more deeply about the experiences of other young people ('What does a boy carry with him?'), particularly Mauricio's feelings at the time.

The final section of the poem moves forward in time and recalls a later stage in the speaker's relationship with Mauricio. His **edgy, unpredictable character** is suggested by the metaphor comparing him to a spool of thread that 'would not stay wound' (line 52). Despite her lasting feelings for him, it became clear that they had no future together. For her, destroying old love letters was an emotional experience ('moths swarmed my eyes') and she remembers him with tenderness.

Indeed, the speaker acknowledges that she is still haunted by casual memories of Mauricio and of what might have been. Another **evocative metaphor** ('the frayed thread of dreams') reflects fondly on the joys and disappointments of young love, a reminder of the previous description of Mauricio as a 'spool'. In Genesis, God decided that it was not good for man to be alone and he created a female companion for him. However, in Mauricio's case, young love was not to be.

In the ==closing lines==, **Smith presents readers with several questions** surrounding the intriguing detail of the wedding band 'Two sizes too loose' for her. Was Mauricio too domineering? He once stood up in a 'crowded room, insisting/I was his wife'. Does this suggest that he assumed the God-given right of 'naming'? Did the speaker need more space and freedom in their relationship?

Yet she still acknowledges just how close she came to marrying Mauricio – even though he wasn't 'the right person' for her. The mood is one of resignation, concluding without judgement or blame – and takes on a more universal significance. In the end, Smith's **bittersweet tone of young love** acts as a kind of confessional for every human who has had similar experiences.

✒ Writing About the Poem

'Tracy K. Smith's sensual poems often explore universal themes of desire and longing.' To what extent is this true of her poem 'Dominion over the Beasts of the Earth'? Develop your answer with reference to the text.

Sample Paragraph

'Dominion over the Beasts of the Earth' has relevance to most young people. Nearly all teenagers experience love – or at least infatuation. Smith describes her obsessive feelings for Mauricio and their sweaty nights full of desire in 'dark rooms' in Mexico. The couple are almost out of control as they rush around an empty hacienda, 'giddy as kid goats'. This sensual image really showed the power of physical attraction. As an adult, she later thinks back to their carefree love and how unsure she was about starting a relationship with him, 'What would've really happened?' Coming-of-age moments like this are normal and the poet still doesn't seem totally sure that she made the right choice – even though she was happy to marry someone else. Many adults would have doubts about choices they made in their teens.

> **EXAMINER'S COMMENT**
>
> *Good top-grade response that traced the progress of thought in the poem and tackled the question's basic elements ('sensual', 'desire' and 'universal'). Varied expression and clear, well-written points, supported by relevant reference and quotation throughout.*

✒ Class/Homework Exercises

1. 'Tracy K. Smith is a natural storyteller who loves to explore how a person can respond in intimate situations.' Discuss this statement, developing your answer with reference to 'Dominion over the Beasts of the Earth'.
2. 'There is often a haunting, dream-like quality to Smith's fascination with the past.' To what extent do you agree with this view? Develop your answer with reference to 'Dominion over the Beasts of the Earth'.

⊙ Points to Consider

- Personal subject matter confronting the theme of emerging adulthood.
- Sub-themes include making choices, destiny and the unreliability of memory.
- Dramatic language and scenes are enlivened by the Mexican setting and culture.
- Changing moods and tones – nostalgic, erotic, reflective, compassionate.
- Effective use of descriptive detail, metaphors, rhythm and rhetorical questions.

3 The Searchers

after the film by John Ford

He wants to kill her for surviving,
For the language she spits,
The way she runs, clutching
Her skirt as if life pools there.

Instead he grabs her, puts her   5
On his saddle, rides back
Into town where faces
She barely remembers

Smile into her fear
With questions and the wish,   10
The impossible wish, to forget.
What does living do to any of us?

And why do we grip it, hang on
As if it's the ribs of a horse
Past commanding? A beast   15
That big could wreck us easily,

Could rise up on two legs,
Or kick its back end up
And send us soaring.
We might land, any moment,   20

Like cheap toys. There's always
A chimney burning in the mind,
A porch where the rocker still rocks,
Though empty. Why

Do we insist our lives are ours?   25
Look at the frontier. It didn't resist.
Gave anyone the chance
To plant shrubs, dig wells.

Watched, not really concerned
With whether it belonged   30
To him or to him. Either way
The land went on living,

Dying. What else could it choose?

Title: famous 1956 Western.

He: Ethan Edwards, uncle of kidnapped girl.
language: abducted niece speaks Comanche.

pools: forms, gathers, combines.

barely: she has been missing for five years.

forget: fail to think of.

Past commanding: beyond control.

soaring: rising very quickly.

in the mind: in memory.
rocker: rocking chair.

frontier: Wild West, American frontier.
chance: opportunity, gamble.

👤 Personal Response

1. Based on the evidence of the poem, briefly describe the dilemma facing the young abducted girl.
2. Select one line or image from the poem that you find particularly interesting. Briefly explain your choice.
3. In your opinion, what is the tone of the poem's conclusion? Briefly explain your response.

👁 Critical Literacy

'The Searchers' comes from Tracy K. Smith's second poetry collection, *Duende*, published in 2007. The title refers to a mischievous house spirit. In her book, the poet includes a comment from the Spanish writer Federico García Lorca, 'The *duende* does not come at all unless he sees that death is possible.' Smith often explores themes of loss, desire, identity with quiet relentless focus. This poem springs from a controversial dramatic scene in a famous Western movie and widens out into a reflection on identity, ownership and attitude to life.

The title of the poem 'The Searchers' and its dedication is a reference to John Ford's melancholic Western about an obsessive quest. Twelve-year-old Debbie, niece of the central character, Ethan Edwards (played by John Wayne), is kidnapped by Native Americans from the Comanche tribe who have lured the men from the homestead with a cattle raid. The Comanche

'He wants to kill her for surviving'

murder Debbie's family and burn their home. Edwards, a world-weary Confederate veteran, spends five years hunting down the tribe who hold the girl. He does not rescue her, however, but shoots her dead. This complex character can be viewed as an anti-hero. He would rather kill his niece than have her live 'with a buck' because in his opinion, 'livin' with the Comanche ain't living'.

Edwards has a **fanatical hatred towards interracial mixing.** Line 1 bluntly states, 'He wants to kill her for surviving'. The first stanza of this lyric shows the situation from Edwards' perspective. He is appalled that his niece now speaks Comanche, revealed by the ugly monosyllabic verb 'spits'. He is shocked that she does not want to be rescued, but runs away 'clutching' her native skirt. Has this young woman decided that her life is now with the Comanche? The evocative verb 'pools' suggests that her new life has merged with the tribe. By running away from her 'rescuer', is she desperately trying to take ownership of her own destiny?

The emphatic adverb 'Instead' in line 5 indicates that Edwards is now deciding his niece's fate. He takes control through a quick series of actions, powerfully portrayed by aggressive monosyllabic verbs, 'grabs', 'puts'. He then 'rides back' to take her home. But is he making a mistake? Can what has happened to the girl be erased? Run-on lines and stanzas capture the **confused response** of the young woman, suddenly catapulted back into a past 'She barely remembers'.

While she is met with well-meaning kindness from the inhabitants of this unfamiliar white world, displayed by their 'Smile', she is also confronted by their inquisitiveness. They bombard her with 'questions'. They also pressure her with an 'impossible' demand, the 'wish' that she should move on from her ordeal and her life with the Comanches. The definite article suggests that it is more their wish than the girl's that she should 'forget' her time among the Native American tribe. The adjective 'impossible' and the repetition of 'wish' point out the futility of this desire to wipe out what occurred (line 11). **The past cannot be erased**.

In lines 13–15, Smith uses the evocative Wild West simile of a rider on an untamed horse to reveal how desperately humans cling to life. The rider cannot rule the horse's spirit, just as the events that occur in life are not always controlled by humans, despite their best efforts. **Ironically, it is people who are at the mercy of fate**. The rider risks serious injury by insisting on mastering a wild horse. The harsh-sounding verb 'wreck' suggests both the horse's and life's potential to hurt. Smith extends the metaphor of the untamed horse rearing up on its hind legs or flicking up its back end to dislodge its rider. This vividly displays the ups and downs of life which are often left 'soaring' beyond control. Hissing sibilance and the elongated sound of the verb in line 19 emphasise how those who sought to control are sometimes placed in an uncontrollable situation, and sent flying helplessly through the air.

The unpredictable situation continues in line 20, 'We might land, any moment'. Both the rider and the individual's irrelevance and unimportance in life's bigger scheme is sharply conveyed in the simile 'Like cheap toys'. Although colourful, they are worthless and easily broken. The poet now presents the reader with two well-known domestic images from life on the frontier, the cosy fire in the homestead and the rocking chair on the porch. But **these exist only in memory**, 'in the mind' (line 22). The stark adjective 'empty' confronts readers with the inescapable truth: that particular time is past. There is now no one there.

A run-on rhetorical question addresses the reader, 'Why/Do we insist our lives are ours?' Human beings cannot control or take possession of something which they are unable to manage. This is rather like the rescuer who will 'insist' on saving someone who does not wish to be rescued. The poet offers us advice in line 26: 'Look at the frontier' as a guide. Careful rhyme, 'insist'/'resist', exposes a startling contrast. **People display a closed attitude to life in comparison to the open frontier landscape which accepts all** and 'Gave anyone the chance'. Homely images ('plant shrubs, dig wells') reflect the lives of the early settlers, illustrating the opportunity to survive and prosper.

Smith personifies the landscape which 'Watched' (line 29), placing it in the role of observer. Unlike humans, who are active participants seeking to control and own, the vast Western frontier stands aloof, 'not really concerned/With whether it belonged/To him or to him'. Run-on lines emphasise the indifferent attitude of this harshly beautiful, open place, 'Either way'. The **concluding stand-alone line accentuates the natural inescapable progression of life towards 'Dying'**. The poem ends with a fatalist rhetorical question, 'What else could it choose?'

This poignant lyric weaves questions about identity and belonging. The overall **tone is darkly meditative**. Should we indulge a nostalgic longing for home and family and the past? Does an anti-hero act out of vengeance or a commitment to honour and decency? Do the very qualities which form the anti-hero make him an outcast in society? The question posed by Smith is whether the displaced, marginalised young victim of abuse should embrace life, adapting to uncontrollable circumstances, or refuse to change and give in to death.

POETRY FOCUS

📝 Writing About the Poem

Discuss how Tracy K. Smith makes effective use of a variety of characters, often in dramatic settings, to probe various personal issues. Develop your response with reference to 'The Searchers'.

Sample Paragraph

'The Searchers' opens with an intense scene from John Ford's famous film. Set in the American Wild West, the story is about an obsessive search for a kidnapped girl. Smith uses this drama to explore personal identity and choices. The open landscape is personified – like another character. This land is open to everybody, 'Gave anyone the chance'. In contrast, the uncle, the film's anti-hero, searching for the girl, is determined that his personal view of life should triumph. Violent verbs, such as 'grabs', highlight his attempts to control others. Smith raises issues about individual rights. Two central characters dominate, the traditional male and the personified Wild West. The first is opposed to change, the second welcoming and inclusive. The conflict between them really made me think about power and powerlessness.

> **EXAMINER'S COMMENT**
> *Clearly written top-grade response that engages with the key aspects of the question. Effective discussion points focus on identity and opposing attitudes to life. Good use of relevant reference and quotation throughout.*

✒️ Class/Homework Exercises

1. 'Tracy K. Smith often explores complex issues of identity and belonging.' Discuss this view with reference to her poem 'The Searchers'.
2. 'The effective use of evocative imagery is a recurring feature of Smith's poetry.' To what extent is this true of 'The Searchers'?

⊙ Points to Consider

- Poignant exploration of loss, revenge, obsession, racism and acceptance.
- Features of style include rhetorical questions, cinematic scenes, irony, personification and contrast.
- Effective extended metaphor – bucking bronco suggesting life's ungovernable events.
- Extensive use of run-on lines to indicate life's unpredictability and the inviting landscape.
- Varied tones: dark, honest, nostalgic, reflective, chilling, questioning.

Letter to a Photojournalist Going-In

TRACY K. SMITH

You go to the pain. City after city. Borders
Where they peer into your eyes as if to erase you.

You go by bus or truck, days at a time, just taking it
When they throw you in a room or kick at your gut,

Taking it when a strong fist hammers person after person   5
A little deeper into the ground. Your camera blinks:

Soldiers smoking between rounds. Bodies
Blown open like curtains. In the neighborhoods,

Boys brandish plastic guns with TV bravado. Men
Ask you to look them in the face and say who's right.   10

At night you sleep, playing it all back in reverse:

The dance of wind in a valley of dirt. Rugs and tools,
All the junk that rises up, resurrected, then disappears

Into newly formed windows and walls. People
Close their mouths and run backwards out of frame.   15

Up late, your voice fits my ear like a secret.
But who can hear two things at once?

Errant stars flare, shatter. A whistle, then the indescribable thud
Of an era spilling its matter into the night. Who can say the word *love*

When everything – everything – pushes back with the promise   20
To grind itself to dust?

      And what if there's no dignity to what we do,
None at all? If our work – what you see, what I say – is nothing

But a way to kid ourselves into thinking we might last? If trust is just
Another human trick that'll lick its lips and laugh as it backs away?   25

Sometimes I think you're right, wanting to lose everything and wander
Like a blind king. Wanting to squeeze a lifetime between your hands

---

erase: delete, remove.

gut: stomach.

rounds: firing weapons.

brandish: display.
bravado: machismo, showing off.

resurrected: revitalised.

Errant: stray.
era: time.

grind: turn.

kid: fool.

And press it into a single flimsy frame. Will you take it to your lips
Like the body of a woman, something to love in passing,

Or set it down, free finally, empty as the camera, 30
Which we all know is just a hollow box, mechanized to obey?

Sometimes I want my heart to beat like yours: from the outside in,
A locket stuffed with faces that refuse to be named. For time

To land at my feet like a grenade.

flimsy: light.

mechanized: set.

locket: pendant that holds a small photo.

grenade: bomb thrown by hand.

'Boys brandish plastic guns'

Personal Response

1. Choose one image from the poem that, in your opinion, conveys the reality of what happens in conflict areas. Comment briefly on the effectiveness of the image.
2. Briefly describe the poem's dramatic qualities. You might refer to some of the following: setting, characters, tension, vivid language.
3. Outline your own immediate thoughts and feelings in response to the poem.

👁 Critical Literacy

Tracy K. Smith has always been drawn to questions about what it means to survive, to endure. 'Letter to a Photojournalist Going-In' (taken from her 2007 collection, *Duende*) paints a poignant scenario of war documented by embedded photojournalists. The poem is divided into two halves, 17 shorter lines and 17 longer lines. The first half describes the day-to-day reality of being a war photographer. In the more reflective second half, Smith addresses issues around the wider impact of the photojournalist's work and its impact on his personal relationships.

The letter-writer (the speaker) addresses the photojournalist directly in the poem's opening line: 'You go to the pain. City after city'. The images are like 'snapshots' recording the tragedy and suffering ('pain') that he photographs in war zones. Brisk **staccato (or jerky) rhythm gives an impression of breathlessness**. We can imagine the everyday dangers faced by working journalists who are often viewed as intrusive outsiders in places of conflict – especially at border checkpoints where suspicious guards 'peer into your eyes'.

This could be the frightful experience of any war correspondent who is **resigned to endure almost anything as part of the job**. Smith focuses on the predictable risks experienced 'days at a time'. The emphasis is on 'taking it', putting up with whatever brutality occurs, 'When they throw you in a room or kick at your gut'. The phrase 'taking it' also suggests a deepening awareness by visiting reporters who suddenly take in and understand **the dehumanising effects of war**. Their shock and disbelief is conveyed through personification: 'Your camera blinks'.

Lines 7–9 include several **graphic images** of soldiers and victims. The poet's unflinching picture of routine atrocities when bodies are 'Blown open like curtains' is **both horrifying and surreal**. The simile emphasises how images of war can open a window to what is happening outside in the real world. Smith's sense of hopelessness is evident in the association of violence with impressionable young boys who 'brandish plastic guns with TV bravado' (line 9).

Photojournalists have often recorded images of innocent children playing war games they have learned from what they have witnessed directly. But in referencing how television can glamourise violence, the poet raises a **disturbing question about the bigger gun culture in society**. Smith has always encouraged readers to think seriously about complex issues, such as the connection between masculine culture, violence and moral confusion: 'Men/Ask you to look them in the face and say who's right'.

Line 11 marks a change in tone, **focusing on the personal relationship between the speaker and the photojournalist**. She imagines him unable to sleep at night. Having seen humanity at its worst, he is 'playing it all back in reverse' and associating haunting memories of everyday conflict ('the junk that rises up') with the destruction and re-building of bombed-out neighbourhoods. Is the poet suggesting that the cycle of violence never ends? As always, she voices her greatest concern for ordinary 'People' who are powerless, the fearful who 'run backwards out of frame'.

The intimate moment between the speaker and journalist (**lines 16–17**) recalls a phone call between them and the mysterious question: 'who can hear two things at once?' She is **reflecting on her love for a photojournalist** who chooses to risk his life and finding it difficult to understand his true feelings. Glimpses of chaos and destruction ('stars flare, shatter') associate battle scenes with their emotional lives. Are the dehumanising consequences of his job as a war correspondent likely to destroy their relationship – 'Who can say the word *love*'?

The final section of the poem centres mainly on **the pressures that threaten their relationship**. Poignant, long-lined couplets are filled with disquieting visions of conflict and inevitable death where everything is destined to 'grind itself to dust' (**line 21**). The speaker is overwhelmed by doubts, questioning their commitment to love each other and fearing that they are trying to 'kid ourselves into thinking we might last'. Once again, she wonders if she can rely on her lover and whether he is more devoted to his adventurous work to ever be 'free finally' of the camera. Does she see the camera as another dangerous weapon coming between them?

The poem's uneasy **ending develops this battle-weary view of romantic love**. The speaker realises that the photojournalist's experiences of war force him to suppress his emotions. But she seems unsure about what she herself wants. There are times when she wants to be like her lover and escape reality by hiding her feelings, so that her heart can 'beat like yours: from the outside in' (**line 32**). The concluding tone is particularly ominous, reflecting her dreadful fear of a future that will 'land at my feet like a grenade'.

The searing simile of an unexploded bomb highlights the lingering tension in the couple's complex relationship. Smith leaves readers in no doubt that **war can make victims of many people** – and not just individuals like the journalist who are directly caught up in the turmoil of conflict.

✒ Writing About the Poem

'In many of her poems, Tracy K. Smith intertwines stories, often linking personal and public experiences.' Discuss this statement in relation to 'Letter to a Photojournalist Going-In'.

Sample Paragraph

'Letter to a Photojournalist' is mainly about the dangerous work of a reporter in parts of the world where wars are taking place. But it's also linked in with a love story. Smith's violent images show the horror of war through the journalist's eyes, 'kick you', 'bodies are blown up like curtains'. He has nightmares 'playing it all back'. But there is another tragic story because his job also affects the poet. Stray bombs could put an end to her partner and their relationship in a flash. This story makes the public life of a journalist personal. The couple's love is over-shadowed by his job as a war correspondent. Smith's personal relationship is always under threat and she has doubts about her love for him, 'At times I think you're right, wanting to lose everything'. Both storylines are closely linked throughout this sad poem.

EXAMINER'S COMMENT

Good high-grade response showing a clear understanding of the two narrative strands in the poem and the overlap between public and private experiences. Critical comments are clearly expressed and supported by relevant reference (although there are some slight misquotations).

✒ Class/Homework Exercises

1. 'Smith's compelling poems often raise questions about the complexity of human relationships.' Discuss this view with reference to 'Letter to a Photojournalist Going-In'.
2. 'Powerful and dramatic imagery is a recurring feature of Tracy K. Smith's most intense poetry.' To what extent is this true of 'Letter to a Photojournalist Going-In'?

⊙ Points to Consider

- Insightful exploration of the photojournalist's experience.
- Themes include conflict, male violence, personal relationships.
- Striking images of conflict – both public and personal.
- Effective use of questions, tension, varied sentence length.
- Contrasting tones – empathic, reflective, self-doubting, anxious.

5 The Universe is a House Party

The universe is expanding. Look: postcards
And panties, bottles with lipstick on the rim,

Orphan socks and napkins dried into knots.
Quickly, wordlessly, all of it whisked into file

With radio waves from a generation ago
Drifting to the edge of what doesn't end,

Like the air inside a balloon. Is it bright?
Will our eyes crimp shut? Is it molten, atomic,

A conflagration of suns? It sounds like the kind of party
Your neighbors forget to invite you to: bass throbbing

Through walls, and everyone thudding around drunk
On the roof. We grind lenses to an impossible strength,

Point them toward the future, and dream of beings
We'll welcome with indefatigable hospitality:

How marvelous you've come! We won't flinch
At the pinprick mouths, the nubbin limbs. We'll rise,

Gracile, robust. *Mi casa es su casa.* Never more sincere.
Seeing us, they'll know exactly what we mean.

Of course, it's ours. If it's anyone's, it's ours.

A Note on the Title

The poem's title, 'The Universe is a House Party' is a metaphor. Smith believes that metaphors allow a person to depart from their normal literal self. They distort our sense of the way the world works so that it can be viewed from another angle. Throughout the 1970s, America was gripped by a craze for all things martian.

The title of Smith's poetry collection, *Life on Mars*, was taken from the song 'Life on Mars?' from David Bowie's pop album *Hunky Dory* (1971). Smith uses science fiction as a means of asking ourselves questions. What characterises our views of ourselves? Are they true? Have we a false opinion of our own importance in the grand scheme of things? Are we prepared to admit that we don't know everything?

👤 Personal Response

1. Based on the evidence of the poem, briefly describe your impression of the universe.
2. The poet includes two phrases in italics which are used by humans greeting the aliens. Do you think Smith is being sarcastic when she imagines this meeting? Give a reason for your response.
3. In your opinion, what is the tone of the poem's concluding line? Is it positive or negative? Briefly explain your response.

👁 Critical Literacy

Tracy K. Smith's third poetry collection, *Life on Mars* (2011), includes the poem, 'The Universe is a House Party'. This book won the Pulitzer Prize in 2012. With wry humour, Smith not only explores a supernatural universe beyond what can be known, but from that future vantage point, she looks back to explore modern life. The limits of human comprehension are contrasted sharply with the vast, mysterious universe.

A short, emphatic statement dramatically opens the poem, 'The universe is expanding'. Smith was very close to her father, an engineer on the Hubble Space Telescope named after the astronomer Edwin Hubble.

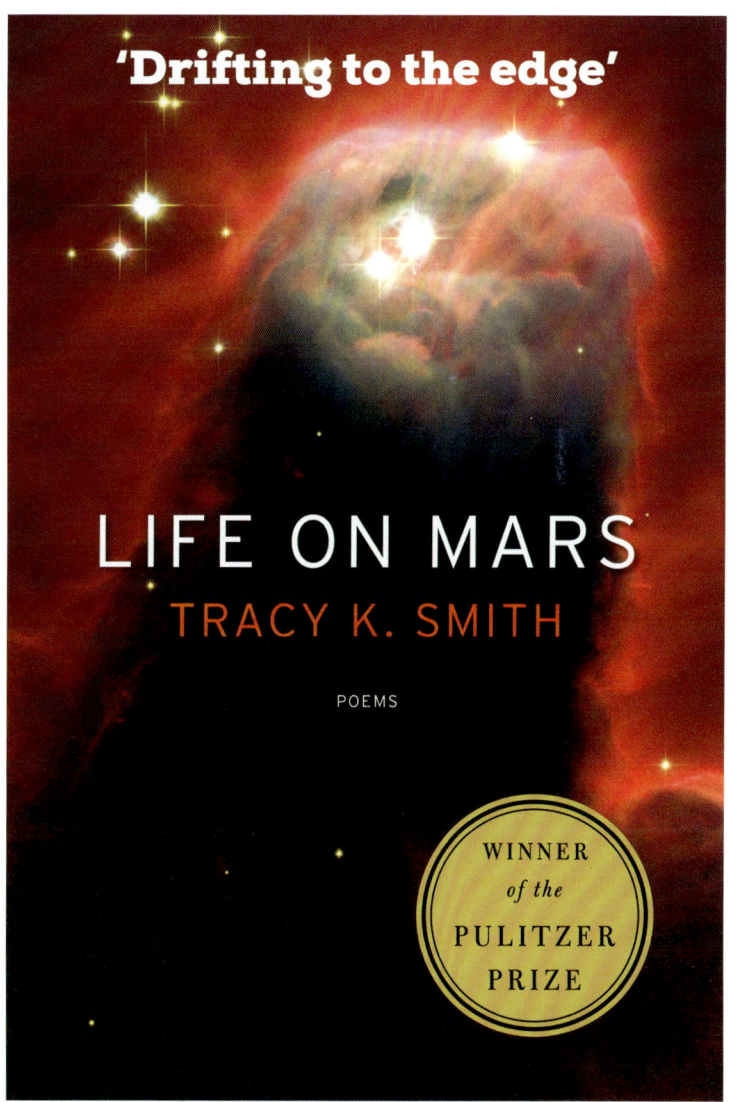

TRACY K. SMITH

The front cover of Life on Mars *shows a dramatic picture from the Hubble Space Telescope of Cone Nebula, a pillar of dust and gas, more than 2,500 light years from Earth.*

POETRY FOCUS

During the 1920s, Hubble had made an astonishing discovery that the universe was not static, as had been believed earlier. He found that it had been growing since its beginning with the Big Bang, over 13 billion years ago. The universe is expanding into itself as the familiar analogy of rising bread dough in the oven illustrates. The galaxies of stars (like the raisins in the dough) are retreating from each other as the universe expands. But just as the raisins remain in the dough, the stars continue to exist in space. This is the **mysterious nature** of the universe.

An insistent command verb, 'Look', in line 1, draws attention to the present. A party's debris-strewn aftermath is vividly highlighted in explosive alliteration and run-on lines, 'postcards/And panties'. Sharply focused cinematic close-ups, 'bottles with lipstick on the rim,/Orphan socks' suggest **a hedonistic lifestyle**. The poet views today's human race as specks in the future's rear-view mirror. Swiftly moving punctuation underlines the busybody humans sweeping the mess into order to the background sound of the radio.

The discovery of 'radio waves' by Hertz in 1880 allowed sound to be transmitted and formed our modern communication system. But radio waves are also transmitted from objects in space to our telescopes, informing us of what is present in space, but which we cannot see. These radio waves travel for ever within the infinite universe, 'to the edge of what doesn't end'. There is a striking contrast between the purposeful human action, 'whisked' in line 4 and the aimless action of **the eternal universe**, 'Drifting'. This also hints at the weightlessness experienced in space, when objects are free from Earth's gravitational pull.

In line 7, Smith compares the radio waves to the air moving around the interior empty space within a balloon. Follow-up **staccato questions** examine the nature of the universe. She wonders if it glows brilliantly, perhaps from the light of the stars? Will it be too much for humans to bear, causing our eyes to 'crimp shut' against the glare? Is it a boiling, fragmentary blaze ('molten', 'atomic', 'conflagration')? According to the Big Bang theory, our universe began as an extremely hot, dense state which later underwent colossal rapid expansion.

The poem turns to modern-day life in line 9 when Smith compares the universe to a noisy house party. The scene is described in terms of sound, a subtle reference to our knowledge of what space contains being comprehended through 'radio waves' on our telescopes. **Onomatopoeic verbs**, 'throbbing', 'thudding', vividly enact the hectic party atmosphere heard 'Through walls'. But a more disquieting tone is struck with the observation that 'Your neighbors forget to invite you'. Is mankind relegated to being a mere listener who is always excluded from the universe's party?

Once again, Smith is examining our confusing, question-riddled relationship with the universe.

Line 12 again references the purposeful action of the humans who pulverise glass, 'grind lenses', to make telescopes to peer into space, to seek to know the unknowable. Poet and astronomer are both trying to further understand the immensity of the universe, 'Point them toward the future'. At this point, **the poem changes dramatically**, becoming a surreal 'dream' where 'beings' suddenly arrive on Earth from space.

The poet imagines people greeting the aliens with 'indefatigable hospitality', almost a relentless or perhaps even forced welcome. An italicised phrase suggests the interchange, '*How marvelous you've come!*' The humans have adopted the role of welcoming hosts. Yet another **unsettling note** is struck, however, by the humans' description of these 'beings'. While they promise not to recoil, 'flinch', their focus is negatively fixated on the strange appearance of the visitors who have 'pinprick mouths' and stunted limbs, 'nubbin limbs'. Slender assonance underlines the aliens' disturbing presence.

Line 16 again stresses the human race's sense of self-importance. Smith emphatically states that humanity will 'rise' to the occasion, nimbly, 'Gracile', and firmly, 'robust'. Another italic phrase is used to show the emphatic welcome offered to the alien visitors, '*Mi casa es su casa*' (My house is your house). But are people speaking from the heart, 'Never more sincere'? The poem shifts focus again, as we look at ourselves from the aliens' perspective with the ironic phrase, 'they'll know exactly what we mean'. Are the humans being hospitable or presumptuous? After nine carefully ordered couplets a stand-alone line suggests a shocking possibility, a new perspective. Are human beings really assuming that the universe belongs solely to them, 'Of course, it's ours', **line 19**. Readers are left wondering about who is the host of the universe's house party. And who are the guests?

TRACY K. SMITH

> ## ✎ Writing About the Poem
>
> **To what extent is your response to Smith's poetry heightened by her use of both provocative and evocative imagery? Develop your answer with reference to her poem 'The Universe is a House Party'.**

Sample Paragraph

'The Universe is a House Party' left me thinking how people can misrepresent what they are truly like to themselves. Provocative images describe the chaos after a party and suggest a decadent lifestyle, 'postcards and panties'. Strong alliteration adds to the self-indulgent mood. I got a sense of human superiority in their reaction to the alien 'beings'. Although humans seem 'indefatigable' in their welcome, it is their negative focus on the creatures' appearance that is emphasised. This is seen in the offensive images, 'pinprick mouths', 'nubbin limbs'. In contrast, powerful sci-fi images highlight the mystery of space. It sends 'radio waves' from unseen objects travelling 'to the edge of what doesn't end'. The mix of disturbing modern images and haunting science fiction imagery helped me reflect on people's desire to control and be the centre of the universe.

> **EXAMINER'S COMMENT**
> Good personal top-grade response that focuses on the main aspects of the question and engages closely with the poem. Effective discussion of contrasting images and their effectiveness. Relevant supportive reference and quotation throughout.

Class/Homework Exercises

1. 'Tracy K. Smith often explores issues of acceptance and rejection'. Discuss this view with reference to her poem 'The Universe is a House Party'.
2. 'The effective use of sound effects is a recurring feature of Smith's poetry.' To what extent is this true of 'The Universe is a House Party'? Develop your answer with reference to the poem.

Points to Consider

- **Thought-provoking exploration of modern life through insightful observation and imaginative perspective.**

- **Revealing contrasts between vast, mysterious universe and narrow and sometimes vacuous human existence.**

- **Stylistic features include irony, pertinent questions and distinctive imagery.**

- **Effective use of metaphor: the image of space to explore contemporary human existence.**

- **Use of present tense adds immediacy and collective pronouns strengthen engagement with the reader.**

6 The Museum of Obsolescence

TRACY K. SMITH

So much we once coveted. So much
That would have saved us, but lived,

Instead, its own quick span, returning
To uselessness with the mute acquiescence

Of shed skin. It watches us watch it: 5
Our faulty eyes, our telltale heat, hearts

Ticking through our shirts. We're here
To titter at gimcracks, the naïve tools,

The replicas of replicas stacked like bricks.
There's green money, and oil in drums. 10

Pots of honey pilfered from a tomb. Books
Recounting the wars, maps of fizzled stars.

In the south wing, there's a small room
Where a living man sits on display. Ask,

And he'll describe the old beliefs. If you 15
Laugh, he'll lower his head to his hands

And sigh. When he dies, they'll replace him
With a video looping on *ad infinitum*.

Special installations come and go. 'Love'
Was up for a season, followed by 'Illness', 20

Concepts difficult to grasp. The last thing you see
(After a mirror – someone's idea of a joke?)

Is an image of the old planet taken from space.
Outside, vendors hawk t-shirts, three for eight.

Title: exhibition of useless outdated things.

coveted: desired.

quick span: short time.
mute acquiescence: silent surrender.

It: the museum.

gimcracks: shoddy knick-knacks.
naïve: simple.

replicas: copies, cheap imitations.

pilfered: stolen.
tomb: burial chamber.
fizzled: burnt out.

wing: section of the museum.

ad infinitum: endlessly.

installations: displays.

Concepts: ideas, experiences.
grasp: understand.

the old planet: Earth.
vendors hawk: street traders sell.
eight: eight dollars.

👤 Personal Response

1. Describe the poet's mood in lines 1–4. Sad? Cynical? Humorous? Hopeful? Briefly explain your response, using reference to the text.
2. Select one image or line from the poem that you find particularly interesting. Briefly explain your choice.
3. In your opinion, what is the central theme or message in this poem? Refer to the text in your response.

'maps of fizzled stars'

👁 Critical Literacy

Tracy K. Smith's 2011 collection, *Life on Mars*, includes several poems that consider the future of humanity. The poet uses the image of outer space to allow her to explore the even bigger concept of life's meaning. Readers are presented with a dystopian future commenting on a dystopian present. Smith writes of stars and oceans, a futuristic planet and the universal sense of loss. 'The Museum of Obsolescence' imagines a public gallery far into the future. The building is full of forgotten and useless artefacts from the human species' time on Earth.

In the poem's opening lines, Smith envisions a time when generations to come will look back on all the things we thought were essential. Biblical language ('we once coveted') suggests that people today are avaricious and obsessed with material possessions. Yet the sad truth is that all of our **greed and wishful thinking have failed us**. Ironically, everything that we hoped 'would have saved us' became outdated and inadequate after lasting for just a 'quick span'.

The graphic metaphor in lines 4–5 compares the museum's exhibits to a body that is slowly but naturally decaying 'with the mute acquiescence/Of shed skin'. A poignant sense of the inevitable cycle of change is evident in the **gentle sounds and elegiac tone**. Smith's poetic voice has the soft sibilant hush of someone almost whispering. Is she saddened by the excessive trust placed in technology that quickly becomes outmoded? Does she feel sympathy for her fellow human beings? Or is she critical of them?

We are invited on a tour of the gallery, but line 5 **personifies the museum: 'It watches us watch it'**. The poet takes a quirky approach, asking us to reflect more closely on our own lives. If we take time to consider ourselves as the exhibits, what do our various moods and feelings ('telltale heat, hearts') reveal about us? Do we have a 'faulty' view of the world? Is Smith focusing on what really defines us as people? Have we been mistaken about the importance of emotions? Are human feelings also destined to become obsolete?

For visitors to this futuristic museum, **our world will simply be a passing attraction**. The poet imagines tourists being entertained by the technology we have today and ridiculing our 'naïve tools' (line 8). She reminds us of the lack of innovation ('replicas of replicas') associated with modern mass consumerism. The simile 'stacked like bricks' adds to the sense of sameness. Smith's catalogue of obsolescence includes 'green money, and oil in drums' (line 10), vivid images of a capitalist world. She is in no doubt that our present economic system will ultimately be looked upon as primitive – and not least because our consumerist system has led to planetary devastation.

The poem's central viewpoint is emphasised in lines 11–12. Everything in **the universe will keep changing**, regardless of successive human civilisations. Images of out-dated paraphernalia, 'honey pilfered from a tomb' and 'Books/Recounting the wars', are reminders that history shows there is no escape from destruction and death. The onomatopoeic adjective 'fizzled' suggests a light being extinguished. All things will pass and even the stars will eventually burn out.

Perhaps the poem's most haunting scene is found in line 14: 'a living man sits on display'. The idea that human beings as we know them are becoming an endangered species reflects **Smith's deep sense of tragedy as well as her dark humour**. Although the man can answer questions about the 'old beliefs', he is often mocked and put to shame. In the dehumanised sci-fi world of the future, he will soon be replaced by a machine, 'a video looping on *ad infinitum*' (line 18), perpetual motion going nowhere.

The dystopian vision intensifies in the closing lines. The poet imagines future generations laughing at many of our current beliefs and values, even consigning key aspects of what makes us human, such as 'Love' and 'Illness', to the museum. The desire to love or to be sympathetic to others is in stark contrast to the material things on display. However, she sees the **tragic irony** of the entire museum. The mirror seems to be 'someone's idea of a joke' (line 22). Through our reflections in the mirror, we now become part of the exhibits in the museum of obsolescence. It's a cruel joke, of course, since it shows us our real selves in light of our own insignificance.

The final exhibit item before the exit is 'an image of the old planet taken from space' (line 23). This is a reproduction of one of the first photographs of the whole Earth, taken from space. Does this bittersweet relic of a bygone era lament a lost connection to Earth as a natural home for the human race? Throughout the poem, Smith has questioned the usefulness of human knowledge and emphasised **our small place in the universe**.

Meanwhile, certain aspects of human nature don't seem to change and commercial life goes on. Outside the museum building, street vendors 'hawk t-shirts', making a living by selling history. The trashy T-shirts are not much different from the old photograph of planet Earth. As she **looks ahead to a time when human individuality has become obsolete**, readers are left wondering if we are rapidly losing an entire shared world. Smith's concluding tone is obviously cynical. But is she also being realistic?

Writing About the Poem

Comment on Smith's use of effective irony throughout this poem. Refer closely to the text in your response.

Sample Paragraph

'The Museum of Obsolescence' is set long after people have abandoned Planet Earth. Human life has evolved and the museum amuses future visitors. They 'titter' at the 'naïve tools' we once thought were so advanced. It's ironic that we always think of ourselves as so developed and superior when everything becomes obsolete so quickly. In space we are insignificant. Smith's tone is gentle, yet she seems really troubled that people are destined be replaced by machines. A 'living man' is on display, but is of little interest. It's just like nowadays, when sightseers make a quick visit to Pompeii to check out life back in AD 79. The irony is most effective when Smith describes special 'installations' including 'Love'. Even people's feelings have died out – something I found really shocking.

EXAMINER'S COMMENT

Good personal response that includes some insightful engagement with the poem. Clear discussion of irony is supported with relevant reference and integrated quotations. A slightly more developed point about the irony of the poet's gentle tone would have improved the answer. Expression is lively and coherent throughout. Overall, a solid high-grade standard.

✒ Class/Homework Exercises

1. 'Tracy K. Smith emphasises the importance of the imagination to raise questions about our lives.' To what extent is this true of 'The Museum of Obsolescence'? Develop your answer with reference to the poem.
2. 'Smith's poems often include strange and disturbing imagery to convey thought-provoking insights.' Discuss this view with reference to 'The Museum of Obsolescence'.

⊙ Points to Consider

- Themes include transience, dehumanisation, loss and human destiny.
- Poet illustrates the significance of the imagination in addressing life's mysteries.
- Effective use of vivid imagery, haunting atmosphere, irony and sound effects.
- Variety of tones: regretful, cynical, reflective, ironic, nostalgic and elegiac.

7 Don't You Wonder, Sometimes?

Title: from David Bowie's song 'Sound and Vision'.

1.

After dark, stars glisten like ice, and the distance they span
Hides something elemental. Not God, exactly. More like
Some thin-hipped glittering Bowie-being – a Starman
Or cosmic ace hovering, swaying, aching to make us see.
And what would we do, you and I, if we could know for sure   5

That someone was there squinting through the dust,
Saying nothing is lost, that everything lives on waiting only
To be wanted back badly enough? Would you go then,
Even for a few nights, into that other life where you
And that first she loved, blind to the future once, and happy?   10

Would I put on my coat and return to the kitchen where my
Mother and father sit waiting, dinner keeping warm on the stove?
Bowie will never die. Nothing will come for him in his sleep
Or charging through his veins. And he'll never grow old,
Just like the woman you lost, who will always be dark-haired   15

And flush-faced, running toward an electronic screen
That clocks the minutes, the miles left to go. Just like the life
In which I'm forever a child looking out my window at the night sky
Thinking one day I'll touch the world with bare hands
Even if it burns.   20

2.

He leaves no tracks. Slips past, quick as a cat. That's Bowie
For you: the Pope of Pop, coy as Christ. Like a play
Within a play, he's trademarked twice. The hours

Plink past like water from a window A/C. We sweat it out,
Teach ourselves to wait. Silently, lazily, collapse happens.   25
But not for Bowie. He cocks his head, grins that wicked grin.

Time never stops, but does it end? And how many lives
Before take-off, before we find ourselves
Beyond ourselves, all glam-glow, all twinkle and gold?

The future isn't what it used to be. Even Bowie thirsts   30
For something good and cold. Jets blink across the sky
Like migratory souls.

elemental: fundamental, essential.
Bowie: influential pop artist.
Starman: alien creature.
cosmic ace: space champion.

squinting: peering.

Pope: supreme leader.
coy: shy, flirtatious.
trademarked: branded.

A/C: air conditioner.

glam: glamorous.

migratory souls: travelling spirits.

TRACY K. SMITH

3.

Bowie is among us. Right here
In New York City. In a baseball cap
And expensive jeans. Ducking into   35
A deli. Flashing all those teeth
At the doorman on his way back up.
Or he's hailing a taxi on Lafayette
As the sky clouds over at dusk.
He's in no rush. Doesn't feel   40
The way you'd think he feels.
Doesn't strut or gloat. Tells jokes.

I've lived here all those years
And never seen him. Like not knowing
A comet from a shooting star.   45
But I'll bet he burns bright,
Dragging a tail of white-hot matter
The way some of us track tissue
Back from the toilet stall. He's got
The whole world under his foot,   50
And we are small alongside,
Though there are occasions

When a man his size can meet
Your eyes for just a blip of time
And send a thought like SHINE   55
SHINE SHINE SHINE SHINE
Straight to your mind. Bowie,
I want to believe you. Want to feel
Your will like the wind before the rain.
The kind everything simply obeys,   60
Swept up in that hypnotic dance
As if something with the power to do so
Had looked its way and said:
      Go ahead.

deli: food shop.

Lafayette: a major street in Lower Manhattan, New York City.

strut or gloat: show off.

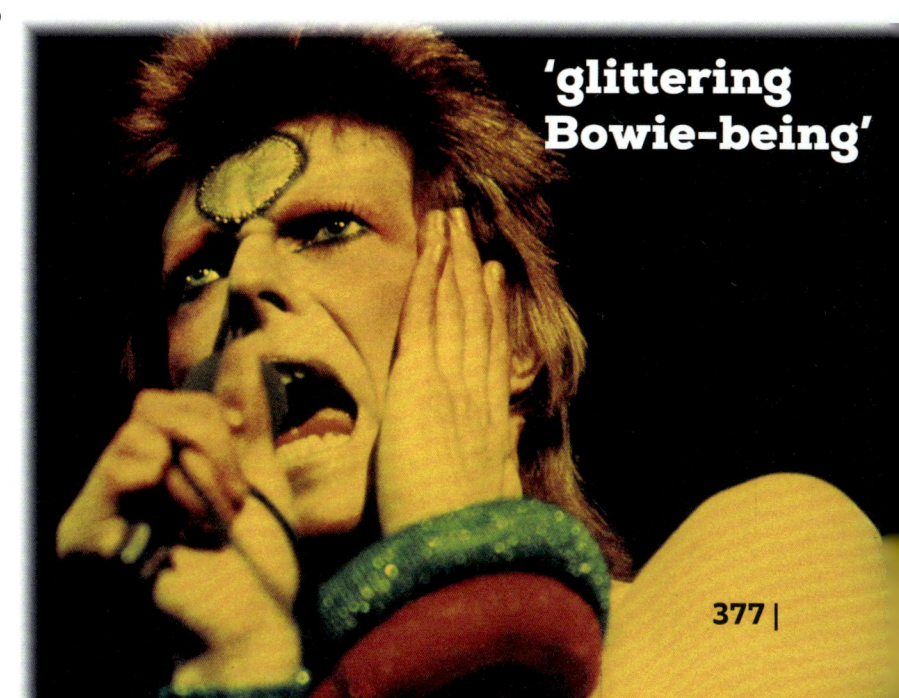

comet: icy body orbiting the sun.
shooting star: meteor.

track: trail.

blip: fleeting moment.

hypnotic: spellbinding.

'glittering Bowie-being'

👤 Personal Response

1. Briefly outline one key question that Tracy K. Smith is exploring and wondering about in her poem 'Don't You Wonder, Sometimes?'
2. Smith uses alliteration extensively in her poem. Choose one example which appealed to you and explain how alliteration is effectively used to convey the poet's ideas.
3. Based on your reading of the poem, what is meant by the concluding italicised phrase, '*Go ahead*'? Briefly explain your response.

👁 Critical Literacy

Tracy K. Smith's poetry often addresses the reality of the human condition, including change and our place in the universe. 'Don't You Wonder, Sometimes?' is taken from her collection *Life on Mars* (2011). Smith's father grew up in pre-civil rights Alabama and subsequently worked as an engineer developing the Hubble Telescope. The poet uses his career to illustrate the collection's central metaphor – outer space as a vast, unknowable infinity. She alters the punctuation of Bowie's song 'Life on Mars?' to make it into a statement rather than a question. Is she asserting that there is hope for a better future? The poet combines pop culture, anecdote and science fiction while working the grief she feels after her father's death into otherworldliness in the three-part poem.

Section 1 of the poem focuses on visions of the future and meditations on outer space. The poem's title comes from the song 'Sound and Vision' by the English musician David Bowie – 'Don't you wonder sometimes/'Bout sound and vision?' – his casual reference to how we primarily experience our reality through hearing and seeing. The poet diverts the reader's eye towards the heavens with the declaration that **something fundamental, 'elemental', is hidden among the stars**. Sibilance and slender vowel sounds in the simile 'stars glisten like ice' softly hint at another reality. Broad assonance ('distance'/'span'/'elemental') suggests the vast expanse and mystery of space.

The notion of hope after 'dark' times begins to emerge: it's 'Not God, exactly' (line 2). **This symbol of eternity takes the form of Bowie's persona Ziggy Stardust**, an alien rock star who looked partly male and partly female. The androgynous messenger was sent to save the world from an impending apocalypse through rock 'n' roll. Compound words, slender vowels and explosive alliteration, 'Some thin-hipped glittering Bowie-being', capture the outlandish appearance of this unique creature in the high-heeled boots and extravagant make-up and costumes of the 1970s glam rock era. The verbs 'hovering, swaying' and a series of run-on lines suggest a character not subject to Earth's limitations. He is longing, 'aching', to share his message, 'make us see'.

Just as Bowie used the Ziggy persona to examine the rock star culture he uneasily occupied, Smith uses Bowie for a similar function, to analyse and comment on human life here on Earth. In line 5, she addresses readers directly: 'And what would we do, you and I'. The tone is intimate, revealing uncertainty when faced with this strange event, 'That someone was there squinting through the dust'. Bowie's Starman offers **the wonderful reassurance that 'nothing is lost'**.

Bowie and the Starman show us the power of the imagination. **By going into the world of science fiction, the poet helps us to escape our mortal world.** We are given the opportunity to reconsider time. A note of hesitancy creeps in when the poet asks 'Would you go' back to a previous 'happy' time even if you would be 'blind', because the future would be unknown. The poet turns the question on herself, 'Would I' return to the secure, comfortable past to sit again with her mother and father at the dining table? The homely visual detail, 'dinner keeping warm on the stove' (line 12) evokes an idyllic family scene.

A short emphatic statement, 'Bowie will never die', interrupts the uncertain, nostalgic mood. The poet sees God in him just as the child saw God in the Starman waiting in the sky, a powerful sign of hope. The wry allusion to Bowie's everlasting youth, 'he'll never grow old', conjures up **the star's mystifying ability to reinvent his image**. He escapes mortality by continually changing, 'Nothing will come for him'.

Bowie's mute presence overhead encourages Smith to articulate the grief animating the poem. His chameleon style, pop idol, glam artist, actor, transcends the limitations of this earthly world and his creativity will endure. **A modern vision of death and eternity emerges.** For the poet, life can be reclaimed through memory and positive acceptance.

Compound words accentuate how her father will remember her deceased mother in her prime, 'dark-haired', 'flush-faced', even though time's clock ticks on, 'the minutes, the miles left to go'. **The poet has returned to the innocent perspective of a child**, just as in Bowie's album, 'I'm forever a child looking out my window', believing everything is possible. 'I'll touch the world with bare hands/Even if it burns' (lines 19–20).

Smith continues to weave **references to sci-fi, popular culture and space** throughout the poem's second section. It begins by conveying Bowie's ability to transcend the limitations of Earth, revealed through short sentences, 'He leaves no tracks. Slips past'. The paradox of his public and private personae is embodied in the conflicting alliterative phrases, 'Pope of Pop, coy as Christ'. Both confer a religious aura on the star, referencing his flamboyant appearance similar to the pomp and ceremony of the Church and his contrasting demure private attitude, comparable to the modesty of Jesus.

TRACY K. SMITH

Bowie has admitted that **he adopted multiple personae** because he was extremely shy. This ambivalence is his intellectual property, 'trademarked twice', because both opposing roles are being played out at the same time, 'Like a play/Within a play'. Time's ongoing momentum is caught in the contemporary detail of the air-conditioning unit, 'The hours/Plink past like water from a window A/C' (lines 23–24). The run-on line and alliteration underline the relentless forward movement of time.

Resigned acceptance of the human condition is described in terms of the discomfort of a hot day, 'We sweat it out'. The inevitable end comes for everyone, described in the present tense, 'collapse happens'. But Bowie rises above it all through his carefree, humorous attitude, 'He cocks his head, grins that wicked grin', a heavenly being not subject to Earth's constraints.

An **unanswerable riddle** is posed in line 27: 'Time never stops, but does it end?' Humans vainly seek the unknowable for solace. A follow-up question asks: 'how many lives' must we live before we 'take-off' into another sphere, 'find ourselves/Beyond ourselves'. Bowie's flashy rock persona is evoked in the shimmering phrase, 'all glam-glow, all twinkle and gold' to suggest existence in this other dimension. The language of science fiction and glam rock are intertwined to imagine this new form of being.

In line 30, Smith paraphrases the French poet Paul Valéry's observation, 'The future isn't what it used to be'. She herself can only guess as to what the new future will be. The modern world is assuming the shape of humankind's mind – unstable and volatile. 'Even Bowie thirsts/For something good and cold'. His song that inspired the poem's title was written at a time when he had decided to live healthily after a period of drug addiction.

The onomatopoeic verb 'blink' captures the fleeting quality of time as everything moves and changes – both 'Jets' and 'migratory souls'. The poet suggests that **wondering about life on other planets is similar to wondering about the afterlife**, attempting to gain an insight into the intangible. Smith's search for spiritual reassurance is central to the poem and she considers Bowie's mythical Starman as the cosmic answer to this elemental need.

Section 3 shifts perspective and presents Bowie as an average person, the celebrity who walks among us, 'Right here/In New York City', lines 33–34. The reality of modern urban life is detailed in casual language and abbreviations, 'Ducking into/A deli', 'hailing a taxi'. But the otherworldliness of the 'star' is suggested by the celluloid imagery, 'Flashing all those teeth'. The real Bowie lacks ego, 'Doesn't strut or gloat' (line 42). He has a sense of humour, 'Tells jokes'.

Ironically, his alter ego, Ziggy Stardust, falls from grace because he gave in to his own inflated sense of self-importance. The poet confesses that she has 'never seen' Bowie, likening it to a lack of knowledge about the difference between a 'comet' which circles the sun, and a 'shooting star' which enters Earth's atmosphere. Both have bright trails in the sky, but only the shooting star comes to Earth, like Bowie, 'among us'. Alliteration and details from the language of space suggest **Bowie's explosive, charismatic personality**, 'But I'll bet he burns bright,/Dragging a tail of white-hot matter' (lines 46–47).

The poet humorously deflates the elevated image of the shooting star by linking it with the banal simile of humans walking from a toilet with a piece of toilet paper stuck to a shoe, two very different trails. Bowie's **star status as a rock god** is accentuated, 'He's got/The whole world under his foot'. Ordinary people are 'small alongside'.

In an enactment of the famous biblical scene when God touches man to inspire him, the poet imagines Bowie meeting 'Your eyes' to motivate and convey a sense of what might be possible. The brief encounter is described in the onomatopoeia of 'a blip of time' (line 54). Capital letters and repetition underline this **special message** to 'SHINE', to twinkle, to be the best that we can be. This advice has been sent without sound and vision, 'Straight to your mind', in a scene reminiscent of a science fiction movie.

The poet's act of faith in Bowie ('I want to believe you') means abandoning self-determination and surrendering to 'Your will', to the elemental pull of this charismatic being, in the same way as the wind is driven before a rainstorm. **Everything 'simply obeys' this primary force of nature.** Everyone is 'Swept up in that hypnotic dance', spellbound because a powerful entity had encouraged and given permission, '*Go ahead*', so that humans can wonder, re-imagine reality and travel into the unknown.

✒ Writing About the Poem

'Tracy K. Smith effectively blends the language of science fiction and pop culture to convey her questions about the limitations of life on Earth.' Discuss this view with reference to her poem 'Don't You Wonder, Sometimes?'

Sample Paragraph

The poem's intimate title, from Bowie's Ziggy Stardust album sets the surreal tone for Smith's gentle questioning of the reality of human life. Like the Starman, she encourages us to look towards the heavens for another take on reality. She successfully combines sci-fi and pop by presenting Bowie's glam rock creation as a godlike presence to transcend our limited lives on Earth. After 'take-off' from Earth, it's 'all

EXAMINER'S COMMENT

Assured top-grade response that addresses the key aspects of a challenging question. Effective critical discussion demonstrates close engagement with the poem. Excellent use of relevant reference and direct quotation throughout.

twinkle and gold'. Smith compares him to a 'shooting star', almost from another world. Bowie bypasses time, so 'nothing is lost'. This is conveyed by science fiction, through 'a blip' in a time machine. His cosmic image is mesmerising 'thin-hipped glittering Bowie-being', 'coy as Christ'. While humans struggle with grief and loss, Bowie is the 'elemental' source of energy which has the 'power' to inspire, 'Go ahead'.

✒ Class/Homework Exercises

1. 'Tracy K. Smith often challenges accepted perspectives of loss and grief.' Discuss this view with reference to her poem 'Don't You Wonder, Sometimes?'
2. 'The effective use of sound effects (sibilance, alliteration, assonance, etc.) is a recurring feature of Smith's poetry.' To what extent is this true of 'Don't You Wonder, Sometimes?'

◎ Points to Consider

- **Smith juxtaposes surreal features from the world of science fiction and pop to question accepted limitations of human life.**
- **Stylistic features include free verse, aural and visual imagery, irony, first-person viewpoint and inclusive personal address to reader.**
- **Balance of extraordinary subject matter with accessible language.**
- **Varied moods: confessional, analytical, imaginative, humorous, optimistic.**

8 It's Not

for Jean

That death was thinking of you or me
Or our family, or the woman
Our father would abandon when he died.
Death was thinking what it owed him:
His ride beyond the body, its garments,   5

Beyond the taxes that swarm each year,
The car and its fuel injection, the fruit trees
Heavy in his garden. Death led him past
The aisles of tools, the freezer lined with meat,
The television saying over and over *Seek*   10

And ye shall find. So why do we insist
He has vanished, that death ran off with our
Everything worth having? Why not that he was
Swimming only through this life – his slow,
Graceful crawl, shoulders rippling,   15

Legs slicing away at the waves, gliding
Further into what life itself denies?
He is only gone so far as we can tell. Though
When I try, I see the white cloud of his hair
In the distance like an eternity.   20

Dedication: The dedication is to Smith's sister, who looked after their mother in her final years.

abandon: leave, forsake.

garments: clothes.

aisles: lines, rows.

Seek/And ye shall find: biblical proverb.

rippling: moving.

gliding: floating.

eternity: infinity, for ever.

TRACY K. SMITH

'the white cloud of his hair'

👤 Personal Response

1. Based on the evidence of the poem, briefly describe your impression of Tracy K. Smith's father.
2. Smith personifies death throughout the poem. Does this add to the sense that death is something to be feared? Or is it a natural part of life? Give a reason for your response.
3. In your opinion, what is the tone of the poem's two concluding lines? Is it positive or negative? Briefly explain your response.

👁 Critical Literacy

Tracy K. Smith frequently addresses themes of loss, grief and memory in her work. 'It's Not' was published in her 2011 collection, *Life on Mars*. Some critics have viewed the book as a work of mourning for her father, an engineer who worked on developing the Hubble Space Telescope. He died in 2008. Smith has said that many of the poems became a way to wrestle with her sorrow and create a satisfying sense of where her father's spirit resided.

The poem's title is part of the first sentence, which ends in line 3. Death is personified as a powerful force which acts independently, regardless of what sadness it causes. Smith's **tone of resentment** is evident in describing the impact of her father's death on 'our family'. The poet highlights how people are shocked by bereavement and often struggle to cope with it. Smith recalls the devastating effect of death and separation. The underlying sense of her own personal feelings of betrayal is also apparent. How dare death and time erode the world that she had become used to?

As Smith reflects on her perception of her father's life, **she considers his passing as a natural progression** beyond the control of every human, 'Death was thinking what it owed him'. The intensity of his spiritual journey through life and death into the unknown is suggested by the dynamic phrase, 'ride beyond the body' (line 5).

With a touch of **wry humour**, the poet notes that dying finally freed her father from his routine concerns and irritations, such as 'the taxes that swarm each year' (line 6). There is an evocative feeling of celebrating key aspects of his vibrant character through a series of everyday images she associates with him. She recalls some of his wide-ranging interests from technology ('fuel injection', 'tools') to gardening ('fruit trees').

Smith draws interesting parallels between her own efforts to accept her father's death and his work as an engineer on the Hubble Telescope. Father and daughter have much in common. He wondered about whether or not there was life on other planets while she now wonders about the possibility of an afterlife. The biblical quotation, '*Seek/And ye shall find*' (lines 10–11) is an ironic reference to their shared inquiring minds. **Is Smith questioning religion?** Does it really provide her with meaningful answers?

Although she understands the sad reality that her father has died, **the poet challenges the view that earthly life is the end**. She still feels cheated by death, which 'ran off' with 'Everything worth having'. Refusing to believe that he 'has vanished', she imagines his athletic body 'Swimming only through this life' (line 14). The metaphor is extended to reflect a loving recollection of her father's qualities, such as his simple dignity ('Graceful crawl') and physical strength ('shoulders rippling').

The vigorous language in line 16 emphasises his determination: 'Legs slicing away at the waves'. But while she accepts the inevitability of death, **Smith converts her mourning into something redemptive**. The poet senses that her father spent his entire life 'gliding' into the unknowable afterlife. She experiences both the thrill and terror of thinking about the cycle of life. The interplay between what she now feels and what she can remember – between love and loss – adds a tender energy to the poem.

The final lines are a reminder that Smith thinks about her father in galactic dimensions. Does this make him less significant? Or does it associate him with a greater universal power? The poet acknowledges the limitations of human knowledge about a possible spiritual existence after death. But for her, **space is a symbol of the unknowable**: 'He is only gone so far as we can tell' (line 18).

She turns her eyes to the stars in search of perspective and consolation, seeing 'the white cloud of his hair' (line 19). This vivid metaphor expresses her hope that his life hasn't ceased, but merely changed – and he is somewhere 'In the distance like an eternity'. In this beautiful sequence, her reflections seem filled with the love of a child for a parent. **Smith converts her own experience into a universal one**, allowing readers to identify the pervasive sense of grief and longing in the poem. The conclusion offers a kind of acceptance mingled with philosophy – life and death are part of a natural progression.

This elegy alternates cosmic context and personal focus. Both in life and in death, the poet's parents gave her a sense of anchoring. It is especially poignant because she seems to imply that her father has gone to a perfect heaven that is also a part of the universe. She has said: 'We all have our own language for what we've lived and what loss feels like.' Imagining the afterlife through the metaphor of outer space helped Smith come to terms with loved ones who had died. Yet **mystery remains** alongside her deep yearning to connect with her father.

✒ Writing About the Poem

'Tracy K. Smith's most compelling poetry is often written as a response to her personal uncertainties.' Discuss this view with reference to her poem 'It's Not'.

Sample Paragraph

'It's Not' is filled with very compelling questions about how the poet deals with her dad dying and leaving this earthly world. Smith isn't too sure about how she feels, except she resents losing him to 'Death' which she looks on as a thief in the night who 'ran off' with him. She wonders if dying is really the end. Has he totally 'vanished' forever? The poem is extremely sad but has a reassuring ending. I found it very compelling that she believes her father 'is only gone as far as we can tell'. In a strange way, she solves her own worries, because she ends up thinking of her dad in the next world with his soul returning to nature like a cloud 'in the distance like an eternity'.

> **EXAMINER'S COMMENT**
>
> *This succinct response addresses the question directly, engages with the text and makes effective use of supportive quotes worked into the commentary. Expression is slightly repetitive and points are reasonably clear, but could have been developed more. A solid middle-grade standard.*

🖋 Class/Homework Exercises

1. 'Tracy K. Smith often explores issues of loss and mystery.' Discuss this view with reference to her poem 'It's Not'.
2. 'The effective use of vivid imagery is a recurring feature of Smith's poetry.' To what extent is this true of 'It's Not'?

◉ Points to Consider

- Moving elegy in tribute to the poet's father.
- Smith juxtaposes some of the mysteries of science with the major questions of life.
- Stylistic features include irony, personification and striking imagery.
- Effective use of metaphor: the image of space to explore the unknowable.
- Varied tones: elegiac, mournful, exhilarated and questioning.

9 The Universe as Primal Scream

Title: all matter and energy as first sound.

TRACY K. SMITH

5pm on the nose. They open their mouths
And it rolls out: high, shrill and metallic.
First the boy, then his sister. Occasionally,
They both let loose at once, and I think
Of putting on my shoes to go up and see 5
Whether it is merely an experiment
Their parents have been conducting
Upon the good crystal, which must surely
Lie shattered to dust on the floor.

Maybe the mother is still proud 10
Of the four pink lungs she nursed
To such might. Perhaps, if they hit
The magic decibel, the whole building
Will lift-off, and we'll ride to glory
Like Elijah. If this is it – if this is what 15
Their cries are cocked toward – let the sky
Pass from blue, to red, to molten gold,
To black. Let the heaven we inherit approach.

Whether it is our dead in Old Testament robes,
Or a door opening onto the roiling infinity of space. 20
Whether it will bend down to greet us like a father,
Or swallow us like a furnace. I'm ready
To meet what refuses to let us keep anything
For long. What teases us with blessings,
Bends us with grief. Wizard, thief, the great 25
Wind rushing to knock our mirrors to the floor,
To sweep our short lives clean. How mean

Our racket seems beside it. My stereo on shuffle.
The neighbor chopping onions through a wall.
All of it just a hiccough against what may never 30
Come for us. And the kids upstairs still at it,
Screaming like the Dawn of Man, as if something
They have no name for has begun to insist
Upon being born.

metallic: harsh, clanging.

good crystal: fine glassware.

decibel: high-pitched volume.
Elijah: biblical prophet, miracle worker.
cocked: pointed.
molten: melted.
inherit: are due to receive.

Old Testament robes: pre-Christian clothes.
roiling: boiling, churning.
furnace: incinerator.

mean: cruel, miserable.

racket: noise, uproar.
stereo: record player.
shuffle: random selection.
hiccough: slip-up, hiccup.

Dawn of Man: beginning of human life

👤 Personal Response

1. Describe the mood and atmosphere created by the poet in the opening stanza.
2. Comment briefly on the impact of Smith's sound effects (alliteration, assonance, onomatopoeia, internal rhyme) in the poem.
3. In your opinion, what is the tone of the poem's conclusion? Is it positive or negative? Briefly explain your response.

👁 Critical Literacy

'The Universe as Primal Scream' was published in Tracy K. Smith's third poetry collection, the Pulitzer Prize-winning *Life on Mars* (2011). This selection of poems searches for a viewpoint and sense of peace while elegising her beloved father, an engineer who worked on the development of the Hubble Telescope. A broad spectrum of modern experience is addressed, including pop culture, astronomy, physics, science and religion. The poet also explores human pain, loss, forgiveness and otherworldliness. Her father was obsessed by the idea of space as the final frontier and Smith brings readers on a cinematic journey to the ends of the galaxy, then reels back, frame by frame, until she focuses on the reality of life on Earth, noisy children in an upstairs apartment.

The **title** is **an interesting simile**, 'The Universe as Primal Scream'. The Big Bang theory is the astronomers' explanation for the creation of the universe. At a particular time in the remote past, all matter was created with a giant explosion. A primal scream is a release of intense frustration and anger that can help people to resolve psychological issues by allowing them to express their emotions in a safe environment. Smith uses her poem to explore the universe through the screams of two young children who live above her in an apartment block.

Stanza 1 opens with a private interior scene, a portrayal of screaming children and the speaker's curiosity about what is happening in the upstairs apartment. A curt colloquial expression, '5pm on the nose' (**line 1**) pinpoints the exact time the yelling begins. This is similar to the specific moment identified when the universe was created by the Big Bang. **The ear-piercing sound suggests a parallel between the birth of a child and the creation of the world.** The use of the present tense, 'They open', and broad assonance, 'rolls out', conveys the overwhelming nature of the noise. High-pitched screeches echo in the slender assonance ('shrill', 'metallic'). The drawn-out racket is mimicked through lengthening the 'o' and 'a' vowels with a double 'l' sound ('roll', 'metallic'). This exceptionally loud noise seems to reach right into the poet's mind, arousing the need to find out what is going on. The primal instinct has spurred a rational response.

The beginning of creation is now evolving with the introduction of the cognitive self, 'I think' (line 4). Smith contrasts the over-emotional squealing children with the mature adult ascending to a higher plane of being, 'go up and see'. The speaker self-consciously dresses ('putting on my shoes') to go out in public, just as Adam and Eve clothed themselves when they became self-aware in the Garden of Eden. She **humorously wonders** why the children are allowed to make such a galactic commotion before offering a sarcastic suggestion that their parents must be conducting 'an experiment'.

TRACY K. SMITH

'high, shrill and metallic'

This places the parents in the elevated role of scientists testing truth. Will their children's shrieks shatter 'the good crystal'? Fortunately, sound vibrations only break the finest leaded crystal. This scientific allusion gives way to a biblical allusion, 'Lie shattered to dust', reminiscent of the phrase 'For you are dust, and unto dust you shall return' (Genesis). The first stanza concludes with the **circular motion of the universe – creation, evolution and death**. The stanza's short opening sentences represent the beginning of creation while the more complex structure ('Occasionally ... on the floor' in lines 3–9) indicates the evolution of the rational thought process in humans.

Exasperated by the continuing din, **the speaker resorts to hyperbole**. In the second stanza, she proposes that 'Maybe' the mother is pleased that she has produced 'four pink lungs' of 'such might'. Run-on lines expose humanity's self-congratulatory sense of its own importance. The poet believes that humans are taking credit for what some other power created. She theorises, 'Perhaps', if the children strike the 'magic decibel', the precise volume, something extraordinary might occur. The speaker imagines this sound propelling the whole apartment building to 'lift-off' like a space rocket soaring into the sky. Like Elijah in the biblical story, she visualises ascending to heaven, a riotous 'ride to glory' (line 14).

The tone suddenly becomes resigned, 'If this is it'. Harsh alliteration introduces a warlike attitude ('cries', 'cocked'), a possible reference to the **two differing opinions on the origin of the universe, one scientific, the other religious**, each introduced by the phrase 'let the'. The changing colours of the sky (line 17) introduce the Doppler effect of the Big Bang theory. The wave frequency changes; red signifies a longer wavelength while blue indicates a shorter one. Black refers to the dark matter and energy thought to make up 95 per cent of the universe. The poet's deceased mother was devoutly Christian and the stanza concludes with the calm acceptance of religious faith, 'Let the heaven we inherit approach'. The wild flurry of noisy activity has been stilled.

In stanza 3, **two opposing viewpoints of the apocalypse** further explore the idea of heaven and how we will be greeted in the afterlife. The poet alternates between the traditional soothing view of heaven, 'our dead in Old Testament robes' (line 19) and a terrifying scientific dystopia, 'the roiling infinity of space'. The serene biblical scene, 'bend down to greet us like a father', is vividly contrasted with the seething turbulence of the black hole of infinity. A petrifying simile, 'swallow us like a furnace' (line 22), implies the utter annihilation of the human being. But the speaker is determined to challenge the threat and is 'ready/To meet' whatever is ahead. She also accuses this power of depriving humans of what they cherish, 'refuses to let us keep anything/For long'.

The **memory of Smith's late father is now subtly introduced**. Negative verbs ('teases', 'Bends') indicate the harshness of this mysterious power which governs human life and death. The speaker calls it a 'Wizard' (line 25), an enchanter who plays tricks. It is a 'thief' who steals from humanity. It is also seen as an uncontrollable elemental force, 'the great/Wind', its strength highlighted by the run-on line. This destructive energy eliminates the self-reflective minds of humans, 'knock our mirrors'. Smith illustrates the finite nature of human existence in the visual image, 'sweep our short lives clean'. The stanza's momentum is halted while readers consider how cruel this spiteful force is in clearing away human existence. As the poem slips into the final stanza, we are left with a sense of how inferior and squalid people's lives are in contrast to the almighty universal power.

The fourth stanza echoes the circular motion of the first, returning to the opening picture of noisy children and the familiar 'racket' of everyday life (line 28). Ordinary pictures of the meaningless activities of human existence reinforce **how puny and insignificant our lives are in contrast to the immense roar of the universe**. Readers are jolted back to the present through commonplace imagery, 'The neighbor chopping onions' and 'My stereo on shuffle'. Even the random selection of music suggests the lack of order in real life.

From Smith's viewpoint, **every human being is shuffled by an incomprehensible power** with no apparent order or reason. People stumble closer to their graves unaware that they approach an inscrutable void. For the poet, humankind is a mere 'hiccough' (line 30), a technical hitch, an interruption in the grand and unknowable scheme of things.

The poem ends as it began with screaming children, 'the kids upstairs still at it'. A tone of weary exasperation notes that people have always cried out – since the beginning of creation, 'like the Dawn of Man' (line 32). The noise heralds the arrival of something new and strange and nameless. The shortest stanza in the poem implies an unfinished work. **Is the speaker suggesting that human life ends incomplete**, cut short by inevitable but unpredictable death?

Throughout the poem, free verse, enjambment, prose-like expression and an absence of rhyme all permit a wide-ranging exploration of the limited nature of human life. **This central theme is supported by the poem's structure**. The four-part shape is contained neatly in four stanzas: a specific incident (children screaming), the relationship of the incident to humanity, then to the entire universe, before finally returning to the initial incident. The neat order of a row of nine-line stanzas is disturbed by the final short seven-line stanza, signifying a life randomly torn apart. Is this a reference to the poet's attitude to her father's death? Does human life have any significant meaning?

✒ Writing About the Poem

Based on your reading of 'The Universe as Primal Scream', to what extent is your emotional response to the poem heightened by Smith's use of both calm and disturbing imagery? Develop your answer with reference to the text.

Sample Paragraph

Biblical and scientific imagery increased my feelings of confusion in this harrowing exploration of the universe and human existence in 'The Universe as Primal Scream'. Although Smith includes joyous biblical details such as Elijah swept to heaven in a whirlwind, 'ride to glory' and a gentle religious scene, 'bend down like a father', the main message is that God causes grief and pain. She calls this almighty power a 'thief' who 'teases us'. She accuses this divine force of being 'mean' to humanity because it removes what is most loved. Smith's scientific imagery is even more terrifying. She paints a horrifying scenario of being 'swallowed' in a 'roiling infinity of space', utter annihilation. The poem concluded with a short stanza, suggesting life cut short by 'the great wind'. I found these contrasting images very unsettling.

EXAMINER'S COMMENT

Clearly written top-grade personal response that addresses the question directly and engages closely with the poem. Effective discussion points focus on how Smith's themes are illustrated through contrasting images. Good use of relevant reference and quotation throughout.

Class/Homework Exercises

1. 'In Tracy K. Smith's poetry, personal anecdote and philosophical questioning are blended to examine the strangeness of contemporary life.' To what extent is this true of 'The Universe as Primal Scream'?
2. 'Smith is well known for the power and energy of her dramatic language.' Discuss this view with reference to her poem 'The Universe as Primal Scream'.

Points to Consider

- Challenging perspectives on human existence and the meaning of life.
- Other themes include God, the universe, loss, death and the hereafter.
- Blend of visual, biblical and scientific imagery.
- Effective use of sounds, contrast and repetition.
- Incomplete poetic structure mirrors the theme of life randomly cut short.
- Ordinary language balances extraordinary subject matter.
- Varied tones: wry humour, exasperation, determination, grief, questioning.

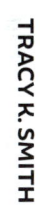

10 The Greatest Personal Privation

Title: Mary Jones complained of privation (deprivation and hardship).

TRACY K. SMITH

The greatest personal privation I have had to endure has been the want of either Patience or Phoebe – tell them I am never, if life is spared us, to be without both of them again.
  – Letter from Mary Jones to Elizabeth Jones Maxwell regarding two of her slaves, 30 August 1849

1.

It is a painful and harassing business
Belonging to her. We have had trouble enough,
Have no comfort or confidence in them,

And they appear unhappy themselves, no doubt
From the trouble they have occasioned. 5
They could dispose of the whole family

Without consulting us – Father, Mother,
Every good cook, washer, and seamstress
Subject to sale. I believe Good shall be

Glad if we may have hope of the loss of trouble. 10
I remain in glad conscience, at peace with God
And the world! I have prayed for those people

Many, many, very many times.

2.

Much as I should miss Mother,
I have had trouble enough 15
And wish no more to be
Only waiting to be sent
Home in peace with God.

3.

In every probability
We may yet discover 20

harassing: annoying.
Belonging: being owned, enslaved.

occasioned: caused.

seamstress: woman whose job is sewing.

glad: happy, clear.

The whole country
Will not come back

From the sale of parent
And child. So far

As I can see, the loss   25
Is great and increasing.

I know they have desired
We should not know

What was for our own good,
But we cannot be all the cause   30

Of all that has been done.

      4.
We wish to act. We may yet.
But we have to learn what their

Character and moral conduct   **moral conduct:** behaviour.
Will present. We have it in   35

Contemplation to wait and see.   **Contemplation:** mind.
If good, we shall be glad; if

Evil, then we must meet evil
As best we can.

      5.
Father, mother, son, daughter, man.   40
And if that family is sold:
      Please –
We cannot –
   Please –
      We have got to –   45
Please –
   The children –
Mother and Father and husband and –
All of you –
     All –   50
      I have no more –
How soon and unexpectedly cut off
Many, many, very many times.

A Note on Erasure Poetry

An erasure poem takes a pre-existing text and makes a poem by *erasing* or removing some of the words. It is sometimes referred to as 'found', 'redacted' or 'blackout' poetry.

Erasure poems are created from any source, including novels, published poems, letters, political publications or newspaper articles. The remaining text can then be framed into lines and/or stanzas on the page as a new poem.

Tracy K. Smith uses erasure poetry to allow those she wishes to honour, and sometimes challenge, to speak for themselves. She reveals the text beneath the text by listening closely to hidden voices. The poems address some of the most troubling events in history and often give voice to the oppressed or marginalised.

The title of Smith's poetry collection *Wade in Water* comes from an African-American spiritual hymn, 'Wade in the water/God's gonna trouble the water'. Many of the poems are rooted in questioning US history and identity through collective reckoning and empathy. The poet has commented: 'You want a poem to unsettle something.'

'Subject for sale'

👤 Personal Response

1. Based on the short extract from the letter in the poem's subtitle, briefly describe your impression of Mary Jones.
2. Repetition is used throughout the poem. Select one example and comment on its effectiveness.
3. In your opinion, what is Smith's key message or viewpoint in this poem? Briefly explain your response.

👁 Critical Literacy

Tracy K. Smith's 2018 collection, *Wade in the Water*, includes this erasure poem, drawn directly from letters between white slave-owners Charles Colcock Jones and his wife, written in the mid-19th century. On one occasion, when she was away from home, Mary Jones wrote about how much she missed the services of two slaves, a mother and daughter. The poem opens with a quote from one of her letters. She considers herself deprived and helpless without them. The poem centres on the slaves' reaction to the news of their upcoming sale. It is a poignant commentary on the violence done to black Americans.

In the **opening section**, Smith inverts the letter-writer's views by turning Jones's own words against her. The great **irony**, of course, is that her self-pitying letter shows no regard for the people enslaved by Jones herself and her family. Instead, the sentimental tone and exaggerated description of her 'greatest personal privation' reinforces Smith's point about the obvious racial injustice involved.

The **dual perspective** is evident in everything that is said. Using the mid-19th-century language from the Jones family's letters, Smith imagines the voices of Patience and Phoebe – and of countless other families who were held in bondage. For them, the reality of 'Belonging' is what is 'painful and harassing'. The quietly insistent tone makes it clear that what is unacceptable today is the idea of any human being ever 'belonging' to another.

Readers get a glimpse of the mercilessness of routine plantation life where slaves who had been accused of causing 'trouble' were 'Subject to sale'. However, the generosity of those who suffered enslavement is highlighted in the simple expression of forgiveness, 'I have prayed for those people'. The **emphatic commentary**, 'Many, many, very many times' (**line 13**) reminds us of how long the injustice of slavery endured.

In the short **second section**, we hear the voice of a daughter who has experienced 'trouble enough' and now seems defeated by a life of oppression. Although distressed about the being separated from her mother, her **religious faith offers consolation** and she hopes to find 'peace with God'. The subdued tone and slow-moving pace add to the powerful impact of her poignant prayer.

Section 3 presents a devastating portrait of American history. Smith recalls the human cost of historical racism directly in a series of **carefully controlled couplets**. The short lines emphasise her considered view of the legacy of slavery: 'The whole country/Will not come back/From the sale of parent/And child'. The sparse diction and simple syntax are compelling.

Smith examines the injustice – at both a political and a personal level – with sharp insight. She **invites her readers to face up to the racist** past when generations of African-Americans were deprived of determining 'What was for our own good'. We are challenged to question the 'cause/Of all that has been done'.

As the poem progresses, it turns from a reflective probing of historical injustice to a more determined desire 'to act'. Section 4 focuses on the need for a communal response, reflected in the repetition of the personal pronoun, 'We'. The haunting **voices of Patience and Phoebe transcend time**, appealing for justice from the people in power who control their lives. But Smith is not particularly confident of social progress and is realistic enough to admit that 'we must meet evil/As best we can'.

The dramatic final section is much more urgent in tone. An agonising chorus of desperate voices call injustice and its perpetrators to account. The fragmented phrasing and use of unfinished sentences filled with cries of '*Please*' have **a timeless quality** – spelling out the experience of enslaved families over generations. The insistent repetition of the pronoun '*We*' emphasises the power of community and elevates compassion as a liberating force.

Smith's use of italics and dashes add to the tension, highlighting the continuing gap between the ideal of universal human rights and the ongoing discrimination against African Americans. The poem's **frantic rhythm** builds to a high point in line 51: '*I have no more*'. Is Smith overwhelmed by her country's history? Or is she still hopeful that despite the failures to eradicate oppression in the past, the world must continue to fight against injustice?

The haunting refrain of 'Many, many, very many times' (line 53) leaves readers in no doubt that lack of freedom and widespread inequality are still found worldwide. In moments like this, the poet's example in creating a spiritual hymn to America's forgotten people makes the point that there is still an ever-increasing amount of work to do.

The poem is a compelling response to the original letter from which it is derived. Smith's choice of **the erasure form works well** because she is primarily highlighting how the truth was erased for centuries. The poet inverts this original erasure of the appalling reality of countless people who were denied the most basic human rights, allowing us to understand the present through the past.

✒ Writing About the Poem

'Tracy K. Smith uses a range of compelling voices to communicate disturbing aspects of American life.' Discuss this view with reference to 'The Greatest Personal Privation'.

Sample Paragraph

The title quotes a letter from a wealthy white woman who owned a plantation in the American South. Although she kept slaves, she had two favourites and depended on them. Her voice is full of self-pity which actually makes the point that she feels no guilt. It's not always clear who is actually speaking in this poem, but it's mainly the voices of the two slaves, 'We have had trouble enough'. I actually believe they represent every person deprived of freedom either during the times of slavery or in the present day. The poem's last lines involve mixed voices chanting the need for an end to racism. The one voice behind all of these is, of course, the actual poet herself. Tracy Smith's tone is angry and persuasive, 'We wish to act', 'We have got to' – and this has a very disturbing impact.

> **EXAMINER'S COMMENT**
> *Confident response that includes some insightful engagement with the poem. Points are expressed clearly – particularly the idea of Smith's own governing voice throughout. Apart from some repetitive expression ('actually'), this is a solid high-grade standard.*

✎ Class/Homework Exercises

1. 'Tracy K. Smith's poems often combine deep compassion with an insistence on hope.' To what extent is this the case in 'The Greatest Personal Privation'? Develop your response with reference to the poem.
2. 'Smith makes effective use of various tones and moods to illustrate her thematic concerns.' Discuss this statement with reference to 'The Greatest Personal Privation'.

⊙ Points to Consider

- **Erasure form weaves together past and present, personal and political.**
- **Effective stylistic features include irony, repetition and a range of speakers.**
- **Contrasting tones: sympathetic, didactic, dramatic and questioning.**
- **Smith urges readers to question governments and challenge injustice and lack of freedom.**

11 I am 60 odd years of age

TRACY K. SMITH

Note: Smith did not give the poem a title initially. This emphasised the lack of identity of African-American soldiers.

(from 'I Will Tell You the Truth About This, I Will Tell You All About It')

I am 60 odd years of age –

I am 62 years of age next month –

I am about 65 years of age –

I reckon I am about 67 years old –

I am about 68 years of age –   5

I am on the rise of 80 years of age –

I am 89 years old –

I am 94 years of age –

I don't know my exact age –

I am the claimant in this case. I have testified before you   10   **claimant:** applicant.
two different times before –

I filed my claim I think first about 12 years ago –   **filed:** put on record.

I am now an applicant for a pension,   **applicant:** person applying.
because I understand
that all soldiers are entitled to a pension –   15   **entitled:** eligible, due.

I claim pension under the general law   **general:** usual, universal.
on account of disease of eyes
as a result of smallpox   **smallpox:** viral disease.
contracted in service –   **contracted:** caught.

The varicose veins came on both my legs   20   **varicose:** swollen, twisted.
soon after the war and the sores were there
when I first put in my claim –

I claim pension for rheumatism   **rheumatism:** chronic pain.
and got my toe broke and I was struck
in the side with the breech of a gun   25   **breech:** rear barrel.
breaking my ribs –

I was a man stout and healthy
over 27 years of age when I enlisted –

When I enlisted I had a little mustache,
and some chin whiskers –   30

I was a green boy right off the farm and did
just what I was told to do –

When I went to enlist the recruiting officer
said to me, your name is John Wilson.
I said, no, my name is Robert Harrison,   35
but he put me down as John Wilson. I was
known while in service by that name –

I cannot read nor write, and I do not know
how my name was spelled when I enlisted
nor do I know how it is spelled now   40
I always signed my name while in the army
by making my mark
I know my name by sound –

My mother said after my discharge that the reason
the officer put my name down as John Wilson   45
was he could draw my bounty –

I am the son of Solomon and Lucinda Sibley –

I am the only living child of Dennis Campbell –

My father was George Jourdan and my mother was Millie Jourdan –

My mother told me that John Barnett was my father –   50

My mother was Mary Eliza Jackson and my father Reuben Jackson –

My name on the roll was Frank Nunn. No sir,
it was not Frank Nearn –

My full name is Dick Lewis Barnett.
I am the applicant for pension   55
on account of having served
under the name Lewis Smith
which was the name I wore before
the days of slavery were over –

My correct name is Hiram Kirkland.   60
Some persons call me Harry and others call me Henry,
But neither is my correct name.

A Note on Erasure Poetry

An erasure poem takes a pre-existing text and makes a poem by erasing or removing some of the words. It is sometimes referred to as 'found', 'redacted' or 'blackout' poetry.

Erasure poems are created from any source, including novels, published poems, letters, political publications or newspaper articles. The remaining text can then be framed into lines and/or stanzas on the page as a new poem.

Tracy K. Smith uses erasure poetry to allow those she wishes to honour, and sometimes challenge, to speak for themselves. She reveals the text beneath the text by listening closely to hidden voices. The poems address some of the most troubling events in history and often give voice to the oppressed or marginalised.

Smith's collection *Wade in Water* includes extracts from letters by African Americans who served in the American Civil War and their surviving relatives. These soldiers and their families speak on their own behalf. They tell of tragedies on and off the battlefield, ask for news of loved ones, and beg President Lincoln for help and the payment of pensions due.

TRACY K. SMITH

'all soldiers are entitled to a pension'

👤 Personal Response

1. Based on the evidence of the poem, what is your understanding of the treatment of the African-American soldiers who served in the Civil War?
2. Choose one image from the poem that you find shocking or disturbing. Comment briefly on its effectiveness.
3. In your opinion, what is the tone of the poem's three concluding lines? Is it positive or negative? Briefly explain your response.

👁 Critical Literacy

Tracy K. Smith's fourth volume of poetry, *Wade in the Water* (2018), examines racial and environmental injustice. Named after a popular slave spiritual, this collection is a spiritual hymn to America's forgotten people. Split into four chapters, each carrying a number rather than a title, the chapters resemble self-contained movements in a piece of music. They invite readers to interact and interpret. The various voices, identified and unidentified, create a communal chorus enabling negative realities to be confronted in a positive way. 'I am 60 odd years of age' forms part of Chapter II which contains agonising near-verbatim letters and statements of African-American Civil War soldiers and their families.

The poet has commented: '*A lot of the blacks who fought in the Civil War while enslaved and who were emancipated didn't have birth certificates; they didn't have marriage licenses; they often changed their names once they were given a say in the matter. And then the government said to them: we can't pay you your pension, because how can you prove to us that you are you?*' (From 'A Conversation with Tracy K. Smith' – *The Adroit Journal*, Issue 22.)

'I am 60 odd years of age' is an extract from 'I Will Tell You the Truth About This, I Will Tell You All About It'. Smith researched the US Bureau of Pensions files and she **fills the poem with fragments** from African-American Civil War soldiers' pension applications. These are accentuated by the use of italics to remind readers that they are the person's actual words. Ironically, the poet uses these official records to reveal the soldiers' lack of recognition in society's formal records of its citizens' lives. The war was fought primarily over the issue of slavery. Smith brings to life the encounters between these soldiers and the system in which they live.

The poem begins in a shy, self-effacing manner, 'I am 60 odd years of age –'. Many speakers **introduce themselves in anonymous phrases** that trail off with a dash. Are these dashes pleading or threatening? The hesitant echoes of these voices register uncertainty regarding their precise age, 'about 65', 'I don't know my exact age' (line 9). Many African-American soldiers were never issued with birth certificates and official records did not list their existence. Is this a symptom of how society viewed these people?

Their **unwavering perseverance in pursuing their entitlement** to a pension is evident in lines 10–12: 'I have testified before you/two different times before', 'I filed my claim I think first about 12 years ago'. The authority of this army of living ghosts is heightened by the use of formal legal language, such as 'claimant' and 'testified'. It is also suggested by the repetition and capitalisation of the first-person singular pronoun, 'I'. The deep pride of these people is unmistakable in their claim for what they are due for their service to the country, 'all soldiers are entitled to a pension' line 15. Their voices combine to cast light on the shadows of history which have obscured their story.

A list of specific injuries sustained while 'in service' begins to illuminate these people as unique individuals. One suffered 'disease of eyes/as a result of smallpox' (lines 17–18). Another claimant described how 'varicose veins came on both my legs/soon after the war'. The violent brutality of conflict is conveyed in the explosive alliterative phrase 'breech of a gun/breaking my ribs'. This carefully collated **collage of archival fragments** has a hypnotic effect. Everyone mentioned is given dignity by being allocated a specific place in the widely spaced poem's canvas. It records their distinguishing characteristics, 'a man stout and healthy', 'I had a little mustache' (line 29). Smith weaves memorable images together with compassion as if making a hand-stitched quilt from treasured fragments of cloth.

One **individual story is developed**, inviting readers further into the narrative and so into their own humanity. The arrogance of a recruiting officer is exposed in his insistence that the young enlistee, the 'green boy', should be recorded by a new name. Despite the young man's protest, 'he put me down as John Wilson' (line 36). Does the officer have so little regard for the new black recruit that he will register him any way he chooses? Or is there a more sinister motive to his action? The vulnerability of the young soldier is evident in his timid disclosure that he did 'just what I was told to do'.

At the time of the American Civil War (1860–65), it was illegal in some states to teach slaves basic literacy. In line 38, a young soldier admits that he 'cannot read nor write'. During his time in the army, he signed his name simply by placing an X ('making my mark'). The soft alliterative phrase foreshadows how easily he could be deceived since he only knew his name 'by sound'. The mother of this 'green boy' exposes the ulterior motives of the recruiting officer's act of renaming her son. The fraud was carried out to steal the young man's initial enlistment payment or 'bounty' (line 46). **Run-on lines accentuate the overwhelming rush of frustration** felt because he could not prove who he was and that he had served his country.

In the final section, Smith emphasises the **importance of one's name to establish identity and status**. Speakers are no longer anonymous, contrasting with those referenced at the beginning of the poem. Instead, the individual is firmly placed within a particular family, 'I am the son of Solomon and Lucinda Sibley' (line 47). The tone here is much more self-assured. These overlooked people are now being treated with due respect. Some have married parents, 'My father was George Jourdan and my mother was Millie Jourdan'. Others have not, 'My mother told me that John Barnett was my father'. The first-person singular pronoun 'I' is replaced by the possessive adjective 'My', indicating that the person's place in society is now reclaimed.

A brief exchange between a claimant and an official illustrates the ongoing battle for recognition: 'My name on the roll was Frank Nunn. No sir,/it was not Frank Nearn' (lines 52–53). The struggle for reclamation of identity is detailed in the fragment from Dick Lewis Barnett who served 'under the name Lewis Smith', his slave name. The verb 'wore' suggests that this slave name was a cloak which hid the soldier's true identity. However, **the poem concludes on a dignified note, establishing one person's 'correct name'**. The two anglicised names sometimes given to Kirkland, 'Henry' and 'Harry', are now set aside and his proper forename, 'Hiram', is finally placed on record (line 60). This biblical name means 'exalted brother'.

In this **poignant erasure poem**, the voices of forgotten people have now asserted their individuality and reinstated their rightful place in history. With characteristic compassion, Smith has stirred things up by making visible the words of the forgotten African-American soldiers who served in the Civil War. The cumulative effect of their simple statements is unexpectedly powerful, a litany of wrongs crying out for redress. The poet is drawing back the curtains to reveal America's historical racism. Her poems, like the great spirituals, witness, protect and raise the roof, because they contribute to the national dialogue.

✒ Writing About the Poem

'Tracy K. Smith's fearless exploration of history constructs a powerful account of misidentifying and discrimination.' Discuss this view with reference to 'I am 60 odd years of age'.

Sample Paragraph

'I am 60 odd years of age' is a collection of extracts from the pension applications of African-American soldiers after the Civil War. Smith builds a powerful poem by using these forgotten voices. Italics emphasise the truth of racial discrimination. The poet fearlessly insists on identifying particular soldiers by describing their injuries, 'smallpox', 'varicose veins', 'rheumatism'. These young black recruits are presented as individuals in both appearance, 'chin whiskers' and personality, 'a green boy'. Smith exposes official misidentification and exploitation, 'he put me down as John Wilson'. She details how the true identity of slaves was hidden by the assumed names they 'wore'. By recording their proper names, 'My correct name is Hiram Kirkland', Smith has challenged historical injustice and corrected the official records.

EXAMINER'S COMMENT

This is a solid top-grade response that addresses the question and engages intelligently with the poem. Good critical commentary is supported by apt reference and accurate quotation. Points are clearly expressed throughout.

Class/Homework Exercises

1. 'Tracy K. Smith often confronts issues of loss and wrong-doing.' Discuss this view with reference to her poem 'I am 60 odd years of age'.
2. 'In "I am 60 odd years of age", the structure of the poem increases the strength of Smith's central message.' To what extent do you agree or disagree? Explore some of the following in your response: the use of italicised fragments, dashes, line spacing, repetition, contrast, run-on lines, etc.

Points to Consider

- **Powerful combination of fragmentary voices from US Bureau of Pensions archives.**
- **Smith awakens reader's awareness of and compassion for forgotten people and their story through the mix of many voices.**
- **Stylistic features include specific details, repetition, contrast, colloquial speech, legal language.**
- **Effective use of alliteration, dashes, replacement of first-person singular pronoun with possessive adjective.**
- **Varied tones: timid, steadfast, moral, demanding, authoritative, moving.**

12 Ghazal

The sky is a dry pitiless white. The wide rows stretch on into
   death.
Like famished birds, my hands strip each stalk of its stolen
   crop: our name.

History is a ship forever setting sail. On either shore: mountains
   of men,
Oceans of bone, an engine whose teeth shred all that is not
   our name.

Can you imagine what will sound from us, what we'll rend and
   claim   5
When we find ourselves alone with all we've ever sought: our
   name?

Or perhaps what we seek lives outside of speech, like a tribe
   of goats
On a mountain above a lake, whose hooves nick away at rock.
   Our name

Is blown from tree to tree, scattered by the breeze. Who am I
   to say what,
In that marriage, is lost? For all I know, the grass has caught
   our name.   10

Having risen from moan to growl, growl to a hound's low bray,
The voices catch. No priest, no sinner has yet been taught
   our name.

Will it thunder up, the call of time? Or lie quiet as bedrock
   beneath
Our feet? Our name our name our name our fraught,
   fraught name.

famished: starved.

shred: cut.

rend: rip up.

sought: wanted.

nick: scratch.

bray: cry.

fraught: tense, oppressed.

A Note on Ghazal Poems

'Ghazal' (often pronounced 'guzzle') means 'the cry of a gazelle when it is cornered by a hunter'. This Arabic form of poetry originated in the 7th century and was made up of a minimum of five couplets (two-line sections).

These short poems have an intricate rhyme scheme and every couplet ends with the same word or phrase (known as the radif). Traditionally, ghazals told stories and were sung by musicians. Popular themes included longing, love, sadness and mysticism.

In this poem, Tracy K. Smith concludes each couplet with the phrase, 'our name', referring to the identity and human rights denied to generations of African Americans.

TRACY K. SMITH

👤 Personal Response

1. Comment briefly on the effectiveness of the imagery in the poem's opening couplet.
2. In your opinion, what does the poet mean when she says: 'History is a ship forever setting sail'?
3. How does the poem make you feel? In your opinion, is it hopeful or despondent? Briefly explain your response, using reference to the text.

'scattered by the breeze'

POETRY FOCUS

👁 Critical Literacy

In her 2018 collection, *Wade in the Water*, Tracy K. Smith reflects on her own racial identity. An awareness of history and her relationship to it also runs throughout the book. 'Wade in the Water' comes from an African-American spiritual which emphasises faith in God during harsh times. It also references how slaves sought to escape captivity by going into water to evade the dogs which were unleashed to hunt them down. 'Ghazal' laments the historical and current traumas that have impacted the African-American 'name'. The poet chose 'our name' as the repeated phrase at the end of each couplet, concluding with a haunting chant for the loss of what has been stolen.

The poem's **opening lines** present a dystopian scene: 'The sky is a dry pitiless white' that stretches 'into death'. Graphic images of decay suggest a future of inescapable hopelessness. This treacherous landscape is arid and lifeless, reflecting the dark parts of America's troubled past. Smith uses this **harrowing setting** to guide readers towards an understanding of the injustice of denying people their identity.

She focuses on the African-American experience, emphasising the basic human rights 'stolen' from successive generations of enslaved plantation workers: 'Like famished birds, my hands strip each stalk'. The **harsh simile highlights their suffering** in being deprived of the freedom they were due, their 'name'.

All through the poem, the long-dead voices of every individual wronged by inequality and neglect call across the centuries across a chasm of suffering. Their **anguished cries** appeal not only to the humanity of those who had none to give, but to those of us alive today who long to express our sympathy.

The despondent mood eases in **line 3** as **Smith reflects on the possibility of change**: 'History is a ship forever setting sail'. She develops the metaphor, charting the waters of the past to illuminate contemporary culture. But while the poet retains some confidence and can almost believe that all is not lost, she still sees American history as male-dominated and an abuse of privilege.

For Smith, **the truth about racism has been erased** by 'mountains of men' and 'Oceans of bone' (**line 4**). These startling images refer to the deaths of thousands of black people down through the centuries. Acutely conscious that the reality of slavery and oppression has been generally 'shredded' from history, she repeats the phrase, 'our name', including their countless individual voices and reclaiming their true story. Smith's poems witness and protest.

She brings great sensitivity to the poem, leading us deeper into other people's lives – and ultimately into our own humanity. She is a curious poet, and her inquisitive nature reflects this thoughtfulness. Smith also believes in the **power of imagination** as a way of sustaining the hope that subjugated people would eventually be free. The rhetorical question posed in lines 5–6 looks ahead to a more optimistic future for black America: 'Can you imagine what will sound from us, what we'll rend and claim'. The poet urges readers to foresee the swelling power that all excluded people have sought and fought for: their 'name'. In giving voice to the voiceless, her resolute vision is both challenging and uplifting.

Line 7 focuses on the difficulty of responding effectively to racial prejudice: 'perhaps what we seek lives outside of speech'. This is an important reminder to any human struggling with how to release emotion. During the period when this poem was written, the names of brutally murdered African Americans began to symbolise the greater injustice their deaths were part of. Those names in turn found their way into public street protests demanding change. The past is pressing up against the present. However, Smith is **realistic about the slow pace of progress**, signified in the timeless image of mountain goats 'whose hooves nick away at rock'. She is the poetic caretaker who calls for collective reckoning and collective empathy.

While being personally uncertain of a way to break the circle of injustice, Smith examines American history with an incisive, yet positive, honesty. In that portrait, she includes the images of her ancestors, those who have come before her. Although 'scattered by the breeze', there is still the possibility that 'the grass has caught our name' (line 10). Despite her abhorrence of the past and society's sins against marginalised people, **the poet's personal compassion remains intact**, even as she questions its power to change anything for the better.

The pattern of animal imagery in line 11 is evocative and resonant, bringing to mind different responses to racial oppression, from endurance to anger and ultimately to a sense of redemption: 'Having risen from moan to growl, growl to a hound's low bray'. Smith is a recorder of destructive realities. **She places herself within the collective movement in support of human rights** – where the 'voices catch'. Such unity of purpose offers the most likely reason to be guardedly hopeful – even though 'No priest, no sinner has yet been taught our name'.

History is never finished, never finite. By posing questions about social justice, the poet asks readers to become involved, to hear the 'sound' that will either 'thunder up' or 'lie quiet as bedrock'. Her concluding tone is both urgent and determined. She asks us to keep reflecting on the African-American past, 'our fraught, fraught name'. Repetition emphasises her deep-rooted sense of loss, lending poignancy to these final lines. As in so many of her most compelling poems, Smith declares her **solidarity with those who are abandoned by history** and unites herself with the voices who

TRACY K. SMITH

cry out for justice. She believes that 'we are accountable to each other'. Tracy K. Smith has commented that 'poems pull me out of my own perspective … and challenge our assumptions of the world'.

✒ Writing About the Poem

'In her most humane poems, Tracy K. Smith shows a tremendous range that often blends disturbing reflective passages with cautious hope.' Discuss this view, with reference to 'Ghazal'.

Sample Paragraph

'Ghazal' is a thoughtful poem that reflects on discrimination against black people going right back to the slave trade. Tracy Smith has a conscience about the prejudice of those 'pitiless' times. She uses disturbing images of cruelty and starvation to show this – 'famished birds', 'oceans of bone'. She also asks questions about whether or not racism is ending – 'Who am I to say'. Yet Smith has not given up. She dares to dream of restoring human rights to victims of racist abuse – their good 'name' – by saying that protests are growing worldwide – 'the voices catch'. This is a more confident point of view. Her own views seem to range over the issue of racism – reflecting different attitudes. She concludes that universal human rights – 'our name' – will 'thunder up'. I think this is quietly hopeful.

> **EXAMINER'S COMMENT**
> *Confident top-grade response that addressed the question's three basic elements ('humane', 'reflective' and 'hope'). Some effective discussion of disturbing images and their impact. Relevant supportive reference and apt quotation throughout.*

✎ Class/Homework Exercises

1. 'Tracy K. Smith often uses effective poetic techniques, such as descriptive detail and repetition, to convey key thematic concerns in her work.' Discuss this statement, with particular reference to 'Ghazal'.
2. 'In her poem "Ghazal", Tracy K. Smith surveys African-American history with an incisively critical mind, but without resorting to bitterness or sentimentality.' To what extent do you agree with this statement? Refer to the text in your response.

◎ Points to Consider

- Perceptive and insightful consideration of racism and injustice.
- Startling images and descriptive details are evocative and resonant.
- Effective use of repetition – 'our name' reinforces the poem's central theme.
- Variety of moods and tones: open-ended conclusion.

Sample Leaving Cert Questions on Smith's Poetry

1. 'Smith makes effective use of language to address universal themes of love, loss and identity.' To what extent do you agree with this statement? Develop your answer with reference to the poetry of Tracy K. Smith on your course.
2. 'In presenting an evocative voice for victims of racism and injustice, Smith makes compelling connections between the current state of American culture and its history.' To what extent do you agree with this view? Develop your answer with reference to the poetry of Tracy K. Smith on your course.
3. Discuss how Smith effectively uses a variety of characters, often in dramatic settings, to probe both personal issues and wider public concerns in her poems. Develop your response with reference to the poetry of Tracy K. Smith on your course.

Understanding the Prescribed Poetry Question

Marks are awarded using the PCLM Marking Scheme: P = 15; C = 15; L = 15; M = 5 Total = 50

- **P** (Purpose = 15 marks) refers to the set question and is the launch pad for the answer. This involves engaging with all of the question. Both theme and language must be addressed, although not necessarily equally.
- **C** (Coherence = 15 marks) refers to the organisation of the developed response and the use of accurate, relevant quotation. Paragraphing is essential.
- **L** (Language = 15 marks) refers to the student's skill in controlling language throughout the answer.
- **M** (Mechanics = 5 marks) refers to spelling and grammar.
- Although no specific number of poems is required, students usually discuss at least 3 or 4 in their written responses.
- Aim for at least 800 words, to be completed within 45–50 minutes.

How do I organise my answer?

(Sample question 1)

'Smith makes effective use of language to address universal themes of love, loss and identity.' To what extent do you agree with this statement? Develop your answer with reference to the poetry of Tracy K. Smith on your course.

Sample Plan 1

Intro: (*Stance: agree with viewpoint in the question*) Smith's poetry is distinguished by her position as witness and recorder. Universal themes include first love, loss of loved ones and self-identity. Varied settings, clever contrasts, interesting use of poetic structure, resonant sound effects and repetition create a powerful examination of this subject matter.

Point 1: (*Loss/racism – poetic structure and aural imagery*) 'Ghazal' repeats key words to emphasise the African-American experience of loss of identity and human rights. Onomatopoeic animal sounds capture the rising confidence of oppressed people. Hopeful conclusion reclaims identity.

POETRY FOCUS

NOTE

In keeping with the PCLM approach, the student has to take a stance by agreeing, disagreeing or partially agreeing that Smith:

- **makes effective use of language** (vivid imagery, striking contrasts, dramatic language, dialogue, varied settings, evocative sound effects, rhetorical questions, direct address to reader, open-ended conclusions, range of moods and tones, etc.)

… to address:

- **universal themes of love, loss and identity** (love of parents/community, loss of loved ones, choices, transition to adulthood, sense of self, awareness of recurring racism and injustice, mysteries of human existence, fascination with the cycle of life and death, etc.)

Point 2: *(Lost love/unreliable memory – exotic setting/religious references)* 'Dominion over the Beasts of the Earth' uses the vivid sensuality of a Mexican setting to emphasise the heady experience of first love. Colloquial Spanish expressions bring to life the young character of Mauricio. Vivid metaphor, 'frayed thread of dreams', expresses unreliability of memory. Bittersweet confessional of lost love.

Point 3: *(Limitations of human life – clever contrast of science fiction/ pop culture)* 'Don't you Wonder, Sometimes?' showcases charismatic pop icon David Bowie to explore the inevitable transcendence of earthly limitations. Mystery of space suggested by broad assonant sounds and soft sibilance, 'stars glisten like ice'. Optimistic ending urges 'Go ahead'.

Point 4: *(Loss of mother – varied settings, powerful metaphors)* 'Joy' is a tender elegy contrasting Smith's mother as carefree child and terminally ill patient. Powerful metaphors, 'The body is memory', 'The body is appetite', explore the physical body's purpose. Vivid symbol, 'a dark chamber around a chord of light' exposes a new reality. Inconclusive and challenging ending: 'What do you believe in?'

Conclusion: Smith's poetry 'speaks to life'. Her carefully crafted poems and sympathetic viewpoint provide consolation to universal concerns about love, loss and identity.

Sample Paragraph: Point 1

Tracy K. Smith's choice of the traditional form of poetry, 'Ghazal', allows her to explore the Afro-American experience. She highlights the deeply felt loss of human rights and identity. The repeated phrase, 'our name', is like a continuous mantra at the end of each stanza, leading to the heart-breaking final 'our fraught, fraught name'. Compelling animal sounds, such as 'moan', 'growl' and 'low bray', convey the rising tension of an oppressed people. We can sense the sorrow, anger and hunt for recognition. The final line's thudding repetition leaves us in no doubt that reclamation of identity and equal rights is happening and will go on being heard.

EXAMINER'S COMMENT

As part of a more developed response to the poem, this is a clearly written top-grade standard. Insightful points succinctly address the question through focusing on the poet's use of repetition and sound effects. Some good close engagement with the text and the supportive quotation is effective.

(Sample question 3)

Discuss how Smith effectively uses a variety of characters, often in dramatic settings, to probe both personal and wider public concerns in her poems. Develop your response with reference to the poetry of Tracy K. Smith on your course.

> **NOTE**
> In keeping with the PCLM approach, the student has to explore poems of Smith's on the course that include:
> - **a variety of characters, often in dramatic settings** (real people from poet's personal life, oppressed African-American communities, real and imaginary figures in futuristic and dangerous settings, cinematic scenes, pop icons from surreal fantasy, etc.)
> … to probe:
> - **personal issues** (identity, loss, conflicted views, search for meaning in life, etc.) **and wider public concerns in her poems** (racial injustice, use and abuse of power, etc.)

Sample Plan 2

Intro: (*Stance: agree with viewpoint in the question*) Smith's poetry creates unforgettable characters in a variety of settings in order to examine personal matters of identity, first love, power and oppression.

Point 1: (*Power – film scene of rescue in Wild West setting*) 'The Searchers' explores male power and female acquiescence/identity through dramatic rescue scene of an abducted girl. Wild West setting exposes not only the dangers of the frontier but also its healing capacity.

Point 2: (*Repression – chorus of voices from aftermath of American Civil War*) 'I am 60 odd years of age' is a collage of archival fragments from pension applications of African-American soldiers. The poignant setting for those attempting to reclaim what is due to them exposes corruption of power and an extinction of identity.

Point 3: (*Young love – vibrant characters in exotic location*) 'Dominion over the Beasts of the Earth' vividly evokes a sultry Mexican setting and the experience of first love with the charismatic character of Mauricio. Male dominance and female identity are questioned.

Point 4: (*Meaning of existence – glamorous pop icon in fantasy setting*) 'Don't You Wonder, Sometimes?' presents David Bowie's mesmerising persona, Ziggy Stardust, as a channel through which to escape the sorrow of this mundane earthly world.

Conclusion: Both private issues and public concerns are explored by Smith through vivid portrayals in a wide variety of settings, including the unpredictable Wild West, the poignant aftermath of the Civil War, the heat of Mexico and the surreal world of science fiction.

Sample Paragraph: Point 1

'The Searchers', focuses on a dramatic scene of the rescue of an abducted girl by a former Confederate soldier. He is furious that the girl has survived and has adapted Comanche customs, so he 'wants to kill her'. Aggressive verbs show the patriarchal power of this angry man – 'grab', 'puts'. His traditional attitude about how things should be is contrasted with the wide-open landscape which accepts everyone, 'Gave anyone the chance'. The Wild West shows us how to exist, by not being concerned with control and possession, 'With whether it belonged to him or to him'. The poet is saying that this ex-soldier was wrong to condemn the girl for 'surviving' the landscape.

> **EXAMINER'S COMMENT**
> Engages quite well with a challenging question – although the 'public concerns' element could be more clearly developed. Some perceptive analysis of dramatic tension through reference to contrasts and language use, e.g. 'Aggressive verbs show the patriarchal power'. Good high-grade standard as part of a full essay response.

> **EXAM FOCUS**
> - As you may not be familiar with some of the poems referred to in the sample plans, substitute poems that you have studied closely.
> - Key points about a particular poem can be developed over more than one paragraph.
> - Paragraphs may also include cross-referencing and discussion of more than one poem.
> - Remember that there is no single 'correct' answer to poetry questions, so always be confident in expressing your own considered response.

Leaving Cert Sample Essay

Discuss how effectively, in your opinion, Tracy K. Smith uses a range of stylistic features to convey both the overwhelming compassion and deep-rooted anger in her work. Develop your response with reference to the poems by Smith on your course.

Sample Essay

1. Tracy K. Smith's poems clearly show her personal sympathy for human beings and her deep outrage at injustice both in today's world and in the past. Her powerful imagery and emotive tones really involve readers and appeal to their dislike of prejudice. She repeatedly explores universal themes, such as grief, racism and the mystery of life. Anger and compassion can sometimes be found in the same poem.

2. Smith's compassion for the forgotten truth about the African-American Civil War soldiers is central to her poem, 'I am 60 odd years of age'. Actual extracts from letters written by the black troops and their families over 160 years ago show them begging the authorities for basic pension rights due to all veterans. Italics are used to emphasise their authentic words

which adds to the anger and compassion Smith obviously feels. Smith also uses dashes to reinforce how lacking in confidence the soldiers were, 'I am about 65 years of age –' and the chorus of voices shows Smith's compassion for these victims of racism. The tragic reality was that some of these unfortunate people were not even given a birth certificate to record that they even existed. As one soldier wrote, 'I don't know my exact age'.

3. Smith tells the story of an innocent volunteer, a 'green boy', who had been a former slave who was always happy to do 'just what I was told to do'. He became the victim of a dishonest army officer who registered the soldier as 'John Wilson' so he could cheat him out of his bounty. The young soldier's signature was just a 'mark' that could be easily forged. Smith's rage is clear in her quiet tone as she reminds us that at this time slaves were often forbidden to read or write. This clearly illustrates both her tender compassion for these soldiers and her outrage at how they were mistreated.

4. 'Ghazal' also deals with the oppression of African-Americans whose basic human rights were 'stolen' by white plantation owners. Smith details the brutal mistreatment of slaves, comparing them to 'famished birds'. This graphic image clearly emphasises the suffering of countless people who were robbed of freedom and their rights as humans, their 'name'. The poet's voice is compassionate throughout. Smith uses another disturbing image, 'oceans of bone', to describe the thousands of black people trafficked from Africa during the 1900s. Her frustration and anger is a reaction to the fact that the full truth about what happened has been 'shredded' from the history books.

5. In 'The Universe as Primal Scream', Smith clearly shows her empathy for anyone struggling to come to terms with the cycle of life and death. She feels angry at the powerlessness of ordinary people to control their own destiny. She lashes out at nature or God or whatever force 'steals' loved ones from their families in death. Her sympathy for those left grieving is seen in the homely image, 'sweep all our short lives clean'. Smith believes that humans cannot find any real answers to the mysteries of creation – either in religion or in science. She is clearly resentful that man's so-called understanding is just an illusion and that every life is cut short by 'the great wind'.

6. Smith also uses disturbing images effectively to convey her sympathy for victims of conflict. In 'Letter to a Photojournalist Going-In', she emphasises the terrible suffering that news photographers witness. Soldiers and civilians are 'blown open like curtains'. Sometimes the journalist can also be arrested and beaten, 'they throw you into a room

---

INDICATIVE MATERIAL

- **Smith is/is not effective in using stylistic features:** (striking imagery – Western, scientific, space, pop culture, etc. – dramatic settings, metaphor, personification, contrasts, accessible language, universal themes, colloquial speech, repetition, run-through lines, unusual structures, evocative/provocative tones – ironic, dark, honest, nostalgic, questioning, hesitant, reflective, etc.)
- **to convey both compassion and anger** (empathy for oppressed people, concern for victims of violence, anger about historical racism, deep resentment of injustice, awareness of the desire for acceptance, shared understanding of the mystery of the universe and human existence, etc.)

TRACY K. SMITH

or kick at your gut'. We are given an insight into the intense dangers some of these reporters face, 'you go to the pain'.

7. Smith's despair is also clearly seen in her description of the effects of war on local children who imitate the violence of the adult world around them. Innocent kids show off by playing war games as if violence is a good thing, 'brandishing their plastic guns with TV bravado'. But the poet has sympathy for other victims of conflict apart from those who are directly involved.

8. The letter writer in the poem worries about the effect on her personal relationship with the photojournalist. She wonders if the awful scenes he has witnessed have caused him to hide his own feelings. The trauma of war seems to be destroying their relationship, turning it onto another battleground. Once again, Smith's imagery is effective in conveying her compassion. The writer ends her letter with a dark image suggesting that the couple's future is in great danger, imagining it 'landing at my feet like a grenade'.

9. Overall, I found Smith's poetry to be very effective. Her imagery and strong tones express her feelings about issues, such as racism. She has a strong social conscience and calls out injustice and oppression in many of her poems.

(805 words)

EXAMINER'S COMMENT

Good solid response that stays focused on how stylistic features convey anger and compassion in Smith's poetry. Most discussion points are developed reasonably well, particularly on the use of imagery (paragraphs 2, 3 and 8). Good use is made of relevant supportive reference. There are slight misquotes, some weaknesses in the notelike expression and the adverb, 'clearly', is over-used.

GRADE: H1
P = 15/15
C = 13/15
L = 13/15
M = 5/5
Total = 46/50

👓 Revision Overview

'Joy'
Tender elegy for Smith's mother addressing universal themes of identity, grief, death and life's great mysteries.

'Dominion over the Beasts of the Earth'
Enlivened by the dramatic Mexican setting, this nostalgic poem reflects on the uneasy transition from childhood to adulthood.

'The Searchers' (OL)
Smith uses the John Ford Western to explore the concept of home while raising questions about memory and how we relate to past experiences.

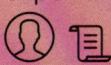

'Letter to a Photojournalist Going-In'
Perceptive reflection on how war makes victims of many people – and not just those directly caught up in conflict.

'The Universe is a House Party'
In comparing the universe to a noisy party, Smith uses science fiction to investigate the significance of the human race.

'The Museum of Obsolescence'
The image of outer space allows Smith to explore life's meaning and imagine the possibility of human beings eventually becoming obsolete.

'Don't You Wonder, Sometimes?'
Outer space as a vast, unknowable infinity and the enduring presence of David Bowie allow the poet to articulate underlying feelings of grief.

'It's Not' (OL)
In a poem written after her father's death, Smith expresses a deep yearning to connect with his spirit while wrestling with the mystery of an afterlife.

'The Universe as Primal Scream'
Reflective poem focusing on the challenge of making sense of everyday life, loss, the universe, and human existence.

'The Greatest Personal Privation' (OL)
Smith's compelling commentary on the history of slavery in America is central to this poignant erasure poem.

'I am 60 odd years of age'
Disadvantaged African-American Civil War soldiers ask President Lincoln for due recognition and equal pension rights.

'Ghazal'
Another searing indictment exposing the historical denial of basic human rights to generations of African Americans.

🗣 Last Words

'Smith is a storyteller who loves to explore how the body can respond to a lover, to family, and to history.'
Hilton Als

'A truly exceptional poet, with an eye for the arresting image.'
Paul Muldoon

'Poetry invites us to listen to other voices.'
Tracy K. Smith

TRACY K. SMITH

SPIRITUALITY | LOSS | IDENTITY | RELATIONSHIPS | WONDER
HISTORY/MEMORY | CONFLICT | MEANING OF LIFE | INJUSTICE

POETRY FOCUS

The Unseen Poem

'Students should be able … to read poetry conscious of its specific mode of using language as an artistic medium.'

(DES English Syllabus, 4.5.1)

Note that responding to the unseen poem is an exercise in aesthetic reading. It is especially important, in assessing the responses of the candidates, to guard against the temptation to assume a 'correct' reading of the poem.

Reward the candidates' awareness of the patterned nature of the language of poetry, its imagery, its sensuous qualities, and its suggestiveness.

SEC Marking Scheme

In the Unseen Poem 20-mark question, you will have 20 minutes to read and respond to a short poem that you are unlikely to have already studied. Targeted reading is essential. **Read over the questions** first to focus your thoughts and feelings.

In your **first reading** of the poem:
- Aim to get an initial sense of what the poet is saying and think about why the poet is writing about that particular subject.
- What is happening? Who is involved? Is there a sense of place and atmosphere?
- Underline interesting words or phrases that catch your attention. Avoid wasting time worrying about any words that you don't understand. Instead, **focus on what makes sense** to you.

Read through the poem **a second time**:
- Who is speaking in the poem? Is it the poet or another character?
- Is the poet describing a scene?
- Or remembering an experience?
- What point is the poet making?
- What do you notice about the poet's language use?
- How does the poem make you feel?
- Did it make you wonder? Trust your own reaction.

Check the **'Glossary of Common Literary Terms'** on GillExplore.ie

- **Theme** (the central idea or message in a poem. There may be more than one theme)
- **Imagery** (includes similes, metaphors, symbols and personification)
- **Sound (aural) effects** – often referred to as onomatopoeia (includes alliteration, assonance, sibilance, rhyme and repetition)
- **Tone** (nostalgic, happy, sad, reflective, angry, optimistic, etc.)
- **Mood** (atmosphere can be relaxed, mysterious, poignant, uneasy, etc.)
- **Rhythm** (the pace or movement of lines, similar to the musical 'beat' of a song. Rhythm often reflects mood and can be slow, regular, rapid, uneven, etc.)
- **Language** (the poet's choice and order of words, including imagery and poetic devices)
- **Style** (the use of language. Poets choose various techniques, such as imagery, tone, etc. to convey meaning and emotion)
- **Lyric** (poem that expresses the poet's thoughts and feelings. Lyric poems are often short and sometimes resemble a song in form or style)
- **Rhyme** (the occurrence of the same or similar sounds – usually at the end of a line. Rhyme often adds emphasis)
- **Stanza** (two or more lines of poetry that together form a section of a poem)
- **Persona** (the speaker or 'voice' in the poem ... This may or may not be the poet)
- **Personification** (where a thing is treated as a living being. In 'Mirror', Sylvia Plath gives an everyday household object human qualities, allowing it to speak – 'I am exact')
- **Enjambment** (when a line doesn't have punctuation at the end. The resulting run-on lines usually add emphasis)
- **Irony** (when there is a different meaning from what is stated, e.g. the title of Plath's poem, 'The Times Are Tidy')
- **Emotive language** (language that affects the reader's feelings, e.g. 'our times have robbed your cradle' in Eavan Boland's 'Child of Our Time')
- **Contrasts** (contrasting themes, tones and images highlight differences and similarities, e.g. Kavanagh contrasts adult life with childhood innocence in 'A Christmas Childhood')
- **Structure and layout** (a poem's form can be identified by analysing its structure or shape. Hopkins's sonnets are fourteen lines only and divided into two parts. The first eight lines are called the octave and often describe a problem, idea or situation. The next six lines are called the sestet and present a response to the octave)

> **REMEMBER!**
> 'This section [Unseen Poetry] was often not answered, resulting in a loss of 20 marks. Omitting questions or parts of questions has a deleterious effect and is often due to poor time management.'
> **Chief Examiner's Report**

Unseen Poem – Practice 1

Read the following poem by Alan Bold and answer **either** Question 1 **or** Question 2 which follow.

1 Autumn

Autumn arrives
Like an experienced robber
Grabbing the green stuff
Then cunningly covering his tracks
With a deep multitude
Of colourful distractions.
And the wind,
The wind is his accomplice
Putting an air of chaos
Into the careful diversions
So branches shake
And dead leaves are suddenly blown
In the faces of inquisitive strangers.
The theft chills the world,
Changes the temper of the earth
Till the normally placid sky
Glows red with a quiet rage.

Alan Bold

---

1. (a) What do you learn about the poet's attitude to autumn in the above poem? Support your answer with reference to the poem. (10)

(b) Identify two images from the poem that make an impact on you and give reasons for your choice. (10)

OR

2. Discuss the appeal of this poem, commenting on its theme, tone and the poet's use of language and imagery. Support your answer with reference to the poem. (20)

Sample Answer 1

Q1. (a) (Poet's attitude to autumn)
(Basic response)

The poet's attitude to autumn is not good at all because he calls autumn an experienced robber which is a negative thing. Alan does not compare the beauty in which nature is full of descriptive scenery of leaves falling in countryside areas. I think he's wrong about autumn to call it a theif in the night because this is not the whole picture at all and he only sees the negative side like storms and trees shaking. There is another story to the beauty of autumn's nature other than the dead leaves which are a reminder of death which is a totally negative side. Alan has a pesimmistic attitude and this is too narrow to be true to life.

EXAMINER'S COMMENT
- Makes one valid point about negativity.
- Little development or use of reference.
- No focus on the varied aspects of autumn.
- Expression is awkward and repetitive.
- Incorrect spellings ('theif', 'pesimmistic').

Marks awarded: 3/10

Sample Answer 2

Q1. (a) (Poet's attitude to autumn)
(Top-grade response)

Alan Bold has a very playful outlook towards the season of autumn. In comparing it to a cunning 'experienced' robber who sneaks in every year to steal 'the green stuff' that grows in summer, he seems fascinated by the way nature changes so secretively. Bold develops the metaphor throughout the poem, closely observing how the wind (autumn's 'accomplice') creates chaos, tossing colourful leaves across the ground. Autumn is depicted as a powerful natural force which not only changes the landscape, but also affects how people feel. This is evident in the poem's final lines where he suggests that autumn marks the transition into winter and is a reminder that nature can be destructive – and even something to be feared. The poet's overall attitude is that the season of autumn warns human beings about our fragile relationship with the natural world.

EXAMINER'S COMMENT
- Insightful answer that engages closely with the poem.
- Interesting final point about nature's destructive power.
- Good use made of supportive quotations throughout.
- Varied sentence length, fluent expression.
- Grammar and spellings are excellent.

Marks awarded: 10/10

Sample Answer 3

Q1. (b) (Two images that make an impact)
(Basic response)

'the faces of inquisitive strangers' This is the first image that makes an impact on me and my reasons for my choice is that it is just as it would happen in reality when people are in parks. This when we see the leaves are blown around into your face during October. If people have young children with them they never stop asking questions about the weather and everything.

'normally placid sky' The second image from the poem that made an impact on me and my reason for my choice is because this is that it is pure Irish weather in which the clouds are grey. It is usually about to rain in Ireland just like the calm before the storm. It does not exactly stay placid for long in this country. This image is detailed and true to life.

EXAMINER'S COMMENT
- Little engagement with the poem's language.
- Limited point about the realism of both images.
- Needs more developed discussion.
- Drifted into general commentary.
- Repetitive, flawed expression throughout.

Marks awarded: 4/10

Sample Answer 4

Q1. (b) (Two images that make an impact)
(Top-grade response)

I thought the 'experienced robber' image was powerful. The simile suggests that autumn is sly – disturbing the peace of summer. Bold cleverly develops the comparison, emphasising the criminal image of the season, with associated words, such as 'covering his tracks' and 'cunningly'. The effect is playful – autumn is fooling everyone into a false sense of security by disguising the changes that are happening to the climate. This lively colourful season is not to be fully trusted.

In a second striking image, the poet personifies the wind, describing it as autumn's 'accomplice' in creating widespread havoc. It creates an air of chaos – literally. This gives nature a human characteristic, which only strengthens its awesome power. The wind shows autumn to be even more terrifying because something so strong is merely its accomplice.

EXAMINER'S COMMENT
- Perceptive analysis of the poet's inventive language.
- Good understanding of the extended metaphor.
- Effective use of apt textual reference.
- Excellent expression throughout.

Marks awarded: 9/10

Unseen Poem – Practice 2

Read the following poem by Grace Nichols and answer **either** Question 1 **or** Question 2 which follow.

2   Roller-Skaters

Flying by
on the winged-wheels
of their heels

Two teenage earthbirds
zig-zagging
down the street

Rising
unfeathered –
in sudden air-leap

Defying law
death and gravity
as they do a wheely

Landing back
in the smooth swoop
of youth

And faces gaping
gawking, impressed
and unimpressed

Only mother watches – heartbeat in her mouth

Grace Nichols

1. (a) What do you think the poet is saying about the relationships between parents and their children in 'Roller-Skaters'? Support your answer with reference to the poem. (10)

  (b) Identify two images from the poem that make an impact on you and give reasons for your choice. (10)

OR

2. Discuss the language, including the imagery, used by the poet throughout this poem. Make detailed reference to the poem in support of your answer. (20)

Sample Answer 1

Q2. (Poet's language use)
(Basic response)

The poet's language including the imagry used by the poet is very detailed. It shows a street where roller skaters are taking place. The details show they are brave doing the wheely and zig zags as they are actually risking their lives for the sport they love. I myself have mixed feelings about the imagry because it shows how they jump in amazing tricks. Like leaps but on the other hand their mother is afraid that he will be hurt. The language describes the danger.

People out in the street are looking at the image of these skaters. This is an image of risking life or just to show off to attract attention. The images make me think of the danger involved behind the first impressions of an exciting sport that attracts kids in every city. At the start it is very exciting because no one is injured so far but as Grace protrays the skaters more in a detailed way the language becomes more dangerous for example when she says there is a risk of death during the wheely. No wonder the mother watching has an image of her heart in her mouth because it is a dangerous situation and she is not too impressed.

EXAMINER'S COMMENT

- *Makes some points about detailed description.*
- *Little development or use of close reference to language.*
- *Minimal focus on the effectiveness of imagery.*
- *Expression is awkward and repetitive at times.*
- *Mechanical errors ('imagry', 'protrays').*
Marks awarded: 6/20

Sample Answer 2

Q2. (Poet's language use)
(Top-grade response)

Vivid imagery and energetic language are key features in this poem. Nichols describes the roller skaters 'Flying by' and having 'winged-wheels'. Both descriptions are metaphors as the skaters are not actually 'flying' nor do they have real 'wings'. The poem can be seen as one developed metaphor that suggests the breakneck actions of the skaters. Short lines and dynamic verbs, such as 'zig-zagging' suggest their speed.

The skaters are compared to 'earthbirds' which is very effective. I can imagine that they will take off into the air at any minute. Later on, they are described as 'unfeathered', which links back to the same idea that they are defying 'death and gravity'. Towards the end, the poet mentions the 'smooth sweep of youth' and suggests that the skaters are enjoying their freedom.

The poem's rhythm is lively throughout and not interrupted by punctuation. This highlights the reckless moves the skaters make. Run-on lines create a sense of continuous movement. Sound effects play a huge part. There is a pattern of slender vowels – e.g. 'winged-wheels' – in the opening lines which increases the pace. The alliteration suggests the repeated actions of the skaters.

The layout is arranged in a series of short lines and this highlights the skaters' lively movement. The final separate line cleverly suggests how the mother is outside of the action and can only watch from a distance as her child takes risks.

EXAMINER'S COMMENT

- Focused on the effectiveness of language throughout.
- Ranges over various aspects, including imagery and sound.
- Well-developed discussion of the bird metaphor.
- Insightful comments on rhythm and structure.
- Good expression (although 'suggests' is overused).

Marks awarded: 18/20

REMEMBER!

There is no single 'correct' reading of the poem. Respond to the poem honestly. How does it make you feel? Trust your own reaction.

Unseen Poem – Practice 3

Read the following poem by David Harmer and answer **either** Question 1 **or** Question 2 which follow.

3   At Cider Mill Farm

I remember my uncle's farm
Still in mid-summer
Heat hazing the air above the red roof tops
Some cattle sheds, a couple of stables
Clustered round a small yard
Lying under the hills that stretched their long back
Through three counties.

I rolled with the dogs
Among the hay bales
Stacked high in the barn he built himself
During a storm one autumn evening
Tunnelled for treasure or jumped with a scream
From a pirate ship's mast into the straw
Burrowed for gold and found he'd buried
Three battered Ford cars deep in the hay.

He drove an old tractor that sweated oil
In long black streaks down the rusty orange
It chugged and whirred, coughed into life
Each day as he clattered across the cattle grids
I remember one night my cousin and I
Dragging back cows from over the common
We prodded them homeward through the rain
And then drank tea from huge tin mugs
Feeling like farmers.

He's gone now, he sold it
But I have been back for one last look
To the twist in the lane that borders the stream
Where Mary, Ruth and I once waded
Water sloshing over our wellies
And I showed my own children my uncle's farm
The barn still leaning over the straw
With for all I know three battered Ford cars
Still buried beneath it.

David Harmer

1. **(a)** What is your impression of the poet's experiences on the farm in 'At Cider Hill Farm'? Support your answer with reference to the poem. **(10)**
   (b) Select two images from the poem that appeal to you and give reasons for your choice. **(10)**

   OR

2. Discuss the language used by the poet, commenting on imagery, tone and sound effects. Support your answer with reference to the poem. **(20)**

Sample Answer 1

Q1. (a) (Poet's experiences on the farm)
(Basic response)

My impression of David Harmer is he remembers spending happy times on his holidays in cider mill farm. It belonged to his uncle who was the farm owner during his childhood, so he would have been there in the holidays. He had happy experiences splashing in the river and messing with the dogs but his best experience is of the one time he drank tea from the mugs belonging to the proper farmers after working with the cattle one evening. But the boy was dissapointed after the farm was sold, any child would naturally suffer from dissapointment by loosing their freedom. Up to then the farm life was very appealing, a good break away from school during the holidays.

EXAMINER'S COMMENT
- Some references to the poet's happy experiences.
- These could have been more effectively supported by quotes.
- Lacks discussion on stylistic features, e.g. nostalgic tone.
- Capital letter errors and misspellings ('dissapointed', 'loosing').
Marks awarded: 4/10

Sample Answer 2

Q1. (a) (Poet's experiences on the farm)
(Top-grade response)

Harmer's reminiscences are of exciting childhood days on his uncle's farm. From the start, his tone is nostalgic, 'Heat hazing the air above the red roof tops'. The vowel sounds and gentle alliteration emphasise the poet's happy memories of far-off times. The images of rural scenes show the impact that the countryside 'under the hills' had on him. I think it's almost as if the changing seasons matched the change in the poet's life as he grew up. The mood is enthusiastic, however. The boy's sense of adventure is seen when exploring new sensations among the farm animals, 'We prodded them homeward through the rain'. He seems fascinated by the 'rusty orange' tractor – 'It chugged and whirred'. As a child, he delighted in creating his own world. It's clear that the time on the farm was important, so much so that he wants to pass on his memories to his own children.

EXAMINER'S COMMENT
- Intuitive response focusing on the poet's idyllic childhood.
- Good range of discussion points.
- Well-supported by suitable quotations.
- Effective reference to imagery, tone and sound effects.
- Confident expression and excellent mechanics.
Marks awarded: 10/10

Sample Answer 3

Q1. (b) (Two appealing images)
(Basic response)

The first appealing image is of 'one night dragging cows' because this shows cows don't hurry and have to be prodded with sticks. They nearly have to get dragged along as the image says, so this is the reason why this is a good image as it really shows farmers totally have their hands full trying to get animals to go anywhere. The next image is 'three battered Ford cars'. This is the second appealing image of cars rusting in a field. This can be seen in parts of the country where cars are dumped and they are a complete and total eyesore to the public who have to look at them. So in one way this is not appealing as an image because some people just dump rubbish anywhere.

EXAMINER'S COMMENT

- Slight points that need to be much more developed.
- Drifts into irrelevant general commentary.
- No attempt to examine the effectiveness of the language.
- Repetitive expression lacks fluency.

Marks awarded: 3/10

Sample Answer 4

Q1. (b) (Two appealing images)
(Top-grade response)

There are many appealing images in this poem. I liked the ones that focused on the poet's carefree childhood, such as 'Heat hazing the air above the red roof tops'. The summer setting has strong associations with warmth and happiness. The poet remembers the haze of bright sunlight and the vivid red colours of the farm buildings. This vibrant imagery suggests an exaggerated childlike memory which is reinforced by the 'h' and 'r' alliteration. The line has a dreamlike quality, suggesting the wonder of the experience. Some of the feelings the poet recalls are reinforced by sound images, for example, 'Water sloshing over our wellies'. The onomatopoeic effect of 'sloshing' echoes the squelching noises made by the children as they splashed through the water. This all contributes to the upbeat mood of the poem. Harmer is re-living a moment when he was totally happy-go-lucky on his uncle's farm.

EXAMINER'S COMMENT

- Perceptive analysis of visual and aural imagery.
- Well-developed discussion examining language closely.
- Points supported by relevant textual reference.
- Excellent expression and varied vocabulary throughout.

Marks awarded: 10/10

Unseen Poem – Practice 4

Read the following poem by Rosita Boland and answer **either** Question 1 **or** Question 2 which follow.

4 Lipstick

Home from work one evening,
I switched the radio on as usual,
chose a knife and started to slice
red peppers, scallions, wild mushrooms.

I started listening to a programme about Iran.
After the Shah fled, Revolutionary Guards
patrolled the streets of Teheran
looking for stray hairs, exposed ankles
and other signs of female disrespect.

The programme ended.
I was left standing in my kitchen
looking at the chopped vegetables on the table;
the scarlet circles of the peppers
delicate mouths, scattered at random.

When they discovered a woman wearing lipstick
they razor-bladed it off:
replaced one red gash with another.

Rosita Boland

1. (a) What do you learn about the kind of person the poet is from reading this poem? Explain your answer with reference to the poem. (10)
   (b) Identify a mood or feeling evoked in 'Lipstick' and explain how the poet creates this mood or feeling. Support your answer with reference to the poem. (10)

   OR

2. What impact did this poem make on you? Refer closely to the text in discussing its theme, tone and the poet's use of language and imagery. (20)

Sample Answer 1

Q2. (Impact of the poem)
(Basic response)

This was a hard to understand poem about a worker who comes home to make a meal. But she starts to listen to the news about what is happening in the war. I think she imagines the soilders running wild attacking people. One soilder uses a knife and attacks an innocent woman who is just dressed up and wearing lipstick which is her basic human right and just out for the evening. This guard should of known better. This is the part of the poem that made the most impact on me personally.

This is the theme of war and the tone of this poem is showing what happens on the back streets in some parts of the world. If your not doing harm you should be left in peace. There is a big difference between the image of the innocent woman out to enjoy herself on a night out as she is intitled and the angry language of the soilder who attacks her for no reason. Unfortunately it is not a state of peace everywhere else which is the main impact of the poem.

EXAMINER'S COMMENT

- Makes one reasonable point about the impact of violence.
- Only slight engagement with the poem.
- No convincing analysis of the poet's language use.
- Expression could have been much more controlled.
- Mechanical errors ('soilder', 'intitled', 'should of', 'your').

Marks awarded: 6/20

Sample Answer 2

Q2. (Impact of the poem)
(Top-grade response)

Although the language is simple in this poem, it actually makes the point that routine violence against women is still common in some societies. This makes a greater impact as the poem develops because the poet's tone is almost relaxed in the first stanza – 'I switched the radio on as usual'. The programme is truly shocking. Boland points out the stark difference between what we take for granted as normality here at home and the grotesque reality of life in conflict areas, such as the Middle East.

The vivid image of the attack on the civilian is horrific. The poet creates a dramatic effect by contrasting the girl's beauty and the brutal violence she experiences. The guard's vicious action is foreshadowed by the earlier image of the poet herself using a kitchen knife to slice vegetables. I can relate to her sense of revulsion as she imagines the Iranian policeman's use of a razor blade to replace 'one red gash with another'.

The quiet tone of the final stanza reflects her sense of failure, 'left standing there in my kitchen'. Vivid images of the half-chopped vegetables, particularly the 'scarlet circles of the peppers', are closely associated with the 'Delicate mouths' of vulnerable women who suffer vicious abuse and injustice.

EXAMINER'S COMMENT

- Convincing personal response to the question.
- Points are clear, incisive and aptly supported.
- Links theme and stylistic features very well.
- Perceptive analysis of tone, imagery and contrast.
- Excellent expression, fluent and varied.

Marks awarded: 20/20

REMEMBER!

Avoid wasting time worrying about any words in an Unseen Poem that you don't understand. Instead, focus on what makes sense to you.

Unseen Poem Revision Points

- **Study the wording of questions** to identify the task that you have to do.
- Express your **key points** clearly.
- Include **supportive reference or quotation** (correctly punctuated).
- Refer to both the poet's **style** (how the poem is written) as well as the **themes** (what the poet is writing about).
- **Select interesting phrases** that give you an opportunity to discuss subject matter and use of language.
- **Avoid summaries** that simply repeat the text of the poem.
- **Engage with the poem** by responding genuinely to what the poet has written.

Unseen Poem – Practice 5

Read the following poem by Pat Boran and answer **either** Question 1 **or** Question 2 which follow. (Allow 20 minutes to complete the answer.)

5 Stalled Train

In the listening carriage, someone's phone cries out for help.
A student frisks himself,
a woman weighs her handbag
then stares into space. Our train
is going nowhere, stalled here
so long now the cattle in this field
have dared come right up close
to chew and gaze. We tell ourselves
that somewhere down the line
things we cannot understand
are surely taking place – the future
almost within reach – and into each
small telephone that rings
or shudders now, like doubt,
we commit (if still in whispers)
our hopes and fears,
our last known
whereabouts.

Pat Boran

1. **(a)** In your opinion, is the dominant mood in the poem positive or negative? Explain your answer with reference to the poem. (10)
   (b) Identify two images from the poem that you find interesting and give reasons for your choice. (10)

   OR

2. Discuss the impact of this poem, with reference to its theme and the poet's use of language and imagery. Refer closely to the text in support of your answer. (20)

PROMPT!
- Think about the poet's attitude to modern life.
- Imagery is vivid, graphic, cinematic.
- Surreal, mysterious, dream-like atmosphere.
- Effective use of personification and symbols.
- Final lines are disturbing.
- Poem raises many interesting questions.

Acknowledgements

The authors and publisher are grateful to the following for permission to reproduce copyrighted material:

'The War Horse', 'Child of Our Time', 'The Famine Road', 'The Shadow Doll', 'White Hawthorn in the West of Ireland', 'Outside History', 'The Black Lace Fan My Mother Gave Me', 'This Moment', 'The Pomegranate' and 'Love' by Eavan Boland, from *New Selected Poems*, 2005. Copyright © Eavan Boland, reproduced by permission of Carcanet Press Limited.

'Lipstick' by Rosita Boland, from *Dissecting the Heart*, 2003. Copyright © Rosita Boland, reproduced by kind permission of the author and The Gallery Press, Loughcrew, Oldcastle, County Meath, Ireland.

'Autumn' by Alan Bold. Copyright © Alan Bold, reprinted by permission of Alice Bold.

'Stalled Train' by Pat Boran, from *Then Again*, 2019. Copyright © Pat Boran, reproduced by kind permission of Dedalus Press.

'There's a certain Slant of light', 'I felt a Funeral, in my Brain', 'A Bird came down the Walk', 'I Heard a fly buzz–when I died', 'The Soul has Bandaged moments', 'I could bring You Jewels–had I a mind to', 'A narrow Fellow in the Grass', 'I taste a liquor never brewed' and 'After great pain, a formal feeling comes' by Emily Dickinson. *The Poems of Emily Dickinson: Variorum Edition*, edited by Ralph W. Franklin, Cambridge, Mass.: The Belknap Press of Harvard University Press. Copyright © 1998 by the President and Fellows of Harvard College. Copyright © 1951, 1955 by the President and Fellows of Harvard College. Copyright © renewed 1979, 1983 by the President and Fellows of Harvard College. Copyright © 1914, 1918, 1919, 1924, 1929, 1930, 1932, 1935, 1937, 1942 by Martha Dickinson Bianchi. Copyright © 1952, 1957, 1958, 1963, 1965 by Mary L. Hampson. Used by permission. All rights reserved.

'The Love Song of J. Alfred Prufrock', 'Preludes', 'Aunt Helen', from *The Waste Land*: 'II: A Game of Chess', 'Journey of the Magi', from *Landscapes*: 'III. Usk' and 'IV. Rannoch, by Glencoe' and from The Four Quartets: 'East Coker, IV' by T. S. Eliot, from *The Complete Poems and Plays*, 2004. Reproduced by permission of Faber and Faber Ltd.

'At Cider Mill Farm' by David Harmer, from *The Works 3*, chosen by Paul Cookson, published by Macmillan Children's Books, 2004. Copyright © David Harmer, used by permission of the author.

'Inniskeen Road: July Evening', 'Shancoduff', from *The Great Hunger:* 'Section I', 'Advent', 'A Christmas Childhood', 'Epic', 'Canal Bank Walk', 'Lines Written on a Seat on the Grand Canal, Dublin', 'The Hospital' and 'On Raglan Road' by Patrick Kavanagh. Reprinted from *Collected Poems*, edited by Antoinette Quinn (Allen Lane, 2004), by kind permission of the Trustees of the Estate of the late Katherine B. Kavanagh, through the Jonathan Williams Literary Agency.

'Grandfather', 'Day Trip to Donegal', 'Ecclesiastes', 'After the *Titanic*', 'As It Should Be', 'A Disused Shed in Co. Wexford', 'Rathlin', 'The Chinese Restaurant in Portrush', 'Kinsale', and 'Antarctica' by Derek Mahon, from *The Poems: 1961–2020*, 2021. Reproduced by kind permission of the author and The Gallery Press, Loughcrew, Oldcastle, County Meath, Ireland.

'Roller-Skaters' by Grace Nichols, from *Give Yourself a Hug*, 1994. Copyright © Grace Nichols, reproduced with permission of Curtis Brown Group Limited, London, on behalf of Grace Nichols.

'Black Rook in Rainy Weather', 'The Times Are Tidy', 'Morning Song', 'Finisterre', 'Mirror', 'Pheasant', 'Elm', 'Poppies in July', 'The Arrival of the Bee Box' and 'Child' by Sylvia Plath, from *Collected Poems*, 2002. Reproduced by permission of Faber and Faber Ltd.

'Joy' and 'Dominion over the Beasts of the Earth' from *The Body's Question*, 2003; 'The Searchers' and 'Letter to a Photojournalist Going-In' from *Duende*, 2007; 'The Universe is a House Party', 'The Museum of Obsolescence', 'Don't You Wonder, Sometimes?', 'It's Not' and 'The Universe as Primal Scream' from *Life on Mars*, 2011; 'The Greatest Personal Privation', 'I am 60 odd years of age– ' from 'I Will Tell You the Truth about This, I Will Tell You All about It' and 'Ghazal' from *Wade in the Water*, 2018, by Tracy K. Smith. Copyright © Tracy K. Smith. All reprinted with the permission of The Permissions Company, LLC on behalf of Graywolf Press, Minneapolis, Minnesota, graywolfpress.org.